D0882483

301.45
C839r

DATE DUE			

Phillips Library
Bethany College
Bethany, W. Va. 26032

Reconstruction,
the Negro,
and the
New South

Reconstruction, the Negro, and the New South

Edited by

LaWanda Cox
and
John H. Cox

UNIVERSITY OF SOUTH CAROLINA PRESS
Columbia, South Carolina

RECONSTRUCTION, THE NEGRO, AND THE NEW SOUTH

Copyright © 1973 by LaWanda Cox and John H. Cox

All rights reserved. Printed in the United States of America. No part of this book may be used or reproduced in any manner without written permission except in the case of brief quotations embodied in critical articles and reviews. For information address Harper & Row, Publishers, Inc., 10 East 53rd Street, New York, N.Y. 10022.

First HARPER TORCHBOOK edition published 1973.

This edition published by the UNIVERSITY OF SOUTH CAROLINA PRESS, Columbia, S.C., 1973, by arrangement with HARPER PAPERBACKS, from whom a paperback edition is available.

Library of Congress Cataloging in Publication Data

Cox, LaWanda C   (Fenlason)   comp.
    Reconstruction, the Negro, and the new South.

    (Documentary history of the United States)
    Includes bibliographical references.
    1. Negroes—History—1863–1877—Sources.
2. Negroes—History—1877–1964—Sources.
3. Negroes—Civil rights—History—Sources.
4. Reconstruction—Sources.   I. Cox, John Henry,
1907–   joint comp.   II. Title.
E185.2.C77   1973   301.45′19′6073075   73-5793
ISBN 0-87249-278-8

To
R.B.M.
Scholar, Editor, Friend

301.45
C 839r

Contents

C. The Continuing Commitment:
Advance and Retreat

PART TWO
FLAWED FREEDOM:
THE SOUTHERN EXPERIENCE, 1868–1900

A. BLACKS SHARE POWER IN THE SOUTH

Introduction

IN EDITING THIS COLLECTION we have approached the subject not as three distinct topics but as one basic problem, that of the status of the freed Negro. This question was central to the national effort to reconstruct the South, an effort that came to an ignominious end in the 1890s with the defeat of the Federal Elections Bill in 1891 and the Plessy v. Ferguson decision in 1896. During the immediate postwar years the question was dominant in national politics. Though its priority gradually diminished on the national scene, it continued as a central theme of Southern history.

The documentation begins with 1866, the year Congress took the first decisive action to transform the freed slave into equal citizen. Between the veto of the Freedmen's Bureau Bill in February, 1866 and the ratification of the Fifteenth Amendment in March, 1870, the national commitment was made. Awareness of the issue antedated the commitment, but during the war years controversy and decision making centered on the question of freeing the slave. The Thirteenth Amendment, which destroyed slavery, had received the necessary two-thirds vote in the House of Representatives only at the end of January, 1865, and as the result of great pressure and skillful lobbying on the part of the Lincoln administration. Its ratification was certified the following December 18, and the accompanying enumeration of the required three-fourths of the states included eight formerly in the Confederacy whose acquiescence was, in effect, imposed by the Johnson administration. Despite the pressure, Mississippi had repudiated the amendment. Both Alabama and South Carolina ratified with qualifications in respect to section two, which gave Congress power of enforcement, South Carolina stating specifically that any attempt by Congress to legislate concerning the political status or civil relations of freedmen would be contrary to the Constitution, in conflict with the president's policy, and an obstacle to the reestablishment of harmony in the Union.

Meanwhile, in the summer and fall of 1865 reports coming out of the South in respect to the treatment of freedmen by their former masters gained wide publicity and aroused grave apprehensions at the North. In November and December the new Mississippi legislature passed a series of laws, the earliest and most notorious of the Black Codes, which made unmistakable the Southern intent to establish a special status for the Negro short of full citizenship, to establish it not as a temporary way station to equality but as a permanent form of second-class citizenship. When the first postwar Congress met on December 4, 1865, it faced the momentous issue of the nation's responsibility for men and women set free but not yet equal before the law.

Part One
The Commitment

In all modern history no development is more astounding than the attempt in the immediate post–Civil War years to raise over 4 million people just released from a legal servitude of special rigidity to a legal status of equality. By legislative enactment and constitutional amendment men who yesterday were property, subject to whatever discipline their owners might impose, were made the equal of their old masters in the right to due process of law, to contract freely, to hold property, to bear arms, to testify from the witness stand, to sit on juries, to enjoy public transportation, inns and theatres, to vote both for local and for national officials, and to themselves hold office. Moreover, the new rights and privileges were conferred upon a people of a distinctive race with the approval of an electorate who believed, except for an articulate dissenting minority, in the racial superiority of whites and the racial inferiority of blacks. The roots of this prejudice ran deep in the history of the country and of the Western world, and in the 1860s prejudice was dignified by the scientific authorities of the day. When the freedman was made equal citizen, the concept of racial inequality, unlike the institution of slavery which had become an anachronism, was still growing in vigor and malignancy. The documents presented in part one focus attention upon the problem of how the national commitment came to be made. They also explore what had been done by the close of the nineteenth century, at the national level, both to honor and to erode the promise of equal citizenship.

Recognition of the mid-nineteenth-century effort to establish civic equality has been equated in recent scholarship with a pledge by the nation to racial equality. This view embodies two misconceptions which can distort judgment of the past. Though a national commitment, it was not made by the nation as a whole. A consensus of white Americans was noticeably lacking; the legal changes were forced by one major political party, with almost no freely given support from Southern whites and in the face of nearly solid opposition in the North from the other major party. Equality was a commitment made for the nation by the Republican party. Nor was the promise an affirmation of racial equality. The pledge was to equality irrespective of race or past servitude in matters of public, as distinct from private, authority. Care need be taken not to assume that the Republican party was identical with "the North" or that the concept of equal citizenship is synonymous with that of the equality of races.

The major documents of the Republican postwar legislative record are included in part one: the civil rights acts of 1866 and 1875, the law continuing the Freedmen's Bureau, the First Reconstruction Act, the two equal rights amendments, and the two most important laws passed in an effort to enforce them. In seeking to understand how this record came about, one cannot overlook the continuing force of religious equalitarianism and of its secularization in the eighteenth-century doctrine of the equal rights of man, nor the continuing deference to the heritage of English law and tradition in respect to freemen. Devoted abolitionist leaders outside Congress, though represented here only by the editorials of Wendell Phillips, the speech of Frederick Douglass, and the selection from the London Freed-Man, played a significant role both on behalf of equal citizenship and in opposition to the concept of racial inequality. Yet these leaders and this patrimony were not in themselves sufficient to effect so sweeping a change, one that went beyond the particulars of the legislation to the very nature of the relationship between the federal government and the states, and between the nation and its citizens. Of critical importance was the reaction of moderate leaders and a major segment of the Northern public, especially their view of injustices imposed upon freedmen by white Southerners. There were not only the Black Codes, but more shockingly, instances of brutality by whites acting individually or together to terrorize blacks, a brutality dramatized in the New Orleans riot of 1866 (doc. 9a). We would like to suggest that equal citizenship, particularly in respect to nationalization of fundamental rights and inclusion of the voting privilege, gained mass support among Northern whites because they saw it as a means by which to attain justice. In conscience, having freed the slave, Republicans could not entrust his well-being to local and state white authority in the South, could not permit legal barriers to his advancement, could not stand by and witness harsh treatment inflicted with impunity. To most Republicans, irrespective of the boundaries of their allegiance to equality, the extension of national authority and national citizenship appeared essential to fair play and meaningful freedom for the former slave. The selections in section A, by illuminating the nature of local justice in the South, suggest a substantial basis for the conviction among Republicans that riot, terror, and isolated incidents could not be discounted as exceptional happenings.

A further explanation for the anomaly of a racist society establishing unqualified equality of civic rights and for the specific nature of the measures taken, lies in the very momentum of events. The chronology of the materials in section B is of basic importance. From the beginning of the clash between President Johnson and the Republican majority, there was at stake the rights of black Southerners, but the form of legislation passed to secure those rights was shaped by the exigencies of the moment. Thus the Freedmen's Bureau Bill passed in July, 1866 differed in significant aspects from the one vetoed in February (doc. 6c)—tempered (though it retained what Republicans considered most essential) in an effort to frame a new measure that would either gain the President's approval or command a two-thirds majority in both houses. The universal suffrage provision of the Reconstruction legislation of early 1867 owed more to the 1866 campaign, the New Orleans riot, and most particularly to the postelection repudiation of the Fourteenth Amendment by Johnson and the Southern States (doc. 9c) than to any Radical blueprint. These two examples also suggest the paradoxical impact of the continuing conflict between Executive and Congress: it resulted in a legislative program of Reconstruction at once more conservative and more extreme than would have been enacted had the two branches of government been in substantial agreement in the early months of 1866.

Contemporary opponents of the Republican majority voiced harsh explanations for the party record, and some have been echoed by historians. Republican policy was attributed to the fanaticism of "negro worshippers," to a vindictive desire to punish and humiliate the defeated white South, and to shrewd calculation designed to further party fortunes including opportunity for patronage and pelf. The charge of narrow partisan self-interest warrants critical attention.

Party considerations did affect Reconstruction legislation. No major party in American politics can afford to disregard the practical political consequences of its actions. Typically, party principle and program have represented compromise within a wide spectrum of opinion and interest, and they have rarely been irreconciliable with those of the opposing party. In the case of the Republican party during the first two decades of its existence, members identified party loyalty with a distinctive cause, a cause that progressed from the containment of slavery, to antislavery, to equality before the law, and finally to equal suffrage. The consequences for the freedman of this identification have received only partial examination. Careful study has been given to party self-interest in relation to Republican policy toward the Negro in the post-1876 decades with the conclusion implied or explicit that concern for party affected adversely the status of the Negro. An alternate perspective, one looking to the black man's interest and extending over the entire postwar period, raises doubt that the harsh assessment on party is generally valid. In respect to a major issue whose resolution would fundamentally affect the national character and experience, the two parties in the 1860s were sharply divided from each other, and each was remarkably cohesive within its own ranks. The sharp ideological cleavage between parties, marked by attitude and policy toward the freedmen, strengthened Republican concern for the Negro and helped mobilize party loyalty in support of legislation that went beyond what would otherwise have been consensus. Partisanship, so often held up to scorn and condemnation in accounts of the period, may well have operated as a powerful force for constructive change. And the lessening of partisanship on the issue of the Negro's status, the weakening of identification between Republicanism and the black man's cause, may well have contributed to the failure of Reconstruction. Such a hypothesis will suggest the possibility of some startling reversals of standard historical judgment. The political tactic of "waving the bloody shirt," illustrated in the debates on the enforcement bill of 1875 (doc. 18), could lose its odium; and the repudiation of party loyalty by the Republican Liberals of 1872 could forfeit its halo.

Whether political partisanship, either by its weakening or by its strength, helped dishonor the Reconstruction commitment to equal citizenship, it is clear that the party role was not so crucial in defeat as it had been in victory. Many elements converged to shatter the expectations of those responsible for the Reconstruction legislation. Most important, in our judgment, was the resistance characterized as "in effect a massive campaign of civil disobedience throughout the South."[1] In opposing equality the white South was united and persistent, both strident and subtle, sometimes open and other times covert. Its spokesmen defended civic inequality by arguments directed northward that were notably inconsistent but remarkably effective (see docs. 21, 22a and c). On the one hand, they denied its existence and gave assurance that the South had accepted the Reconstruction amendments; on the other, they argued directly that race inferiority constituted a danger which made white supremacy imperative. Facing the South's concentrated resolve was a North long divided on the issue, weary from the battles of war and Reconstruction, anxious for peace and reconciliation, increasingly concerned with the burgeoning problems of industrialization and urbanization: depression, strikes, poverty alongside riches, outraged farmers, and a proliferation of corruption responsive to the opportunities offered by a rapidly advancing technology. In addition the authority of science and the new social sciences, instead of aiding those who would keep the faith, was increasingly invoked against them. And as the Democratic South wrested state after state from Republican control, it cast the opposition into an image of unparalleled oppression, incompetence, and corruption, a distortion so convincingly publicized that many who had thought to befriend and vindicate the Negro by giving him the ballot recoiled in dismay.

What should surprise the student of the First Reconstruction is not that it failed, but that within the ranks of the Republican party, despite defections, there remained enough commitment to persist. Without the congressional majorities necessary to pass legislation from the spring of 1875 until 1889 (a predominance soon lost in the elections of 1890 and 1892), the Republicans after more than a decade resumed the old battle. Senator George F.

1.   David Donald, *Charles Sumner and the Rights of Man* (New York: Alfred A. Knopf, 1970), p. 420.

Hoar, a good exemplar of the old faith, fought valiantly for the Federal Elections Bill of 1890 (doc. 23a). The fate of that measure should not obscure the fact that Republicans pushed it through the House and would have done so in the Senate except for a handful of senators who put special interest above party pledge. Moreover, a close look at the record of the Hayes administration (doc. 19), the usual target of censure, casts doubt upon the charges of abandonment and betrayal in the late 1870s.

The congressional reconstructionists who sought guarantees that black men would not be reduced to a state of second-class citizenship by white Southerners looked principally to two instruments: the federal courts and the ballot box. Use of the military was reluctant, limited, and brief. How justified was their confidence in the power of the ballot, our twentieth-century experience may eventually test—certainly, no fair trial occurred in the post–Civil War decades. It is worth noting that their confidence was fully shared by the very radical Wendell Phillips (doc. 14a).

The federal courts at best proved ineffectual and at worst obstructed the clear intent behind the Reconstruction laws and amendments. In a series of decisions extending over more than two decades the Supreme Court reduced the laws to impotence and interpreted the amendments so narrowly as to deny their basic purpose. In effect the court held that under them neither Congress nor the Supreme Court itself had power to safeguard the fundamental rights of freemen. The relevant decisions are not included here for they will be printed in Alan F. Westin's volume of this documentary history. Readers who finish part one and then study these cases will recognize a firmer grasp of Reconstruction history in the minority dissents of Ward Hunt and John M. Harlan than in the key majority decisions written by Morris R. Waite, Joseph P. Bradley, and Henry Billings Brown.[2]

How to account for the striking failure of a Republican Supreme Court to uphold the legislative achievements of the Republican

2. Of the decisions the most important for our purpose are Chief Justice Waite's opinions in *United States* v. *Reese* and *United States* v. *Cruikshank* together with Justice Hunt's dissent in the former (March 1876), Justice Bradley's opinion and Justice Harlan's dissent in the civil rights cases (October 1883), Justice Samuel Miller's opinion in *Ex Parte* Yarbrough (March 1884), and Justice Brown's opinion together with Harlan's dissent in *Plessy* v. *Ferguson* (May 1896).

party presents an unresolved problem. Part of the answer lies in the fact that the vitiation was a gradual process, not without counter-vailing tendencies. It began with the Slaughter-house cases in 1873 while the Republican resolve was not only strong but still politi-cally dominant; it was completed in 1896 with Plessy v. Ferguson when that resolve had been not only defeated but shattered.

The first decision of the Supreme Court on the meaning of the Fourteenth Amendment, by a bare five to four majority, came in a case having nothing to do with the protection of black men. The butchers of New Orleans were contesting the authority of the Louisiana legislature to grant a slaughter-house monopoly which deprived them of the right to exercise their trade. The 1873 deci-sion was written by Justice Samuel Miller, both a strong antislavery man and a commanding figure on the bench, with no intent to weaken the power of the national government to safeguard the Negro and apparently with no awareness that such would be the result. Shocked by the far-reaching implications if the amendment were recognized as transferring the protection of all civil rights from the states to Congress and the federal judiciary, Miller decided such had not been the intent of the amendment. His decision narrowly delimited those rights pertaining to United States citizen-ship. Had the case involved the Negro directly, as did the Cruik-shank and Reese decisions three years later, it is unlikely that the rights traditional in American society would have been eliminated from the "privileges and immunities of citizens of the United States," at least where those citizens were black men. It is worth noting that in 1875 a part of Miller's Slaughter-house opinion was cited in support of the Republican effort to pass the ill-fated Enforcement Bill of that session (doc. 18) and that the Yarbrough decision which he also wrote was similarly used by Senator Hoar in 1890 to defend the so-called Force Bill (doc. 23a).

By the time the court on March 27, 1876 passed judgment in cases involving flagrant attack upon the rights of black men, not only were the justices bound by the earlier Slaughter-house deci-sion but also they were operating in a climate of public opinion increasingly critical of federal intervention in the South and de-sirous of reconciliation between the sections. The same considera-tions which led President Grant by 1875 to deny military support to Southern Republican regimes and President Hayes two years later to inaugurate a new Southern policy (doc. 19) may well have been influential with the court. In the Reese and Cruikshank cases there had been a long interval between hearing argument and rendering opinion, and also a change of mind, for the court originally agreed simply to throw out the indictments on technicalities. Chance could have chosen no less propitious time than the spring of 1876 for a major decision affecting the freedmen. Action under the enforcement laws had become a political liability to the Republicans; support for a policy of "home rule" was gaining momentum in the North; and disillusionment with the pledges of New South leaders waited upon future events. Timing was not the only disadvantage born by the government in the two cases. The attorney general and the solicitor general were no match for the brilliant array of legal talent available to the defendants, with Henry Stanbery one of two counselors for Reese, and in the more important Cruikshank case the eight defense attorneys included former Democratic Senator Reverdy Johnson and David Dudley Field, brother of Justice Stephen J. Field.

The narrow interpretation of "privileges and immunities," to which the court consistently held after the Slaughter-house decision, was but one of the two major arguments with which the legislative effort to protect the freedman was turned aside. The phraseology of the Fourteenth Amendment, despite intent (see doc. 15c), and of the Fifteenth Amendment as well, was vulnerable, particularly at a time when logic rather than experience appeared the surer judicial guide. For logic, if not history, gave support to a devastating line of argument barely stated in the 1876 Cruikshank decision but fully developed in later ones, notably in United States v. Harris (January 1883) and the civil rights cases (October 1883). Since the amendments had enjoined the states from denying civil rights, the court held that the enforcement authority granted Congress could be used only against the states. This reasoning left the national government with no power under the amendments to safeguard blacks against the most outrageous infringements of their rights even by armed bands if committed by whites acting as individuals rather than as agents of local or state governments.

At the time of the earlier decisions the full impact of the two arguments was not yet apparent. Conflicting directions are evident within the opinions and reappear in later ones. The court in 1876 had clearly acknowledged a new and critically important right that Congress might protect: exemption from discrimination in voting on account of race. In effect Chief Justice Waite had suggested that more careful indictments and a revision of the laws would make this right enforceable. Revision proved politically impossible, but the court in Justice Miller's strong, unanimous opinion of 1884 (Ex Parte Yarbrough) found other basis for upholding federal protection of voters.

This counterdirection supportive of federal action on behalf of Negroes but partially offset the impact of Justice Bradley's 1883 civil rights opinion, which overturned those provisions of the Civil Rights Act of 1875 that provided equal access to transportation, inns, and places of amusement. While the decision opened the way for the segregation laws of the 1890s, Bradley based the opinion on a lack of congressional authority to pass the legislation; he did not argue that Jim Crow was reconcilable with the equal protection of the laws. Indeed, he conceded that equal access to such facilities might be a legal right under the Fourteenth Amendment; but if violated, he held that redress must be sought from the state, or if state laws were adverse, by corrective legislation in Congress directed at state action. In contrast the Plessy decision thirteen years later was unrelieved in its racial insensitivity and unequivocal in upholding enforced segregation:

> A statute which implies merely a legal distinction between the white and colored races—a distinction which is founded in the color of the two races, and which must always exist so long as white men are distinguished from the other race by color—has no tendency to destroy the legal equality of the two races.

In the 1880s, reaction to the civil rights decision, reenforced by Harlan's brilliant dissent, had moved Northern states to take action in the opposite direction. Within two years, eleven states had enacted civil rights laws prohibiting segregation. The Plessy decision stirred no comparable political counterattack in the 1890s when the climate of public opinion reflected both increasing racism and the urgency of other national problems.

The process sketched above does not, of course, provide a full explanation for the action of the post–Civil War Supreme Court in respect to the rights of black men. That must wait upon further studies, including one that would probe with subtlety the relationship between the race attitudes of justices and their decision making. Like the history of the Reconstruction laws and amendments, the ringing dissents of Justice Harlan, former slaveholder and opponent of the Thirteenth Amendment, suggest that a commitment to racial equality was not a prerequisite for commitment to justice irrespective of race. In counterbalance, passages from the majority opinions indicate that the assumption of race superiority endemic in white America, North as well as South, reached the Supreme Court bench and helped undermine judicial support for the commitment to equal justice.

Whatever the explanation, the responsibility of the nineteenth-century Supreme Court was monumental. In fairness it must be pointed out again that the court did not close off all avenues to the security promised black men, at least in respect to some essential rights. Perhaps it should be added that in the face of Democratic opposition at the national level and widespread local obstruction, even full support from the federal judiciary would probably not have saved the First Reconstruction.

Part Two
Flawed Freedom

Modern scholarship has destroyed the stereotypes from which white Southerners fashioned the myth of their humiliation and oppression under the yoke of "black" Reconstruction. Gone are the hordes of venal "carpetbaggers," the renegade "scalawags," the swaggering blacks who elbowed whites from the sidewalks and turned legislative halls into forums of buffoonery. The assumed outrage of "Negro dominance" has yielded to historic facts: Negroes as legislators and officeholders constituted a minority in the Republican state governments. Constructive achievement marked the period, particularly the new constitutions and the free school systems. Both within and without the seats of government, blacks displayed more often than not a spirit of moderation and magnanimity toward old masters. White defiance and white terror, not black incompetence or crime or belligerency, are now recognized as the critical forces undermining law and order during the Republican years.[3]

Understanding the Southern experience during Republican Reconstruction and the years of Conservative control that followed

3. The most comprehensive study is Allen W. Trelease, White Terror: The Ku Klux Klan Conspiracy and Southern Reconstruction (New York: Harper & Row, 1971).

requires more than the discard of old misconceptions. A number of the documents presented in part two suggest the need for a fresh synthesis. If there was no black dominance riding roughshod over white supremacy, blacks nonetheless shared political power during the Republican years and exercised it with a sense of group interest and individual dignity. Republican regimes rested upon black votes and survived longest in those states where blacks were most numerous. When Republican strength was broken beyond recovery, the fact that considerable numbers of blacks continued to vote brought concessions and at some times and places during the years of Redeemer dominance, even a measure of local power (doc. 26). And however many were cowed into silence, there were also men like C. H. Johnson, a porter in Columbus, Georgia, who "aint of that sort. Whatever I want to say, I am going to say it." (doc. 34.)

As indicated by the appeal of white South Carolinians to Congress (doc. 24c), the leaders of the old South did not wait upon experience to condemn the new order. Indeed, a chronological approach to Southern "Redemption" can be misleading. In Virginia the state was "redeemed" without ever having passed into Republican control. Throughout the South, victory for the Conservative Democratic opposition represented not so much a reaction against the Republican years as the triumph of a continuing resolve to concede to a victorious North little more than the renunciation of independent nationhood and of property rights in human beings.

The tragic inability of Republican state governments to maintain the rights of Negro citizens is nowhere more poignantly documented than in the case of Mississippi (doc. 28a). The unquestionable integrity of the state's carpetbag governor, Adelbert Ames, did not save him from impeachment charges once the Democrats through violence, intimidation, and perfidy had gained control of the state legislature. His case illustrates the manner in which white Southerners sought to legitimize their own seizure of power by indiscriminate accusations of official misconduct on the part of their political opponents. It also suggests the skill with which "Redeemers" turned their own defiance of law into an asset in manipulating Northern public opinion. That opinion was increasingly repelled by the continuing turbulence and call for military intervention in the southland, as white Southerners defeated the expectation of moderate Republicans that social change could be enforced through the peaceful instruments of the ballot and the courts.

The "New South" is a term of monumental ambiguity, most often associated with the decade of the eighties and the ardor for industrial development (docs. 21, 22a and c, 36). The phrase became current in the 1870s, and its key concepts emerged even earlier. Statements in the seventies linked the material progress projected for the future with freedom from past bondage to slavery, which one white Southerner termed the "malignant cancer" responsible for the backwardness of the South. The implication for the freedman was unclear. There were doubts of his ability to meet the need for more efficient and skilled labor; his future in the South was termed a "mystery."[4] By the eighties, however, it was evident that blacks would not be displaced as a major labor force of the region, and spokesmen for the New South creed, which matured during that decade, saw a secure place for the Negro in the developing prosperity. Repudiating repression and violence, they viewed their goals as dependent upon cooperation between the races and benefiting both whites and blacks. The documents in part two dealing with the black man's condition during the 1880s suggest that blacks did in fact share in the greater abundance of the optimistic years between the depression seventies and the depression nineties. The documents also reveal, however, that the cooperation offered by whites in the pursuit of regional progress was limited and sometimes viciously cruel. The most shocking exploitation of blacks by whites was administered through the convict lease system (doc. 35). Ironically, while Negroes who applied found few open doors to employment in the new industrial order, those held under restraints were eagerly sought for work in its mines and railroad construction.

The economic expansion acclaimed in the South appeared so minimal in retrospect that the New South title passed to succeeding generations. The material advances of the eighties have recently been characterized as nothing more than "The Emperor's

4. John C. Reed, The Old and New South (pamphlet, New York: A. S. Barnes and Co., 1876), pp. 11–24.

New Clothes,"[5] and a scholarly summation of New South histori-
ography reports a consensus among historians and economists that
"no great leap or qualitative change occurred in the economy of the
South until after 1940."[6] Yet behind the exaggerated rhetoric and
booster psychology, the eighties did not stand naked of economic
achievement. Statistical comparisons of per capita income and
wealth in 1880 and 1900, a key element in the examination of the
South's economic development, take no account of the slippage in
the depression nineties; and indeed, it would be an almost impossible task to assess quantitatively the economic advance in the years
from 1879 through 1892. Whether mirage or reality, the promise of
the eighties was not fulfilled. This meant that in the pursuit of a
decent livelihood black men faced both racial barriers and the wall
of economic disadvantage that separated the South, both black and
white, from the rest of the nation.

Since the 1930s the most commonly accepted explanation for
the South's disadvantaged position has placed the blame on Northern exploitation, a "colonial-imperialistic conspiracy thesis" cur-
rently held untenable by economists and some historians.[7] Internal
factors which they have identified as contributing to the region's
lagging economic growth are numerous and formidable, ranging
from the dominant values of the Southern tradition to the inadequate supply of money and credit, lagging urbanization, and local
markets too limited to sustain profitability either in industry or in
agriculture. There is a special irony in the elements of parallel
between post–World War II prescriptions for continuing economic
growth in the South and the programs of Republican Reconstruction regimes. Both championed effective education, rejected the
elitist concept of inevitable low-income status for large numbers of
Southerners, welcomed industrial enterprise as essential to economic prosperity, and sought to unshackle the South from its
heritage of racial discrimination. Qualified by less fervor for educa-

5. Paul M. Gaston, *The New South Creed: A Study in Southern Myth-
making* (New York: Alfred A. Knopf, 1970), pp. 202–207.
6. Sheldon Hackney, "Origins of the New South in Retrospect," *Journal of
Southern History*, XXXVIII (May 1972), 209.
7. A key article is that of Clarence H. Danhof, "Four Decades of Thought
on the South's Economic Problems," in Melvin L. Greenhut and W. Tate
Witman, eds., *Essays in Southern Economic Development* (Chapel Hill,
N.C.: University of North Carolina Press, 1964), pp. 7–68.

tion and a significantly different concept of appropriate race relationships, the New South creed of the Redeemers in the 1880s also embraced the essentials of the old Republican–new economists' approach to plenty.

The economic status and well being of most black Southerners directly depended not upon the new order but upon the old agricultural staples. While the limitations imposed by a predominantly agrarian economy have been recognized in general, insufficient study has been given to the detailed relationship between its vagaries and the emergence of a poverty-ridden, largely-landless black peasantry. Selections in section C, part two, suggest that "King Cotton" failed the black man in peace as decisively as the white Southerner in war. Indeed, its indirect impact may have been as important as its immediate consequences. To sustain the promising growth of the eighties, their developing local credit and capital, markets and urbanization, a relatively stable prosperous commercial agriculture may well have been indispensable. It is reasonable to assume that cotton prices had been an element essential to the relative prosperity of the decade. Though low as compared to the postwar expectations of the sixties, prices during the eighties neither followed the wide fluctuations of the preceding years nor dropped to the impossibly low levels of the depression nineties.

Modern scholarship has absolved the furnishing merchant and the crop lien system of much of the opprobrium heaped upon them by contemporaries and by later analysts. References in several selections of section C suggest something of the contradictory nature of their role as both instruments of economic bondage and the means through which a precarious agricultural economy kept functioning and men newly freed from legal servitude found an alternative to abject dependence upon old masters. It has taken a century after the First Reconstruction for Southern agriculture finally to approach a reasonably secure economic status. This has been attained through a partial displacement of old staples by grasslands, poultry production, dairy, and food cattle combined with the mechanization of its primary crops, both developments precipitating a massive out-migration of poverty-ridden rural laborers. A comparable agricultural revolution, though in some of its aspects anticipated by agricultural reformers of the earlier years, was impossible to effect precipitously. In freedom as in slavery the black man's fate was largely tied to cotton production.

In the immediate post–Civil War period, yearly contracts embodied a variety of labor arrangements—wages, seldom paid in full until the crop year's end, group sharing in crop production, individual or family tenancy, often a combination within the limits of a single plantation (see doc. 31b). By the freedmen's friends, these were seen as temporary, transitional devices that would start the black man up the agricultural ladder to independent land ownership. He was expected to follow the example of countless propertyless white Americans, both natives and newcomers, who had found on the land dignity and economic opportunity. The nation's past experience gave an aura of reality to this expectation of the 1860s, but it was one that could not be realized in the last decades of the nineteenth century, a period that developed into a time of troubles for all of rural America.

Historians looking for an answer to the freedmen's plight have focused attention upon the nation's failure to provide land. Some attribute to this omission the failure of the First Reconstruction, a conclusion with which we cannot agree. Land ownership could not have created the profitable agriculture essential to the black man's economic security, nor would it have provided a sufficient defense against the assault of determined white supremacists. Yet land ownership would have added to his new status a dimension of dignity and some measure of independence both political and economic.

The freedman's desire for land was great, and his expectations justified. The Freedmen's Bureau Act of 1865 had promised to assign forty acres of abandoned or confiscated land to every male freedman, not without charge, but with reasonable provision for rental and purchase. The promise went unfulfilled. Many factors entered into that nonfulfillment, but first responsibility for its abnegation—and perhaps ultimate responsibility as well—rested with President Andrew Johnson. The essential sequence of events in 1865 and early 1866 can be followed in the report and correspondence of Commissioner O. O. Howard (doc. 30a). President Johnson restored lands which would otherwise have been allotted to freedmen and in effect abandoned execution of the confiscation acts adopted during the war as inappropriate to a time of peace. In historical perspective there is considerable justification for this course of action. The forty-acre mandate carried a dubious property title for it had been contingent upon a confiscation that would not extend beyond the lifetime of the rebel owner. Further, the uncertainty as to land titles would surely have complicated economic recovery of the defeated southland.

President Johnson's subsequent policy, however, does not invite an equally generous judgment. He refused to consider, apparently without any hesitation, the suggestion that his pardon to large landowners include a requirement that they provide small homesteads for their former bondsmen. In the bitter contention over lands assigned by General Sherman's order to freedmen in the sea islands of South Carolina and Georgia, the president undercut the Freedmen's Bureau chief and placed the influence of the executive office at the service of the old slaveholding aristocracy. When he vetoed the Freedmen's Bureau Bill of February, 1866, President Johnson singled out its land provisions for special condemnation. According to the veto message, they represented an improper exercise of congressional authority; the general provisions favored "one class or color of our people more than another," and those in respect to the sea islands would "keep the mind of the freedman in a state of uncertain expectation and restlessness," a source of "constant and vague apprehension" for his neighbors (doc. 6b).

In early 1866 it had been possible for Republican leadership to gain congressional approval for proposals designed to meet in some measure the wartime commitment to the freedmen. A close comparison of sections three through six of the vetoed bill (doc. 6c) with the Freedmen's Bureau Law enacted the following July (doc. 6d) will reveal that the bill, but not the law, embodied a general land program, one usually overlooked by historians but not by the Democrats in Congress who opposed it. The substitute program was premised not upon a dubious confiscation but upon governmental land purchase plus the allocation of 3 million acres of public domain and provision for supplying transportation, clothing, fuel, and temporary shelter to homesteaders who were destitute. This delimited but viable program was a casualty of the conflict between President Johnson and the Republican Congress. As battlelines were drawn, Republicans abandoned the land program as particularly vulnerable before the president's appeal to race prejudice, traditional laissez-faire individualism, and concern for frugality in public expenditures. Friends of the freedman gave first priority to defense of his basic civil rights. With the Fourteenth and Fifteenth Amendments secured, a remnant of the antislavery forces sought federal legislation for a land program reminiscent of the one abandoned in 1866. They proposed a national land commission empowered to spend $2 million to finance land purchases for Negroes. But when this belated effort was made in the winter of 1869, the time was no longer propitious for such a measure to become the law of the land.

PART ONE
The Issue of Civil Rights:
The National Commitment
to Equity for the
Freedmen, 1866–1896

A. Local Justice in the South

THE REPORT and letters included in this section were written by Southerners whose testimony carries a special conviction and conveys as well
an intimate view of the failure of local justice. As early as the summer
of 1865, the problem was evident and entered into party contentions
over Reconstruction. No foolproof solution was ever found despite all
congressional efforts to insure equity, which included authorizing military
jurisdiction through the Freedmen's Bureau, enlarging the role of federal
courts in the protection of civil rights, providing freedmen with the
ballot, and insisting upon their right to testify and to act as jurors. During its lifetime the bureau showed continuing concern but followed no
consistent policy largely because President Johnson pressed for early recognition of local civil authority and disapproved special bureau courts.
Note that the Texan Unionist (doc. 3), unlike most Northern friends
of the freedmen, assumed that equal justice would not follow upon
Negro enfranchisement. The first selection was extracted from an Arkansas report and forwarded to Commissioner Howard. It was written
by a prominent Arkansas ex-Confederate turned Union supporter during
the war, who in 1866 was working for the bureau in the southwestern
part of the state with the title of general superintendent. The Fleming
letter (doc. 2) was addressed to the bureau's assistant commissioner for
South Carolina.

1. Report of Honorable E. W. Gantt, Arkansas Freedmen's Bureau, May 27, 1866

I did intend to write at length in reference to the orders turning
over to the civil authorities cases in which the protection or punishment of the freedmen is involved, but I dislike to state a proposition and not give my reasons for it.

SOURCE: Quoted in report of John W. Sprague, June 7, 1866, Records of
the Bureau of Refugees, Freedmen, and Abandoned Lands, War Records Division, National Archives, Washington, D.C. (hereafter referred to as Freedmen's Bureau Records).

I will say in brief however that so far as relates to *felonies* of negroes, I see no other plan but for offences *less than felony* committed on the persons of freedmen I regard it as quite a different thing.

For instance: an employer tells a freedman that he does not work well or that he has stolen his meat, or has told a lie; the negro says, "No massa I hasn't"; the white man replies "dont say you havent* you insolent fellow." The negro says "he is free and has a right to make the denial." The white man knocks him down, or whips him, or kicks him off his place, and the agent of the Bureau turns the case over to the civil authorities. The justice of the peace hears the proof, and decides that the "nigger" "sauced" the white man, and that the white man did right and he would knock down any impertinent negro.

Now then, Gen'l I know our people and such would be the fate of nine tenths of the cases.

A case occurred in this place, a week ago today. A colored woman went to a Mrs Vaughn's (I believe is the name) and remarked that she had come after her little girl. Mrs V. refused to give her up. There had been no contract for her hire. The woman insisted that she would have her child. Mrs V. abused and threatened her; the negro after many provoking words replied "I am as free as you madam." Mrs V. thereupon became enraged and struck her, after this the woman left and in going out of the gate met the wife's husband. He was told that the negro "sauced" his wife, and he immediately "horsewhipped" her, and after that clubbed his whip and struck her severely over the head. She came to me bleeding and looking very badly, while her little girls were in tears, and seemed half frightened to death. I at once addressed a note to Mr Williams, local superintendent, urging immediate action in the matter. He proceeded I thought reluctantly, carelessly and slowly. Today I sent him instructions referred to. My impression is that he will turn the case over to the civil authorities, if referred I do not believe a solitary thing will be done. I feel certain that a jury from this town would never convict the man, even for *an assault with a whip upon a woman*, because that woman is a negro & "sauced" the other woman, who is white. Can the colored people expect

* Spelling has been reprinted as it originally appeared in the documents without the use of *sic* to indicate instances where the original was erroneous.—Eds.

protection from such authorities yet a while? I shall watch this case with interest should it be referred.

On yesterday I was in Mr Williams office, who is the District Superintendent for this county, a gentleman came in and reported that a negro had sauced him, and he struck him. Mr W. asked me if *legally* such a man were amenable to the laws. I replied that "no words justified an assault, but were I on a jury, I should be for inflicting the lightest penalty upon any person who struck another in consequence of very abusive or threatening language." A very respectable old citizen in the room at the time swore "that, if he could not thrash a negro who insulted him, he would leave the country"; this feeling of blows for impudence as it existed under the old system is hard to eradicate from the minds of our people. *It can only be done*, in my opinion, by the frequent infliction of a penalty, coupled with explanations as to the law and the justice thereof, *and this by officers holding authority directly under the United States Government.* Officers elected by the people in the Southern States would enforce no penalty for wrongs done a negro, less than felony.

The people are not up to it, and our public men, especially those of small calibre and great pretensions, fear the people, not one of them could be "reelected," and there are the fewest number who can brave public opinion, face demagogues, and standing on the right, maintain it until the people come to them in the end.

I believe that intelligent, discreet and conscientious officers, responsible not to the people directly, that is not holding office directly from them, can so chasten the unpatriotic and the brutal, and so educate the well disposed persons in our midst that in a year or two, a public sentiment would grow up which would elect civil authorities before whom all these questions could safely go. A course other than this, might crystalize a public sentiment, and intensify a wrongful prejudice, that might at last have to be broken by force, or result in the extinction of the colored race in our midst.

The term "impudence" or "sauce" (which should have been explained in its proper place in this communication) meant usually any words returned for the grossest charges; a meek denial of having done wrong was by some declared impudence, "not shutting his mouth" when told to do so by master or mistress, when the slave should protest his innocence of grave or light charges; not "holding down his other hand" when their mistress was whipping them (but raising them up to break the force of the blow, always considered *voluntary*, no difference how hard the infliction) was always regarded as the extreme of impudence. To respond "I have done all the work I can" to a charge of "laziness" was always quite insolvent; to walk slowly when told to "run" was insupportable insolence. I was an indulgent master, but remember myself whipping a little rascal because he wouldn't run fast when I called him. The point I desire to make is that a court of justice plucked from a public sentiment of that kind, catches the hue of its surroundings, and until that public sentiment advances, there is but little hope of fair dealing. But after all I am hopeful of great changes and a bright future for all, even the most obdurate in our midst, provided always that too many opportunities are not thrown away in this and the coming step of final adjustment of sectional difficulties.

2. Julius J. Fleming to General R. K. Scott, South Carolina, February 8, 1867

Sumter, S.C., Febry, 8th 1867

Brig. Genl R. K. Scott Asst. Comr. Bureau F. and A.L. for S.C.

Sir: As partially illustrating the history of the times, I submit for your consideration and that of the Government, the subjoined copies of letters . . . addressed by me to Judge Aldrich and Gov. Orr of this State.

Sumter, S.C. Nov 3rd. 1866

Hon Judge Aldrich,
Presiding at Fall Term of Sessions for Sumter District:

I beg leave to invite your Honor's attention to the fact that many persons in this District need instruction as to their duty toward the negroes in the new relation they now sustain as freed-men. As a Magistrate, I have necessarily become apprised of much which has escaped the public eye and I regret to say that cases in which negro men and women have been beaten, shot, stabbed and maimed, are sufficiently numerous to demand a public rebuke from the presiding Judge. It is also an unhappy fact, that a conscientious Magistrate, however pure his past record, and however far beyond

SOURCE: Freedmen's Bureau Records.

suspicion as a true Carolinian his antecedents may have been, is greatly denounced and abused in some quarters for simply extending the protection of the law to these unhappy people. If this sentiment is not corrected, it must soon be evident that no high-toned gentleman who values his reputation & peace of mind, will consent to act as a Magistrate. The result will be that none but ignorant and prejudiced persons will accept the position, at a time when only the most judicious and prudent should be selected. When I have issued warrants on the complaints of wounded & bleeding negroes, I have even requested the Sheriff or Constable to inform by note the offender that a warrant had been issued, and request attendance to give bond, without the annoyance of an arrest at home & this course has been pursued; and yet I have been obliged on several occasions to threaten fine & imprisonment for contempt, on account of language reflecting on the Magistrate used by persons thus brought before me. It is true that apologies have followed, but it makes the duty very unpleasant when the faithful and impartial Magistrate is popularly censured for doing what is actually for the public good. For it is well known to me that serious disturbances in the country have been prevented by my course in assuring the freedmen that the law was amply sufficient and that they should have the benefit of the usual remedies which it provides.

In such Courts as we have heretofore had, I have represented both races as counsel and in every case where I have appeared for freedmen, I have been fully sensible of the fact that the popular current was against my client, although the law and evidence forced a decision in his favor (in the *Provost* Court). And planters have told me frankly that they did not believe that any lawyer should act as counsel for a negro. And if a lawyer knows that in thus acting, he is serving a client too poor to pay, and incurs popular odium by his humanity, what prospect is there for these unhappy people in our Courts? For one, I have steadfastly pursued the line of duty uninfluenced by popular favor or prejudices—but for the good of the country I most earnestly wish that a better sentiment prevailed among our people at large. As a Magistrate I was sometimes censored in former days by these very people for enforcing the law against *slaves*, when their owners employed the best counsel and did all they could to defeat the law, even where the negro was guilty of the most atrocious crimes, as rape (of white women) burglary, deadly assault, &c. Now, when they are free (&

helpless), it is maintained that they should not have even a fair trial. A *senator* could then appear as counsel for *a slave* involved in horrible guilt, without compromise of position; but *now*, any lawyer must expect abuse if he gives a *freedman* the benefit of his services, when his client is not the wrong-doer, but the victim of injustice and outrage. *O Tempora! O Mores!* hackneyed and trite the exclamation may be, but Cicero himself never had better cause for its utterance!

I have thought it my duty to address this communication to your Honor. Although a native Carolinian and a slaveholder as long as the institution lasted, I believe that the interests of both races demand that the negroes should be treated kindly & justly, and that they should have all the protection which their necessities demand, and all the sympathies which their very ignorance and helplessness inspire; and the kindred sentiments in your Honor's charge at the extra Court, I am sorry to say, need repetition in "line upon line."

Very Respectfully,
Yr. obt Servt.
(Sgd) Julius J. Fleming

. . . The letter to Judge Aldrich was given to him before the opening of Court, & he *did* charge the Grand Jury in accordance with its suggestions. But in two cases tried at that term, of white men for killing freedmen, the juries promptly acquitted the accused, although *the fact* of the killing in each case was admitted. And in said cases, his Honor's charges to the Petit Juries amounted to plain *instructions to acquit.* The circumstances when explained might *palliate*, but could scarcely *justify* the taking of life. . . .

Under the existing *regime*, a freed(?)man can be deprived of his personal liberty at any moment by an arrest on the most trivial grounds, (as to keep the peace &c.) on account of his *inability to give bail.*

The District Court may be considered as *the* tribunal which the State has provided for the freedmen. In *the city,* under the eye of the Bureau and the military, it may meet out justice—but will it do this in the rural districts? . . .

It is presided over by a judge nominated and virtually appointed by the district delegation in the legislature—a judge belonging to the locality and mixed up with its passions and prejudices, and having the right to practice as an attorney in the higher courts, a prudent regard for which practice will naturally indispose him to offend any who in the future might become profitable clients.

The juries in an agricultural country must be composed chiefly of *planters*—the very class with whom the freedmen have their principal difficulties. Can such juries be expected to act without bias in any case in which a freedman appears as plaintiff or defendant, with a planter as his adversary?

The costs are required of the plaintiff *in advance*—$2.00 to the Clerk and the same to the Sheriff, before the case is docketed. A freedman may have $100 due him and be unable to sue for the want of the $4.00 thus required. Besides, where are they to find counsel, without funds to pay?

Each party litigant looks generally to its own color for witnesses —and in weighing the testimony, it seems to be taken for granted, that a negro *cannot* tell the truth, and that it is impossible for a white person to swear falsely—a conclusion which is unjust & fatal to the freedman, & which facts often reverse.

The court allows colored witnesses to be brow-beaten and bullied in a manner never allowed towards others, and well calculated to confuse and involve them in hopeless (yet innocent) contradictions—and this is then commented on by counsel as evidence of falsehood and perjury. . . .

The *desideratum* is a Provost Court—fairly & fearlessly conducted—holding its sessions only as occasion requires—and which shall do no injustice and give no just cause of complaint to the white population, but at the same time shall extend to the freedmen the protection which others enjoy. . . .

3. William Pressick of Texas to Thomas D. Eliot, January 24, 1868

Malagorda City [Texas], 24 January 1868

To T. D. Elliott
Chairman of the Committee of Freedmens Affairs

Dear Sir: Your communication of 9th Dec. 1867 is received to wit: That the Committee on Freedmens affairs be directed to ascertain what reasons there are, if any why the Freedmens Beaureau

SOURCE: T. D. Eliot Papers, Freedmen's Bureau Records.

should be continued beyond the time now limited by law, and report by bill or otherwise &c. And requesting me to state any causes that may have come to my knowledge on the subject." I have been a resident of Texas since 1835 and well know the deep and ineradicable feelings of the white population, with regard to blacks. I am satisfied that fair and equal justice cannot be meeted out even by the Union party to the black man, much less can he have it from the died in the wool secessionist.

If the Beaureau were removed, the rights of the negro would be adjudicated by a jury mostly white and the chance of equal justice would be a very poor one. The evidence of a negro is always received with suspicion. This state has since the close of the rebellion, had one state legislature and clearly foreshadoed how the state if left to itself clear of all control of congress would act towards the negro. It is true that in the unjust and unequal laws then passed the negro was seldom mentioned but the negro nevertheless was the person meant, see Law of June 1866 page [omitted] Texas House of Representatives—"If any *labourer* (negro was here mainly aimed at, if the blow hit a white person, it was because he was in the way) shall use profane language he shall be fined one dollar—If the employer swore thare was no offence." If any labourer shall absent himself from labor part of a day—fine of 25 cents per hour—disrespectful language—fine one dollar. Suppose a labourer hired at $15 per month, one hours absence fine one ¼ dollar. A girl at $3 pr month fine the same. It is true that the next legislature will not again committ such another blunder. Not from a returning sense of justice, but because the negro would not hire under the laws and because it was found out that no white labor would come into the country. Now if such laws, can be passed in a state where the Freedmens Beaureau is in operation, I ask what would be the state of the negro, in the absence of all United States control. If such a law could be passed in 1866, a person that believes that equal justice can be meeted out to the negro in 1868 or even 1878 by the same state, has the bump of credulity much more largely developed in him than it is with me. . . . I shall conclude by saying that if the congress relinquishes all control and withdraws all protection from the negro—and thus leaves him to the protection of the weak Union element existing in the southern states, we shall have to abide by it and must perforce give the negro up, and leve his cause to the protection of the Eternal. And as the Russian proverb has it, when he speaks of the impossibility of obtaining Justice—Heaven is high and the Emperor a long way off.

I am respectfully

William Pressick

President—board of Registration Malagorda Co Texas

P.S. I have just seen the Colored Registrar of the board, and have asked him this question. Now Henry Kennan tell me can you negroes get along without the Freedmans Beaureau, or any protection from the United States government. After I made him understand the question clearly, he answered No Sir, we could not get along at all; we have use for them.

B. Conflict between President and Congressional Majority

4. Clash on Amending the Constitution

IN DECEMBER and January, with the beginning of the first postwar session of Congress, numerous proposals for amending the Constitution were presented, both directly to the House or Senate and to the Joint Committee of Fifteen on Reconstruction, to which both houses had given responsibility for formulating the terms on which Southern representatives would be readmitted. Most such proposals were variants of what was to become the Fourteenth Amendment's civil rights provisions (section 1) or its modification of apportionment linked to suffrage (section 2). In the selection below from the Congressional Globe, Thaddeus Stevens is presenting on behalf of the joint committee a formula for reapportioning representatives which passed the House but was defeated in the Senate by a combination of Democrats and of equal-suffrage Republicans under Charles Sumner's leadership.

On the day of the debate the joint committee had changed its amendment by omitting reference to taxation, which may have been in part a concession to President Johnson's views as published two days earlier. However, the president's general disparagement of the effort underway to formulate amendments, followed the next day by a report of his criticism of Congress for placing the Reconstruction question in the hands of a "secret" committee, had stirred excitement and resentment. Despite the tension, note that this first public attack by Stevens on the president, which is said to have created a sensation, was quite incidental until pursued by Green Clay Smith of Kentucky, a Unionist who a few weeks later was to support Johnson's civil rights veto and soon thereafter received appointment as governor of Montana territory.

Old Thad's amusing appeal to Robert C. Schenck to join in trying "to be practical" illustrates an essential aspect of Stevens' parliamentary leadership, as indeed does his argument as a whole. However extreme his own goals, and they included confiscation, equality of rights, and general Negro suffrage, he could accept half a loaf and defend it as vigorously as a whole one. In pushing the representation proposal, note that Stevens frankly avowed the purpose of keeping political power out of the hands of Southern whites and their Northern Democratic allies, a frankness often cited by his critics in order to damn him.

a. President Johnson's Interview with Senator Dixon, January 28, 1866

January 28, 1866—The following is the substance of the conversation, as telegraphed that night over the country:

The President said he doubted the propriety at this time of making further amendments to the Constitution. One great amendment had already been made, by which slavery had forever been abolished within the limits of the United States, and a national guarantee thus given that the institution should never exist in the land. Propositions to amend the Constitution were becoming as numerous as preambles and resolutions at town meetings called to consider the most ordinary questions connected with the administration of local affairs. All this, in his opinion, had a tendency to diminish the dignity and prestige attached to the Constitution of the country, and to lessen the respect and confidence of the people in their great charter of freedom. If, however, amendments are to be made to the Constitution, changing the basis of representation and taxation, (and he did not deem them at all necessary at the present time,) he knew of none better than a simple proposition, embraced in a few lines, making in each State the number of qualified voters the basis of representation, and the value of property the basis of direct taxation. Such a proposition could be embraced in the following terms:

"Representatives shall be apportioned among the several States which may be included within this Union according to the number of qualified voters in each State.

"Direct taxes shall be apportioned among the several States which may be included within this Union according to the value of all taxable property in each State."

An amendment of this kind would, in his opinion, place the basis of representation and direct taxation upon correct principles. . . .

Such an amendment, the President also suggested, would re-

SOURCE: Edward McPherson, A Handbook of Politics for 1868 (Washington, D.C.: 1868), pp. 51–52.

move from Congress all issues in reference to the political equality of the races. It would leave the States to determine absolutely the qualifications of their own voters with regard to color; and thus the number of Representatives to which they would be entitled in Congress would depend upon the number upon whom they conferred the right of suffrage. . . .

b. Thaddeus Stevens in the House of Representatives, January 31, 1866

MR. STEVENS. Mr. Speaker, all I shall attempt on this occasion is to place before the House distinctly, and I hope intelligibly, the true meaning of the proposition submitted by the committee, noticing slightly the objections which have been made to it.

It is true we have been informed by high authority, at the other end of the avenue, introduced through an unusual conduit, that no amendment is necessary to the Constitution as our fathers made it, and that it is better to let it stand as it is. Now, sir, I think very differently, myself, for one individual. I believe there is intrusted to this Congress a high duty, no less important and no less fraught with the weal or woe of future ages than was intrusted to the august body that made the Declaration of Independence. I believe now, if we omit to exercise that high duty, or abuse it, we shall be held to account by future generations of America, and by the whole civilized world that is in favor of freedom, and that our names will go down to posterity with some applause, or with black condemnation if we do not treat the subject thoroughly, honestly, and justly, in reference to every human being on this continent. . . .

God forbid I should so adopt the principle of the gentleman from New York, [MR. RAYMOND,] that this Constitution needs no amendment. I would rather not live than live and be so disgraced by such a sentiment. . . .

MR. RAYMOND. I rise simply to remark that if the gentleman understood me to say no amendments whatever were needed to the Constitution, and the Constitution was better without them, he misunderstood me, for I expressly said on this very point of representation that some amendment was necessary.

MR. STEVENS. I refer not only to the gentleman from New York,

SOURCE: U.S. *Congressional Globe*, 39 Cong., 1st Sess. (January 31, 1866), pp. 536–537.

but to what I take to be an authorized utterance of one at the other end of the avenue. I am glad the gentleman has explained it in that way.

Now, sir, since I have referred to that, I believe I am right, for I have no doubt that this is the proclamation, the command of the President of the United States, made and put forth by authority in advance, and at a time when this Congress was legislating on this very question; made, in my judgment, in violation of the privileges of this House; made in such a way that centuries ago, had it been made to Parliament by a British king, it would have cost him his head. But, sir, we pass that by; we are tolerant of usurpation in this tolerant Government of ours.

Now, sir, let me consider what is the meaning of the proposition made by the committee; how far it ought to be affected by any modifications. It has been amended by the committee in obedience to what is supposed to be the sense of the House. The committee have reported back the simple proposition that representation shall be apportioned among the States in proportion to their numbers, provided that when the elective franchise shall be denied or abridged in any State on account of race or color, all persons therein of such race or color shall be excluded from the basis of representation. . . .

Now, sir, I say no more strong inducement could ever be held out to them, no more severe punishment could ever be inflicted upon them as States. If they exclude the colored population they will lose at least thirty-five Representatives in this Hall. If they adopt it they will have eighty-three votes. Take it away from them and they will have only from forty-five to forty-eight votes, all told, in this Hall: and then, sir, let them have all the copperhead assistance they can get, and liberty will still be triumphant. Now, I prefer that to an immediate declaration that all shall be represented; for if you make them all voters and let them into this Hall, not one beneficial act for the benefit of the freedmen or for the benefit of the country could ever be passed. Their eighty-three votes, with the Representatives of the Five Points and other dark corners, would be sufficient to overrule the friends of progress here, and this nation would be in the hands of secessionists at the very next congressional election and at the very next presidential election. I do not, therefore, want to grant them this privilege at least for some years. I want, in the mean time, that our Christian men shall go among the freedmen and teach them what their duties are as citizens; they know them now much better than their masters, and I hope their masters will take notice of what they learn. I say I want our Christian men to go among them, the philanthropists of the North, the honest Methodists, my friends, the Hardshell Baptists, and all others; and then, four or five years hence, when these freedmen shall have been made free indeed, when they shall have become intelligent enough, and there are sufficient loyal men there to control the representation from those States, I shall be glad to see them admitted here. But I do not want them to have representation—I say it plainly—I do not want them to have the right of suffrage before this Congress has done the great work of regenerating the Constitution and laws of this country according to the principles of the Declaration of Independence.

Hence I object to the amendment of my friend from Ohio, [MR. SCHENCK.] He says that if we allow these people representation in proportion as they extend the suffrage we shall encourage them to extend it to the colored race. Well, that is the very objection. They will give the suffrage to their menials, their house servants, those they can control, and elect whom they please to make our laws. That is not the kind of increase of suffrage I want. I want all such men cut off from it. But when they have said to all the freedmen, to the former slaves, "You are men and you shall be represented," then let them come here. I shall not be here to see them, as I did their masters, who a few years since drew pistols and daggers upon me when I was making such a speech as this, yet a free people will be here represented, and they will take care of themselves.

But I have another objection to the amendment of my friend from Ohio. His proposition is to apportion representation according to the male citizens of the States. Why has he put in that word "male?" It was never in the Constitution of the United States before. Why make a crusade against women in the Constitution of the nation? [Laughter.] Is my friend as much afraid of their rivalry as the gentlemen on the other side of the House are afraid of the rivalry of the negro? [Laughter.] I do not think we ought to disfigure the Constitution with such a provision. I find that every unmarried man is opposed to the proposition. Whether married men have particular reason for dreading interference from that quarter I know not. [Laughter.] I certainly shall never vote to insert the word "male" or the word "white" in the national Constitution. Let those things be attended to by the States.

Now, sir, there is another fatal objection to the proposition of my friend from Ohio. If I have been rightly informed as to the number, there are from fifteen to twenty Representatives in the northern States founded upon those who are not citizens of the United States. In New York I think there are three or four Representatives founded upon the foreign population, three certainly. And so it is in Wisconsin, Iowa, and other northern States. There are fifteen or twenty northern Representatives that would be lost by that amendment and given to the South whenever they grant the elective franchise to the negro.

Now, sir, while I have not any particular regard for any foreigner who goes against me, yet I do not think it would be wise to put into the Constitution or send to the people a proposition to amend the Constitution which would take such Representatives from those States, and which therefore they will never adopt. I have no hope that any such proposition would ever be adopted. Let us try to be practical. On the 5th day of December last I introduced a proposition to amend the Constitution founding representation upon the voting basis and excluding the foreign population, as the proposition of my friend from Ohio does. It was dear to my heart, for I had been gestating it for three months. [Laughter.] But when I came to consult the committee of fifteen and found that the States would not adopt it, I surrendered it. Now, cannot my friend from Ohio give up his darling, too? [Laughter.]

I had another proposition, which I hope may again be brought forward. It is this:

> All national and State laws shall be equally applicable to every citizen, and no discrimination shall be made on account of race or color.

There is the genuine proposition; that is the one I love; that is the one which I hope, before we separate, we shall have educated ourselves up to the idea of adopting, and that we shall have educated our people up to the point of ratifying. But it would not be wise to entangle the present proposition with that one. The one might drag down the other; and although I have not obtained what I want, I am content to take what, after comparing ideas with others, I believe we can carry through the States; and I believe we can carry this proposition.

Now, the question is narrowed down to the sole question of a choice between the proposition of the committee and the proposition of the gentleman from Ohio, [MR. SCHENCK.] There is no necessity, then, unless I desire to exhibit myself, for my proceeding any further in this matter. Nor do I propose to go into an examination of what was perhaps the not quite pertinent argument of the gentleman from New York, [MR. RAYMOND.] All I want is that two thirds of each branch of this Congress shall vote affirmatively on this question. And while I should take pleasure in having the President approve of our conduct, yet he has nothing to say about it on this question. We do not send it to him and ask his opinion about it, and therefore it was all the more kind in him to send us his opinion without being asked for it.

MR. SMITH. I would ask the gentleman from Pennsylvania [MR. STEVENS] to permit to be read the paper which has called forth his remarks, so that we may understand to what he alludes when he speaks of the President undertaking to dictate to Congress.

MR. STEVENS. I have no objection to having it read, except that it will take more time than its importance warrants.

Several MEMBERS. Let it be read.

The Clerk read, as follows: . . . [doc. 4a.]

MR. STEVENS. I am rather glad the gentleman from Kentucky [MR. SMITH] called for the reading of that paper, because it shows that the President and I agree exactly, on one point at least; for he leaves out the word "male" in condemnation of the gentleman from Ohio, [MR. SCHENCK.] I am very glad he called for the reading of the paper.

MR. INGERSOLL. I would like to ask a question of the gentleman from Pennsylvania, [MR. STEVENS.]

MR. STEVENS. Very well.

MR. INGERSOLL. I would like to ask the gentleman by what authority does he claim that the paper just read expresses the views of the President?

MR. STEVENS. I think I have good reasons for saying that it emanated from the President.

MR. INGERSOLL. Has the gentleman any objection to stating what those reasons are?

MR. STEVENS. I have no right to tell the secrets of the Executive. [Laughter.]

But we know perfectly well that the President has nothing to do with this matter. The passage of this amendment by a two-thirds vote of both Houses of Congress will carry it before the State Legislatures for ratification without regard to the approval or disapproval of the President. It is true that the constitutional amendment for the abolition of slavery was, after its passage by both Houses of Congress, sent inadvertently to President Lincoln for his signature. But although he signed it because he approved it, yet, acting with the sagacity and the modesty which were so characteristic of him, he sent to Congress a message stating that that body, in sending him that joint resolution for approval, had done what the Constitution did not require. We shall not trouble President Johnson by sending him this amendment if it should be passed by Congress, because it is not necessary to submit it to him for his approval. . . .

5. Exchange between the President and Negro Spokesmen on Suffrage

Johnson's position on suffrage is here clearly stated, and despite logical inconsistencies and bias, parts of his argument cannot be lightly dismissed. What may not be suggested in reading the printed interview is his resentment of Frederick Douglass, of whom he spoke bitterly in private after the delegation had left. The letter from Benjamin B. French reflected a tendency among men of similar race attitudes, particularly in the Border States and the South, to look to the president as their champion.

a. Interview and Reply of the Delegation February 7, 1866

February 7, 1866—The delegation of colored representatives from different States of the country, now in Washington, to urge the interests of the colored people before the Government, had an interview with the President.

The President shook hands kindly with each member of the delegation.

Address of George T. Downing

Mr. George T. Downing then addressed the President as follows:

We present ourselves to your Excellency, to make known with pleasure the respect which we are glad to cherish for you—a respect

Source: McPherson, *Handbook for 1868*, pp. 53–56.

which is your due, as our Chief Magistrate. It is our desire for you to know that we come feeling that we are friends meeting a friend. We should, however, have manifested our friendship by not coming to further tax your already much burdened and valuable time; but we have another object in calling. We are in a passage to equality before the law. God hath made it by opening a Red Sea. We would have your assistance through the same. . . .

Our coming is a marked circumstance, noting determined hope that we are not satisfied with an amendment prohibiting slavery, but that we wish it enforced with appropriate legislation. This is our desire. We ask for it intelligently, with the knowledge and conviction that the fathers of the Revolution intended freedom for every American; that they should be protected in their rights as citizens, and be equal before the law. We are Americans, native born Americans. We are citizens; we are glad to have it known to the world that you bear no doubtful record on this point. On this fact, and with confidence in the triumph of justice, we base our hope. We see no recognition of color or race in the organic law of the land. It knows no privileged class, and therefore we cherish the hope that we may be fully enfranchised, not only here in this District, but throughout the land. . . .

ADDRESS OF FRED. DOUGLASS

Following upon Mr. Downing, Mr. Fred. Douglass advanced and addressed the President, saying:

Mr. President, we are not here to enlighten you, sir, as to your duties as the Chief Magistrate of this Republic, but to show our respect, and to present in brief the claims of our race to your favorable consideration. In the order of Divine Providence you are placed in a position where you have the power to save or destroy us, to bless or blast us—I mean our whole race. Your noble and humane predecessor placed in our hands the sword to assist in saving the nation, and we do hope that you, his able successor, will favorably regard the placing in our hands the ballot with which to save ourselves.

We shall submit no argument on that point. The fact that we are the subjects of Government, and subject to taxation, subject to volunteer in the service of the country, subject to being drafted, subject to bear the burdens of the State, makes it not improper that we should ask to share in the privileges of this condition.

I have no speech to make on this occasion. I simply submit these observations as a limited expression of the views and feelings of the delegation with which I have come.

RESPONSE OF THE PRESIDENT

In reply to some of your inquiries, not to make a speech about this thing, for it is always best to talk plainly and distinctly about such matters, I will say that if I have not given evidence in my course that I am a friend of humanity, and to that portion of it which constitutes the colored population, I can give no evidence here. Everything that I have had, both as regards life and property, has been perilled in that cause, and I feel and think that I understand—not to be egotistic—what should be the true direction of this question, and what course of policy would result in the melioration and ultimate elevation, not only of the colored, but of the great mass of the people of the United States. . . . If I know myself, and the feelings of my own heart, they have been for the colored man. I have owned slaves and bought slaves, but I never sold one. I might say, however, that practically, so far as my connection with slaves has gone, I have been their slave instead of their being mine. Some have even followed me here, while others are occupying and enjoying my property with my consent. For the colored race my means, my time, my all has been perilled; and now at this late day, after giving evidence that is tangible, that is practical, I am free to say to you that I do not like to be arraigned by some who can get up handsomely-rounded periods and deal in rhetoric, and talk about abstract ideas of liberty, who never perilled life, liberty, or property. This kind of theoretical, hollow, unpractical friendship amounts to but very little. While I say that I am a friend of the colored man, I do not want to adopt a policy that I believe will end in a contest between the races, which if persisted in will result in the extermination of one or the other. God forbid that I should be engaged in such a work!

Now, it is always best to talk about things practically and in a common sense way. Yes, I have said, and I repeat here, that if the colored man in the United States could find no other Moses, or any Moses that would be more able and efficient than myself, I would be his Moses to lead him from bondage to freedom; that I would pass him from a land where he had lived in slavery to a land (if it were in our reach) of freedom. Yes, I would be willing to pass with him through the Red sea to the Land of Promise, to the land of liberty; but I am not willing, under either circumstance, to adopt a policy which I believe will only result in the sacrifice of his life and the shedding of his blood. I think I know what I say. I feel what I say; and I feel well assured that if the policy urged by some be persisted in, it will result in great injury to the white as well as to the colored man. There is a great deal of talk about the sword in one hand accomplishing an end, and the ballot accomplishing another at the ballot-box. . . .

Now, let us get closer up to this subject, and talk about it. [The President here approached very near to Mr. Douglass.] What relation has the colored man and the white man heretofore occupied in the South? I opposed slavery upon two grounds. First, it was a great monopoly, enabling those who controlled and owned it to constitute an aristocracy, enabling the few to derive great profits and rule the many with an iron rod, as it were. And this is one great objection to it in a government, it being a monopoly. I was opposed to it secondly upon the abstract principle of slavery. Hence, in getting clear of a monopoly, we are getting clear of slavery at the same time. So you see there were two right ends accomplished in the accomplishment of the one.

MR. DOUGLASS. Mr. President, do you wish—

THE PRESIDENT. I am not quite through yet.

Slavery has been abolished. A great national guarantee has been given, one that cannot be revoked. I was getting at the relation that subsisted between the white man and the colored men. A very small proportion of white persons compared with the whole number of such owned the colored people of the South. I might instance the State of Tennessee in illustration. There were there twenty-seven non-slaveholders to one slaveholder, and yet the slave power controlled the State. Let us talk about this matter as it is. Although the colored man was in slavery there, and owned as property in the sense and in the language of that locality and of that community, yet, in comparing his condition and his position there with the non-slaveholder, he usually estimated his importance just in proportion to the number of slaves that his master owned with the non-slaveholder.

Have you ever lived upon a plantation?

MR. DOUGLASS. I have, your excellency.

THE PRESIDENT. When you would look over and see a man who

had a large family, struggling hard upon a poor piece of land, you thought a great deal less of him than you did of your own master's negro, didn't you?

MR. DOUGLASS. Not I!

THE PRESIDENT. Well, I know such was the case with a large number of you in those sections. Where such is the case we know there is an enmity, we know there is a hate. The poor white man, on the other hand, was opposed to the slave and his master; for the colored man and his master combined kept him in slavery, by depriving him of a fair participation in the labor and productions of the rich land of the country. . . .

The colored man went into this rebellion a slave; by the operation of the rebellion he came out a freedman—equal to a freeman in any other portion of the country. Then there is a great deal done for him on this point. The non-slaveholder who was forced into the rebellion, who was as loyal as those that lived beyond the limits of the State, but was carried into it, lost his property, and in a number of instances the lives of such were sacrificed, and he who has survived has come out of it with nothing gained, but a great deal lost.

Now, upon the principle of justice, should they be placed in a condition different from what they were before? On the one hand, one has gained a great deal; on the other hand, one has lost a great deal, and, in a political point of view, scarcely stands where he did before.

Now, we are talking about where we are going to begin. We have got at the hate that existed between the two races. The query comes up, whether these two races, situated as they were before, without preparation, without time for passion and excitement to be appeased, and without time for the slightest improvement, whether the one should be turned loose upon the other, and be thrown together at the ballot-box with this enmity and hate existing between them. The query comes up right there, whether we don't commence a war of races. I think I understand this thing, and especially is this the case where you force it upon a people without their consent.

You have spoken about government. Where is power derived from? We say it is derived from the people. Let us take it so, and refer to the District of Columbia by way of illustration. Suppose, for instance, here, in this political community, which, to a certain extent, must have government, must have laws, and putting it now upon the broadest basis you can put it—take into consideration the relation which the white has heretofore borne to the colored race— is it proper to force upon this community, without their consent, the elective franchise, without regard to color, making it univer- sal? . . . Do you deny that first great principle of the right of the people to govern themselves? Will you resort to an arbitrary power, and say a majority of the people shall receive a state of things they are opposed to?

MR. DOUGLASS. That was said before the war.

THE PRESIDENT. I am now talking about a principle; not what somebody else said.

MR. DOWNING. Apply what you have said, Mr. President, to South Carolina, for instance, where a majority of the inhabitants are colored.

THE PRESIDENT. Suppose you go to South Carolina; suppose you go to Ohio. That doesn't change the principle at all. . . .

Each community is better prepared to determine the depository of its political power than anybody else, and it is for the Legisla- ture, for the people of Ohio to say who shall vote, and not for the Congress of the United States. I might go down here to the ballot- box to-morrow and vote directly for universal suffrage; but if a great majority of the people said no, I should consider it would be tyrannical in me to attempt to force such upon them without their will. It is a fundamental tenet in my creed that the will of the people must be obeyed. Is there anything wrong or unfair in that?

MR. DOUGLASS (smiling.) A great deal that is wrong, Mr. Presi- dent, with all respect.

THE PRESIDENT. It is the people of the States that must for themselves determine this thing. I do not want to be engaged in a work that will commence a war of races. I want to begin the work of preparation, and the States, or the people in each community, if a man demeans himself well, and shows evidence that this new state of affairs will operate, will protect him in all his rights and give him every possible advantage when they become reconciled socially and politically to this state of things. Then will this new order of things work harmoniously; but forced upon the people before they are prepared for it, it will be resisted, and work inhar- moniously. I feel a conviction that driving this matter upon the people, upon the community, will result in the injury of both races, and the ruin of one or the other. God knows I have no desire but the good of the whole human race. I would it were so that all you advocate could be done in the twinkling of an eye; but it is not in the nature of things, and I do not assume or pretend to be wiser than Providence, or stronger than the laws of nature. . . .

God knows that anything I can do I will do. In the mighty process by which the great end is to be reached, anything I can do to elevate the races, to soften and ameliorate their condition I will do, and to be able to do so is the sincere desire of my heart.

I am glad to have met you, and thank you for the compliment you have paid me.

MR. DOUGLASS. I have to return to you our thanks, Mr. President, for so kindly granting us this interview. We did not come here expecting to argue this question with your excellency, but simply to state what were our views and wishes in the premises. If we were disposed to argue the question, and you would grant us permission, of course we would endeavor to controvert some of the positions you have assumed.

MR. DOWNING. Mr. Douglass, I take it that the President, by his kind expressions and his very full treatment of the subject, must have contemplated some reply to the views which he has advanced, and in which we certainly do not concur, and I say this with due respect.

THE PRESIDENT. I thought you expected me to indicate to some extent what my views were on the subjects touched upon in your statement.

MR. DOWNING. We are very happy, indeed, to have heard them.

MR. DOUGLASS. If the President will allow me, I would like to say one or two words in reply. You enfranchise your enemies and disfranchise your friends.

THE PRESIDENT. All I have done is simply to indicate what my views are, as I supposed you expected me to, from your address.

MR. DOUGLASS. My own impression is that the very thing that your excellency would avoid in the southern States can only be avoided by the very measure that we propose, and I would state to my brother delegates that because I perceive the President has taken strong grounds in favor of a given policy, and distrusting my own ability to remove any of those impressions which he has expressed, I thought we had better end the interview with the expression of thanks. (Addressing the President.) But if your excellency will be pleased to hear, I would like to say a word or two in regard to that one matter of the enfranchisement of the blacks as a means of preventing the very thing which your excellency seems to apprehend—that is a conflict of races.

THE PRESIDENT. I repeat, I merely wanted to indicate my views in reply to your address, and not to enter into any general controversy, as I could not well do so under the circumstances.

Your statement was a very frank one, and I thought it was due to you to meet it in the same spirit.

MR. DOUGLASS. Thank you, sir.

THE PRESIDENT. I think you will find, so far as the South is concerned, that if you will all inculcate there the idea in connection with the one you urge, that the colored people can live and advance in civilization to better advantage elsewhere than crowded right down there in the South, it would be better for them.

MR. DOUGLASS. But the masters have the making of the laws, and we cannot get away from the plantation.

THE PRESIDENT. What prevents you?

MR. DOUGLASS. We have not the single right of locomotion through the Southern States now.

THE PRESIDENT. Why not; the government furnishes you with every facility.

MR. DOUGLASS. There are six days in the year that the negro is free in the South now, and his master then decides for him where he shall go, where he shall work, how much he shall work—in fact, he is divested of all political power. He is absolutely in the hands of those men.

THE PRESIDENT. If the master now controls him or his action, would he not control him in his vote?

MR. DOUGLASS. Let the negro once understand that he has an organic right to vote, and he will raise up a party in the Southern States among the poor, who will rally with him. There is this conflict that you speak of between the wealthy slaveholder and the poor man.

THE PRESIDENT. You touch right upon the point there. There is this conflict, and hence I suggest emigration. If he cannot get employment in the South, he has it in his power to go where he can get it.

In parting, the PRESIDENT said that they were both desirous of accomplishing the same ends, but proposed to do so by following different roads.

MR. DOUGLASS, on turning to leave, remarked to his fellow delegates: "The President sends us to the people, and we go to the people."

THE PRESIDENT. Yes, sir; I have great faith in the people. I believe they will do what is right.

———

Reply of the Colored Delegation to the President.
To the Editor of the Chronicle:

Will you do us the favor to insert in your columns the following reply of the colored delegation to the President of the United States?

GEO. T. DOWNING
In behalf of the Delegation

MR. PRESIDENT. In consideration of a delicate sense of propriety, as well as your own repeated intimations of indisposition to discuss or to listen to a reply to the views and opinions you were pleased to express to us in your elaborate speech to-day, the undersigned would respectfully take this method of replying thereto. Believing as we do that the views and opinions you expressed in that address are entirely unsound and prejudicial to the highest interests of our race as well as our country at large, we cannot do other than expose the same, and, as far as may be in our power, arrest their dangerous influence. It is not necessary at this time to call attention to more than two or three features of your remarkable address:

1. The first point to which we feel especially bound to take exception is your attempt to found a policy opposed to our enfranchisement, upon the alleged ground of an existing hostility on the part of the former slaves toward the poor white people of the South. We admit the existence of this hostility, and hold that it is entirely reciprocal. But you obviously commit an error by drawing an argument from an incident of a state of slavery, and making it a basis for policy adapted to a state of freedom. . . .

There was no earthly reason why the blacks should not hate and dread the poor whites when in a state of slavery, for it was from this class that their masters received their slave-catchers, slave-drivers, and overseers. They were the men called in upon all occasions by the masters when any fiendish outrage was to be committed upon the slave. Now, sir, you cannot but perceive that, the cause of this hatred removed, the effect must be removed also. . . .

2. Besides, even if it were true, as you allege, that the hostility of the blacks toward the poor whites must necessarily project itself into a state of freedom, and that this enmity between the two races is even more intense in a state of freedom than in a state of slavery, in the name of Heaven, we reverently ask, how can you, in view of your professed desire to promote the welfare of the black man, deprive him of all means of defence, and clothe him whom you regard as his enemy in the panoply of political power? Can it be that you would recommend a policy which would arm the strong and cast down the defenceless? Can you, by any possibility of reasoning, regard this as just, fair, or wise? Experience proves that those are oftenest abused who can be abused with the greatest impunity. Men are whipped oftenest who are whipped easiest. Peace between races is not to be secured by degrading one race and exalting another, by giving power to one race and withholding it from another; but by maintaining a state of equal justice between all classes. . . .

3. On the colonization theory you were pleased to broach, very much could be said. It is impossible to suppose, in view of the usefulness of the black man in time of peace as a laborer in the South, and in time of war as a soldier at the North, and the growing respect for his rights among the people, and his increasing adaptation to a high state of civilization in this his native land, there can ever come a time when he can be removed from this country without a terrible shock to its prosperity and peace. . . .

b. Commendation: Benjamin French to Andrew Johnson,
February 8, 1866

Washington, Feby. 8, 1866.

Andrew Johnson
President of the United States

My Dear Sir:

I cannot forbear to express to you the great pleasure I felt on reading your remarks to the colored men who visited you yesterday.

SOURCE: Andrew Johnson Papers, Library of Congress, Washington, D.C.

The principles you enunciated are the same expressed to me in a conversation I had with you last Autumn, and in which I fully agreed with you. You said to me then that every one would and must admit that the white race was superior to the black, and that while we ought to do our best to bring them up to our present level, that, in doing so we should, at the same time raise our own intellectual status so that the relative position of the two races would be the same. I think that was about your idea, and, if success attended the efforts to exalt the black race, which I some doubt, the result would doubtless be that the white race would still hold its natural place above them. Man, with his puny arm, cannot annul the decrees of God!

I am astonished, and more than astonished, at the persistency with which the radical idea of placing negroes on an equality with whites, *in every particular*, is pressed in Congress. And with solemnity I say, that, in my opinion our Union is at this moment in greater danger from the fanatical zeal with which this false idea is pressed, than it was from the Rebellion itself! Give the colored race the unlimited right of suffrage, and a fire brand is cast among the people that cannot be extinguished until it is quenched in the blood of hostile factions.

I hope, & trust, and pray that the vision of the sovereign people will be so far carried into the future by the common Father of us all, that they will avert the danger by vetoing, not only the *measures* which tend to so awful a result, but the *men* who initiated and supported them.

I am only one humble citizen, but I love my Country and her Constitution, and I desire, beyond all things, the prosperity, and the honor of that Country. Until the tide of fanaticism, which is now in full flood, shall turn, as it must, unless sanity has departed from the people, we must place our trust in you to keep us safe "from the pestilence that walketh in darkness, and the destruction that wasteth at noon-day."

Permit me to ask if you have read a most forcible article on the races of men, published in the Intelligencer of this morning, from the pen of a Doctor Nott? If you have not read it, I commend it to your perusal.

Pardon me for writing to you at such length. I have known you so long, and so well, and esteemed and respected you so much, that I could not forbear to express my unalloyed pleasure at the noble position you hold as a statesman and a patriot. If my feeble tongue or arm are needed for your defence they are always ready.

With high respect

Your faithful friend & obt Servt.

B. B. French

6. The First Presidential Veto and Extension of the Freedmen's Bureau

THE FREEDMEN'S BUREAU BILL was fathered by moderate men and had the overwhelming support of Republicans in Congress. The New York Herald's position is an example of distortion, one perpetuated by an earlier generation of historians who confused the paper's claim to political independence with objectivity. Two days after the editorial Johnson's veto was released, and a telegram went from the White House to the Herald, commending its editorial position in respect to the bureau. Because the president's final "grave objection" to the bill challenged congressional authority in a manner virtually precluding reconciliation, the importance of substantive disagreement over the role of the bureau, evident in the vote as well as in the editorial, has often been minimized.

Nor has adequate attention been given to the differences between the vetoed bill and the measure passed five months later; a close comparison will justify the reader's effort. Despite significant modifications, the second bill was vetoed by President Johnson on the ground that it merited the objections he had voiced to the first and additional ones as well. He asserted that freedmen could obtain ample redress through civil tribunals, attacked the integrity of bureau agents, and argued that the bill's provisions in respect to the sea island lands (sections 6–11) jeopardized the property rights of some citizens in the interest of a "favored class." The whole measure he condemned as class legislation that would encourage certain citizens to hope for support "whether they pursue a life of indolence or of labor." No Democratic senator or representative voted for either the February or the July bill to extend the bureau.

A century after the First Reconstruction, two major criticisms are leveled against the legislative program pushed through by the Republican majority. First, no land was provided for the freedmen, thereby denying them a secure economic base for freedom. Second, the bureau was discontinued prematurely at a time when there was need of a continuing national agency to provide what the twentieth century would call compensatory support for the former slaves. Had the Freedmen's Bureau Bill of February 1866 (c) been signed by President Johnson there would in *all likelihood have been both a modest land program (see introduction to doc. 30) and a continuance of major bureau activities beyond the end of 1868.*

a. New York Herald *Editorial on Freedmen's Bureau Bill,* February 17, 1866

THE FREEDMEN'S BUREAU BILL BEFORE THE PRESIDENT— WHAT OUGHT HE TO DO WITH IT?

The new bill to enlarge the powers of the Freedmen's Bureau, which finally passed the House of Representatives with the Senate amendments on the 9th of this month, now lies before the President for his action. . . . The radicals are particularly nervous, because this bill is a trap they have set with which to catch the President. The *Tribune* and other kindred negro-worshipping sheets, as well as members of Congress of that stamp, have been very coaxing and persuasive to the President since last Friday. . . . The prey is not so easily to be caught, however; and we believe they will not be able to entangle him in their web. He will veto, probably, this monstrous piece of legislation, and give full and conclusive reasons for doing so.

The bill ought to be called an act to support the negroes in idleness by the honest labor of white people, or an act to establish a gigantic and corrupt political machine for the benefit of the radical faction and a swarm of office holders. Either would be its correct title. There might have been some excuse for the establishment of a freedmen's bureau during the war and before the negroes were placed on an equal footing with white people by the amendment to the constitution. There is not the least excuse for it now. Instead of enlarging its powers as this bill enlarges them, the former act ought to be repealed. In whatever point of view we look at the measure it is full of evil. The professed object of the bill, which, in fact, is not the real object—to protect and benefit the negroes— cannot be attained by any such legislation. On the contrary, it will destroy that very independence of character and action which inspires a feeling of manhood, by making them dependent upon government. Never disposed to work more than they could help, and having always been taught to rely upon others to provide for

SOURCE: *New York Herald*, February 17, 1866.

and direct them, they naturally will be shiftless, idle, dependent and useless to themselves or others under the special guardianship and control of government. . . .

Then, how can the planters and other employers get along with these people as laborers when the caprices, corruption, passions or arbitrary will of the thousands of agents of the bureau scattered all over the country stand in the way? The system would be bad enough if we were sure of having honest and intelligent agents; but we know this will not be the case except in a few instances. The greater part would be ignorant, arbitrary or corrupt, and the temptation to exercise undue power or to make money out of both employers and employed, would be too great to resist. And where could the victims of this gigantic and arbitrary machine find redress? Let the negroes and white people of the South—the laborers and employers—make their own arrangements, conduct their own affairs and take care of themselves, as people in the North and elsewhere do. They know what is best to be done for their mutual interest. The negroes are free and cannot be enslaved in any manner whatever. Their old masters are willing to employ them, and indeed wish to do so, as free laborers. They understand the negroes better than any other people do, and, as a class, are more kindly disposed toward them. Why then should we not allow the natural laws that govern labor and capital, employer and employed at the North, to operate there? Why should we be burdened with a great charitable institution to support the negroes in idleness at a cost of many millions—maybe twenty millions or more—a year? Why should the white working people of the North pay for this, as well as the necessary army of office holders that would be required to carry out the law? It would really be a monstrous fraud upon the country and a great evil to both negroes and whites in the South.

The bill is neither more nor less than a political machine, and has been skilfully engineered through Congress. . . . If he should sign the bill it would be considered in opposition to his general policy, and the radicals would claim that he had gone over to them. If he should veto it they would be able to raise a hue and cry about the poor negro. They would be able to find some isolated cases of negro suffering, and could appeal to the sympathies of all the old women sentimentalists of New England, who never see similar cases of white people's suffering at their own doors. Should the bill not become law in consequence of the President refusing to sign it, we can imagine what horrifying details of oppression and misery among the poor negroes Mr. Sumner and the other negro worshippers will give us. However, we hope the President may find it to be his duty, after mature consideration, to veto the bill, notwithstanding the abuse he may receive and the ghosts of negro suffering that may be raised. The issue between him and the radicals has to be made, and it is better that it should be made now and on this measure than hereafter. Let the bill go back to Congress with a full rc..iew of its features and his general policy as connected with it, and the country will sustain him. If Congress should pass it over his veto let them do so. He will have done his duty, he will find out who are with him and who against, and the question will then be fairly laid before the public.

b. Veto Message, February 19, 1866

WASHINGTON, February 19, 1866.
To the Senate of the United States:

I have examined with care the bill, which originated in the Senate and has been passed by the two Houses of Congress, to amend an act entitled "An act to establish a bureau for the relief of freedmen and refugees," and for other purposes. Having with much regret come to the conclusion that it would not be consistent with the public welfare to give my approval to the measure, I return the bill to the Senate with my objections to its becoming a law.

I might call to mind in advance of these objections that there is no immediate necessity for the proposed measure. The act to establish a bureau for the relief of freedmen and refugees, which was approved in the month of March last, has not yet expired. It was thought stringent and extensive enough for the purpose in view in time of war. Before it ceases to have effect further experience may assist to guide us to a wise conclusion as to the policy to be adopted in time of peace.

I share with Congress the strongest desire to secure to the freed-men the full enjoyment of their freedom and property and their entire independence and equality in making contracts for their

SOURCE: James D. Richardson, *A Compilation of the Messages and Papers of the Presidents, 1787–1897* (Washington, D.C.: 1900), VI: 398–405.

labor, but the bill before me contains provisions which in my opinion are not warranted by the Constitution and are not well suited to accomplish the end in view.

The bill proposes to establish by authority of Congress military jurisdiction over all parts of the United States containing refugees and freedmen. It would by its very nature apply with most force to those parts of the United States in which the freedmen most abound, and it expressly extends the existing temporary jurisdiction of the Freedmen's Bureau, with greatly enlarged powers, over those States "in which the ordinary course of judicial proceedings has been interrupted by the rebellion." The source from which this military jurisdiction is to emanate is none other than the President of the United States, acting through the War Department and the Commissioner of the Freedmen's Bureau. The agents to carry out this military jurisdiction are to be selected either from the Army or from civil life; the country is to be divided into districts and subdistricts, and the number of salaried agents to be employed may be equal to the number of countries or parishes in all the United States where freedmen and refugees are to be found.

The subjects over which this military jurisdiction is to extend in every part of the United States include protection to "all employees, agents, and officers of this bureau in the exercise of the duties imposed" upon them by the bill. In eleven States it is further to extend over all cases affecting freedmen and refugees discriminated against "by local law, custom, or prejudice." In those eleven States the bill subjects any white person who may be charged with depriving a freedman of "any civil rights or immunities belonging to white persons" to imprisonment or fine, or both, without, however, defining the "civil rights and immunities" which are thus to be secured to the freedmen by military law. This military jurisdiction also extends to all questions that may arise respecting contracts. The agent who is thus to exercise the office of a military judge may be a stranger, entirely ignorant of the laws of the place, and exposed to the errors of judgment to which all men are liable. The exercise of power over which there is no legal supervision by so vast a number of agents as is contemplated by the bill must, by the very nature of man, be attended by acts of caprice, injustice, and passion.

The trials having their origin under this bill are to take place without the intervention of a jury and without any fixed rules of law or evidence. The rules on which offenses are to be "heard and determined" by the numerous agents are such rules and regulations as the President, through the War Department, shall prescribe. No previous presentment is required nor any indictment charging the commission of a crime against the laws; but the trial must proceed on charges and specifications. The punishment will be, not what the law declares, but such as a court-martial may think proper, and from these arbitrary tribunals there lies no appeal, no writ of error to any of the courts in which the Constitution of the United States vests exclusively the judicial power of the country.

While the territory and the classes of actions and offenses that are made subject to this measure are so extensive, the bill itself, should it become a law, will have no limitation in point of time, but will form a part of the permanent legislation of the country. I can not reconcile a system of military jurisdiction of this kind with the words of the Constitution which declare that "no person shall be held to answer for a capital or otherwise infamous crime unless on a presentment or indictment of a grand jury, except in cases arising in the land or naval forces, or in the militia when in actual service in time of war or public danger," and that "in all criminal prosecutions the accused shall enjoy the right to a speedy and public trial by an impartial jury of the State and district wherein the crime shall have been committed." The safeguards which the experience and wisdom of ages taught our fathers to establish as securities for the protection of the innocent, the punishment of the guilty, and the equal administration of justice are to be set aside, and for the sake of a more vigorous interposition in behalf of justice we are to take the risks of the many acts of injustice that would necessarily follow from an almost countless number of agents established in every parish or county in nearly a third of the States of the Union, over whose decisions there is to be no super-vision or control by the Federal courts. The power that would be thus placed in the hands of the President is such as in time of peace certainly ought never to be intrusted to any one man.

If it be asked whether the creation of such a tribunal within a State is warranted as a measure of war, the question immediately presents itself whether we are still engaged in war. Let us not unnecessarily disturb the commerce and credit and industry of the country by declaring to the American people and to the world that the United States are still in a condition of civil war. At present there is no part of our country in which the authority of the United States is disputed. Offenses that may be committed by individuals should not work a forfeiture of the rights of whole communities. The country has returned, or is returning, to a state of peace and industry, and the rebellion is in fact at an end. The measure, therefore, seems to be as inconsistent with the actual condition of the country as it is at variance with the Constitution of the United States.

If, passing from general considerations, we examine the bill in detail, it is open to weighty objections.

In time of war it was eminently proper that we should provide for those who were passing suddenly from a condition of bondage to a state of freedom. But this bill proposes to make the Freedmen's Bureau, established by the act of 1865 as one of many great and extraordinary military measures to suppress a formidable rebellion, a permanent branch of the public administration, with its powers greatly enlarged. I have no reason to suppose, and I do not understand it to be alleged, that the act of March, 1865, has proved deficient for the purpose for which it was passed, although at that time and for a considerable period thereafter the Government of the United States remained unacknowledged in most of the States whose inhabitants had been involved in the rebellion. The institution of slavery, for the military destruction of which the Freedmen's Bureau was called into existence as an auxiliary, has been already effectually and finally abrogated throughout the whole country by an amendment of the Constitution of the United States, and practically its eradication has received the assent and concurrence of most of those States in which it at any time had an existence. I am not, therefore, able to discern in the condition of the country anything to justify an apprehension that the powers and agencies of the Freedmen's Bureau, which were effective for the protection of freedmen and refugees during the actual continuance of hostilities and of African servitude, will now, in a time of peace and after the abolition of slavery, prove inadequate to the same proper ends. If I am correct in these views, there can be no necessity for the enlargement of the powers of the Bureau, for which provision is made in the bill.

The third section of the bill authorizes a general and unlimited grant of support to the destitute and suffering refugees and freedmen, their wives and children. Succeeding sections make provision for the rent or purchase of landed estates for freedmen, and for the erection for their benefit of suitable buildings for asylums and schools, the expenses to be defrayed from the Treasury of the whole people. The Congress of the United States has never heretofore thought itself empowered to establish asylums beyond the limits of the District of Columbia, except for the benefit of our disabled soldiers and sailors. It has never founded schools for any class of our own people, not even for the orphans of those who have fallen in the defense of the Union, but has left the care of education to the much more competent and efficient control of the States, of communities, of private associations, and of individuals. It has never deemed itself authorized to expend the public money for the rent or purchase of homes for the thousands, not to say millions, of the white race who are honestly toiling from day to day for their subsistence. A system for the support of indigent persons in the United States was never contemplated by the authors of the Constitution; nor can any good reason be advanced why, as a permanent establishment, it should be founded for one class or color of our people more than another. Pending the war many refugees and freedmen received support from the Government, but it was never intended that they should thenceforth be fed, clothed, educated, and sheltered by the United States. The idea on which the slaves were assisted to freedom was that on becoming free they would be a self-sustaining population. Any legislation that shall imply that they are not expected to attain a self-sustaining condition must have a tendency injurious alike to their character and their prospects.

The appointment of an agent for every county and parish will create an immense patronage, and the expense of the numerous officers and their clerks, to be appointed by the President, will be great in the beginning, with a tendency steadily to increase. The appropriations asked by the Freedmen's Bureau as now established, for the year 1866, amount to $11,745,000. It may be safely estimated that the cost to be incurred under the pending bill will require double that amount—more than the entire sum expended in any one year under the Administration of the second Adams. If the presence of agents in every parish and county is to be considered as a war measure, opposition, or even resistance, might be provoked; so that to give effect to their jurisdiction troops would have to be stationed within reach of every one of them, and thus a large standing force be rendered necessary. Large appropriations would therefore be required to sustain and enforce military jurisdiction in every county or parish from the Potomac to the Rio Grande. The condition of our fiscal affairs is encouraging, but in order to sustain the present measure of public confidence it is necessary that we practice not merely customary economy, but, as far as possible, severe retrenchment.

In addition to the objections already stated, the fifth section of the bill proposes to take away land from its former owners without any legal proceedings being first had, contrary to that provision of the Constitution which declares that no person shall "be deprived of life, liberty, or property without due process of law." It does not appear that a part of the lands to which this section refers may not be owned by minors or persons of unsound mind, or by those who have been faithful to all their obligations as citizens of the United States. If any portion of the land is held by such persons, it is not competent for any authority to deprive them of it. If, on the other hand, it be found that the property is liable to confiscation, even then it can not be appropriated to public purposes until by due process of law it shall have been declared forfeited to the Government.

There is still further objection to the bill, on grounds seriously affecting the class of persons to whom it is designed to bring relief. It will tend to keep the mind of the freedman in a state of uncertain expectation and restlessness, while to those among whom he lives it will be a source of constant and vague apprehension.

Undoubtedly the freedman should be protected, but he should be protected by the civil authorities, especially by the exercise of all the constitutional powers of the courts of the United States and of the States. His condition is not so exposed as may at first be imagined. He is in a portion of the country where his labor can not well be spared. Competition for his services from planters, from those who are constructing or repairing railroads, and from capitalists in his vicinage or from other States will enable him to command almost his own terms. He also possesses a perfect right to change his place of abode, and if, therefore, he does not find in one community or State a mode of life suited to his desires or proper remuneration for his labor, he can move to another where that labor is more esteemed and better rewarded. In truth, however, each State, induced by its own wants and interests, will do what is necessary and proper to retain within its borders all the labor that is needed for the development of its resources. The laws that regulate supply and demand will maintain their force, and the wages of the laborer will be regulated thereby. There is no danger that the exceedingly great demand for labor will not operate in favor of the laborer.

Neither is sufficient consideration given to the ability of the freedmen to protect and take care of themselves. It is no more than justice to them to believe that as they have received their freedom with moderation and forbearance, so they will distinguish themselves by their industry and thrift, and soon show the world that in a condition of freedom they are self-sustaining, capable of selecting their own employment and their own places of abode, of insisting for themselves on a proper remuneration, and of establishing and maintaining their own asylums and schools. It is earnestly hoped that instead of wasting away they will by their own efforts establish for themselves a condition of respectability and prosperity. It is certain that they can attain to that condition only through their own merits and exertions.

In this connection the query presents itself whether the system proposed by the bill will not, when put into complete operation, practically transfer the entire care, support, and control of 4,000,000 emancipated slaves to agents, overseers, or taskmasters, who, appointed at Washington, are to be located in every county and parish throughout the United States containing freedmen and refugees. Such a system would inevitably tend to a concentration of power in the Executive which would enable him, if so disposed, to control the action of this numerous class and use them for the attainment of his own political ends.

I can not but add another very grave objection to this bill. The Constitution imperatively declares, in connection with taxation, that each State *shall* have at least one Representative, and fixes the rule for the number to which, in future times, each State shall be entitled. It also provides that the Senate of the United States *shall* be composed of two Senators from each State, and adds with peculiar force "that no State, without its consent, shall be deprived of its equal suffrage in the Senate." The original act was necessarily passed in the absence of the States chiefly to be affected, because their people were then contumaciously engaged in the rebellion. Now the case is changed, and some, at least, of those States are attending Congress by loyal representatives, soliciting the allowance of the constitutional right for representation. At the time, however, of the consideration and the passing of this bill there was no Senator or Representative in Congress from the eleven States which are to be mainly affected by its provisions. The very fact that reports were and are made against the good disposition of the people of that portion of the country is an additional reason why they need and should have representatives of their own in Congress to explain their condition, reply to accusations, and assist by their local knowledge in the perfecting of measures immediately affecting themselves. While the liberty of deliberation would then be free and Congress would have full power to decide according to its judgment, there could be no objection urged that the States most interested had not been permitted to be heard. The principle is firmly fixed in the minds of the American people that there should be no taxation without representation. Great burdens have now to be borne by all the country, and we may best demand that they shall be borne without murmur when they are voted by a majority of the representatives of all the people. I would not interfere with the unquestionable right of Congress to judge, each House for itself, "of the elections, returns, and qualifications of its own members;" but that authority can not be construed as including the right to shut out in time of peace any State from the representation to which it is entitled by the Constitution. At present all the people of eleven States are excluded—those who were most faithful during the war not less than others. The State of Tennessee, for instance, whose authorities engaged in rebellion, was restored to all her constitutional relations to the Union by the patriotism and energy of her injured and betrayed people. Before the war was brought to a termination they had placed themselves in relations with the General Government, had established a State government of their own, and, as they were not included in the emancipation proclamation, they by their own act had amended their constitution so as to abolish slavery within the limits of their State. I know no reason why the State of Tennessee, for example, should not fully enjoy "all her constitutional relations to the United States."

The President of the United States stands toward the country in a somewhat different attitude from that of any member of Congress. Each member of Congress is chosen from a single district or State; the President is chosen by the people of all the States. As eleven States are not at this time represented in either branch of Congress, it would seem to be his duty on all proper occasions to present their just claims to Congress. There always will be differences of opinion in the community, and individuals may be guilty of transgressions of the law, but these do not constitute valid objections against the right of a State to representation. I would in no wise interfere with the discretion of Congress with regard to the qualifications of members; but I hold it my duty to recommend to you, in the interests of peace and the interests of union, the admission of every State to its share in public legislation when, however insubordinate, insurgent, or rebellious its people may have been, it presents itself, not only in an attitude of loyalty and harmony, but in the persons of representatives whose loyalty can not be questioned under any existing constitutional or legal test. It is plain that an indefinite or permanent exclusion of any part of the country from representation must be attended by a spirit of disquiet and complaint. It is unwise and dangerous to pursue a course of measures which will unite a very large section of the country against another section of the country, however much the latter may preponderate. The course of emigration, the development of industry and business, and natural causes will raise up at the South men as devoted to the Union as those of any other part of the land; but if they are all excluded from Congress, if in a permanent statute they are declared not to be in full constitutional relations to the country, they may think they have cause to become a unit in feeling and sentiment against the Government. Under the political education of the American people the idea is inherent and ineradicable that the consent of the majority of the whole people is necessary to securing a willing acquiescence in legislation.

The bill under consideration refers to certain of the States as though they had not "been fully restored in all their constitutional relations to the United States." If they have not, let us at once act together to secure that desirable end at the earliest possible moment. It is hardly necessary for me to inform Congress that in my own judgment most of those States, so far, at least, as depends upon their own action, have already been fully restored, and are to be deemed as entitled to enjoy their constitutional rights as members of the Union. Reasoning from the Constitution itself and from the actual situation of the country, I feel not only entitled but bound to assume that with the Federal courts restored and those of the several States in the full exercise of their functions the rights and interests of all classes of people will, with the aid of the military in cases of resistance to the laws, be essentially protected against unconstitutional infringement or violation. Should this expectation unhappily fail, which I do not anticipate, then the Executive is already fully armed with the powers conferred by the act of March, 1865, establishing the Freedmen's Bureau, and hereafter, as heretofore, he can employ the land and naval forces of the country to suppress insurrection or to overcome obstructions to the laws.

In accordance with the Constitution, I return the bill to the Senate, in the earnest hope that a measure involving questions and interests so important to the country will not become a law, unless upon deliberate consideration by the people it shall receive the sanction of an enlightened public judgment.

ANDREW JOHNSON.

c. The Vetoed Freedmen's Bureau Bill

AN ACT to amend an act entitled "An act to establish a Bureau for the relief of Freedmen and Refugees," and for other purposes.

Be it enacted, &c., That the act to establish a bureau for the relief of freedmen and refugees, approved March three, eighteen hundred and sixty-five, shall continue in force until otherwise provided by law, and shall extend to refugees and freedmen in all parts of the United States; and the President may divide the section of country containing such refugees and freedmen into districts, each containing one or more States, not to exceed twelve in number, and, by and with the advice and consent of the Senate, appoint an assistant commissioner for each of said districts, who shall give like bond, receive the compensation, and perform the duties prescribed by this and the act to which this is an amendment; or said bureau may, in the discretion of the President, be placed under a commissioner and assistant commissioners, to be detailed from the army; in which event each officer so assigned to duty shall serve without increase of pay or allowances.

SEC. 2. That the commissioner, with the approval of the President, and when the same shall be necessary for the operations of

SOURCE: McPherson, *Handbook for 1868,* pp. 72–74. Republicans indicated by regular type, Democrats by italics.

the bureau, may divide each district into a number of sub-districts, not to exceed the number of counties or parishes in such district, and shall assign to each sub-district at least one agent, either a citizen, officer of the army, or enlisted man, who, if an officer, shall serve without additional compensation or allowance, and if a citizen or enlisted man, shall receive a salary of not less than five hundred dollars nor more than twelve hundred dollars annually, according to the services rendered, in full compensation for such services; and such agent shall, before entering on the duties of his office, take the oath prescribed in the first section of the act to which this is an amendment. And the commissioner may, when the same shall be necessary, assign to each assistant commissioner not exceeding three clerks, and to each of said agents one clerk, at an annual salary not exceeding one thousand dollars each, provided suitable clerks cannot be detailed from the army. And the President of the United States, through the War Department and the commissioner, shall extend military jurisdiction and protection over all employés, agents, and officers of this bureau in the exercise of the duties imposed or authorized by this act or the act to which this is additional.

Sec. 3. That the Secretary of War may direct such issues of provisions, clothing, fuel, and other supplies, including medical stores and transportation, and afford such aid, medical or otherwise, as he may deem needful for the immediate and temporary shelter and supply of destitute and suffering refugees and freedmen, their wives and children, under such rules and regulations as he may direct: *Provided*, That no person shall be deemed "destitute," "suffering," or "dependent upon the Government for support," within the meaning of this act, who, being able to find employment, could by proper industry and exertion avoid such destitution, suffering, or dependence.

Sec. 4. That the President is hereby authorized to reserve from sale, or from settlement, under the homestead or pre-emption laws, and to set apart for the use of freedmen and loyal refugees, male or female, unoccupied public lands in Florida, Mississippi, Alabama, Louisiana, and Arkansas, not exceeding in all three millions of acres of good land; and the commissioner, under the direction of the President, shall cause the same from time to time to be allotted and assigned, in parcels not exceeding forty acres each, to the loyal refugees and freedmen, who shall be protected in the use and enjoyment thereof for such term of time and at such annual rent as may be agreed on between the commissioner and such refugees or freedmen. The rental shall be based upon a valuation of the land, to be ascertained in such manner as the commissioner may, under the direction of the President, by regulation prescribe. At the end of such term, or sooner, if the commissioner shall assent thereto, the occupants of any parcels so assigned, their heirs and assigns, may purchase the land and receive a title thereto from the United States in fee, upon paying therefor the value of the land ascertained as aforesaid.

SEC. 5. That the occupants of land under Major General Sherman's special field order, dated at Savannah, January sixteen, eighteen hundred and sixty-five, are hereby confirmed in their possession for the period of three years from the date of said order, and no person shall be disturbed in or ousted from said possession during said three years, unless a settlement shall be made with said occupant, by the former owner, his heirs or assigns, satisfactory to the commissioner of the Freedmen's Bureau: *Provided,* That whenever the former owners of lands occupied under General Sherman's field order shall make application for restoration of said lands, the commissioner is hereby authorized, upon the agreement and with the written consent of said occupants, to procure other lands for them by rent or purchase, not exceeding forty acres for each occupant, under the terms and conditions named in section four of this act, or to set apart for them, out of the public lands assigned for that purpose in section four of this act, forty acres each, upon the same terms and conditions.

SEC. 6. That the commissioner shall, under the direction of the President, procure in the name of the United States, by grant or purchase, such lands within the districts aforesaid as may be required for refugees and freedmen dependent on the Government for support; and he shall provide or cause to be erected suitable buildings for asylums and schools. But no such purchase shall be made, nor contract for the same entered into, nor other expense incurred, until after appropriations shall have been provided by Congress for such purposes. And no payment shall be made for lands purchased under this section, except for asylums and schools, from any moneys not specifically appropriated therefor. And the commissioner shall cause such lands from time to time to be valued, allotted, assigned, and sold in manner and form provided in the fourth section of this act, at a price not less than the cost thereof to the United States.

SEC. 7. That whenever in any State or district in which the ordinary course of judicial proceedings has been interrupted by the rebellion, and wherein, in consequence of any State or local law, ordinance, police or other regulation, custom, or prejudice, any of the civil rights or immunities belonging to white persons, including the right to make and enforce contracts, to sue, be parties, and give evidence, to inherit, purchase, lease, sell, hold and convey real and personal property, and to have full and equal benefit of all laws and proceedings for the security of persons and estate, including the constitutional right of bearing arms, are refused or denied to negroes, mulattoes, freedmen, refugees, or any other persons, on account of race, color, or any previous condition of slavery or involuntary servitude, or wherein they or any of them are subjected to any other or different punishment, pains, or penalties, for the commission of any act or offence than are prescribed for white persons committing like acts or offences, it shall be the duty of the President of the United States, through the commissioner, to extend military protection and jurisdiction over all cases affecting such persons so discriminated against.

SEC. 8. That any person who, under color of any State or local law, ordinance, police, or other regulation or custom, shall, in any State or district in which the ordinary course of judicial proceedings has been interrupted by the rebellion, subject, or cause to be subjected, any negro, mulatto, freedman, refugee, or other person, on account of race or color, or any previous condition of slavery or involuntary servitude, or for any other cause, to the deprivation of any civil right secured to white persons, or to any other or different punishment than white persons are subject to for the commission of like acts or offences, shall be deemed guilty of a misdemeanor, and be punished by fine not exceeding one thousand dollars, or imprisonment not exceeding one year, or both; and it shall be the duty of the officers and agents of this bureau to take jurisdiction of, and hear and determine all offences committed against the provisions of this section, and also of all cases affecting negroes, mulattoes, freedmen, refugees, or other persons who are discriminated against in any of the particulars mentioned in the preceding section of this act, under such rules and regulations as the President of the United States, through the War Department, shall prescribe. The jurisdiction conferred by this and the preceding section on the officers and agents of this bureau shall cease and determine whenever the discrimination on account of which it is conferred ceases, and in no event to be exercised in any State in which the ordinary course of judicial proceedings has not been interrupted by the rebellion, nor in any such State after said State shall have been fully restored in all its constitutional relations to the United States, and the courts of the State and of the United States within the same are not disturbed or stopped in the peaceable course of justice.

SEC. 9. That all acts, or parts of acts, inconsistent with the provisions of this act, are hereby repealed.

The votes on passing this bill were:

IN SENATE.

1866, January 25—The bill passed—yeas 37, nays 10

IN HOUSE.

February 6—The bill passed—yeas 137, nays 33

February 21—In Senate, the vote on passing the bill, notwithstanding the objections of the President, was—yeas 30, nays 18, as follow:

YEAS—Messrs. Anthony, Brown, Chandler, Clark, Conness, Cragin, Creswell, Fessenden, Foster, Grimes, Harris, Henderson, Howard, Howe, Kirkwood, Lane of Indiana, Lane of Kansas, Morrill, Nye, Poland, Pomeroy, Ramsey, Sherman, Sprague, Sumner, Trumbull, Wade, Williams, Wilson, Yates—30.

NAYS—Messrs. *Buckalew, Cowan, Davis, Dixon, Doolittle, Guthrie, Hendricks, Johnson, McDougall, Morgan, Nesmith, Norton, Riddle, Saulsbury, Stewart, Stockton,* Van Winkle, *Willey*—18.

Two-thirds not having voted therefor, the bill failed.

d. The Act to Extend the Bureau, July 16, 1866

—*An Act to continue in force and to amend "An Act to establish a Bureau for the Relief of Freedmen and Refugees," and for other Purposes.* [July 16, 1866.]

Be it enacted by the Senate and House of Representatives of the

SOURCE: U.S., *Statutes at Large*, XIV:173–177.

United States of America in Congress assembled, That the act to establish a bureau for the relief of freedmen and refugees, approved March third, eighteen hundred and sixty-five, shall continue in force for the term of two years from and after the passage of this act.

SEC. 2. *And be it further enacted,* That the supervision and care of said bureau shall extend to all loyal refugees and freedmen, so far as the same shall be necessary to enable them as speedily as practicable to become self-supporting citizens of the United States, and to aid them in making the freedom conferred by proclamation of the commander-in-chief, by emancipation under the laws of States, and by constitutional amendment, available to them and beneficial to the republic.

SEC. 3. *And be it further enacted,* That the President shall, by and with the advice and consent of the Senate, appoint two assistant commissioners, in addition to those authorized by the act to which this is an amendment. . . . And the commissioner shall, under the direction of the President, and so far as the same shall be, in his judgment, necessary for the efficient and economical administration of the affairs of the bureau, appoint such agents, clerks, and assistants as may be required for the proper conduct of the bureau. Military officers or enlisted men may be detailed for service and assigned to duty under this act; and the President may, if in his judgment safe and judicious so to do, detail from the army all the officers and agents of this bureau; but no officer so assigned shall have increase of pay or allowances. Each agent or clerk, not heretofore authorized by law, not being a military officer, shall have an annual salary of not less than five hundred dollars, nor more than twelve hundred dollars, according to the service required of him. And it shall be the duty of the commissioner, when it can be done consistently with public interest, to appoint, as assistant commissioners, agents, and clerks, such men as have proved their loyalty by faithful service in the armies of the Union during the rebellion. And all persons appointed to service under this act and the act to which this is an amendment, shall be so far deemed in the military service of the United States as to be under the military jurisdiction, and entitled to the military protection of the government while in discharge of the duties of their office.

SEC. 4. *And be it further enacted,* That officers of the veteran reserve corps or of the volunteer service, now on duty in the

Freedmen's Bureau as assistant commissioners, agents, medical officers, or in other capacities, whose regiments or corps have been or may hereafter be mustered out of service, may be retained upon such duty as officers of said bureau, with the same compensation as is now provided by law for their respective grades; and the Secretary of War shall have power to fill vacancies until other officers can be detailed in their places without detriment to the public service.

SEC. 5. *And be it further enacted,* That the second section of the act to which this is an amendment shall be deemed to authorize the Secretary of War to issue such medical stores or other supplies and transportation, and afford such medical or other aid as here may be needful for the purposes named in said section: *Provided,* That no person shall be deemed "destitute," "suffering," or "dependent upon the government for support," within the meaning of this act, who is able to find employment, and could, by proper industry or exertion, avoid such destitution, suffering, or dependence.

SEC. 6. Whereas, by the provisions of an act approved February sixth, eighteen hundred and sixty-three, entitled "An act to amend an act entitled 'An act for the collection of direct taxes in insurrectionary districts within the United States, and for other purposes,' approved June seventh, eighteen hundred and sixty-two," certain lands in the parishes of St. Helena and Saint Luke, South Carolina, were bid in by the United States at public tax sales, and by the limitation of said act the time of redemption of said lands has expired; and whereas, in accordance with instructions issued by President Lincoln on the sixteenth day of September, eighteen hundred and sixty-three, to the United States direct tax commissioners for South Carolina, certain lands bid in by the United States in the parish of Saint Helena, in said State, were in part sold by the said tax commissioners to "heads of families of the African race," in parcels of not more than twenty acres to each purchaser; and whereas, under said instructions, the said tax commissioners did also set apart as "school farms" certain parcels of land in said parish, numbered on their plats from one to thirty-three, inclusive, making an aggregate of six thousand acres, more or less: Therefore, *be it further enacted,* That the sales made to "heads of families of the African race," under the instructions of President Lincoln to the United States direct tax commissioners for South Carolina, of date of September sixteenth, eighteen hundred and sixty-three, are hereby confirmed and established; and all leases which have been made to such "heads of families," by said direct tax commissioners, shall be changed into certificates of sale in all cases wherein the lease provides for such substitution; and all the lands now remaining unsold, which come within the same designation, being eight thousand acres, more or less, shall be disposed of according to said instructions.

SEC. 7. *And be it further enacted,* That all other lands bid in by the United States at tax sales, being thirty-eight thousand acres more or less, and now in the hands of the said tax commissioners as the property of the United States, in the parishes of Saint Helena and Saint Luke, excepting the "school farms," as specified in the preceding section, and so much as may be necessary for military and naval purposes at Hilton Head, Bay Point, and Land's End, and excepting also the city of Port Royal, on Saint Helena Island, and the town of Beaufort, shall be disposed of in parcels of twenty acres, at one dollar and fifty cents per acre, to such persons and to such only as have acquired and are now occupying lands under and agreeably to the provisions of General Sherman's special field order, dated at Savannah, Georgia, January sixteenth, eighteen hundred and sixty-five; and the remaining lands, if any, shall be disposed of in like manner to such persons as had acquired lands agreeably to the said order of General Sherman, but who have been dispossessed by the restoration of the same to former owners: *Provided,* That the lands sold in compliance with the provisions of this and the preceding section shall not be alienated by their purchasers within six years from and after the passage of this act.

SEC. 8. [Town lots and houses in Beaufort & Port Royal and "school farms" of Saint Helena, S.C., held by United States tax commissioners to be sold at auction and proceeds invested in United States bonds, the interest appropriated to the support of local schools without distinction of color or race.]

SEC. 9. *And be it further enacted,* That the assistant commissioners for South Carolina and Georgia are hereby authorized to examine all claims to lands in their respective States which are claimed under the provisions of General Sherman's special field order, and to give each person having a valid claim a warrant upon the direct tax commissioners for South Carolina for twenty acres of land; and the said direct tax commissioners shall issue to every person, or to his or her heirs, but in no case to any assigns, presenting such warrant, a lease of twenty acres of land, as provided for in section seven, for the term of six years; but at any time thereafter, upon the payment of a sum not exceeding one dollar and fifty cents per acre, the person holding such lease shall be entitled to a certificate of sale of said tract of twenty acres from the direct tax commissioner or such officer as may be authorized to issue the same; but no warrant shall be held valid longer than two years after the issue of the same.

SEC. 10. *And be it further enacted,* That the direct tax commissioners for South Carolina are hereby authorized and required at the earliest day practicable to survey the lands designated in section seven into lots of twenty acres each, with proper metes and bounds distinctly marked, so that the several tracts shall be convenient in form, and as near as practicable have an average of fertility and woodland. . . .

SEC. 11. *And be it further enacted,* That restoration of lands occupied by freedmen under General Sherman's field order dated at Savannah, Georgia, January sixteenth, eighteen hundred and sixty-five, shall not be made until after the crops of the present year shall have been gathered by the occupants of said lands, nor until a fair compensation shall have been made to them by the former owners of such lands, or their legal representatives, for all improvements or betterments erected or constructed thereon, and after due notice of the same being done shall have been given by the assistant commissioner.

SEC. 12. [The commissioner may sell all buildings and lands held by the so-called confederate states and not disposed of and use proceeds for the education of the freed people; and when the bureau ceases to exist the sums remaining shall go to such states as have made provision for the education of their citizens without distinction of color.]

SEC. 13. *And be it further enacted,* That the commissioner of this bureau shall at all times co-operate with private benevolent associations of citizens in aid of freedmen, and with agents and teachers, duly accredited and appointed by them, and shall hire or provide by lease buildings for purposes of education whenever such associations shall, without cost to the government, provide suitable teachers and means of instruction; and he shall furnish such protection as may be required for the safe conduct of such schools.

SEC. 14. *And be it further enacted,* That in every State or district where the ordinary course of judicial proceedings has been interrupted by the rebellion, and until the same shall be fully restored, and in every State or district whose constitutional relations to the government have been practically discontinued by the rebellion, and until such State shall have been restored in such relations, and shall be duly represented in the Congress of the United States, the right to make and enforce contracts, to sue, be parties, and give evidence, to inherit, purchase, lease, sell, hold, and convey real and personal property, and to have full and equal benefit of all laws and proceedings concerning personal liberty, personal security, and the acquisition, enjoyment, and disposition of estate, real and personal, including the constitutional right to bear arms, shall be secured to and enjoyed by all the citizens of such State or district without respect to race or color, or previous condition of slavery. And whenever in either of said States or districts the ordinary course of judicial proceedings has been interrupted by the rebellion, and until the same shall be fully restored, and until such State shall have been restored in its constitutional relations to the government, and shall be duly represented in the Congress of the United States, the President shall, through the commissioner and the officers of the bureau, and under such rules and regulations as the President, through the Secretary of War, shall prescribe, extend military protection and have military jurisdiction over all cases and questions concerning the free enjoyment of such immunities and rights, and no penalty or punishment for any violation of law shall be imposed or permitted because of race or color, or previous condition of slavery, other or greater than the penalty or punishment to which white persons may be liable by law for the like offence. But the jurisdiction conferred by this section upon the officers of the bureau shall not exist in any State where the ordinary course of judicial proceedings has not been interrupted by the rebellion, and shall cease in every State when the courts of the State and the United States are not disturbed in the peaceable course of justice, and after such State shall be fully restored in its constitutional relations to the government, and shall be duly represented in the Congress of the United States.

SEC. 15. *And be it further enacted,* That all officers, agents, and employés of this bureau, before entering upon the duties of their office shall take the oath prescribed in the first section of the act to which this is an amendment; and all acts or parts of acts inconsistent with the provisions of this act are hereby repealed.

7. Johnson's Speech on Washington's Birthday, February 22, 1866

THIS PASSIONATE *extemporaneous speech, coming shortly after the first veto, greatly exacerbated the growing political conflict. Johnson's friends, as well as subsequent apologists, considered it an unfortunate political indiscretion provoked by the abusive language of his radical critics (see doc. 4b). Johnson himself never repudiated its sentiments or charges nor did he take care in later speeches to avoid the same tasteless self-identification with martyrdom.*

SPEECH OF THE 22D FEBRUARY, 1866.
[*Report of National Intelligencer.*]

After returning his thanks to the committee which had waited upon him and presented him with the resolutions which had been adopted, the President said: The resolutions, as I understand them, are complimentary of the policy which has been adopted and pursued by the Administration since it came into power. I am free to say to you on this occasion that it is extremely gratifying to me to know that so large a portion of our fellow-citizens indorse the policy which has been adopted and which is intended to be carried out.

This policy has been one which was intended to restore the glorious Union—to bring these great States, now the subject of controversy, to their original relations to the Government of the United States. . . . I stand before you as I did in the Senate of the United States in 1860. I denounced there those who wanted to disrupt the Government, and I portrayed their true character. I told them that those who were engaged in the effort to break up the Government were traitors. I have not ceased to repeat that, and, as far as endeavor could accomplish it, to carry out the sentiment. I remarked, though, that there were two parties. One would

SOURCE: McPherson, *Handbook for 1868*, pp. 58–63.

destroy the Government to preserve slavery; the other would break up the Government to destroy slavery. The objects to be accomplished were different, it is true, so far as slavery was concerned; but they agreed in one thing—the destruction of the Government, precisely what I was always opposed to; and whether the disunionists came from the South or from the North, I stand now where I did then, vindicating the Union of these States and the Constitution of our country. . . .

I came into power under the Constitution of the country, and with the approbation of the people, and what did I find? I found eight millions of people who were convicted, condemned under the law, and the penalty was death; and, through revenge and resentment, were they all to be annihilated? Oh! may I not exclaim, how different would this be from the example set by the Founder of our holy religion, whose divine arch rests its extremities on the horizon while its span embraces the universe! Yes, He that founded this great scheme came into the world and saw men condemned under the law, and the sentence was death. What was his example? Instead of putting the world or a nation to death, He went forth on the cross and testified with His wounds that He would die and let the world live. Let them repent; let them acknowledge their rashness; let them become loyal, and let them be supporters of our glorious stripes and stars, and the Constitution of our country. I say let the leaders, the conscious, intelligent traitors, meet the penalties of the law. But as for the great mass, who have been forced into the rebellion—misled in other instances—let there be clemency and kindness, and a trust and a confidence in them. But, my countrymen, after having passed through this rebellion, and having given as much evidence of enmity to it as some who croak a great deal about the matter—when I look back over the battle-field and see many of those brave men in whose company I was, in localities of the rebellion where the contest was most difficult and doubtful, and who yet were patient; when I look back over these fields, and where the smoke has scarcely passed away; where the blood that has been shed has scarcely been absorbed—before their bodies have passed through the stages of decomposition—what do I find? The rebellion is put down by the strong arm of the Government in the field. But is this the only way in which we can have rebellions? This was a struggle against a change and a revolution of the Government, and before we fully get from the battle-fields—when our brave men have scarcely returned to their homes and renewed the ties of affection and love to their wives and their children—we are now almost inaugurated into another rebellion.

One rebellion was the effort of States to secede, and the war on the part of the Government was to prevent them from accomplishing that, and thereby changing the character of our Government and weakening its power. When the Government has succeeded, there is an attempt now to concentrate all power in the hands of a few at the federal head, and thereby bring about a consolidation of the Republic, which is equally objectionable with its dissolution. We find a power assumed and attempted to be exercised of a most extraordinary character. We see now that governments can be revolutionized without going into the battle-field; and sometimes the revolutions most distressing to a people are effected without the shedding of blood. That is, the substance of your Government may be taken away, while there is held out to you the form and the shadow. And now, what are the attempts, and what is being proposed? We find that by an irresponsible central directory nearly all the powers of Congress are assumed, without even consulting the legislative and executive departments of the Government. By a resolution reported by a committee, upon whom and in whom the legislative power of the Government has been lodged, that great principle in the Constitution which authorizes and empowers the legislative department, the Senate and House of Representatives, to be the judges of elections, returns, and qualifications of its own members, has been virtually taken away from the two respective branches of the national legislature, and conferred upon a committee, who must report before the body can act on the question of the admission of members to their seats. By this rule they assume a State is out of the Union, and to have its practical relations restored by that rule, before the House can judge of the qualifications of its own members. What position is that? You have been struggling for four years to put down a rebellion. You contended at the beginning of that struggle that a State had not a right to go out. You said it had neither the right nor the power, and it has been settled that the States had neither the right nor the power to go out of the Union. And when you determine by the executive, by the military, and by the public judgment, that these States cannot have any right to go out, this committee turns around and assumes that they are out, and that they shall not come in.

I am free to say to you, as your Executive, that I am not prepared to take any such position. I said in the Senate, in the very inception of this rebellion, that the States had no right to secede. That question has been settled. Thus determined, I cannot turn round and give the lie direct to all that I profess to have done during the last four years. I say that when the States that attempted to secede comply with the Constitution, and give sufficient evidence of loyalty, I shall extend to them the right hand of fellowship, and let peace and union be restored. I am opposed to the Davises, the Toombses, the Slidells, and the long list of such. But when I perceive, on the other hand, men—[A voice, "Call them off"]—I care not by what name you call them—still opposed to the Union, I am free to say to you that I am still with the people. I am still for the preservation of these States, for the preservation of this Union, and in favor of this great Government accomplishing its destiny.

[Here the President was called upon to give the names of three of the members of Congress to whom he had alluded as being opposed to the Union.]

The gentleman calls for three names. I am talking to my friends and fellow-citizens here. Suppose I should name to you those whom I look upon as being opposed to the fundamental principles of this Government, and as now laboring to destroy them. I say Thaddeus Stevens, of Pennsylvania; I say Charles Sumner, of Massachusetts; I say Wendell Phillips, of Massachusetts. [A voice, "Forney!"]

I do not waste my fire on dead ducks. I stand for the country, and though my enemies may traduce, slander, and vituperate, I may say, that has no force.

In addition to this, I do not intend to be governed by real or pretended friends, nor do I intend to be bullied by my enemies. An honest conviction is my sustenance, the Constitution my guide. I know, my countrymen, that it has been insinuated—nay, said directly, in high places—that if such a usurpation of power had been exercised two hundred years ago, in particular reigns, it would have cost an individual his head. What usurpation has Andrew Johnson been guilty of? [Cries of "None."] My only usurpation has been committed by standing between the people and the encroachments of power. And because I dared say in a conversation with a fellow-citizen and a Senator too, that I thought amendments to the constitution ought not to be so frequent, lest the instrument lose all its sanctity and dignity, and be wholly lost sight of in a short time, and because I happened to say in conversation that I thought that such and such an amendment was all that ought to be adopted, it was said that I had suggested such a usurpation of power as would have cost a king his head in a certain period! In connection with this subject, one has exclaimed that we are in the "midst of earthquakes and he trembled." Yes, there is an earthquake approaching, there is a groundswell coming, of popular judgment and indignation. The American people will speak, and by their instinct, if in no other way, know who are their friends, when and where and in whatever position I stand—and I have occupied many positions in the government, going through both branches of the legislature. Some gentleman here behind me says, "And was a tailor." Now, that don't affect me in the least. When I was a tailor I always made a close fit, and was always punctual to my customers, and did good work.

[A voice. No patchwork.]

THE PRESIDENT. No, I did not want any patchwork. But we pass by this digression. Intimations have been thrown out—and when principles are involved and the existence of my country imperiled, I will, as on former occasions, speak what I think. Yes! Cost him his head! Usurpation! When and where have I been guilty of this? Where is the man in all the positions I have occupied, from that of alderman to the Vice Presidency, who can say that Andrew Johnson ever made a pledge that he did not redeem, or ever made a promise that he violated, or that he acted with falsity to the people!

They may talk about beheading; but when I am beheaded I want the American people to be the witness. I do not want by inuendoes of an indirect character in high places to have one say to a man who has assassination broiling in his heart, "there is a fit subject," and also exclaim that the "presidential obstacle" must be got out of the way, when possibly the intention was to institute assassination. Are those who want to destroy our institutions and change the character of the Government not satisfied with the blood that has been shed? Are they not satisfied with one martyr? Does not the blood of Lincoln appease the vengeance and wrath of the opponents of this Government? Is their thirst still unslaked? Do they want more blood? Have they not honor and courage enough to effect the removal of the presidential obstacle otherwise than through the hands of the assassin? I am not afraid of assassins; but if it must be, I would wish to be encountered where one brave man can oppose another. I hold him in dread only who strikes cowardly. But if they have courage enough to strike like men, (I know they are willing to wound, but they are afraid to strike;) if my blood is to be shed because I vindicate the Union and the preservation of this Government in its original purity and character, let it be so; but when it is done, let an altar of the Union be erected, and then, if necessary, lay me upon it, and the blood that now warms and animates my frame shall be poured out in a last libation as a tribute to the Union; and let the opponents of this Government remember that when it is poured out the blood of the martyr will be the seed of the church. The Union will grow. It will continue to increase in strength and power, though it may be cemented and cleansed with blood. . . .

8. Veto and Passage of the Civil Rights Bill

AFTER THE FIRST VETO moderate Republican leaders still sought to work with the president. The letters of Edwin D. Morgan, senator from New York and close political associate of Secretary Seward and Thurlow Weed, document that effort and also identify the nonnegotiable issue. This second veto, like the first, was a composite of several drafts apparently invited from associates and then worked into a single document by secretaries under Johnson's close direction. The pledge of cooperation contained in the next-to-the-last paragraph was included at Seward's urgent request and is inconsistent with the spirit of the message as a whole. In the vote that passed the measure over the veto, five Republicans in the Senate and seven in the House supported the president; no Democrat voted for the Civil Rights Bill either then or on its original passage.

The detailed provisions of the law in respect to enforcement suggest that Republican legislators were not unmindful of the difficulties ahead. These sections might be compared with similar ones in the earlier Freedmen's Bureau legislation (doc. 6c and d) and the later Enforcement Acts (doc. 15a and b). The general analysis made by the London Freed-Man (doc. 8d) is of special interest not only because of the journal's distance from the heat of American politics but also because its editors, in their desire to promote British-American unity, generally avoided taking sides on political issues that divided Americans.

a. The Veto Message, March 27, 1866

WASHINGTON, D.C., March 27, 1866.

To the Senate of the United States:

I regret that the bill, which has passed both Houses of Congress, entitled "An act to protect all persons in the United States in their civil rights and furnish the means of their vindication," contains provisions which I can not approve consistently with my sense of duty to the whole people and my obligations to the Constitution of the United States. I am therefore constrained to return it to the Senate, the House in which it originated, with my objections to its becoming a law.

By the first section of the bill all persons born in the United States and not subject to any foreign power, excluding Indians not taxed, are declared to be citizens of the United States. This provision comprehends the Chinese of the Pacific States, Indians subject to taxation, the people called gypsies, as well as the entire race designated as blacks, people of color, negroes, mulattoes, and persons of African blood. Every individual of these races born in the United States is by the bill made a citizen of the United States. It does not purport to declare or confer any other right of citizenship than Federal citizenship. It does not purport to give these classes of persons any status as citizens of States, except that which may result from their status as citizens of the United States. The power to confer the right of State citizenship is just as exclusively with the several States as the power to confer the right of Federal citizenship is with Congress.

The right of Federal citizenship thus to be conferred on the several excepted races before mentioned is now for the first time proposed to be given by law. If, as is claimed by many, all persons who are native born already are, by virtue of the Constitution, citizens of the United States, the passage of the pending bill can not be necessary to make them such. If, on the other hand, such persons are not citizens, as may be assumed from the proposed legislation to make them such, the grave question presents itself whether, when eleven of the thirty-six States are unrepresented in Congress at the present time, it is sound policy to make our entire colored population and all other excepted classes citizens of the

SOURCE: Richardson, *Messages of the Presidents*, VI:405–413.

United States. Four millions of them have just emerged from slavery into freedom. Can it be reasonably supposed that they possess the requisite qualifications to entitle them to all the privileges and immunities of citizens of the United States? Have the people of the several States expressed such a conviction? It may also be asked whether it is necessary that they should be declared citizens in order that they may be secured in the enjoyment of the civil rights proposed to be conferred by the bill. Those rights are, by Federal as well as State laws, secured to all domiciled aliens and foreigners, even before the completion of the process of naturalization; and it may safely be assumed that the same enactments are sufficient to give like protection and benefits to those for whom this bill provides special legislation. Besides, the policy of the Government from its origin to the present time seems to have been that persons who are strangers to and unfamiliar with our institutions and our laws should pass through a certain probation, at the end of which, before attaining the coveted prize, they must give evidence of their fitness to receive and to exercise the rights of citizens as contemplated by the Constitution of the United States. The bill in effect proposes a discrimination against large numbers of intelligent, worthy, and patriotic foreigners, and in favor of the negro, to whom, after long years of bondage, the avenues to freedom and intelligence have just now been suddenly opened. He must of necessity, from his previous unfortunate condition of servitude, be less informed as to the nature and character of our institutions than he who, coming from abroad, has, to some extent at least, familiarized himself with the principles of a Government to which he voluntarily intrusts "life, liberty, and the pursuit of happiness." Yet it is now proposed, by a single legislative enactment, to confer the rights of citizens upon all persons of African descent born within the extended limits of the United States, while persons of foreign birth who make our land their home must undergo a probation of five years, and can only then become citizens upon proof that they are "of good moral character, attached to the principles of the Constitution of the United States, and well disposed to the good order and happiness of the same."

The first section of the bill also contains an enumeration of the rights to be enjoyed by these classes so made citizens "in every State and Territory in the United States." These rights are "to make and enforce contracts; to sue, be parties, and give evidence;

to inherit, purchase, lease, sell, hold, and convey real and personal property," and to have "full and equal benefit of all laws and proceedings for the security of person and property as is enjoyed by white citizens." So, too, they are made subject to the same punishment, pains, and penalties in common with white citizens, and to none other. Thus a perfect equality of the white and colored races is attempted to be fixed by Federal law in every State of the Union over the vast field of State jurisdiction covered by these enumerated rights. In no one of these can any State ever exercise any power of discrimination between the different races. In the exercise of State policy over matters exclusively affecting the people of each State it has frequently been thought expedient to discriminate between the two races. By the statutes of some of the States, Northern as well as Southern, it is enacted, for instance, that no white person shall intermarry with a negro or mulatto. Chancellor Kent says, speaking of the blacks, that—

> Marriages between them and the whites are forbidden in some of the States where slavery does not exist, and they are prohibited in all the slaveholding States; and when not absolutely contrary to law, they are revolting, and regarded as an offense against public decorum.

I do not say that this bill repeals State laws on the subject of marriage between the two races, for as the whites are forbidden to intermarry with the blacks, the blacks can only make such contracts as the whites themselves are allowed to make, and therefore can not under this bill enter into the marriage contract with the whites. I cite this discrimination, however, as an instance of the State policy as to discrimination, and to inquire whether if Congress can abrogate all State laws of discrimination between the two races in the matter of real estate, of suits, and of contracts generally Congress may not also repeal the State laws as to the contract of marriage between the two races. Hitherto every subject embraced in the enumeration of rights contained in this bill has been considered as exclusively belonging to the States. They all relate to the internal police and economy of the respective States. They are matters which in each State concern the domestic condition of its people, varying in each according to its own peculiar circumstances and the safety and well-being of its own citizens. I do not mean to say that upon all these subjects there are not Federal restraints—as, for instance, in the State power of legislation over contracts there is a Federal limitation that no State shall pass a law impairing the obligations of contracts; and, as to crimes, that no State shall pass an ex post facto law; and, as to money, that no State shall make anything but gold and silver a legal tender; but where can we find a Federal prohibition against the power of any State to discriminate, as do most of them, between aliens and citizens, between artificial persons, called corporations, and natural persons, in the right to hold real estate? If it be granted that Congress can repeal all State laws discriminating between whites and blacks in the subjects covered by this bill, why, it may be asked, may not Congress repeal in the same way all State laws discriminating between the two races on the subjects of suffrage and office? If Congress can declare by law who shall hold lands, who shall testify, who shall have capacity to make a contract in a State, then Congress can by law also declare who, without regard to color or race, shall have the right to sit as a juror or as a judge, to hold any office, and, finally, to vote "in every State and Territory of the United States." As respects the Territories, they come within the power of Congress, for as to them the lawmaking power is the Federal power; but as to the States no similar provision exists vesting in Congress the power "to make rules and regulations" for them.

The object of the second section of the bill is to afford discriminating protection to colored persons in the full enjoyment of all the rights secured to them by the preceding section. It declares—

That any person who, under color of any law, statute, ordinance, regulation, or custom, shall subject, or cause to be subjected, any inhabitant of any State or Territory to the deprivation of any right secured or protected by this act, or to different punishment, pains, or penalties on account of such person having at any time been held in a condition of slavery or involuntary servitude, except as a punishment for crime whereof the party shall have been duly convicted, or by reason of his color or race, than is prescribed for the punishment of white persons, shall be deemed guilty of a misdemeanor, and on conviction shall be punished by fine not exceeding $1,000, or imprisonment not exceeding one year, or both, in the discretion of the court.

This section seems to be designed to apply to some existing or future law of a State or Territory which may conflict with the provisions of the bill now under consideration. It provides for counteracting such forbidden legislation by imposing fine and imprisonment upon the legislators who may pass such conflicting laws, or upon the officers or agents who shall put or attempt to put them into execution. It means an official offense, not a common crime committed against law upon the persons or property of the black race. Such an act may deprive the black man of his property, but not of the *right* to hold property. It means a deprivation of the right itself, either by the State judiciary or the State legislature. It is therefore assumed that under this section members of State legislatures who should vote for laws conflicting with the provisions of the bill, that judges of the State courts who should render judgments in antagonism with its terms, and that marshals and sheriffs who should, as ministerial officers, execute processes sanctioned by State laws and issued by State judges in execution of their judgments could be brought before other tribunals and there subjected to fine and imprisonment for the performance of the duties which such State laws might impose. The legislation thus proposed invades the judicial power of the State. It says to every State court or judge, If you decide that this act is unconstitutional; if you refuse, under the prohibition of a State law, to allow a negro to testify; if you hold that over such a subject-matter the State law is paramount, and "under color" of a State law refuse the exercise of the right to the negro, your error of judgment, however conscientious, shall subject you to fine and imprisonment. I do not apprehend that the conflicting legislation which the bill seems to contemplate is so likely to occur as to render it necessary at this time to adopt a measure of such doubtful constitutionality.

In the next place, this provision of the bill seems to be unnecessary, as adequate judicial remedies could be adopted to secure the desired end without invading the immunities of legislators, always important to be preserved in the interest of public liberty; without assailing the independence of the judiciary, always essential to the preservation of individual rights; and without impairing the efficiency of ministerial officers, always necessary for the maintenance of public peace and order. The remedy proposed by this section seems to be in this respect not only anomalous, but unconstitutional; for the Constitution guarantees nothing with certainty if it does not insure to the several States the right of making and executing laws in regard to all matters arising within their jurisdiction, subject only to the restriction that in cases of conflict with the Constitution and constitutional laws of the United States the latter should be held to be the supreme law of the land.

The third section gives the district courts of the United States exclusive "cognizance of all crimes and offenses committed against the provisions of this act," and concurrent jurisdiction with the circuit courts of the United States of all civil and criminal cases "affecting persons who are denied or can not enforce in the courts or judicial tribunals of the State or locality where they may be any of the rights secured to them by the first section." The construction which I have given to the second section is strengthened by this third section, for it makes clear what kind of denial or deprivation of the rights secured by the first section was in contemplation. It is a denial or deprivation of such rights "in the courts or judicial tribunals of the State." It stands, therefore, clear of doubt that the offense and the penalties provided in the second section are intended for the State judge who, in the clear exercise of his functions as a judge, not acting ministerially but judicially, shall decide contrary to this Federal law. In other words, when a State judge, acting upon a question involving a conflict between a State law and a Federal law, and bound, according to his own judgment and responsibility, to give an impartial decision between the two, comes to the conclusion that the State law is valid and the Federal law is invalid, he must not follow the dictates of his own judgment, at the peril of fine and imprisonment. The legislative department of the Government of the United States thus takes from the judicial department of the States the sacred and exclusive duty of judicial decision, and converts the State judge into a mere ministerial officer, bound to decide according to the will of Congress.

It is clear that in States which deny to persons whose rights are secured by the first section of the bill any one of those rights all criminal and civil cases affecting them will, by the provisions of the third section, come under the exclusive cognizance of the Federal tribunals. It follows that if, in any State which denies to a colored person any one of all those rights, that person should commit a crime against the laws of a State—murder, arson, rape, or any other crime—all protection and punishment through the courts of the State are taken away, and he can only be tried and punished in the Federal courts. How is the criminal to be tried? If the offense is provided for and punished by Federal law, that law, and not the State law, is to govern. It is only when the offense does not happen to be within the purview of Federal law that the Federal courts are to try and punish him under any other law. Then resort is to be had to "the common law, as modified and changed" by State legislation, "so far as the same is not inconsistent with the Constitution and laws of the United States." So that over this vast domain of criminal jurisprudence provided by each State for the protection of its own citizens and for the punishment of all persons who violate its criminal laws, Federal law, whenever it can be made to apply, displaces State law. The question here naturally arises, from what source Congress derives the power to transfer to Federal tribunals certain classes of cases embraced in this section. The Constitution expressly declares that the judicial power of the United States "shall extend to all cases, in law and equity, arising under this Constitution, the laws of the United States, and treaties made or which shall be made under their authority; to all cases affecting ambassadors, other public ministers, and consuls; to all cases of admiralty and maritime jurisdiction; to controversies to which the United States shall be a party; to controversies between two or more States, between a State and citizens of another State, between citizens of different States, between citizens of the same State claiming lands under grants of different States, and between a State, or the citizens thereof, and foreign states, citizens, of subjects." Here the judicial power of the United States is expressly set forth and defined; and the act of September 24, 1789, establishing the judicial courts of the United States, in conferring upon the Federal courts jurisdiction over cases originating in State tribunals, is careful to confine them to the classes enumerated in the above-recited clause of the Constitution. This section of the bill undoubtedly comprehends cases and authorizes the exercise of powers that are not, by the Constitution, within the jurisdiction of the courts of the United States. To transfer them to those courts would be an exercise of authority well calculated to excite distrust and alarm on the part of all the States, for the bill applies alike to all of them—as well to those that have as to those that have not been engaged in rebellion.

It may be assumed that this authority is incident to the power granted to Congress by the Constitution, as recently amended, to enforce, by appropriate legislation, the article declaring that—

> Neither slavery nor involuntary servitude, except as a punishment for crime whereof the party shall have been duly convicted, shall exist within the United States or any place subject to their jurisdiction.

It can not, however, be justly claimed that, with a view to the enforcement of this article of the Constitution, there is at present any necessity for the exercise of all the powers which this bill confers. Slavery has been abolished, and at present nowhere exists within the jurisdiction of the United States; nor has there been, nor is it likely there will be, any attempt to revive it by the people or the States. If, however, any such attempt shall be made, it will then become the duty of the General Government to exercise any and all incidental powers necessary and proper to maintain inviolate this great constitutional law of freedom.

The fourth section of the bill provides that officers and agents of the Freedmen's Bureau shall be empowered to make arrests, and also that other officers may be specially commissioned for that purpose by the President of the United States. It also authorizes circuit courts of the United States and the superior courts of the Territories to appoint, without limitation, commissioners, who are to be charged with the performance of quasi judicial duties. The fifth section empowers the commissioners so to be selected by the courts to appoint in writing, under their hands, one or more suitable persons from time to time to execute warrants and other processes described by the bill. These numerous official agents are made to constitute a sort of police, in addition to the military, and are authorized to summon a posse comitatus, and even to call to their aid such portion of the land and naval forces of the United States, or of the militia, "as may be necessary to the performance of the duty with which they are charged." This extraordinary power is to be conferred upon agents irresponsible to the Government and to the people, to whose number the discretion of the commissioners is the only limit, and in whose hands such authority might be made a terrible engine of wrong, oppression, and fraud. The general statutes regulating the land and naval forces of the United States, the militia, and the execution of the laws are believed to be adequate for every emergency which can occur in time of peace. If it should prove otherwise, Congress can at any time amend those laws in such manner as, while subserving the public welfare, not to jeopard the rights, interests, and liberties of the people.

The seventh section provides that a fee of $10 shall be paid to each commissioner in every case brought before him, and a fee of $5 to his deputy or deputies "for each person he or they may arrest and take before any such commissioner," "with such other fees as may be deemed reasonable by such commissioner," "in general for performing such other duties as may be required in the premises." All these fees are to be "paid out of the Treasury of the United States," whether there is a conviction or not; but in case of conviction they are to be recoverable from the defendant. It seems to me that under the influence of such temptations bad men might convert any law, however beneficent, into an instrument of persecution and fraud.

By the eighth section of the bill the United States courts, which sit only in one place for white citizens, must migrate with the marshal and district attorney (and necessarily with the clerk, although he is not mentioned) to any part of the district upon the order of the President, and there hold a court, "for the purpose of the more speedy arrest and trial of persons charged with a violation of this act;" and there the judge and officers of the court must remain, upon the order of the President, "for the time therein designated."

The ninth section authorizes the President, or such person as he may empower for that purpose, "to employ such part of the land or naval forces of the United States, or of the militia, as shall be necessary to prevent the violation and enforce the due execution of this act." This language seems to imply a permanent military force, that is to be always at hand, and whose only business is to be the enforcement of this measure over the vast region where it is intended to operate.

I do not propose to consider the policy of this bill. To me the details of the bill seem fraught with evil. The white race and the black race of the South have hitherto lived together under the relation of master and slave—capital owning labor. Now, suddenly, that relation is changed, and as to ownership capital and labor are divorced. They stand now each master of itself. In this new relation, one being necessary to the other, there will be a new adjustment, which both are deeply interested in making harmonious. Each has equal power in settling the terms, and if left to the laws that regulate capital and labor it is confidently believed that they will satisfactorily work out the problem. Capital, it is true, has more intelligence, but labor is never so ignorant as not to understand its own interests, not to know its own value, and not to see that capital must pay that value.

This bill frustrates this adjustment. It intervenes between capital and labor and attempts to settle questions of political economy through the agency of numerous officials whose interest it will be to foment discord between the two races, for as the breach widens their employment will continue, and when it is closed their occupation will terminate.

In all our history, in all our experience as a people living under Federal and State law, no such system as that contemplated by the details of this bill has ever before been proposed or adopted. They establish for the security of the colored race safeguards which go infinitely beyond any that the General Government has ever provided for the white race. In fact, the distinction of race and color is by the bill made to operate in favor of the colored and against the white race. They interfere with the municipal legislation of the States, with the relations existing exclusively between a State and its citizens, or between inhabitants of the same State—an absorption and assumption of power by the General Government which, if acquiesced in, must sap and destroy our federative system of limited powers and break down the barriers which preserve the rights of the States. It is another step, or rather stride, toward centralization and the concentration of all legislative powers in the National Government. The tendency of the bill must be to resuscitate the spirit of rebellion and to arrest the progress of those influences which are more closely drawing around the States the bonds of union and peace.

My lamented predecessor, in his proclamation of the 1st of January, 1863, ordered and declared that all persons held as slaves within certain States and parts of States therein designated were and thenceforward should be free; and further, that the executive government of the United States, including the military and naval authorities thereof, would recognize and maintain the freedom of such persons. This guaranty has been rendered especially obligatory and sacred by the amendment of the Constitution abolishing slavery throughout the United States. I therefore fully recognize the obligation to protect and defend that class of our people whenever and wherever it shall become necessary, and to the full extent compatible with the Constitution of the United States.

Entertaining these sentiments, it only remains for me to say that I will cheerfully cooperate with Congress in any measure that may be necessary for the protection of the civil rights of the freedmen, as well as those of all other classes of persons throughout the

United States, by judicial process, under equal and impartial laws, in conformity with the provisions of the Federal Constitution.

I now return the bill to the Senate, and regret that in considering the bills and joint resolutions—forty-two in number—which have been thus far submitted for my approval I am compelled to withhold my assent from a second measure that has received the sanction of both Houses of Congress.

ANDREW JOHNSON

b. Civil Rights Act, April 9, 1866

An Act to protect all Persons in the United States in their Civil Rights, and furnish the Means of their Vindication. [April 9, 1866.]

Be it enacted by the Senate and House of Representatives of the United States of America in Congress assembled, That all persons born in the United States and not subject to any foreign power, excluding Indians not taxed, are hereby declared to be citizens of the United States; and such citizens, of every race and color, without regard to any previous condition of slavery or involuntary servitude, except as a punishment for crime whereof the party shall have been duly convicted, shall have the same right, in every State and Territory in the United States, to make and enforce contracts, to sue, be parties, and give evidence, to inherit, purchase, lease, sell, hold, and convey real and personal property, and to full and equal benefit of all laws and proceedings for the security of person and property, as is enjoyed by white citizens, and shall be subject to like punishment, pains, and penalties, and to none other, any law, statute, ordinance, regulation, or custom, to the contrary notwithstanding.

SEC. 2. *And be it further enacted,* That any person who, under color of any law, statute, ordinance, regulation, or custom, shall subject, or cause to be subjected, any inhabitant of any State or Territory to the deprivation of any right secured or protected by this act, or to different punishment, pains, or penalties on account of such person having at any time been held in a condition of slavery or involuntary servitude, except as a punishment for crime whereof the party shall have been duly convicted, or by reason of his color or race, than is prescribed for the punishment of white persons, shall be deemed guilty of a misdemeanor, and, on convic-

SOURCE: U.S., *Statutes at Large,* XIV:27–29.

tion, shall be punished by fine not exceeding one thousand dollars, or imprisonment not exceeding one year, or both, in the discretion of the court.

SEC. 3. *And be it further enacted,* That the district courts of the United States, within their respective districts, shall have, exclusively of the courts of the several States, cognizance of all crimes and offences committed against the provisions of this act, and also, concurrently with the circuit courts of the United States, of all causes, civil and criminal, affecting persons who are denied or cannot enforce in the courts or judicial tribunals of the State or locality where they may be any of the rights secured to them by the first section of this act; and if any suit or prosecution, civil or criminal, has been or shall be commenced in any State court, against any such person, for any cause whatsoever, or against any officer, civil or military, or other person, for any arrest or imprisonment, trespasses, or wrongs done or committed by virtue or under color of authority derived from this act or the act establishing a Bureau for the relief of Freedmen and Refugees, and all acts amendatory thereof, or for refusing to do any act upon the ground that it would be inconsistent with this act, such defendant shall have the right to remove such cause for trial to the proper district or circuit court in the manner prescribed by the "Act relating to habeas corpus and regulating judicial proceedings in certain cases," approved March three, eighteen hundred and sixty-three, and all acts amendatory thereof. The jurisdiction in civil and criminal matters hereby conferred on the district and circuit courts of the United States shall be exercised and enforced in conformity with the laws of the United States, so far as such laws are suitable to carry the same into effect; but in all cases where such laws are not adapted to the object, or are deficient in the provisions necessary to furnish suitable remedies and punish offences against law, the common law, as modified and changed by the constitution and statutes of the State wherein the court having jurisdiction of the cause, civil or criminal, is held, so far as the same is not inconsistent with the Constitution and laws of the United States, shall be extended to and govern said courts in the trial and disposition of such cause, and, if of a criminal nature, in the infliction of punishment on the party found guilty.

SEC. 4. *And be it further enacted,* That the district attorneys, marshals, and deputy marshals of the United States, the commissioners appointed by the circuit and territorial courts of the United States, with powers of arresting, imprisoning, or bailing offenders against the laws of the United States, the officers and agents of the Freedmen's Bureau, and every other officer who may be specially empowered by the President of the United States, shall be, and they are hereby, specially authorized and required, at the expense of the United States, to institute proceedings against all and every person who shall violate the provisions of this act, and cause him or them to be arrested and imprisoned, or bailed, as the case may be, for trial before such court of the United States or territorial court as by this act has cognizance of the offence. And with a view to affording reasonable protection to all persons in their constitutional rights of equality before the law, without distinction of race or color, or previous condition of slavery or involuntary servitude, except as a punishment for crime, whereof the party shall have been duly convicted, and to the prompt discharge of the duties of this act, it shall be the duty of the circuit courts of the United States and the superior courts of the Territories of the United States, from time to time, to increase the number of commissioners, so as to afford a speedy and convenient means for the arrest and examination of persons charged with a violation of this act; and such commissioners are hereby authorized and required to exercise and discharge all the powers and duties conferred on them by this act, and the same duties with regard to offences created by this act, as they are authorized by law to exercise with regard to other offences against the laws of the United States.

SEC. 5. *And be it further enacted*, That it shall be the duty of all marshals and deputy marshals to obey and execute all warrants and precepts issued under the provisions of this act, when to them directed; and should any marshal or deputy marshal refuse to receive such warrant or other process when tendered, or to use all proper means diligently to execute the same, he shall, on conviction thereof, be fined in the sum of one thousand dollars, to the use of the person upon whom the accused is alleged to have committed the offence. And the better to enable the said commissioners to execute their duties faithfully and efficiently, in conformity with the Constitution of the United States and the requirements of this act, they are hereby authorized and empowered, within their counties respectively, to appoint, in writing, under their hands, any one or more suitable persons, from time to time, to execute all such warrants and other process as may be issued by them in the lawful performance of their respective duties; and the persons so appointed to execute any warrant or process as aforesaid shall have authority to summon and call to their aid the bystanders or posse comitatus of the proper country, or such portion of the land or naval forces of the United States, or of the militia, as may be necessary to the performance of the duty with which they are charged, and to insure a faithful observance of the clause of the Constitution which prohibits slavery, in conformity with the provisions of this act; and said warrants shall run and be executed by said officers anywhere in the State or Territory within which they are issued.

SEC. 6. *And be it further enacted,* That any person who shall knowingly and wilfully obstruct, hinder, or prevent any officer, or other person charged with the execution of any warrant or process issued under the provisions of this act, or any person or persons lawfully assisting him or them, from arresting any person for whose apprehension such warrant or process may have been issued, or shall rescue or attempt to rescue such person from the custody of the officer, other person or persons, or those lawfully assisting as aforesaid, when so arrested pursuant to the authority herein given and declared, or shall aid, abet, or assist any person so arrested as aforesaid, directly or indirectly, to escape from the custody of the officer or other person legally authorized as aforesaid, or shall harbor or conceal any person for whose arrest a warrant or process shall have been issued as aforesaid, so as to prevent his discovery and arrest after notice or knowledge of the fact that a warrant has been issued for the apprehension of such person, shall, for either of said offences, be subject to a fine not exceeding one thousand dollars, and imprisonment not exceeding six months, by indictment and conviction before the district court of the United States for the district in which said offence may have been committed, or before the proper court of criminal jurisdiction, if commited within any one of the organized Territories of the United States.

SEC. 7. [Regulates fees for officials involved in execution of the law and provides payment from United States Treasury, recoverable from defendants.]

SEC. 8. *And be it further enacted,* That whenever the President of the United States shall have reason to believe that offences have been or are likely to be committed against the provisions of this act within any judicial district, it shall be lawful for him, in his discretion, to direct the judge, marshal, and district attorney of such district to attend at such place within the district, and for such time as he may designate, for the purpose of the more speedy arrest and trial of persons charged with a violation of this act; and it shall be the duty of every judge or other officer, when any such requisition shall be received by him, to attend at the place and for the time therein designated.

SEC. 9. *And be it further enacted,* That it shall be lawful for the President of the United States, or such person as he may empower for that purpose, to employ such part of the land or naval forces of the United States, or of the militia, as shall be necessary to prevent the violation and enforce the due execution of this act.

SEC. 10. *And be it further enacted,* That upon all questions of law arising in any cause under the provisions of this act a final appeal may be taken to the Supreme Court of the United States.

c. Senator Edwin D. Morgan to Thurlow Weed and John Jay, April and May 1866

UNITED STATES SENATE CHAMBER

Washington Apl 8 1866

Dear Mr Weed

Three days before we came to the vote on the Civil rights bill, I made [as indicated in my letter to Judge Balcom] most earnest efforts with Mr. Fessenden and with the President to have a Compromise bill agreed upon and passed. It looked hopeful at one time but failed. The difficulty really was the President's objections to the *first* Section of the bill. It was then *this* bill or *nothing*. I believed something should pass both Houses of Congress and *this* will. It will be out of the way as an issue in the Elections. There are many ways in which it will do good. The South will become much more sensible and there is need enough of that. The President will

SOURCE: Thurlow Weed Papers, Rhees Library, University of Rochester, Rochester, N.Y., and Edwin D. Morgan Papers, New York State Library at Albany, N.Y.

not be weakened or harmed. When he failed to approve upon his own conviction of duty as I am sure he did *all* responsibility was off from him and *on* Congress.

It is unfortunate perhaps that the bill was not signed. But if it had been returned with the Presidents objection to the Second Section *only* we could have got along with it very well and maintained ourselves which is a matter of *some* consideration, and we could under such circumstances have strengthened the President. Aside from the very natural desire of being sustained on *all* measures, the President will be, or perhaps I should say *may be*, in a better position than if the bill had been defeated by those who voted for it when it first passed the Senate. We must however at least expect delay before these general views will be concur'd in by him.

I thank you for your excellent letter.

Yours very truly
E. D. Morgan

May 16, [186]6

Dear Mr Jay,

I wish it was in my power to send to you cheering news in relation to our political situation. I am scarcely able to do this. The President is not likely to change as to his policy, while Congress is equally firm in maintaining the stand it has taken. In all probability the Fall Elections must decide it. I am much pleased to learn that you approve the passage of the "Civil Rights Bill" over the veto which never should have been sent to the Senate in the sweeping manner in which it came. If the President in returning the bill had disavowed objections to *the Principle* and pointed out the defects of the *details*, the Senate would have amended and passed the bill without any break or serious trouble, as we all knew that the *second* section was objectionable. But the first section, declaring the Blacks citizens, we could not, and would not give up. Next week the Senate will take up the proposed amendment to the Constitution, and the Bills, as reported from the Select Committee of 15. We shall pass *something* beyond any serious doubt and go to the People, who are patriotic, firm and determined. I write this hasty note chiefly as an apology for not writing you before, and hoping to get a better opportunity to write you more fully a few days hence, the session will not terminate before 4th July. Congratulating you upon the improved health of your daughter, and with best regards of Mrs Morgan and myself, to all the members of your family. I remain

Very truly your friend
E. D. Morgan

Mr John Jay
. . . London

d. London Freed-Man Editorial, June 1, 1866

THE CIVIL RIGHTS BILL

As many persons are in uncertainty as to the exact intent and nature of this bill, a short explanation may be useful. The Civil Rights Bill was passed by Congress in the usual way and submitted to President Johnson for his assent, when, to the surprise of the world, it received his veto. The friends of the coloured free people felt aggrieved and indignant at the refusal of the President to place his imprimatur on this act of the legislature, inasmuch as a draft of the bill had been submitted to the President before its introduction, to which at the time he took no exception. That the President had a legal right to veto the bill, no person denies, but he could not do so after he had given, as was supposed, his general approval to its introduction without being charged with double-dealing. If Mr. Johnson had given the explanation which he has given since the bill has been passed a second time in the Senate by a vote of 33 to 15, and in the House of Representatives by one of 122 to 12, that he wished so important a statute simply to receive a second and more careful revision by the legislature, the very grave suspicion that was raised against his integrity, might have been avoided. Such an explanation, however, from his lips, after his boisterous menace against Mr. Sumner and others—well-known patriots and friends of freedom—comes too late, and only serves to change our condemnation of his conduct into unmitigated contempt. The real issue between Congress and Mr. Johnson is very simple. The President believes that the Government of the United States is a Government of white men, and exists for white men alone. Congress believes that it is a Government of citizens without reference

SOURCE: London Freed-Man, June 1, 1866.

to the colour of its citizens. Mr. Sumner has all along asserted that the law needed no alteration—that the constitution embraced all citizens—that the decision in the Dred Scot case, which decided that a black man though free had no rights which a white man was bound to respect—was an infamous violation of the constitution of the United States. The Civil Rights Bill then gives no new Article to the constitution, but like our own Great Charta, and the twenty-ninth chapter of it in particular, declares in relation to the freedom of the citizen and the protection of that freedom, only the fundamental law of the State. It authoritatively strikes out colour as an integer in the great political sum. It is an assertion of the triumph of freedom against the cruel ravening demon of slavery. It reserves the essential principles of citizenship from that destruction to which Mr. Johnson seemed to be willing to surrender them. It tells in unmistakeable terms that the war having terminated in the defeat of the Southern oligarchs, an era of justice—justice for all—equality before the tribunals alike for white and black, is to dawn upon those fair and promising Southern lands.

And what is this terrible declaratory enactment, which some of our countrymen who have never seen it or read it suppose to be intended as a means to fling those who were formerly slaves offensively before the faces of their quondam masters? We will give, not in our language but in the words of the statute, the first section, and then it will be manifest what it is, and what an outrage Mr. Johnson endeavoured to perpetrate upon freedom by his presidential veto.

> Be it enacted, &c., That all persons born in the United States, and not subject to any foreign power, excluding Indians not taxed, are hereby declared to be citizens of the United States; and such citizens of every race and colour, without regard to any previous condition of slavery or involuntary service, except as a punishment for crime whereof the party shall have been duly convicted, shall have the same right in every State and Territory to make and enforce contracts, to sue, to be sued, be parties and give evidence, to inherit, purchase, lease, sell, hold and convey real and personal property; and to full and equal benefit of all laws and proceedings for the security of person and property as is enjoyed by white citizens; and shall be subject to like punishments, pains, and penalties, and to none other, any law, statute, ordinance, regulation, or custom to the contrary notwithstanding.

And this is the method the Sumners, the Wilsons, the Stevens of the United States have resolved to employ to consolidate their

CONFLICT BETWEEN PRESIDENT AND CONGRESS   77

nation and to conserve liberty—a method which at once tells us that these men at least are well-read in the laws of their ancestors, and that they have determined to crown the triumph of the arms of the nation in the field by the greater triumph of law and justice in the forum.

A writer of an article full of confusion and falsehood in "Blackwood's Magazine"—falsehood rendered the more odious because the writer professes to know—a profession we very much doubt—from personal experience something of the negro about whom he ventures to write—proposes in cold blood as a remedy for the negro difficulty one of two things. First—let not our readers be startled—EXTERMINATION, or, secondly, to reduce them to constrained labour, or in plain English the reintroduction of SLAVERY. Is the writer serious, or does he pen his foolish sentences to please a clique that has aimed to involve us with our own kin, across the western wave. We have no word for these ribald scribes. The world moves on, and it will neither tolerate Extermination nor endure Slavery. Twenty years with black people in and out of slavery enable us to affirm what this writer does not know—that the negro is faithful, industrious and religious. God knows this is more than we can say for the whites, whether the mean-whites or the would-be oligarchs of the South. We repeat for the hundredth time, that it is not the "irrepressible nigger" that makes the difficulty in the South, but the impracticable, ignorant and oppressive white man. To those who aim at a solution of the negro question we say: in your calculations assume that the negro is not idle, and that he is influenced by the same motives that avail with ourselves.

9. The Campaign and Election Results of 1866

THE CAMPAIGN OF 1866 was the most important midterm congressional election in American history. Had a victory gone to President Johnson and his supporters, there would have been no Fourteenth Amendment, no Fifteenth Amendment, and no period of so-called Black Reconstruction governments in the South. The rhetoric of the contest was profuse, exaggerated, and offensive but not atypical of American politics. For an older generation of historians the rhetoric tended to obscure the central issue, which is succinctly stated in the New York Times editorial (doc. b). Henry J. Raymond, its editor, had supported the president in Congress and in his newspaper. The October date of the editorial may come as a surprise; but a century ago, congressional elections were not all held in the month of November, and the president's October losses came in key swing states. As the exchange of telegrams between Governor Parsons and the president (doc. c) makes clear, Johnson rejected the advice of the Times.

The New Orleans riot had a major impact upon the 1866 election campaign, with President Johnson charging that it was a radical revolutionary plot and his Republican opposition publicizing its horrors and placing responsibility for them upon the president and his policy. The eye-witness account printed below (doc. a) was apparently written just hours after the event and was addressed to Nathaniel P. Banks, at the time a member of Congress. As a general with more political than military skill, Banks had been entrusted by Lincoln with the administration of Louisiana and the wartime effort to reconstruct the state. Shortly after acceding to the presidency, Johnson replaced Banks and, in effect, set the stage for the return to power in Louisiana of Conservative Democratic ex-Confederates, including John T. Monroe, who in the spring of 1866 won election as mayor of New Orleans. Monroe and his fellow Democrats were determined to maintain and exercise the power they had won, and without concession to local Unionists, white or black. The white unionists were equally determined to challenge the Confederate return to power, and black leaders stubbornly refused to surrender all prospect of obtaining the ballot, which they had long demanded and which Banks had promised them in the name of Abraham Lincoln. Such was the background for the reconvening of the constitutional convention of 1864 and the tension that resulted in over forty dead and 150 wounded, overwhelmingly Negroes and their white friends.

a. New Orleans Riot: An Eye Witness Letter, July 30, 1866

New Orleans July 30 1866

To the honorable N P Banks,
    Dear Sir

by the time this reaches you you will be apprized of the riot that took place in our rebel city. I shall minuitly discribe all that transpired within my obscrvation on the memerble thirty (30th) of July the riot they blame the negroes and Dr. Dostie with. Comenced about twenty minutes past twelve (M) in this manner. There was a collerd persesion marching up Bergundy Street as the head of the persesion arrived at Canal St. a policeman stept out aloud this was a pretty set of dam negroes to be invested with political rights

Source: Nathaniel P. Banks Papers, Library of Congress.

(mark you this prosesion was composed of first Louisiana native Guards or 73 Regament who have so galantly fought in this war) They all ought to be on there masters plantation put in stocks and whiped to death. At this the collerd people ordered him away so that the prosesion could proceed but instead of departing he drew his revolver and commence fireing on the prosesion wounded one (1) man. The drumer began beating his drum for assistance and the police gathered in crowds each minute as soon as the colerd people ran to where the drumer was beating and the police moved of and allowd the prosesion proceede on there way. All this time the collerd people had not fired a shot nor struck a white person. Then they march in the hall where the Convention was in session after arriving in the hall firing began again on the outside of the building. Union White men and collerd men was shot down like dogs. The second disturbanc comence thus, the police was divided into two (2) divissions onc commanded by Lucien Adams (who was sent to fort Jackson by Gen. Butler and the other by Col Adams Chief of police who was Col in the Rebbel Armey the whole under our loyal Major John T. Monroe one of Gen. Butler's prissoners who was Fort Jackson for treasonable sentiments in his Official Capacity as Mayor for the same citezen that he now rules and represents they are the same now as then. Some of the police sent a small boy (white) to begin the quarel he began in this maner. They bore such taunts for some time. The boy saw he could not provoke them to quarel in that maner began to beat them with a stick and to throw bricks this was undurable. One of the party rushed at him and he ran to the corner of Canal and Dryades Street. The police then rushed out of there place of concealment and shot every collerd man they met after succeeding in driving of all collerd person one rebel got upon the iron railing around the Medical College and made a move to hang Michael Hahn and Dr. Dostie which was unamusly applauded by the infuriated mob of citizens and police and moveover to kill every negro they should meat. They suited there actions to there words by shooting every colerd person they saw without regard to age or sex. They would also cry out remember *Port Hudson Fort Wagner* and before *Richmond* &c. Such words recieved with universal acclamation by all. There was a girl and two boys shot on account of color what goes further to show there bitterness. A colerd man was short down and was crying for mercy a common prostitute came out of her house and exterminated him by beating his brains out with a brick. A police officer encouraged her on. There was a colerd man twice commission in the *United States* army as *Captain* that was fired on about twenty times with the words take that damed smoked Yankee son of a bitch. After they got up to the door of the hall they closed it and as fast as any Union man came out he was shot and cut at as long as they could see him. Then Michael Hahn formerly governor of the State was shot and stabbed as he came out the door. Dr Dostie Wm Show formerly a deputy sheriff was also shot and considerable mutilated by the infuriated mob. There was about sixty killed and about one hundred or two wounded in and around the hall. All this was done because men wanted *Equal Rights* at the ballot. Dr. Dostie was informed by one of his danger as I overherd a conversation between a civilian and two policeman. They also threatened to exterminate the negroes because to the negroes they attributed there defeat and *Hahn* and *Dostie* as accomplices—because they were Union men and the black mans friend and out of them we must have our revenge. Said civilian minutely stated where the troops were station and said that we can hang *Dostie & Hahn* and they negroes before they can be musterd for servace. The police fired the first shot & the last shot killed Union men yet they exhonerate themselves and attached all blame to the negroes. A colerd man going home peaceabley from his place of buiseness was accorsted by a policeman and asked him what he was doing out so late. He gave a proper awnswer and passed on. As soon as he had gon a short distance the policeman ran after him and shot him in the back. Being a short distance from home he reached his home but his door being fasten could not get in and before he could arouse any one another policeman came up caught and held the wounded man whilst the other shot him again then both beats him with clubs, expected to die. I omited to state the rebel police fired upon the American flag when it was put out of the window and also fired on a *United States* officer in uniform at the same time remarking there is a dam yankee son of a bitch and all the white person that was supposed to have anything to do with the convention. The policeman all are lately returned rebels. To prove my assertion no man could obtain employment on the police or in the City who did or had not fought four years in the Con-

federate Survice as several appointment that have been made were
found to have been in the employ of the Yankees were amediately
discharged and four years rebels to recieved the posision. A Loyal
man can obtain no employment in the City without they can be
employed Union men or men that did not know that the employe
was Union man—

I remain your humble servent—
formerly an Employe of the Government—
Mr. John Gibbons

b. The People's Verdict: New York Times Editorial, October 11, 1866

The verdict pronounced by the people of four States is merely
the fulfillment of an expectation entertained by every man who
had watched honestly the temper and purposes of the country. The
boasting of the Democratic Press during the progress of the canvass
has not misled anybody. . . . The party statistician will deem it
his duty to ponder every return—to compare the figures of this year
with the figures of other years and to study the causes of every
change. The people, however, have little relish for these fine-drawn
distinctions. Gains or losses here or there matter comparatively
little to them. They have no taste for the casuistry that would
convert defeat into victory, or for the philosophy that would suck
consolation out of irretrievable disaster. The general result is all
that concerns them. They know that Pennsylvania, which has been
the theatre of one of the hottest contests ever known, has rejected
the overtures of the Democracy, and has planted itself more firmly
than ever on the side of the party represented by Congress. They
know that Ohio and Indiana have contributed their quota toward
the maintenance of Republican supremacy, and that Iowa has not
wavered in the faith which made her Congressional delegation an
unit in support of the Union Party. All else is, in the popular
judgment, a matter of indifference. For it concludes, rightly and
reasonably, that the impulses and convictions which on Tuesday
impelled four States to follow the lead of Maine and Vermont, will
as surely determine the contest in New York, and in the States
which have yet to pass judgment on the issues before them.

SOURCE: New York Times, October 11, 1866.

The one great result which has now been reached is the ratification by the people of the position assumed by Congress in relation to the President and the South. This has been the test to which every candidate, every platform, has been subjected. Shall the President be sustained in his plan for restoring the Union by the immediate admission of the Southern States to the Capitol? Or shall the recommendations of the President be repudiated, and the action of Congress endorsed? The question may have been more or less modified in particular localities, as in that represented by Mr. Thaddeus Stevens, but as a rule this has been its shape—the President or Congress? The immediate admission of the South, or the exaction of preliminary conditions embodied in the Constitutional Amendment? And the answer leaves room neither for equivocation nor doubt. It is overwhelmingly against the President—clearly, unmistakably, decisively in favor of Congress and its policy.

Seldom, indeed, has a contest been conducted with so exclusive reference to a single issue. True, the antecedents of candidates during the war have had much to do with the matter of individual eligibility. Clymer has been consigned to private life because his sympathies and efforts were against the war and the Union while Grant's were heroically in its support. But, after all, there have been few of the considerations which in ordinary times have entered into party controversy. The tariff, internal improvements, the currency, the foreign relations of the Government, have been discussed only incidentally. Everywhere the conditions of national unity and peace have formed the theme of debate, and the standard by which party nominations have been weighted and judged. Minor questions, therefore, cannot be pleaded in abatement of the account as it now stands. It is a settlement which can be altered only to be made more stringent. It is a declaration of the popular determination to exact from the south guarantees for the maintenance of the Union as the war has made it; a Union assuring national citizenship to black and white, assuring equality before the law, the just representation of the sections, and the inviolability of the loyal debt, and providing effectually against the future assumption of the rebel debts or claims. This is the sum and substance of Tuesday's verdict. Not negro suffrage—not confiscation—not harsh or vindictive penalties; but the plan of restoration dictated by Congress, and designed to be a final adjustment of our national difficulties.

It is too late to say that the popular verdict hardly comes up to the rigid constitutional standard. It would avail nothing now to argue that the Amendment, equitable and moderate though it is, ought not to be a condition of restoration. Equally useless were it to consider by what possible combinations and compromises the view for which we have contended might have acquired greater prominence and support. The people have been heard from, and from their decision our form of government provides no appeal. The South, if wise, will hearken and comply. And the President, if politic, will not refuse to listen to a verdict which especially concerns himself and the plan to which he is committed.

At least one source of apprehension has been removed. Had these elections ended adversely to Congress—had promises been held out of any considerable change in the complexion of that body—the idea of a second House with the Southern representatives unconstitutionally admitted, might possibly have assumed dangerous dimensions. The proposition that a second Congress should be organized, and that the President should recognize the one favorable to his plan, might then have been more plausible. Fortunately this beginning of revolution has been obviated. Not the faintest pretext can now be found for impugning the validity of the Congressional decision, or for mooting the legitimacy of any other body. The people have taken care that this threatened peril shall not be heard of more. They have decreed, not only that Congress as it now is, faithfully represents their convictions and purposes, but that the Congress which will come after shall sustain substantially the same policy. Neither the South nor the President, then, has aught to expect from delay. The South must choose between prolonged exclusion, with the probability of more stringent terms, and the acceptance of the overture already submitted to them. The President must be content to see Congress push forward its new method of settlement, despite protestations and vetoes, or must frankly accept the verdict pronounced by the people who elected him, and use his opportunities to hasten restoration on the only basis that is practicable. He has stated his own case, and the people have refused to accept it. The part of statesmanship surely is to concede graciously and promptly to the popular requirements, and to exert the influence of the executive in support of the compromise now tendered to the Southern States.

c. President Johnson Rejects the Election Verdict, January 17, 1867

Montgomery, Alabama
January 17, 1867

Legislature in session. Efforts making to re-consider vote on constitutional amendment. Report from Washington says it is probable an enabling act will pass. We do not know what to believe. I find nothing here.

Lewis E. Parson
Exchange Hotel

His Excellency Andrew Johnson, President.

United States Military Telegraph,
Executive Office,
Washington, D.C., January 17, 1867.

What possible good can be obtained [attained] by reconsidering the constitutional amendment? I know of none in the present posture of affairs; and I do not believe the people of the whole country will sustain any set of individuals in attempts to change the whole character of our Government by enabling acts or otherwise. I believe, on the contrary, that they will eventually uphold all who have the patriotism and courage to stand by the Constitution, and who place their confidence in the people. There should be no faltering on the part of those who are honest in their determination to sustain the several co-ordinate departments of the Government, in accordance with its original design.

Andrew Johnson.

Hon. Lewis E. Parsons,
Montgomery, Alabama.

Source: McPherson, Handbook for 1868, 252–253.

10. The Fourteenth Amendment and Its Ratification, June 13, 1866–July 28, 1868

First the framing, and then the acceptance, of the omnibus postwar amendment took a torturous path. With the exception of section four its provisions represented a distillation of numerous proposals in the heat of a developing major political conflict. The amendment passed Congress by a strict party vote, no Democrat voting "yea" and only four Republican adherents of the president, all senators, voting "nay" as against 171 Republican votes on final passage through the House and Senate. The documents below suggest the unprecedented process through which the amendment became the law of the land. (Note also section five of the Reconstruction Act, doc. 11.) Seward's final proclamation was lengthy and repetitious, but extracts from its concluding paragraphs are included so that the reader may see that the secretary of state as well as seven Southern states bowed to congressional coercion before the official date of ratification.

Had President Johnson encouraged, rather than discouraged, ratification after the 1866 election returns clearly indicated that no lesser terms would be exacted for readmission (doc. 9b and c), in all probability there would have been no military rule nor immediate, universal Negro suffrage in the South. For an authoritative statement of the intent behind sections one and five of the amendment, see Bingham's statement (doc. 15c).

FOURTEENTH CONSTITUTIONAL AMENDMENT

Be it resolved by the Senate and House of Representatives of the United States of America, in Congress assembled, (two-thirds of both Houses concurring,) That the following article be proposed to the Legislatures of the several States as an amendment to the Constitution of the United States, which, when ratified by three-fourths of said Legislatures, shall be valid as part of the Constitution, namely:

ARTICLE XIV

SECTION 1. All persons born or naturalized in the United States, and subject to the jurisdiction thereof, are citizens of the United States and of the State wherein they reside. No State shall make or enforce any law which shall abridge the privileges or immunities of citizens of the United States; nor shall any State deprive any person of life, liberty, or property, without due process of law, nor deny to any person within its jurisdiction the equal protection of the laws.

SEC. 2. Representatives shall be apportioned among the several States according to their respective numbers, counting the whole number of persons in each State, excluding Indians not taxed. But when the right to vote at any election for the choice of electors for President and Vice President of the United States, representatives in Congress, the executive and judicial officers of a State, or the members of the Legislature thereof, is denied to any of the male

SOURCE: McPherson, Handbook for 1868, pp. 191, 379–380; U.S., Statutes at Large, XV:710–711.

inhabitants of such State, being twenty-one years of age, and citizens of the United States, or in any way abridged, except for participation in rebellion or other crime, the basis of representation therein shall be reduced in the proportion which the number of such male citizens shall bear to the whole number of male citizens twenty-one years of age in such State.

SEC. 3. No person shall be a Senator or Representative in Congress, or elector of President and Vice President, or hold any office, civil or military, under the United States, or under any State, who, having previously taken an oath as a member of Congress, or as an officer of the United States, or as a member of any State Legislature, or as an executive or judicial officer of any State, to support the Constitution of the United States, shall have engaged in insurrection or rebellion against the same, or given aid or comfort to the enemies thereof. But Congress may, by a vote of two-thirds of each House, remove such disability.

SEC. 4. The validity of the public debt of the United States, authorized by law, including debts incurred for payment of pensions and bounties for services in suppressing insurrection or rebellion, shall not be questioned. But neither the United States nor any State shall assume or pay any debt or obligation incurred in aid of insurrection or rebellion against the United States, or any claim for the loss or emancipation of any slave; but all such debts, obligations, and claims shall be held illegal and void.

SEC. 5. That Congress shall have power to enforce, by appropriate legislation, the provisions of this article.

Passed June 13, 1866.

Certificate of Mr. Secretary Seward respecting the Ratification of the Fourteenth Amendment to the Constitution, July 20, 1868.

And whereas neither the act just quoted from [of April 20, 1818], nor any other law, expressly or by conclusive implication, authorizes the Secretary of State to determine and decide doubtful questions as to the authenticity of the organizaion of State legislatures, or as to the power of any State legislature to recall a previous act or resolution of ratification of any amendment proposed to the Constitution;

And whereas it appears from official documents on file in this Department that the amendment to the Constitution of the United States, proposed as aforesaid, has been ratified by the legislatures of the States of Connecticut, New Hampshire, Tennessee, New Jersey, Oregon, Vermont, New York, Ohio, Illinois, West Virginia, Kansas, Maine, Nevada, Missouri, Indiana, Minnesota, Rhode Island, Wisconsin, Pennsylvania, Michigan, Massachusetts, Nebraska, and Iowa;

And whereas it further appears, from documents on file in this Department, that the amendment to the Constitution of the United States, proposed as aforesaid, has also been ratified by newly-constituted and newly-established bodies avowing themselves to be, and acting as, the legislatures, respectively, of the States of Arkansas, Florida, North Carolina, Louisiana, South Carolina, and Alabama;

And whereas it further appears from official documents on file in this Department that the legislatures of two of the States first above enumerated, to wit: Ohio and New Jersey, have since passed resolutions respectively withdrawing the consent of each of said States to the aforesaid amendment; and whereas it is deemed a matter of doubt and uncertainty whether such resolutions are not irregular, invalid, and therefore ineffectual for withdrawing the consent of the said two States, or of either of them, to the aforesaid amendment;

And whereas the whole number of States in the United States is thirty-seven. . . .

And whereas the twenty-three States first hereinbefore named, whose legislatures have ratified the said proposed amendment, and the six States next thereafter named, as having ratified the said proposed amendment by newly-constituted and established legislative bodies, together constitute three-fourths of the whole number of States in the United States:

Now, therefore, be it known, that I, William H. Seward, Secretary of State of the United States, by virtue and in pursuance of the second section of the act of Congress, approved the twentieth of April, eighteen hundred and eighteen, hereinbefore cited, do hereby certify that if the resolutions of the legislatures of Ohio and New Jersey ratifying the aforesaid amendments are to be deemed as remaining in full force and effect, notwithstanding the subsequent resolutions of the legislatures of those States which purport to withdraw the consent of said States from such ratification, then the aforesaid amendment has been ratified in the manner hereinbefore mentioned, and so has become valid, to all intents and purposes, as a part of the Constitution of the United States.

CONCURRENT RESOLUTION OF CONGRESS ON THE SAME
SUBJECT, JULY 21, 1868

Whereas the legislatures of the States of Connecticut, Tennessee, New Jersey, Oregon, Vermont, West Virginia, Kansas, Missouri, Indiana, Ohio, Illinois, Minnesota, New York, Wisconsin, Pennsylvania, Rhode Island, Michigan, Nevada, New Hampshire, Massachusetts, Nebraska, Maine, Iowa, Arkansas, Florida, North Carolina, Alabama, South Carolina, and Louisiana, being three-fourths and more of the several States of the Union, have ratified the fourteenth article of amendment to the Constitution of the United States, duly proposed by two-thirds of each House of the Thirty-Ninth Congress; therefore

Resolved by the Senate, (the House of Representatives concurring.) That said fourteenth article is hereby declared to be a part of the Constitution of the United States, and it shall be duly promulgated as such by the Secretary of State.

PROCLAMATION OF RATIFICATION, JULY 28, 1868

Now, therefore, be it known that I, WILLIAM H. SEWARD, Secretary of State of the United States, in execution of the aforesaid act, and of the aforesaid concurrent resolution of the 21st of July, 1868, and in conformance thereto, do hereby. . . . certify that the said proposed amendment has been adopted in the manner hereinbefore mentioned by the States specified in the said concurrent resolution . . . the States thus specified being more than three-fourths of the States of the United States.

And I do further certify that the said amendment has become valid to all intents and purposes as a part of the Constitution of the United States.

11. The First Reconstruction Act, March 2, 1867

WITH THE continued recalcitrance of the Southern states, Republicans in Congress had to take decisive action in order to secure the objectives formalized in the still pending amendment, but there was no party consensus on how this could or should be accomplished. The First Reconstruction Bill was therefore the result of stormy compromise reached *under pressure to pass some law before the Thirty-ninth Congress would end on March 3. Ironically, in the face of persistent presidential opposition, by February 1867 universal Negro suffrage had become an instrument of moderation in the search for a viable congressional plan to reunite the nation with a guarantee of justice for the freedman. It appeared to offer an alternative to drastic white disenfranchisement or prolonged military occupation of the South.*

An Act to Provide for the More Efficient Government of the Rebel States

WHEREAS no legal State governments or adequate protection for life or property now exists in the rebel States of Virginia, North Carolina, South Carolina, Georgia, Mississippi, Alabama, Louisiana, Florida, Texas, and Arkansas; and whereas it is necessary that peace and good order should be enforced in said States until loyal and republican State governments can be legally established: Therefore,

Be it enacted by the Senate and House of Representatives of the United States of America in Congress assembled, That said rebel States shall be divided into military districts and made subject to the military authority of the United States as hereinafter prescribed, and for that purpose Virginia shall constitute the first district; North Carolina and South Carolina the second district; Georgia, Alabama, and Florida the third district; Mississippi and Arkansas the fourth district; and Louisiana and Texas the fifth district.

SEC. 2. *And be it further enacted,* That it shall be the duty of the President to assign to the command of each of said districts an officer of the army, not below the rank of brigadier-general, and to detail a sufficient military force to enable such officer to perform his duties and enforce his authority within the district to which he is assigned.

SEC. 3. *And be it further enacted,* That it shall be the duty of each officer assigned as aforesaid, to protect all persons in their rights of person and property, to suppress insurrection, disorder, and violence, and to punish, or cause to be punished, all disturbers of the public peace and criminals; and to this end he may allow local civil tribunals to take jurisdiction of and to try offenders, or, when in his judgment it may be necessary for the trial of offenders,

SOURCE: U.S., *Statutes at Large,* XIV:428–429.

he shall have power to organize military commissions or tribunals for that purpose, and all interference under color of State authority with the exercise of military authority under this act, shall be null and void.

SEC. 4. *And be it further enacted*, That all persons put under military arrest by virtue of this act shall be tried without unnecessary delay, and no cruel or unusual punishment shall be inflicted, and no sentence of any military commission or tribunal hereby authorized, affecting the life or liberty of any person, shall be executed until it is approved by the officer in command of the district, and the laws and regulations for the government of the army shall not be affected by this act, except in so far as they conflict with its provisions: *Provided*, That no sentence of death under the provisions of this act shall be carried into effect without the approval of the President.

SEC. 5. *And be it further enacted*, That when the people of any one of said rebel States shall have formed a constitution of government in conformity with the Constitution of the United States in all respects, framed by a convention of delegates elected by the male citizens of said State, twenty-one years old and upward, of whatever race, color, or previous condition, who have been resident in said State for one year previous to the day of such election, except such as may be disfranchised for participation in the rebellion or for felony at common law, and when such constitution shall provide that the elective franchise shall be enjoyed by all such persons as have the qualifications herein stated for electors of delegates, and when such constitution shall be ratified by a majority of the persons voting on the question of ratification who are qualified as electors for delegates, and when such constitution shall have been submitted to Congress for examination and approval, and Congress shall have approved the same, and when said State, by a vote of its legislature elected under said constitution, shall have adopted the amendment to the Constitution of the United States, proposed by the Thirty-ninth Congress, and known as article fourteen, and when said article shall have become a part of the Constitution of the United States, said State shall be declared entitled to representation in Congress, and senators and representatives shall be admitted therefrom on their taking the oath prescribed by law, and then and thereafter the preceding sections of this act shall be inoperative in said State: *Provided*, That no person excluded from the privilege of holding office by said proposed amendment to the Constitution of the United States, shall be eligible to election as a member of the convention to frame a constitution for any of said rebel States, nor shall any such person vote for members of such convention.

SEC. 6. *And be it further enacted,* That, until the people of said rebel States shall be by law admitted to representation in the Congress of the United States, any civil governments which may exist therein shall be deemed provisional only, and in all respects subject to the paramount authority of the United States at any time to abolish, modify, control, or supersede the same; and in all elections to any office under such provisional governments all persons shall be entitled to vote, and none others, who are entitled to vote, under the provisions of the fifth section of this act; and no person shall be eligible to any office under any such provisional governments who would be disqualified from holding office under the provisions of the third *article* of said constitutional amendment.

12. President Johnson on the Reconstruction Acts, December 3, 1867

BOTH MILITARY RULE *and Negro suffrage lacked popular support in the North, and the immediate result of the 1867 Reconstruction legislation was a series of political defeats for Republicans. Johnson was pleased and reassured, as is evident from his reference to the 1867 elections in this message. His allusion to "negro domination" and his statement that the laws had given blacks "a clear majority in all elections in the Southern States" are distortions that were to become part of the mythology of Reconstruction.*

It is manifestly and avowedly the object of these laws to confer upon negroes the privilege of voting and to disfranchise such a number of white citizens as will give the former a clear majority at all elections in the Southern States. This, to the minds of some persons, is so important that a violation of the Constitution is justified as a means of bringing it about. The morality is always false

SOURCE: Richardson, *Messages of the Presidents,* VI:564–569.

which excuses a wrong because it proposes to accomplish a desirable end. We are not permitted to do evil that good may come. But in this case the end itself is evil, as well as the means. The subjugation of the States to negro domination would be worse than the military despotism under which they are now suffering. It was believed beforehand that the people would endure any amount of military oppression for any length of time rather than degrade themselves by subjection to the negro race. Therefore they have been left without a choice. Negro suffrage was established by act of Congress, and the military officers were commanded to superintend the process of clothing the negro race with the political privileges torn from white men.

The blacks in the South are entitled to be well and humanely governed, and to have the protection of just laws for all their rights of person and property. If it were practicable at this time to give them a Government exclusively their own, under which they might manage their own affairs in their own way, it would become a grave question whether we ought to do so, or whether common humanity would not require us to save them from themselves. But under the circumstances this is only a speculative point. It is not proposed merely that they shall govern themselves, but that they shall rule the white race, make and administer State laws, elect Presidents and members of Congress, and shape to a greater or less extent the future destiny of the whole country. Would such a trust and power be safe in such hands?

The peculiar qualities which should characterize any people who are fit to decide upon the management of public affairs for a great state have seldom been combined. It is the glory of white men to know that they have had these qualities in sufficient measure to build upon this continent a great political fabric and to preserve its stability for more than ninety years, while in every other part of the world all similar experiments have failed. But if anything can be proved by known facts, if all reasoning upon evidence is not abandoned, it must be acknowledged that in the progress of nations negroes have shown less capacity for government than any other race of people. No independent government of any form has ever been successful in their hands. On the contrary, wherever they have been left to their own devices they have shown a constant tendency to relapse into barbarism. In the Southern States, however, Congress has undertaken to confer upon them the privilege of the ballot. Just released from slavery, it may be doubted whether as a class they know more than their ancestors how to organize and regulate civil society. Indeed, it is admitted that the blacks of the South are not only regardless of the rights of property, but so utterly ignorant of public affairs that their voting can consist in nothing more than carrying a ballot to the place where they are directed to deposit it. I need not remind you that the exercise of the elective franchise is the highest attribute of an American citizen, and that when guided by virtue, intelligence, patriotism, and a proper appreciation of our free institutions it constitutes the true basis of a democratic form of government, in which the sovereign power is lodged in the body of the people. A trust artificially created, not for its own sake, but solely as a means of promoting the general welfare, its influence for good must necessarily depend upon the elevated character and true allegiance of the elector. It ought, therefore, to be reposed in none except those who are fitted morally and mentally to administer it well; for if conferred upon persons who do not justly estimate its value and who are indifferent as to its results, it will only serve as a means of placing power in the hands of the unprincipled and ambitious, and must eventuate in the complete destruction of that liberty of which it should be the most powerful conservator. I have therefore heretofore urged upon your attention the great danger—

to be apprehended from an untimely extension of the elective franchise to any new class in our country, especially when the large majority of that class, in wielding the power thus placed in their hands, can not be expected correctly to comprehend the duties and responsibilities which pertain to suffrage. Yesterday, as it were, 4,000,000 persons were held in a condition of slavery that had existed for generations; to-day they are freemen and are assumed by law to be citizens. It can not be presumed, from their previous condition of servitude, that as a class they are as well informed as to the nature of our Government as the intelligent foreigner who makes our land the home of his choice. In the case of the latter neither a residence of five years and the knowledge of our institutions which it gives nor attachment to the principles of the Constitution are the only conditions upon which he can be admitted to citizenship; he must prove in addition a good moral character, and thus give reasonable ground for the belief that he will be faithful to the obligations which he assumes as a citizen of the Republic. Where a people—the source of all political power—speak by their suffrages through the instrumentality of the ballot box, it must be carefully guarded against the control of those who are corrupt in principle and enemies of free institutions, for it can only become to our political and social system a safe conductor of healthy popular sentiment when kept free from demoralizing influences. Controlled through fraud and usurpation by the designing, anarchy and despotism must inevitably follow. In the hands of the patriotic and worthy our Government will be preserved upon the principles of the Constitution inherited from our fathers. It follows, therefore, that in admitting to the ballot box a new class of voters not qualified for the exercise of the elective franchise we weaken our system of government instead of adding to its strength and durability.

I yield to no one in attachment to that rule of general suffrage which distinguishes our policy as a nation. But there is a limit, wisely observed hitherto, which makes the ballot a privilege and a trust, and which requires of some classes a time suitable for probation and preparation. To give it indiscriminately to a new class, wholly unprepared by previous habits and opportunities to perform the trust which it demands, is to degrade it, and finally to destroy its power, for it may be safely assumed that no political truth is better established than that such indiscriminate and all-embracing extension of popular suffrage must end at last in its destruction.

I repeat the expression of my willingness to join in any plan within the scope of our constitutional authority which promises to better the condition of the negroes in the South, by encouraging them in industry, enlightening their minds, improving their morals, and giving protection to all their just rights as freedmen. But the transfer of our political inheritance to them would, in my opinion, be an abandonment of a duty which we owe alike to the memory of our fathers and the rights of our children.

The plan of putting the Southern States wholly and the General Government partially into the hands of negroes is proposed at a time peculiarly unpropitious. The foundations of society have been broken up by civil war. Industry must be reorganized, justice reestablished, public credit maintained, and order brought out of confusion. To accomplish these ends would require all the wisdom and virtue of the great men who formed our institutions originally. I confidently believe that their descendants will be equal to the arduous task before them, but it is worse than madness to expect that negroes will perform it for us. Certainly we ought not to ask their assistance till we despair of our own competency.

The great difference between the two races in physical, mental, and moral characteristics will prevent an amalgamation or fusion of them together in one homogeneous mass. If the inferior obtains the ascendency over the other, it will govern with reference only to its own interests—for it will recognize no common interest—and create such a tyranny as this continent has never yet witnessed. Already the negroes are influenced by promises of confiscation and plunder. They are taught to regard as an enemy every white man who has any respect for the rights of his own race. If this continues it must become worse and worse, until all order will be subverted, all industry cease, and the fertile fields of the South grow up into a wilderness. Of all the dangers which our nation has yet encountered, none are equal to those which must result from the success of the effort now making to Africanize the half of our country.

I would not put considerations of money in competition with justice and right; but the expenses incident to "reconstruction" under the system adopted by Congress aggravate what I regard as the intrinsic wrong of the measure itself. It has cost uncounted millions already, and if persisted in will add largely to the weight of taxation, already too oppressive to be borne without just complaint, and may finally reduce the Treasury of the nation to a condition of bankruptcy. We must not delude ourselves. It will require a strong standing army and probably more than $200,000,-000 per annum to maintain the supremacy of negro governments after they are established. The sum thus thrown away would, if properly used, form a sinking fund large enough to pay the whole national debt in less than fifteen years. It is vain to hope that negroes will maintain their ascendency themselves. Without military power they are wholly incapable of holding in subjection the white people of the South.

I submit to the judgment of Congress whether the public credit may not be injuriously affected by a system of measures like this. With our debt and the vast private interests which are complicated with it, we can not be too cautious of a policy which might by possibility impair the confidence of the world in our Government. That confidence can only be retained by carefully inculcating the principles of justice and honor on the popular mind and by the most scrupulous fidelity to all our engagements of every sort. Any serious breach of the organic law, persisted in for a considerable time, can not but create fears for the stability of our institutions. Habitual violation of prescribed rules, which we bind ourselves to observe, must demoralize the people. Our only standard of civil duty being set at naught, the sheet anchor of our political morality is lost, the public conscience swings from its moorings and yields to every impulse of passion and interest. If we repudiate the Constitution, we will not be expected to care much for mere pecuniary obligations. The violation of such a pledge as we made on the 22d day of July, 1861, will assuredly diminish the market value of our other promises. Besides, if we acknowledge that the national debt was created, not to hold the States in the Union, as the taxpayers were led to suppose, but to expel them from it and hand them over to be governed by negroes, the moral duty to pay it may seem much less clear. I say it may *seem* so, for I do not admit that this or any other argument in favor of repudiation can be entertained as sound; but its influence on some classes of minds may well be apprehended. The financial honor of a great commercial nation, largely indebted and with a republican form of government administered by agents of the popular choice, is a thing of such delicate texture and the destruction of it would be followed by such unspeakable calamity that every true patriot must desire to avoid whatever might expose it to the slightest danger.

The great interests of the country require immediate relief from these enactments. Business in the South is paralyzed by a sense of general insecurity, by the terror of confiscation, and the dread of negro supremacy. The Southern trade, from which the North would have derived so great a profit under a government of law, still languishes, and can never be revived until it ceases to be fettered by the arbitrary power which makes all its operations unsafe. That rich country—the richest in natural resources the world ever saw—is worse than lost if it be not soon placed under the protection of a free constitution. Instead of being, as it ought to be, a source of wealth and power, it will become an intolerable burden upon the rest of the nation.

Another reason for retracing our steps will doubtless be seen by Congress in the late manifestations of public opinion upon this subject. We live in a country where the popular will always enforces obedience to itself, sooner or later. It is vain to think of opposing it with anything short of legal authority backed by overwhelming force. It can not have escaped your attention that from the day on which Congress fairly and formally presented the proposition to govern the Southern States by military force, with a view to the ultimate establishment of negro supremacy, every expression of the general sentiment has been more or less adverse to it. The affections of this generation can not be detached from the institutions of their ancestors. Their determination to preserve the inheritance of free government in their own hands and transmit it undivided and unimpaired to their own posterity is too strong to be successfully opposed. Every weaker passion will disappear before that love of liberty and law for which the American people are distinguished above all others in the world.

How far the duty of the President "to preserve, protect, and defend the Constitution" requires him to go in opposing an unconstitutional act of Congress is a very serious and important question, on which I have deliberated much and felt extremely anxious to reach a proper conclusion. Where an act has been passed according to the forms of the Constitution by the supreme legislative authority, and is regularly enrolled among the public statutes of the country, Executive resistance to it, especially in times of high party excitement, would be likely to produce violent collision between the respective adherents of the two branches of the Government. This would be simply civil war, and civil war must be resorted to only as the last remedy for the worst of evils. Whatever might tend to provoke it should be most carefully avoided. A faithful and conscientious magistrate will concede very much to honest error, and something even to perverse malice, before he will endanger the public peace; and he will not adopt forcible measures, or such as might lead to force, as long as those which are peaceable remain open to him or to his constituents. It is true that cases may occur in which the Executive would be compelled to stand on its rights, and maintain them regardless of all consequences. If Congress should pass an act which is not only in palpable conflict with the Constitution, but will certainly, if carried out, produce immediate and irreparable injury to the organic structure of the Government, and if there be neither judicial remedy for the wrongs it inflicts nor power in the people to protect themselves without the official aid of their elected defender—if, for instance, the legislative department should pass an act even through all the forms of law to abolish a coordinate department of the Government—in such a case the President must take the high responsibilities of his office and save the life of the nation at all hazards. The so-called reconstruction acts, though as plainly unconstitutional as any that can be imagined, were not believed to be within the class last mentioned.

The people were not wholly disarmed of the power of self-defense. In all the Northern States they still held in their hands the sacred right of the ballot, and it was safe to believe that in due time they would come to the rescue of their own institutions. It gives me pleasure to add that the appeal to our common constituents was not taken in vain, and that my confidence in their wisdom and virtue seems not to have been misplaced.

13. The 1868 Election and the Civil Rights Issue

PRIOR TO the meeting of the Democratic convention, the Republican Congress authorized the readmission of seven states and before the session ended in July both seated their representatives, and declared the Fourteenth Amendment ratified. Yet congressional reconstruction and the status of the Negro were very much at stake in the presidential election of 1868. The unanimous first-ballot nomination of Frank Blair as vice-president reflected wide approval among Democrats for Blair's belligerent position (doc. c). Notice that both Republicans and Democrats made an issue of civil rights—one for the rights of black men, the other for the rights of white immigrants and white Southerners.

a. From Republican Party Platform, Chicago, May 21, 1868

The National Republican party of the United States, assembled in national convention in the city of Chicago, on the twenty-first day of May, 1868, make the following declaration of principles:—

1. We congratulate the country on the assured success of the reconstruction policy of Congress, as evinced by the adoption, in the majority of the States lately in rebellion, of constitutions securing equal civil and political rights to all; and it is the duty of the government to sustain those institutions, and to prevent the people of such States from being remitted to a state of anarchy.

2. The guarantee by Congress of equal suffrage to all loyal men at the South was demanded by every consideration of public safety, of gratitude, and of justice, and must be maintained; while the question of suffrage in all the loyal States properly belongs to the people of those States. . . .

SOURCE: For platforms, Edward Stanwood, A History of the Presidency from 1788 to 1897 (Boston and New York: 1898), pp. 318–320, 322–325.

13. We highly commend the spirit of magnanimity and forbearance with which men who have served in the rebellion, but who now frankly and honestly cooperate with us in restoring the peace of the country and reconstructing the southern state governments upon the basis of impartial justice and equal rights, are received back into the communion of the loyal people; and we favor the removal of the disqualifications and restrictions imposed upon the late rebels in the same measure as the spirit of disloyalty will die out, and as may be consistent with the safety of the loyal people.

14. We recognize the great principles laid down in the immortal Declaration of Independence as the true foundation of democratic government; and we hail with gladness every effort toward making these principles a living reality on every inch of American soil.

b. From Democratic Party Platform, New York, July 7, 1868

The Democratic party, in national convention assembled, reposing its trust in the intelligence, patriotism, and discriminating justice of the people, standing upon the Constitution as the foundation and limitation of the powers of the government, and the guarantee of the liberties of the citizen, and recognizing the questions of slavery and secession as having been settled, for all time to come, by the war, or the voluntary action of the Southern States in constitutional conventions assembled, and never to be renewed or reagitated, do, with the return of peace, demand,—

1. Immediate restoration of all the States to their rights in the Union under the Constitution, and of civil government to the American people.

2. Amnesty for all past political offences, and the regulation of the elective franchise in the States by their citizens. . . .

6. Economy in the administration of the government; the reduction of the standing army and navy; the abolition of the freedmen's bureau, and all political instrumentalities designed to secure negro supremacy. . . .

8. Equal rights and protection for naturalized and native-born citizens, at home and abroad; the assertion of American nationality which shall command the respect of foreign powers, and furnish an example and encouragement to peoples struggling for national integrity, constitutional liberty, and individual rights, and the maintenance of the rights of naturalized citizens against the abso-

lute doctrine of immutable allegiance, and the claims of foreign powers to punish them for alleged crime committed beyond their jurisdiction.

In demanding these measures and reforms, we arraign the Radical party for its disregard of right, and the unparalleled oppression and tyranny which have marked its career.

After the most solemn and unanimous pledge of both Houses of Congress to prosecute the war exclusively for the maintenance of the government and the preservation of the Union under the Constitution, it has repeatedly violated that most sacred pledge under which alone was rallied that noble volunteer army which carried our flag to victory. Instead of restoring the Union it has, so far as in its power, dissolved it, and subjected ten States, in the time of profound peace, to military despotism and negro supremacy. It has nullified there the right of trial by jury; it has abolished the *habeas corpus*, that most sacred writ of liberty; it has overthrown the freedom of speech and the press; it has substituted arbitrary seizures and arrests, and military trials and secret star-chamber inquisitions, for the constitutional tribunals; it has disregarded, in time of peace, the right of the people to be free from searches and seizures; it has entered the post and telegraph offices, and even the private rooms of individuals, and seized their private papers and letters without any specific charge or notice or affidavit, as required by the organic law; it has converted the American Capitol into a bastille; it has established a system of spies and official espionage to which no constitutional monarchy of Europe would now dare to resort; it has abolished the right of appeal, on important constitutional questions, to the supreme judicial tribunals, and threatened to curtail or destroy its original jurisdiction, which is irrevocably vested by the Constitution; while the learned chief justice has been subjected to the most atrocious calumnies, merely because he would not prostitute his high office to the support of the false and partisan charges preferred against the President. Its corruption and extravagance have exceeded anything known in history, and, by its frauds and monopolies, it has nearly doubled the burden of the debt created by the war. It has stripped the President of his constitutional power of appointment, even of his own cabinet. Under its repeated assaults the pillars of the government are rocking on their base, and should it succeed in November next, and inaugurate its President, we will meet, as a subjected and conquered people, amid the ruins of liberty and the scattered fragments of the Constitution.

And we do declare and resolve that, ever since the people of the United States threw off all subjection to the British crown, the privilege and trust of suffrage have belonged to the several States, and have been granted, regulated, and controlled exclusively by the political power of each State respectively, and that any attempt by Congress, on any pretext whatever, to deprive any State of this right, or interfere with its exercise, is a flagrant usurpation of power, which can find no warrant in the Constitution, and, if sanctioned by the people, will subvert our form of government, and can only end in a single centralized and consolidated government, in which the separate existence of the States will be entirely absorbed, and unqualified despotism be established in place of a federal Union of coequal States. And that we regard the reconstruction acts (so called) of Congress, as such, as usurpations, and unconstitutional, revolutionary, and void. . . .

That the President of the United States, Andrew Johnson, in exercising the powers of his high office in resisting the aggressions of Congress upon the constitutional rights of the States and the people, is entitled to the gratitude of the whole American people, and in behalf of the Democratic party we tender him our thanks for his patriotic efforts in that regard.

Upon this platform the Democratic party appeal to every patriot, including all the conservative element and all who desire to support the Constitution and restore the Union, forgetting all past differences of opinion, to unite with us in the present great struggle for the liberties of the people; and that to all such, to whatever party they may have heretofore belonged, we extend the right hand of fellowship, and hail all such cooperating with us as friends and brethren.

c. Reconstruction Views of Frank P. Blair, Democratic Vice Presidential Nominee

WASHINGTON, *June* 30, 1868.

Colonel JAMES O. BRODHEAD.

DEAR COLONEL: In reply to your inquiries, I beg leave to say, that I leave to you to determine, on consultation with my friends

SOURCE: McPherson, *Handbook for 1868*, pp. 380–382.

from Missouri, whether my name shall be presented to the Democratic Convention, and to submit the following as what I consider the real and only issue in this contest.

The reconstruction policy of the Radicals will be complete before the next election; the States so long excluded will have been admitted, Negro suffrage established, and the carpet-baggers installed in their seats in both branches of Congress. There is no possibility of changing the political character of the Senate, even if the Democrats should elect their President and a majority of the popular branch of Congress. We cannot, therefore, undo the Radical plan of reconstruction by congressional action; the Senate will continue a bar to its repeal. Must we submit to it? How can it be overthrown? It can only be overthrown by the authority of the Executive, who is sworn to maintain the Construction, and who will fail to do his duty if he allows the Constitution to perish under a series of congressional enactments which are in palpable violation of its fundamental principles.

If the President elected by the Democracy enforces or permits others to enforce these reconstruction acts, the Radicals, by the accession of twenty spurious Senators and fifty Representatives, will control both branches of Congress, and his administration will be as powerless as the present one of Mr. Johnson.

There is but one way to restore the Government and the Constitution, and that is for the President elect to declare these acts null and void, compel the army to undo its usurpations at the South, disperse the carpet-bag State governments, allow the white people to reorganize their own governments, and elect Senators and Representatives. The House of Representatives will contain a majority of Democrats from the North, and they will admit the Representatives elected by the white people of the South, and, with the cooperation of the President, it will not be difficult to compel the Senate to submit once more to the obligations of the Constitution. It will not be able to withstand the public judgment, if distinctly invoked and clearly expressed on this fundamental issue, and it is the sure way to avoid all future strife to put the issue plainly to the country.

I repeat, that this is the real and only question which we should allow to control us: Shall we submit to the usurpations by which the Government has been overthrown; or shall we exert ourselves for its full and complete restoration? It is idle to talk of bonds,

greenbacks, gold, the public faith, and the public credit. What can a Democratic President do in regard to any of these, with a Congress in both branches controlled by the carpet-baggers and their allies? He will be powerless to stop the supplies by which idle negroes are organized into political clubs—by which an army is maintained to protect these vagabonds in their outrages upon the ballot. These, and things like these, eat up the revenues and resources of the Government and destroy its credit—make the difference between gold and greenbacks. We must restore the Constitution before we can restore the finances, and to do this we must have a President who will execute the will of the people by trampling into dust the usurpations of Congress known as the reconstruction acts. I wish to stand before the convention upon this issue, but it is one which embraces everything else that is of value in its large and comprehensive results. It is the one thing that includes all that is worth a contest, and without it there is nothing that gives dignity, honor, or value to the struggle.
Your friend,

FRANK P. BLAIR.

SPEECH OF FRANCIS P. BLAIR, JR., ACCEPTING THE NOMINATION, JULY 10, 1866.

MR. CHAIRMAN: I accept the platform of resolutions passed by the late Democratic Convention, and I accept their nomination with feelings of profound gratitude; and, sir, I thank you for the very kind manner in which you have already conveyed to me the decision of the Democratic Convention. I accept the nomination with the conviction that your nomination for the Presidency is one which will carry us to certain victory, and because I believe that the nomination is the most proper nomination that could be made by the Democratic party. The contest which we wage is for the restoration of constitutional government, and it is proper that we should make this contest under the lead of one who has given his life to the maintenance of constitutional government. We are to make the contest for the restoration of those great principles of government which belong to our race. And, my fellow-citizens, it is most proper that we should select for our leader a man not from military life, but one who has devoted himself to civil pursuits; who has given himself to the study and the understanding of the Constitution and its maintenance with all the force of reason and judgment. My fellow-citizens, I have said that the contest before us was one for the restoration of our government; it is also one for the restoration of our race. It is to prevent the people of our race from being exiled from their homes—exiled from the government which they formed and created for themselves and for their children, and to prevent them from being driven out of the country or trodden under foot by an inferior and semi-barbarous race. In this country we shall have the sympathy of every man who is worthy to belong to the white race. What civilized people on earth would refuse to associate with themselves in all the rights and honors and dignity of their country such men as Lee and Johnston? What civilized country on earth would fail to do honor to those who, fighting for an erroneous cause, yet distinguished themselves by gallantry in that service? In that contest, for which they are sought to be dis-franchised and to be exiled from their homes—in that contest, they have proved themselves worthy to be our peers. My fellow-citizens, it is not my purpose to make any long address, (cries of "go on,") but simply to express my gratitude for the great and distinguished honor which has been conferred upon me—

A VOICE. "You are worthy of it."

General Blair—and from my heart to reiterate the words of thanks that fell from my lips when I arose.

C. The Continuing Commitment: Advance and Retreat

14. The Fifteenth Amendment

THE FIFTEENTH AMENDMENT, like the Fourteenth, was a Republican party measure, formulated in the face of sharp intraparty contention and ratified under stern party discipline or, in the case of four Southern states, under coercion. There is a certain irony in finding the radical of Radicals, Wendell Phillips, urging moderation at a critical point in the bill's legislative history (doc. a). His influence may have affected the outcome, for the necessary two-thirds majority in both House and Senate was obtained only through Republican abstentions, a substantial portion from anti-slavery men who wished a more comprehensive measure, and with reluctant "yeas" from some of their fellow radicals. The amendment in some respects did represent a retreat from the 1867 legislation, first in theory but later in practice. The 1867 law had mandated the vote to black men in ten Southern states; for them, the amendment merely meant that it could not be taken away because they were black. This left the door open to evasion through property, literacy, and poll tax requirements, devices widely used in the South after 1890. On the other hand, in eleven Northern and five Border States where black men had no right to vote in 1869, the Fifteenth Amendment, negative in form, meant a positive grant of suffrage. The Northern experience may yet confound those historians who have held up to mockery the contemporary confidence in the amendment by Phillips when he termed it "the completion and guaranty of emancipation." Further, the second section of the amendment was not routine; it granted to Congress new power.

a. Wendell Phillips's Editorials, February and March 1869

CONGRESS

We see the action of the Senate touching the Constitutional Amendment with great anxiety. The House had passed a simple measure, one covering all the ground that the people are ready to occupy. It answered completely the lesson of the war. Its simplicity gave it all the chance that exists for any form of Amendment being ratified.

Why was it not left in that shape? . . . We exhort every man who professes himself a friend of liberty to drop all undue attachment to any form of words and to cooperate, heartily, earnestly, with the great body of the members in carrying through as promptly as possible, any form which includes the substance of a Constitutional protection to the vote and right to office of the colored race . . .

Our disappointment is the greater because we had reason to believe that the Senators who have this matter in charge, would be the last men to forget themselves at such a crisis. . . . For the first time in our lives we beseech them to be a little more *politicians*—and a little less *reformers*—as those functions are usually understood.

THE CONSTITUTIONAL AMENDMENT

Our cause has always adopted the policy of concentrating its own attention, and trying to concentrate that of the public, on one thing at a time. The step immediately next is usually very definitely marked. Today the next move for us is the ratification of the Constitutional Amendment. . . .

Its recommendation by Congress and the President is the most advanced step taken by the Nation. Its ratification will be the completion and guaranty of emancipation itself. Of course it is not all we could wish; nor is it in just the form some would ask. But it covers the whole Negro race, North and South, and it contains the essential guaranty. It is the grandest and most Christian act ever contemplated or accomplished by any Nation—lifting, in a time of

SOURCE: Editorials in the *National Anti-Slavery Standard*, February 20 and March 20, 1869.

peace, a lately enslaved and still hated race to the full level of citizenship. Though it does not cover all it ought, in present circumstances,—still it contains within itself the cure for all its own defects. A man with a ballot in his hand is the master of the situation. He defines all his other rights. What is not already given him, he takes. As soon as the negro holds the ballot at the South, whatever he suffers will be largely now, and in future wholly, his own fault. Present poverty, ignorance and lack of combination will postpone the full use of his power; but, in the end, the ballot makes every class sovereign over its own fate. Corruption may steal from a man his independence, money may starve and intrigue fetter him at times. But against all these his vote, intelligently and honestly cast, is, in the long run, his full protection. If in the struggle his fort surrenders, it is only because it is betrayed from within. The ballot is the civil panacea. No civil war in a land of universal suffrage. Mexico and some of the bastard Republics may seem to prove otherwise. But Mexico is only a galvanized corpse, pretending to life and a soul.

The Ballot is opportunity, education, fair play, right to office, and elbow-room. Compare the New England of 1820 with the England of that year—one, after two hundred years of timid and heartless caste, and you see the fruit of the ballot. Then take the England of to-day and you see what the imitation of her child, in this particular, has done for her in forty years. What the Alphabet is in Literature the Vote is in the State.

Now, for the first time in our history, God opens to us this grand opportunity. Party necessity craves it, the peace of one whole section demands it. The welfare of the Negro race in the West Indies and throughout the world depends on the position the race attains in the management of the Great Empire on this Continent. Congress, three to one, recommends it. The Republican party lifts it as a party symbol. The idol of the Nation, its President, begs for its ratification. Never were the signs so auspicious. Never were the elements of success so abundant.

Let the veteran toilers of forty years gird themselves for a vigorous, tireless and final effort. We must insure success. Besiege your Legislatures, give your leading men no rest. Weary them with continual coming. Now is our hour. One effort now is worth months of common work. While the whole land waits breathless, for every word Grant utters, be sure that it never is allowed to forget the grandest one he ever spoke; not "peace," but the path to peace, "Justice." When the great soldier, so tardy a convert, consents to lead the way, who of us shall slacken in the following?

What would we not have given, a year ago, to have been assured that today we should see such a vote at the Capitol, and hear such a word from the White House? Can our gratitude for such success find content in anything but the *utmost effort of which we are capable* to make that word the mightiest blow even his sword ever struck for humanity and justice.

WENDELL PHILLIPS

b. Proclamation of Ratification, March 30, 1870

ARTICLE XV.

SECTION 1. The right of citizens of the United States to vote shall not be denied or abridged by the United States or by any State on account of race, color, or previous condition of servitude.

SECTION 2. The Congress shall have power to enforce this article by appropriate legislation.

. . . that it appears from official documents on file in this Department that the amendment to the Constitution of the United States, proposed as aforesaid, has been ratified by the legislatures of the States of North Carolina, West Virginia, Massachusetts, Wisconsin, Maine, Louisiana, Michigan, South Carolina, Pennsylvania, Arkansas, Connecticut, Florida, Illinois, Indiana, New York, New Hampshire, Nevada, Vermont, Virginia, Alabama, Missouri, Mississippi, Ohio, Iowa, Kansas, Minnesota, Rhode Island, Nebraska, and Texas, in all twenty-nine States.

And further, that it appears from an official document on file in this Department that the legislature of the State of New York has since passed resolutions claiming to withdraw the said ratification of the said amendment which had been made by the legislature of that State, and of which official notice had been filed in this Department.

And, further, that it appears from an official document on file in this Department that the legislature of Georgia has by resolution ratified the said proposed amendment:

SOURCE: U.S., *Statutes at Large*, XVI:1131–1132.

Now, therefore, be it known that I, HAMILTON FISH, Secretary of State of the United States. . . . do hereby certify that the amendment aforesaid has become valid to all intents and purposes as part of the Constitution of the United States.

15. Congressional Effort to Enforce the Civil Rights Amendments, 1870–1871

THE FIRST ACT to enforce the Fifteenth Amendment began its way through Congress even before ratification and during the journey expanded into a comprehensive civil rights law. Condemned by an earlier generation of historians as extreme, unconstitutional, and obnoxious party legislation, recent scholarship has established it as "an honest attempt to deal with a real problem."[1] The reader need not be put off by its numerous provisions; they (as well as those of the later act) suggest both the variety of means white Southerners were using to negate Reconstruction and the care with which Republicans sought to counter the obstruction. The conspiracy sections (number six of the first law and number two of the Ku Klux Act) were used by the government in the prosecutions that led to the Cruikshank and Harris cases, both of which involved flagrant violence against black men and both of which the government lost in the Supreme Court.

On the question of constitutional power to enact the laws, the statement of John Bingham is of special interest. It is an authoritative explanation of what the principal framer of the first section of the Fourteenth Amendment intended. Also worthy of special notice is the legal argument of section three of the Ku Klux Act, which equates the failure of a state, for whatever cause, to protect the basic rights of its people with denial of "equal protection of the laws." The argument, that no action constituted a positive offense, was disregarded by the Supreme Court majority; but it has received scholarly sanction in the twentieth century.

a. First Enforcement Act, May 31, 1870

—An Act to enforce the Right of Citizens of the United States to vote in the several States of this Union, and for other Purposes.

1. Everette Swinney, "Suppressing the Ku Klux Klan: The Enforcement of the Reconstruction Amendments, 1870–1874" (Ph.D. diss., University of Texas, 1966), p. 57.
SOURCE: U.S., Statutes at Large, XVI:140–146.

Be it enacted by the Senate and House of Representatives of the United States of America in Congress assembled, That all citizens of the United States who are or shall be otherwise qualified by law to vote at any election by the people in any State, Territory, district, county, city, parish, township, school district, municipality, or other territorial subdivision, shall be entitled and allowed to vote at all such elections, without distinction of race, color, or previous condition of servitude; any constitution, law, custom, usage, or regulation of any State or Territory, or by or under its authority, to the contrary notwithstanding.

SEC. 2. *And be it further enacted,* That if by or under the authority of the constitution or laws of any State, or the laws of any Territory, any act is or shall be required to be done as a prerequisite or qualification for voting, and by such constitution or laws persons or officers are or shall be charged with the performance of duties in furnishing to citizens an opportunity to perform such prerequisite, or to become qualified to vote, it shall be the duty of every such person and officer to give to all citizens of the United States the same and equal opportunity to perform such prerequisite, and to become qualified to vote without distinction of race, color, or previous condition of servitude; and if any such person or officer shall refuse or knowingly omit to give full effect to this section, he shall, for every such offence, forfeit and pay the sum of five hundred dollars to the person aggrieved thereby, to be recovered by an action on the case, with full costs, and such allowance for counsel fees as the court shall deem just, and shall also, for every such offence, be deemed guilty of a misdemeanor, and shall, on conviction thereof, be fined not less than five hundred dollars, or be imprisoned not less than one month and not more than one year, or both, at the discretion of the court.

SEC. 3. [The offer of a citizen to perform an act prerequisite to voting shall be deemed a performance when the act is wrongfully prevented by an election officer.]

SEC. 4. *And be it further enacted,* That if any person, by force, bribery, threats, intimidation, or other unlawful means, shall hinder, delay, prevent, or obstruct, or shall combine and confederate with others to hinder, delay, prevent, or obstruct, any citizen from doing any act required to be done to qualify him to vote or from voting at any election as aforesaid, such person shall for every such offence forfeit and pay the sum of five hundred dollars to the person aggrieved thereby, to be recovered by an action on the case, with full costs, and such allowance for counsel fees as the court shall deem just, and shall also for every such offence be guilty of a misdemeanor, and shall, on conviction thereof, be fined not less than five hundred dollars, or be imprisoned not less than one month and not more than one year, or both, at the discretion of the court.

SEC. 5. *And be it further enacted,* That if any person shall prevent, hinder, control, or intimidate, or shall attempt to prevent, hinder, control, or intimidate, any person from exercising or in exercising the right of suffrage, to whom the right of suffrage is secured or guaranteed by the fifteenth amendment to the Constitution of the United States, by means of bribery, threats, or threats of depriving such person of employment or occupation, or of ejecting such person from rented house, lands, or other property, or by threats of refusing to renew leases or contracts for labor, or by threats of violence to himself or family, such person so offending shall be deemed guilty of a misdemeanor, and shall, on conviction thereof, be fined not less than five hundred dollars, or be imprisoned not less than one month and not more than one year, or both, at the discretion of the court.

SEC. 6. *And be it further enacted,* That if two or more persons shall band or conspire together, or go in disguise upon the public highway, or upon the premises of another, with intent to violate any provision of this act, or to injure, oppress, threaten, or intimidate any citizen with intent to prevent or hinder his free exercise and enjoyment of any right or privilege granted or secured to him by the Constitution or laws of the United States, or because of his having exercised the same, such persons shall be held guilty of felony, and, on conviction thereof, shall be fined or imprisoned, or both, at the discretion of the court,—the fine not to exceed five thousand dollars, and the imprisonment not to exceed ten years,—and shall, moreover, be thereafter ineligible to, and disabled from holding, any office or place of honor, profit, or trust created by the Constitution or laws of the United States.

SEC. 7. *And be it further enacted,* That if in the act of violating any provision in either of the two preceding sections, any other felony, crime, or misdemeanor shall be committed, the offender, on conviction of such violation of said sections, shall be punished for the same with such punishments as are attached to the said felonies, crimes, and misdemeanors by the laws of the State in which the offence may be committed.

SEC. 8. [District courts of the United States to have jurisdiction of offenses under this act, exclusive of state courts, and concurrently with the circuit court.]

SEC. 9. *And be it further enacted,* That the district attorneys, marshals, and deputy marshals of the United States, the commissioners appointed by the circuit and territorial courts of the United States, with powers of arresting, imprisoning, or bailing offenders against the laws of the United States, and every other officer who may be specially empowered by the President of the United States, shall be, and they are hereby, specially authorized and required, at the expense of the United States, to institute proceedings against all and every person who shall violate the provisions of this act, and cause him or them to be arrested and imprisoned, or bailed, as the case may be, for trial before such court of the United States or territorial court as has cognizance of the offense. And with a view to afford reasonable protection to all persons in their constitutional right to vote without distinction of race, color, or previous condition of servitude, and to the prompt discharge of the duties of this act, it shall be the duty of the circuit courts of the United States, and the superior courts of the Territories of the United States, from time to time, to increase the number of commissioners, so as to afford a speedy and convenient means for the arrest and examination of persons charged with a violation of this act [and grants them authority to enforce the act.]

SEC. 10. [Marshals and deputies who refuse to execute all warrants to be fined $1000 and commissioners may appoint suitable persons to execute process with authority to call upon bystanders or the United States forces.]

SEC. 11. [Persons obstructing arrests under this act subject to fine and imprisonment.]

SEC. 12. *And be it further enacted,* That the commissioners, district attorneys, the marshals, their deputies, and the clerks of the said district, circuit, and territorial courts shall be paid for their services the like fees as may be allowed to them for similar services in other cases. . . .

SEC. 13. *And be it further enacted,* That it shall be lawful for the President of the United States to employ such part of the land or naval forces of the United States, or of the militia, as shall be necessary to aid in the execution of judicial process issued under this act.

[SEC. 14 and SEC. 15. Provisions for enforcing third section of Fourteenth Amendment, disqualifying some Southerners from office-holding.]

SEC. 16. *And be it further enacted,* That all persons within the jurisdiction of the United States shall have the same right in every State and Territory in the United States to make and enforce contracts, to sue, be parties, give evidence, and to the full and equal benefit of all laws and proceedings for the security of person and property as is enjoyed by white citizens, and shall be subject to like punishment, pains, penalties, taxes, licenses, and exactions of every kind, and none other, any law, statute, ordinance, regulation, or custom to the contrary notwithstanding. No tax or charge shall be imposed or enforced by any State upon any person immigrating thereto from a foreign country which is not equally imposed and enforced upon every person immigrating to such State from any other foreign country; and any law of any State in conflict with this provision is hereby declared null and void.

SEC. 17. *And be it further enacted,* That any person who, under color of any law, statute, ordinance, regulation, or custom, shall subject, or cause to be subjected, any inhabitant of any State or Territory to the deprivation of any right secured or protected by the last preceding section of this act, or to different punishment, pains, or penalties on account of such person being an alien, or by reason of his color or race, than is prescribed for the punishment of citizens, shall be deemed guilty of a misdemeanor, and, on conviction, shall be punished by fine not exceeding one thousand dollars, or imprisonment not exceeding one year, or both, in the discretion of the court.

SEC. 18. *And be it further enacted,* That the act to protect all persons in the United States in their civil rights, and furnish the means of their vindication, passed April nine, eighteen hundred and sixty-six, is hereby re-enacted; and sections sixteen and seventeen hereof shall be enforced according to the provisions of said act.

SEC. 19. [Fine and punishment provided for any persons preventing a qualified voter from voting or interfering with an election officer.]

Sec. 20. [Like penalties provided for interference with the registration of lawful voters.]

Sec. 21. [Whenever any candidate for congressional office is on the ballot along with candidates for state and local office, it shall be presumptive evidence that offences of preceding sections were committed with reference to the election of such representative to Congress.]

Sec. 22. [Election officers subject to prosecution and punishment for violation of duties or for fraudulent returns even if appointed under state or municipal authority.]

Sec. 23. *And be it further enacted,* That whenever any person shall be defeated or deprived of his election to any office, except elector of President or Vice-President, representative or delegate in Congress, or member of a State legislature, by reason of the denial to any citizen or citizens who shall offer to vote, of the right to vote, on account of race, color, or previous condition of servitude, his right to hold and enjoy such office, and the emoluments thereof, shall not be impaired by such denial; and such person may bring any appropriate suit or proceeding to recover possession of such office, and in cases where it shall appear that the sole question touching the title to such office arises out of the denial of the right to vote to citizens who so offered to vote, on account of race, color, or previous condition of servitude, such suit or proceeding may be instituted in the circuit or district court of the United States of the circuit or district in which such person resides. And said circuit or district court shall have, concurrently with the State courts, jurisdiction thereof so far as to determine the rights of the parties to such office by reason of the denial of the right guaranteed by the fifteenth article of amendment to the Constitution of the United States, and secured by this act.

Approved, May 31, 1870.

b. Third Enforcement (Ku Klux) Act,
April 20, 1871

An Act to enforce the Provisions of the Fourteenth Amendment to the Constitution of the United States, and for other Purposes.

Be it enacted by the Senate and House of Representatives of the United States of America in Congress assembled, That any person

Source: U.S., *Statutes at Large,* XVII:13–15.

who, under color of any law, statute, ordinance, regulation, custom, or usage of any State, shall subject, or cause to be subjected, any person within the jurisdiction of the United States to the deprivation of any rights, privileges, or immunities secured by the Constitution of the United States, shall, any such law, statute, ordinance, regulation, custom, or usage of the State to the contrary notwithstanding, be liable to the party injured [through proceedings in the United States district or circuit courts.]

SEC. 2. That if two or more persons within any State or Territory of the United States shall conspire together to overthrow, or to put down, or to destroy by force the government of the United States, or to levy war against the United States, or to oppose by force the authority of the government of the United States, or by force, intimidation, or threat to prevent, hinder, or delay the execution of any law of the United States, or by force to seize, take, or possess any property of the United States contrary to the authority thereof, or by force, intimidation, or threat to prevent any person from accepting or holding any office or trust or place of confidence under the United States, or from discharging the duties thereof, or by force, intimidation, or threat to induce any officer of the United States to leave any State, district, or place where his duties as such officer might lawfully be performed, or to injure him in his person or property on account of his lawful discharge of the duties of his office, or to injure his person while engaged in the lawful discharge of the duties of his office, or to injure his property so as to molest, interrupt, hinder, or impede him in the discharge of his official duty, or by force, intimidation, or threat to deter any party or witness in any court of the United States from attending such court, or from testifying in any matter pending in such court fully, freely, and truthfully, or to injure any such party or witness in his person or property on account of his having so attended or testified, or by force, intimidation, or threat to influence the verdict, presentment, or indictment, of any juror or grand juror in any court of the United States, or to injure such juror in his person or property on account of any verdict, presentment, or indictment lawfully assented to by him, or on account of his being or having been such juror, or shall conspire together, or go in disguise upon the public highway or upon the premises of another for the purpose, either directly or indirectly, of depriving any person or any class of persons of the equal protection of the laws, or of equal privileges or immunities under the laws, or for the purpose of preventing or hindering the constituted authorities of any State from giving or securing to all persons within such State the equal protection of the laws, or shall conspire together for the purpose of in any manner impeding, hindering, obstructing, or defeating the due course of justice in any State or Territory, with intent to deny to any citizen of the United States the due and equal protection of the laws, or to injure any person in his person or his property for lawfully enforcing the right of any person or class of persons to the equal protection of the laws, or by force, intimidation, or threat to prevent any citizen of the United States lawfully entitled to vote from giving his support or advocacy in a lawful manner towards or in favor of the election of any lawfully qualified person as an elector of President or Vice-President of the United States, or as a member of the Congress of the United States, or to injure any such citizen in his person or property on account of such support or advocacy, [such persons deemed guilty of high crime and punishable through United States courts by fine of $500 to $5000 or imprisonment for six months to six years, or both; the injured person may recover damages through United States courts against any one or more such conspirators.]

SEC. 3. That in all cases where insurrection, domestic violence, unlawful combinations, or conspiracies in any State shall so obstruct or hinder the execution of the laws thereof, and of the United States, as to deprive any portion or class of the people of such State of any of the rights, privileges, or immunities, or protection, named in the Constitution and secured by this act, and the constituted authorities of such State shall either be unable to protect, or shall, from any cause, fail in or refuse protection of the people in such rights, such facts shall be deemed a denial by such State of the equal protection of the laws to which they are entitled under the Constitution of the United States; and in all such cases, or whenever any such insurrection, violence, unlawful combination, or conspiracy shall oppose or obstruct the laws of the United States or the due execution thereof, or impede or obstruct the due course of justice under the same, it shall be lawful for the President, and it shall be his duty to take such measures, by the employment of the militia or the land and naval forces of the United States, or of either, or by other means, as he may deem necessary for the suppression of such insurrection, domestic violence, or combinations; and any person who shall be arrested under the provisions of this and the preceding section shall be delivered to the marshal of the proper district, to be dealt with according to law.

Sec. 4. That whenever in any State or part of a State the unlawful combinations named in the preceding section of this act shall be organized and armed, and so numerous and powerful as to be able, by violence, to either overthrow or set at defiance the constituted authorities of such State, and of the United States within such State, or when the constituted authorities are in complicity with, or shall connive at the unlawful purposes of, such powerful and armed combinations; and whenever, by reason of either or all of the causes aforesaid, the conviction of such offenders and the preservation of the public safety shall become in such district impracticable, in every such case such combinations shall be deemed a rebellion against the government of the United States, and during the continuance of such rebellion, and within the limits of the district which shall be so under the sway thereof, such limits to be prescribed by proclamation, it shall be lawful for the President of the United States, when in his judgment the public safety shall require it, to suspend the privileges of the writ of habeas corpus, to the end that such rebellion may be overthrown: *Provided*, That all the provisions of the second section of an act entitled "An act relating to habeas corpus, and regulating judicial proceedings in certain cases," approved March third, eighteen hundred and sixty-three, which relate to the discharge of prisoners other than prisoners of war, and to the penalty for refusing to obey the order of the court, shall be in full force so far as the same are applicable to the provisions of this section: *Provided further*, That the President shall first have made proclamation, as now provided by law, commanding such insurgents to disperse: *And provided also*, That the provisions of this section shall not be in force after the end of the next regular session of Congress.

Sec. 5. That no person shall be a grand or petit juror in any court of the United States upon any inquiry, hearing, or trial of any suit, proceeding, or prosecution based upon or arising under the provisions of this act who shall, in the judgment of the court, be in complicity with any such combination or conspiracy; and every such juror shall, before entering upon any such inquiry, hearing, or trial, take and subscribe an oath in open court that he has never, directly or indirectly, counselled, advised, or voluntarily aided any such combination or conspiracy [with penalty for perjury.]

Sec. 6. [Persons knowing of conspiracy to commit wrongs enumerated in Sec. 2 and not aiding to prevent them held liable to person injured.]

SEC. 7. That nothing herein contained shall be construed to supersede or repeal any former act or law except so far as the same may be repugnant thereto; and any offences heretofore committed against the tenor of any former act shall be prosecuted, and any proceeding already commenced for the prosecution thereof shall be continued and completed, the same as if this act had not been passed, except so far as the provisions of this act may go to sustain and validate such proceedings.

APPROVED, April 20, 1871.

c. John A. Bingham on Congressional Power under the Fourteenth Amendment, March 31, 1871

MR. BINGHAM said:

MR. SPEAKER: . . . . I have been endeavoring to demonstrate that the legislation of the country in all the past was an exercise of the general power to legislate as proposed by this bill. If it was competent heretofore to give the President power to enforce by arms the faithful execution of the laws against unlawful combinations of men, surely it is equally competent, to make the fact of such combinations a crime punishable in your courts. The powers of the States have been limited and the powers of Congress extended by the last three amendments of the Constitution. *These last amendments—thirteen, fourteen, and fifteen—do, in my judgment, vest in Congress a power to protect the rights of citizens against States, and individuals in States,* [italics added] never before granted. It is my purpose, as far as I may be able in the limited time allowed me, to make this statement good.

Mr. Speaker, the honorable gentleman from Illinois [MR. FARNSWORTH] did me unwittingly, great service, when he ventured to ask me why I changed the form of the first section of the fourteenth article of amendment from the form in which I reported it to the House in February, 1866, from the Committee on Reconstruction. I will answer the gentleman, sir, and answer him truthfully. I had the honor to frame the amendment as reported in February, 1866, and the first section, as it now stands, letter for letter and syllable

SOURCE: U.S., *Congressional Globe*, 42 Cong., 1st sess. (March 31, 1871), Appendix, pp. 81–86.

for syllable, in the fourteenth article of the amendments to the Constitution of the United States, save the introductory clause defining citizens. The clause defining citizens never came from the joint Committee on Reconstruction, but the residue of the first section of the fourteenth amendment did come from the committee precisely as I wrote it and offered it in the Committee on Reconstruction, and precisely as it now stands in the Constitution, to wit:

> No State shall make or enforce any law which shall abridge the privileges or immunities of citizens of the United States: nor shall any State deprive any person of life, liberty, or property, without due process of law, nor deny to any person within its jurisdiction the equal protection of the laws.

The fourteenth amendment concludes as follows: "The Congress shall have power, by appropriate legislation, to enforce the provisions of this article."

That is the grant of power. It is full and complete. The gentleman says that amendment differs from the amendment reported by me in February; differs from the provision introduced and written by me, now in the fourteenth article of amendments. It differs in this: that it is, as it now stands in the Constitution, more comprehensive than as it was first proposed and reported in February, 1866. It embraces all and more than did the February proposition.

MR. FARNSWORTH. I wish simply to call your attention—

MR. BINGHAM. Well, what is it?

MR. FARNSWORTH. The fourteenth amendment embraced other provisions which require legislation. The last clause gives Congress power—

MR. BINGHAM. I thank the gentleman for that word. The fourteenth amendment closes with the words, "the Congress shall have power to enforce, by appropriate legislation, the provisions of this article"—the whole of it, sir; all the provisions of the article; every section of it.

MR. FARNSWORTH rose.

MR. BINGHAM. The gentleman from Illinois must not further interrupt me. He is not now enlightening me on this subject, though doubtless he is capable of doing so when he has the time.

The gentleman ventured upon saying that this amendment does not embrace all of the amendment prepared and reported by me with the consent of the committee in February, 1866. The amendment reported in February, and to which the gentleman refers, is as follows:

> The Congress shall have power to make all laws which shall be necessary and proper to secure to the citizens of each State all the privileges and immunities of citizens in the several States, and to all persons in the several States equal protection in the rights of life, liberty, and property.

That is the amendment, and the whole of it, as reported in February, 1866. That amendment never was rejected by the House or Senate. A motion was made to lay it on the table, which was a test vote on the merits of it, and the motion failed—only forty-one votes for the motion, and one hundred and ten against it. I consented to and voted for the motion to postpone it till the second Tuesday of April. Afterward, in the joint Committee on Reconstruction, I introduced this amendment, in the precise form, as I have stated, in which it was reported, and as it now stands in the Constitution of my country. It contains the words, among others—"Nor deny to any person within its jurisdiction the equal protection of the laws." . . .

The power to enforce this provision by law is as full as any other grant of power to Congress. It is, "the Congress shall have power, by appropriate legislation," to enforce this and every other provision of this article. . . .

I answer the gentleman, how I came to change the form of February to the words now in the first section of the fourteenth article of amendment, as they stand, and I trust will forever stand, in the Constitution of my country. I had read—and that is what induced me to attempt to impose by constitutional amendments new limitations upon the power of the States—the great decision of Marshall in Barron *vs.* the Mayor and City Council of Baltimore, wherein the Chief Justice said, in obedience to his official oath and the Constitution as it then was:

> The amendments [to the Constitution] contain no expression indicating an intention to apply them to the State governments. This court cannot so apply them.—7 *Peters,* p. 250.

. . . They secured, in short, all the rights dear to the American citizen. And yet it was decided, and rightfully, that these amendments, defining and protecting the rights of men and citizens, were only limitations on the power of Congress, not on the power of the States.

In reëxamining that case of Barron, Mr. Speaker, after my struggle in the House in February, 1866, to which the gentleman has alluded, I noted and apprehended as I never did before, certain words in that opinion of Marshall. Referring to the first eight articles of amendments to the Constitution of the United States, the Chief Justice said: "Had the framers of these amendments intended them to be limitations on the powers of the State governments they would have imitated the framers of the original Constitution, and have expressed that intention." Barron vs. The Mayor, &c. 7 Peters, 250.

Acting upon this suggestion I did imitate the framers of the original Constitution. As they had said "no State shall emit bills of credit, pass any bill of attainder, ex post facto law, or law impairing the obligations of contracts"; imitating their example and imitating it to the letter, I prepared the provision of the first section of the fourteenth amendment as it stands in the Constitution, as follows:

> No State shall make or enforce any law which shall abridge the privileges or immunities of the citizens of the United States, nor shall any State deprive any person of life, liberty, or property without due process of law, nor deny to any person within its jurisdiction the equal protection of the laws.

I hope the gentleman now knows why I changed the form of the amendment of February, 1866.

Mr. Speaker, that the scope and meaning of the limitations imposed by the first section, fourteenth amendment of the Constitution may be more fully understood, permit me to say that the privileges and immunities of citizens of the United States, as contradistinguished from citizens of a State, are chiefly defined in the first eight amendments to the Constitution of the United States.

16. "New Departure" Politics of 1872

THE YEAR 1872 may be viewed as a watershed in the politics of Reconstruction. The Liberal Republican movement corroded the unity of antislavery Republicans and foreshadowed the Hayes withdrawal policy of 1877 and the New South ideology in respect to race relations. Avow-

SOURCE: Stanwood, History of the Presidency, pp. 341–344.

ing the old objectives, the liberals repudiated reliance upon the national government as the instrument for attaining them. Plank four of their platform must be read in the light of the Enforcement Acts and the vigorous, successful efforts of the Grant administration to suppress the Ku Klux Klan, culminating in martial law over nine South Carolina counties in October 1871 and the arrest of more than 500 persons there by the end of February 1872. If Liberals retreated, the Democratic party advanced by adopting the Liberal Republican platform. By this act it officially accepted the "new departure" policy that some northern leaders had been urging, thereby breaking the open identification of party and white racism characteristic of Democratic politics in the 1850s and 1860s.

The impetus behind the Liberal movement derived from various sources, most importantly in this context from a desire for national reconciliation with an end to violence and from a growing conviction that federal coercion was an ineffectual tool for achieving just treatment of black Southerners by white Southerners. Although the Greeley ticket was overwhelmed in the elections of 1872, the shift in attitudes that it embodied continued to gain momentum affecting both congressional and executive decision-making in the second Grant administration.

Southern Policy of
Liberal Republican Platform Adopted by the
Democratic Party, July 10, 1872

They [the partisans of the administration] have kept alive the passions and resentments of the late civil war, to use them for their own advantage; they have resorted to arbitrary measures in direct conflict with the organic law, instead of appealing to the better instincts and latent patriotism of the Southern people by restoring to them those rights the enjoyment of which is indispensable to a successful administration of their local affairs, and would tend to revive a patriotic and hopeful national feeling. . . .

We, the Liberal Republicans of the United States, in national convention assembled at Cincinnati, proclaim the following principles as essential to just government:

1. We recognize the equality of all men before the law, and hold that it is the duty of government, in its dealings with the people, to mete out equal and exact justice to all, of whatever nativity, race, color, or persuasion, religious or political.

2. We pledge ourselves to maintain the union of these States, emancipation, and enfranchisement, and to oppose any reopening of the questions settled by the Thirteenth, Fourteenth, and Fifteenth Amendments of the Constitution.

3. We demand the immediate and absolute removal of all disabilities imposed on account of the rebellion, which was finally

THE CONTINUING COMMITMENT

subdued seven years ago, believing that universal amnesty will result in complete pacification in all sections of the country.

4. Local self-government, with impartial suffrage, will guard the rights of all citizens more securely than any centralized power. The public welfare requires the supremacy of the civil over the military authority, and the freedom of the person under the protection of the *habeas corpus*. We demand for the individual the largest liberty consistent with public order, for the State self-government, and for the nation a return to the methods of peace and the constitutional limitations of power.

17. Beyond Political Equality: Attack on Jim Crow

WITH DEMOCRATIC VICTORIES in the elections of 1874 Republicans lost control of Congress until the Harrison administration; and the Civil Rights Bill, passed earlier by the Senate in deference to Charles Sumner's deathbed wish and pushed through the House by Ben Butler in the last days of the Forty-third Congress, represented the last successful party effort at the national level on behalf of the Negro. This final achievement has been discredited on the grounds that the measure was "emasculated" by the elimination of the school clause and that its passage was a cover for other narrowly partisan or "jobbing" legislation. Since the presumably disreputable legislation failed, the latter argument is hardly substantial. The omission of provision for desegregating schools may have saved the bill in the House. Nor were friends of the freedmen agreed on the school clause, as the letter of Albion Tourgee (doc. b) makes clear. Tourgee's views cannot be lightly discounted for he was one of the best and most effective of Northern carpetbaggers and never abandoned his active concern for the equal rights of blacks (doc. 22b). Note that most of the preamble was lifted from the Liberal Republican-Democratic platform of 1872, a stratagem which failed to dent the solid Democratic opposition to the act's provisions. Section one, the heart of the law, was held unconstitutional in the famous civil rights decision of 1883; section four in respect to juries survived judicial review.

a. Civil Rights Act of 1875

An act to protect all citizens in their civil and legal rights.

Whereas, it is essential to just government we recognize the equality of all men before the law, and hold that it is the duty of

SOURCE: U.S., *Statutes at Large*, XVIII:335–337.

government in its dealings with the people to mete out equal and exact justice to all, of whatever nativity, race, color, or persuasion, religious or political; and it being the appropriate object of legislation to enact great fundamental principles into law: Therefore,

Be it enacted by the Senate and House of Representatives of the United States of America in Congress assembled, That all persons within the jurisdiction of the United States shall be entitled to the full and equal enjoyment of the accommodations, advantages, facilities, and privileges of inns, public conveyances on land or water, theaters, and other places of public amusement; subject only to the conditions and limitations established by law, and applicable alike to citizens of every race and color, regardless of any previous condition of servitude.

SEC. 2. That any person who shall violate the foregoing section by denying to any citizen, except for reasons by law applicable to citizens of every race and color, and regardless of any previous condition of servitude, the full enjoyment of any of the accommodations, advantages, facilities, or privileges in said section enumerated, or by aiding or inciting such denial, shall, for every such offense, forfeit and pay the sum of five hundred dollars to the person aggrieved thereby, to be recovered in an action of debt, with full costs; and shall also, for every such offense, be deemed guilty of a misdemeanor, and, upon conviction thereof, shall be fined not less than five hundred nor more than one thousand dollars, or shall be imprisoned not less than thirty days nor more than one year. . . .

SEC. 3. That the district and circuit courts of the United States shall have, exclusively of the courts of the several States, cognizance of all crimes and offenses against, and violations of, the provisions of this act; and actions for the penalty given by the preceding section may be prosecuted in the territorial, district, or circuit courts of the United States wherever the defendant may be found, without regard to the other party; and the district attorneys, marshals, and deputy marshals of the United States, and commissioners appointed by the circuit and territorial courts of the United States, with powers of arresting and imprisoning or bailing offenders against the laws of the United States, are hereby specially authorized and required to institute proceedings against every person who shall violate the provisions of this act. . . . and any district attorney who shall willfully fail to institute and prosecute the proceedings herein required, shall, for every such offense, forfeit and pay the sum of five hundred dollars to the person aggrieved thereby, to be recovered by an action of debt, with full costs, and shall, on conviction thereof, be deemed guilty of a misdemeanor, and be fined not less than one thousand nor more than five thousand dollars. . . .

SEC. 4. That no citizen possessing all other qualifications which are or may be prescribed by law shall be disqualified for service as grand or petit juror in any court of the United States, or of any State, on account of race, color, or previous condition of servitude; and any officer or other person charged with any duty in the selection or summoning of jurors who shall exclude or fail to summon any citizen for the cause aforesaid shall, on conviction thereof, be deemed guilty of a misdemeanor, and be fined not more than five thousand dollars.

SEC. 5. That all cases arising under the provisions of this act in the courts of the United States shall be reviewable by the Supreme Court of the United States, without regard to the sum in controversy, under the same provisions and regulations as are now provided by law for the review of other causes in said court.

Approved, March 1, 1875.

b. The School Issue: Albion W. Tourgée's Letter, May 11, 1874

Greensboro, N.C.,
May 11th 1874

My Dear Doctor*:

Your letter is rec'd and places me under new obligations for your kindness. You would hardly write so coolly of my election—I suppose—if you knew the situation fully—I am hardly sure of the nomination. . . .

The worst thing will be the Civil Rights Bill—Sumner's Suplementary—I know the maxim De mortuis nihil &c but I have no use for those who prescribe for diseases without knowing their nature —Sumner knew no more of the actual condition of the colored man here than he realized his condition on the Gold Coast—The bill with all respects to its author, is just like a blister-plaster put on a dozing man whom it is desirable to soothe to sleep—The most

* Dr. M. B. Anderson, University of Rochester
SOURCE: Albion W. Tourgee Papers, Chautauqua County Historical Museum, Westfield, New York.

important thing in the world is to let the South forget the negro for a bit:—let him acquire property, stability and self-respect; let as many as possible be educated; in short let the race itself get used to freedom self-dependence and proper self assertion; and then let this bill come little by little if necessary.—Of course, if it becomes law, it will be constantly avoided—No man can frame a statue which some other cannot avoid. For all its beneficent purposes it will be a dead letter—For its evil influences it will be vivid and active—It will be like the firebrands between the tails of Samson's foxes. It is just pure folly and results from what I have so long claimed, that the people of the North and our Legislators, will not study the people of the South—reasonably. They will not remember that a prejudice 250 years old (at least) should only be legislated against when *positively harmful*, and should always be let alone when it only conflicts with good doctrine—fine theory. It will utterly destroy the bulk of our common schools at the South. These States will throw them aside at once and the people, except in those where there is a colored majority,—will approve—They are not over fond of education here at the best. Our poor white people have to be fed a heap of soft corn to get them to take much stock in it, and the old slave owners *et cet.* do not see any great need in general education—A tax for free schools is as unwelcome as a vapor bath in dog days—If we get this fools' notion imposed on us, good bye schools in the South. It simply delays—puts back the thorough and complete rehabilitation of the South ten or twenty years—It is the idea of a visionary quack who prescribes for the disease without having made a diagnosis—

But pardon me. I did not mean to write all this—. . . .

Yrs,

Albion W. Tourgee

18. Unfinished Business:
Debates on the Enforcement Bill of 1875

DURING THE LAST DAYS of the Forty-third Congress, Republican success in passing the Civil Rights Act was offset by failure to enact a sup-

SOURCE: U.S., *Congressional Record*, 43 Cong., 2 sess. (February 27, 1875), extracts from pp. 1885–1911.

plementary enforcement bill, passed in the House but too late for Senate action. The measure sought to prevent the intimidation of voters by armed combinations and check the complicity of local authorities, to counter evasive registration practices, to protect ballot boxes against fraud or theft, and to safeguard state governments against violent overthrow. It would have extended to rural counties the provisions of the Second Enforcement Act, applicable only to cities and towns of over 20,000, providing election commissioners and deputy marshalls with effective power to oversee elections. In addition it would have authorized the president to suspend the writ of habeas corpus, his power under the Ku Klux Act of 1871 having expired in 1872. Its impact, had the bill become law, is uncertain; possibly it might have affected the situation in Mississippi (doc. 28) and the course of Supreme Court decisions.

In the selections below from the House debates, the man speaking in opposition to the bill was a Republican and a New Englander, Henry L. Pierce of Boston, which indicates the growing division within the party over Southern policy. The arguments of Joseph G. Cannon, Benjamin F. Butler, and Charles G. Williams are examples of "waving the bloody shirt."

MR. PIERCE. Mr. Speaker, I deplore the introduction of this measure into this House in the last hours of an expiring Congress; for in my judgment it is ill-timed, unnnecessary, and worse than useless. Impressed with its injustice and impolicy, I should fall short of my duty did I content myself with giving a silent vote against it. It is a political measure, intended, as its advocates aver, to secure in the country the ascendency of the political party to which they belong. To this end it provides for the increase of the power of the President, and clothes him with additional authority to interfere in the internal affairs of the several States. For one I am opposed to this increase and to this interference. Nothing but an exigency of the gravest character would justify special legislation of this kind at the very close of the session of a House of Representatives that is to be succeeded by one of adverse political opinion.

Are we not at the bottom working simply and solely for the continuance of political party supremacy? Are we not aiming, or do not those who advocate this bill aim, if not exclusively, mainly at party success by this instrumentality? Is not that in fact the motive to the introduction of the bill? Sir, gentlemen know it is. We are told, by high authority, that one hundred and thirty-eight electoral votes of the reconstructed States rightfully belong to the republican party; and that if the bill now pending in the House becomes a law it will secure these votes to that party, and otherwise they will be lost.

The pretense of redressing personal grievances and protecting individual liberty by this bill is not sufficiently plausible to free the action of its supporters from this criticism. I assert, Mr. Speaker, that we have ample legislation already; sufficiently rigorous and effective laws to accomplish all that is necessary in the Southern States. The Revised Statutes not only permit, but by implication enjoin upon the President and subordinate authorities the suppres- , sion of insurrectionary manifestations; the protection of the States against domestic violence and the rights of citizens in the exercise of suffrage. Why, then, add to the laws this extreme power, these extreme penalties? Are we mindful that constitutional liberty has meaning or force? Do we consider the States as provinces of the General Government that we may obtrude upon them at our pleasure our officers, civil and military, sending them all through the country with utter disregard for their authorities?

If domestic violence exists in the Southern States, the President is empowered to crush it. He has exercised his powers in Louisiana, Arkansas, and other States; and certainly order and tranquillity reign in Arkansas and in Louisiana. We hear of none but political troubles to-day. And yet in the midst of peace we propose to enact a new force bill, with cruel and unusual penalties, and to suspend the writ of *habeas corpus*, that great writ of personal privilege and personal protection, that sole and simple barrier between liberty and despotism that distinguishes this nation and Great Britain from all other nations of the world.

Sir, it is not in the interest of the republican party that this should be done. The people I more immediately represent and the people of Massachusetts as well ask for no such violent remedy. They do not believe the occasion for it exists; and with all kindness toward those who are managing and urging this measure, I say that I doubt if in their heart of hearts these gentlemen believe that any such occasion exists now or is likely to arise in the future. . . .

MR. CANNON, of Illinois . . . I had the honor to be designated by the House as one of a special committee during the present session to proceed to the State of Alabama for the purpose of taking testimony concerning the condition of alleged outrages in the State and make report in the premises to the House. Prior to that committees had been appointed to make similar inquiries in the States of Mississippi, Louisiana, and Arkansas, all of these committees have performed the dutes with which they were charged, and have made reports to the House. . . .

I can only pause long enough to refer to the fact that bad men, organized and armed, stand ready, in defiance of all law, to go from Texas to Mississippi, from Mississippi to Alabama, and from all of these States to Louisiana, to subvert all law, both State and Federal, and with a strong hand hunt down republicans, kill negroes, burn churches and school-houses, depose officers of a State or county, or subvert and revolutionize a State government. The testimony of the different investigating committees shows all this and much more. I do not mean to say that all democrats in Alabama and elsewhere South commit these outrages or approve them. On the contrary, there are many good men South, democrats, who deplore this condition of society. But it is also true that these bad men are sufficient in numbers to boldly and defiantly commit all these acts and so control public opinion that no redress whatever for outrages of this kind can be had in the courts. And while I have no doubt, so far as judges of courts are concerned, in most instances, that they declare the law correctly when called upon to make rulings, yet cases ordinarily can only be disposed of with the aid of juries and healthy public opinion. With the foregoing state of society as a rule, the juries will not or do not help administer the law so as to protect republican citizens, especially negroes, in their rights, so far as personal security is concerned, and punish men who commit political crimes heretofore spoken of; and while Justice may perhaps be still, so far as the judges are concerned, represented with her eyes bandaged, holding the balances, yet she should also be represented as bound both hand and foot by public opinion, and powerless to make and enforce her decrees; and, strange as it may appear, the testimony shows since the war but one white man has been convicted for homicide of a negro in the whole State of Alabama, yet when our democratic friends are called upon to explain, justify, or condemn this state of affairs, they generally deny, or if they admit in part seek to palliate or justify, by saying that the people of Alabama have been under the rule of the republican carpet-baggers, who are fattening upon the misfortunes of the people, and that those manifestations are only the violent protests of a generous people against such a state of things. . . .

Grave responsibilities are resting upon the people of Alabama and other Southern States. Many of the whites are ignorant and lawless, and most of the negroes are ignorant, ordinarily well disposed, but owing to their poverty and former condition many of them incline to commit petit larcenies and smaller grades of offenses. What is needed is a thorough enforcement of the law, protection to all citizens; especially in their rights of personal security, and general education, and until all these are given I do not see much chance for prosperity in the South. But our democratic friends tell us that the difficulty is that the negroes are ignorant and will not divide their votes between the parties, but insist on voting the republican ticket. I have no doubt it would be better if all parties would acknowledge the equality of all men before the law in practice as well as theory; and until this is done by democrats South, instead of resorting to force and intimidation, how can they expect the negroes will vote with them, and how can they criticise with justice the negroes for not dividing their votes between the two parties when the more intelligent whites are seeking to divide on the color line, and resort to ostracism, proscription, and some of them to murder and assassination to accomplish their purpose?

But it is useless to speak further of these matters. All will acknowledge the necessity for action. The gentleman from Connecticut, for whom I entertain great respect, acknowledges the wrongs to be remedied; also that the States have not and probably will not remedy them, and that they will have to go without a remedy, for the reason the United States has no power in the premises. I agree with him that Congress can only give relief by legislation where authority is given under the Constitution, but I also claim that the Constitution covers the proposed legislation.

I have no patience with some gentlemen who admit the necessity for action, but quietly fold their arms, while the blood of the slain cries from the ground and the moan of the widow and orphan are heard as protests against the most foul taking-off of the husband and father, and search with a microscope for a fancied want of power to legislate, or cry conciliation and peace, peace, when there is no peace for these citizens of the United States, if they persist in exercising their rights in voting as they see proper, but the peace of the grave. . . .

Gentlemen on the other side say, however, why not leave this legislation to the next Congress? I will tell them, among others, for the reason that the House of Representatives in the next Congress is composed of many men, enough to make a majority, who the history of the last fourteen years shows will not favor legislation to secure the equality of all before the law, many of whom from the North the records of this House show to have done all they dared do to embarrass the United States in putting down the rebellion, and many of whom from the South sought the life of the nation by war, and nearly all of whom, both from the North and South, have made war on reconstruction, upon the adoption of the constitutional amendments, and from time to time have opposed all legislation to insure a free ballot; who in 1871 first denied the existence of the Ku-Klux and their outrages, and if possible more bitterly denounced the Ku-Klux act than they do this proposed legislation; who have for ten years from time to time ignored, apologized for, or defended ostracism, proscription, riot, murder, and assassination; and who can only hope to get into power and control the United States by a united South, which is only possible by a reign of terror in many parts of the South, under which a free ballot cannot be had. . . .

In conclusion, I want to say in all kindness to gentlemen, North and South, that in my opinion there neither can nor ought to be peace and prosperity until all citizens, as a rule, wherever they may be throughout the Union, are equal before the law in fact as well as in theory. . . .

MR. BUTLER, of Massachusetts . . . I want to say again that the great advantage of suspending the writ of *habeas corpus* is that it allows the military officer, when he arrests a man that rides at night, to take him to the marshal and have a complaint made against him and hold him until he can get him before the court.

One word more, and I will pass from this discussion, and perhaps forever. I sat here, at the risk of my health and life, twenty-odd hours, through the long watches of the night, fighting to bring this bill before the House for consideration against the filibustering motions of the other side, believing it to be my duty so to do. There were men of the republican majority who chose to go to their beds and take their rest. They now come in here and are very anxious that this debate shall be continued and of extending the time for debate to the factious minority. . . .

Now let me tell those gentlemen that if by their conduct they have allowed the minority to stave off this bill so that it is too late to pass it at this session, when they shall hear of a church burned, or a man being murdered at the South, and shall see his widowed wife and orphaned children—

MR. ELDREDGE. I insist upon order being maintained. We cannot hear what the gentleman is saying.

THE SPEAKER. Gentlemen standing in the aisles will please resume their seats.

MR. BUTLER, of Massachusetts. I hope this does not come out of my time.

After a pause.

THE SPEAKER said: The gentleman will proceed.

MR. BUTLER, of Massachusetts. When they hear the shriek of "murder" and see the widowed wife and orphaned children coming north, fleeing from the white-leaguers and Ku-Klux raiders, I trust their sleep will be as sweet as it was on that night when I was standing here for the safety of these poor creatures, at the risk of health, and they were at home sweetly sleeping. When they hereafter meet a widow of some murdered soldier from the South who asks for alms, do not send them to me, but let them give all that is necessary to sustain that poor creature themselves. Let each one of them say to that starving widow, "I am sorry that I did not stand up and defend you by the passage of a proper law; I am responsible; you need not trouble General BUTLER; he did sit up, and he has got to pay his physicians' bills and I have not, and I will take care of you."

And hereafter, Mr. Speaker, when you meet in Augusta, Maine, or in some other beautiful town in that State some poor, wretched refugee who went down South with his knapsack on his back and remained there—a carpet-bagger, if you please—until he was driven out for want of a law to protect, and he complains that you did not pass the law, tell him that parliamentary law required you to allow the democratic minority to control us, the republican majority, for hours, so that the golden opportunity was lost; that you were sorry for it; and be very sure to say at the same time, "What can I do to relieve you?" You never will forget to do that, I am sure.

Gentlemen of the House of Representatives, the question of life and death for hundreds of true men, black and white; the question of good government, anarchy, of peace or war, in my judgment, is to be decided now and here by our votes. Let us have no delay. . . .

MR. WILLIAMS, of Wisconsin. . . Mr. Speaker, we have never yet had, and we shall not have in this country a government which even begins to realize the object for which ours was ordained, namely, "to establish justice, insure domestic tranquillity, provide for the common defense, promote the general welfare, and secure the blessings of liberty to ourselves and our posterity," until the citizens of each State and of all the States can pass freely to and fro, select their domiciles where they will and avow their sentiments as they please, unawed by the assassin's knife and unterrified by the rifle or revolver which sends the deadly bullet crashing through their houses in the night-time, and fills the air with shrieks of horror and distress. But what "justice" is that where law is defied, where courts are overthrown, where judges are sent fleeing for their lives under the cover of night? And what "domestic tranquillity" is "insured" where unarmed and defenseless men can be shot down on their own door-sills, and the missiles of death sent whistling through the beds of sleeping children? And what "blessings of liberty" are secured where men are hunted like wild beasts to the canebrake; their houses robbed; their wives and children terrified; their fields laid waste; their cattle, horses, and mules driven off, and no offender brought to justice, and no attempt made to restore to them the property of which they have thus been despoiled? Sir, a government which permits these things to be done, and to continue, without furnishing a remedy for their correction, not only fails in the highest functions of government, but to these poor victims it becomes a mockery and a curse. . . .

Thus, Mr. Speaker, it will be seen that the thirteenth amendment emancipated the slave, but virtually left him an outlaw; the fourteenth amendment clothed him with citizenship; and the fifteenth gave him the right of suffrage. The three combined raised him to the dignity of a man, and invested him with the rights, the privileges, and immunities of a citizen. The court say: [Slaughterhouse Cases]

> On the most casual examination of the language of these amendments no one can fail to be impressed with the one pervading purpose found in them all, lying at the foundation of each, and without which none of them would have been suggested. We mean the freedom of the slave race, the security and firm establishment of that freedom, and the protection of the newly made freeman and citizen from the oppression of those who had formerly exercised unlimited domination over him.

We do not say that any one else cannot share in this protection; . . . but what we do say, and what we wish to be understood, is, that in any fair and just construction of any section or phrase of these amendments it is necessary to look at the purpose which we have said was the pervading spirit of them all, the evil which they were designed to remedy, and the process of continued addition to the Constitution until that purpose was supposed to be accomplished as far as constitutional law can accomplish it.

Here, Mr. Speaker, we are brought face to face with our duty to protect by every constitutional means this class of citizens; and the only question here to-day is, will we perform this duty or will we shirk it? Will we protect these men or will we leave them to be overborne and butchered? That, sir, is all there is of it. If we will not or cannot protect them, then let us say so. Let us admit that our system of government breaks down at this vital point; but let us prate no more about the "equal protection" of all men under the law; let us talk no longer of the glories of free institutions if, under them, unoffending citizens can be more cruelly persecuted than in Austria or Russia. . . .

Gentlemen of the South, it remains for you to determine what the result of all this shall be. I have stood but twice upon your soil. I have met many of you in the political and social walks of life in this city, and I joyfully bear testimony to your generous hospitality and your genial ways. But upon you, and you alone, rests the fearful responsibility of saying whether these outrages shall continue or whether they shall cease altogether; whether peace shall in fact dawn upon this country or whether war with all its woes shall afflict it again. . . . Let the leading men of the South . . . determine that these disorders shall cease; let them give the colored man a fair chance in the race of life; let them encourage him in acquiring property and protect him in its enjoyment; let all men be secure in the full and free avowal of their sentiments, whether religious or political; let the large landed estates be divided into such tracts as can be most profitably cultivated; let capital feel that its home is in the South, and that its possessor shall be neither socially nor politically ostracized—in short, gentlemen, let every energy be put forth to develop and build up the better rather than the baser elements of human nature, and we will then shake hands, not across a "bloody chasm," but across a country teeming with life, filled with the blessings of peace, and crowned with a prosperity such as no other land has ever seen beneath the sun. Grant us this, and we will consent that the suspension of the writ of *habeas corpus* may be dispensed with forevermore.

[Here the hammer fell.]

19. President Hayes's Southern Policy

WHEN RUTHERFORD B. HAYES assumed the presidency, no state of the former Confederacy was firmly in the hands of Republicans, and the national mood was one of reconciliation. The historic task of the Republican party had been to unshackle the slave, grant him the basic rights of a freeman, and as their guarantee, provide review by the federal courts and the power of the ballot. By 1877 it was clear that in the face of white resistance the black power base had crumbled. An increasing number of Republican spokesmen of goodwill saw only failure and violence as the grim harvest of past efforts to coerce the white South through federal officials and military force. With the lower house of Congress in the control of the Democrats, the country in the midst of a great depression, and reports from the South feeding a growing disillusionment with the black voter in politics, the choice lay between a new weaponry and abandonment of the goal of equal citizenship. Hayes chose not to abandon the Negro but to accept the pledges of Southern white leaders. In return for the withdrawal of federal troops and the reestablishment of "home rule," that is, federal acquiescence in the return to power of white ex-Confederates, the Southern Conservatives pledged to accept and safeguard the civil and political equality of black men in their midst. Had there been no disputed presidential election and no "bargain" to settle the resulting crisis of 1877, in all probability Hayes's Southern policy would have been substantially the same. The argument that only the free consent of white Southerners could in fact secure black Southerners protection and civil rights appeared a not unreasonable conclusion after a decade of turmoil and frustration (see part two, section B). With party "stalwarts" urging strong measures and reformers charging them with caring for nothing more than party interest, Hayes tried to transform basic racial justice from a partisan cause to a nonpartisan reality.

The documents below reveal his disillusionment and his futile effort to reverse direction, short of a resort to military force. In the words of the *Topeka Colored Citizen*, a sharp presidential critic, "President Hayes offered the olive branch to the ex-Confederates, but they refused it. He has since been trying the birch." Prosecutions under the enforcement acts in the South went from twenty-five with no convictions and forty-four cases pending for the fiscal year 1877–1878 to 122 prosecutions with thirty-three convictions and 294 cases pending in the year that followed. But the President could win only a rear guard action. In a special session from March 18 to July 1, 1879, the Democrats, who had gained control of the Senate as well as the House in the 1878 elections, tried to emasculate federal enforcement legislation. In that short period Hayes vetoed five such measures, four of them riders to appropriation bills, voicing strong objection to their substance as well as to the device of a rider. The Democratic Congress ignored the appeals of the president and his attorney general for larger appropriations and new means to protect voters and discourage election fraud. (One method recommended was that elections be administered by federal rather than state officials.) Meantime, the ingenuity of white Southerners was fashioning indirect methods, less susceptible to legal prosecution, to replace violent and open defiance of the Reconstruction amendments. (Compare doc. 29b)

From Inaugural Address, March 5, 1877

. . . The sweeping revolution of the entire labor system of a large portion of our country and the advance of 4,000,000 people from a condition of servitude to that of citizenship, upon an equal footing with their former masters, could not occur without presenting problems of the gravest moment, to be dealt with by the emancipated race, by their former masters, and by the General Government, the author of the act of emancipation. That it was a wise, just, and providential act, fraught with good for all concerned, is now generally conceded throughout the country. That a moral obligation rests upon the National Government to employ its constitutional power and influence to establish the rights of the people it has emancipated, and to protect them in the enjoyment of those rights when they are infringed or assailed, is also generally admitted.

The evils which afflict the Southern States can only be removed or remedied by the united and harmonious efforts of both races, actuated by motives of mutual sympathy and regard; and while in duty bound and fully determined to protect the rights of all by every constitutional means at the disposal of my Administration, I am sincerely anxious to use every legitimate influence in favor of honest and efficient local self-government as the true resource of those States for the promotion of the contentment and prosperity of their citizens. In the effort I shall make to accomplish this purpose I ask the cordial cooperation of all who cherish an interest in the welfare of the country, trusting that party ties and the prejudice of race will be freely surrendered in behalf of the great purpose

Source: Richardson, *Messages of the Presidents*, VII:443–444.

to be accomplished. In the important work of restoring the South it is not the political situation alone that merits attention. The material development of that section of the country has been arrested by the social and political revolution through which it has passed, and now needs and deserves the considerate care of the National Government within the just limits prescribed by the Constitution and wise public economy.

But at the basis of all prosperity, for that as well as for every other part of the country, lies the improvement of the intellectual and moral condition of the people. Universal suffrage should rest upon universal education. To this end, liberal and permanent provision should be made for the support of free schools by the State governments, and, if need be, supplemented by legitimate aid from national authority.

Let me assure my countrymen of the Southern States that it is my earnest desire to regard and promote their truest interests—the interests of the white and of the colored people both and equally—and to put forth my best efforts in behalf of a civil policy which will forever wipe out in our political affairs the color line and the distinction between North and South, to the end that we may have not merely a united North or a united South, but a united country. . . .

THE PRESIDENT INDIGNANT

HE SAYS THE INTEGRITY OF AMERICAN CITIZENSHIP
HAS BEEN GROSSLY VIOLATED IN THE SOUTH
AND MUST AND SHALL BE VINDICATED

Washington, Nov. 12.—The following will appear in *The National Republican* to-morrow morning.

Very naturally, in view of the Democratic conduct of the late campaign [1878] in the Southern States, the President has been frequently interviewed by leading Republicans from all sections of the country, and especially from the South. The fact that the Democrats of that section have violated all the pledges made to him to accord to the blacks their rights and privileges of citizenship, and have thereby robbed the Republican party of its due proportion of representation in the next House, has prompted these interviews, the ultimate design being to urge the President to exhaust the

SOURCE: *New York Daily Tribune*, November 13, 1878.

legitimate resources of his office in bringing the perpetrators of these great crimes to justice. But the President, in his utterances at these interviews, has carefully and persistently refused to take a partisan view of the situation.

His attention was called yesterday to an editorial paragraph in the morning *National Republican* announcing that the Southern situation would be earnestly discussed at the regular Cabinet meeting. To this he replied: "that is a mistake: the time for discussion has passed. It is now too late for anything but the most determined and vigorous action. This determination was reached several days ago, and the deliberations of the Cabinet on this subject since then have been comparatively brief, and confined mainly to the consideration of the duty of the Attorney-General in the premises."

To these remarks the interviewer replied approvingly, and then asked the President how he accounted for the result of a Solid South in the face of the pledges of fair dealing by leading Southern Democrats?

The President—That question leads directly to a discussion of what has been latterly termed the Southern policy of the Administration. When that policy was inaugurated it was with an earnest desire to conciliate the Southern leaders, to round off the sharp angles of sectional difference, and to soften the asperities of political strife. No one will deny that the attempt to enforce this policy was most earnestly made, nor that it was carried out with a conscientious desire to accomplish the result for which it had been inaugurated. Of the personal and partisan sacrifices I made in this effort, and of the consequent interruption of certain relations which had previously existed between myself and some of my supporters, I have nothing to say just now. But it appears that the leaders who made these pledges either did not exert themselves to keep them or were unable to do so. In fact, I am reluctantly forced to admit that the experiment was a failure. The first election of importance held since it was attempted has proved that fair elections with free suffrage for every voter in the South are an impossibility under the existing condition of things.

Interviewer—And the Republican party, except in North Carolina, has thereby been wiped out of existence in the South.

The President—It is not because the Republican party appears as the sufferer in these results that I complain. It is because free suffrage and freedom of political rights have been interfered with, that I am called upon to take cognizance of these disturbances. If the facts were exactly reversed, and if the Republicans had committed these outrages upon the Democrats my duty would be the same. It will not do for me or for any official before whom these questions may come to treat them otherwise than in a non-partisan way. The partisan press will naturally take a partisan view of the case, and I will be held to account for aiding the Republicans—the "Stalwarts," I mean—in flaunting the bloody shirt, as it is called.

Interviewer—Yes: it has been charged that you are following in the footsteps of your predecessor.

The President—Well, I expect that; all that and more. I can't expect to hold the office I do without being kicked and cuffed a little, you know. But for all that, I shall do my duty as the Chief Magistrate of the people, Democrats and Republicans alike; and if in the faithful execution of the laws justice shall demand the punishment of this or that man, whatever his political connections may be, I shall not be deterred by partisan criticism. All I know is that great crimes have been committed, and it is my duty to aid in the punishment of the criminals."

Interviewer—And you do not think that the Southern leaders— the Democrats, I mean—who have promised so often to protect the blacks of the South in the exercise of their rights, are responsible for these crimes?

The President—Frankly, I do not. Governor Hampton, for example, has tried repeatedly to repress the violence which has characterized the campaign in South Carolina, and failed. Such Republicans as Julge Lee and Mr. Rainey, and ex-State Senator Swails of that State, have advised me of these facts. They say that Hampton cannot control the "Red Shirts," as they call them, and they have repeatedly informed me of speeches he has made deprecating violence in the conduct of the campaign. And it appears that Governor Nichols in Louisiana is earnestly opposed to these proceedings and the same kind of violence in his State.

Interviewer—Then the officers of the Department of Justice have been instructed to carry out the proceedings already begun against the depredators.

The President—Not only against those who have already been arrested, but against others who will soon be arrested. It is proposed to make a clean sweep of this business and exhaust every legal resource in the execution of justice. The integrity of American citizenship has been grossly violated in widespread localities. It must and shall be vindicated.

Interviewer—Will it be necessary to make any removals or changes among the District-Attorneys in the Southern States?

The President—I hope not, and believe not; but if it is discovered that any officer of the class you refer to is not earnestly endeavoring to do his whole duty in the matter, there will be no hesitation in taking proper steps to replace him, and to secure a vigorous prosecution of these cases.

From Report of the Attorney General, December 2, 1878

THE ELECTION LAWS

Information, which I received from various sources, led me to believe previous to the recent Congressional election that such interference with the canvass preceding it had taken place, and was reasonably to be expected with the election itself, that the attention of the officers of this department should in certain localities be called to infractions of the laws which had occurred, or which might be expected, and to the necessity of doing all in their power to prevent them and to secure a fair election. In some instances it was deemed to have been fully shown that peaceful meetings lawfully called for the advocacy of particular candidates for Congress had been intruded upon by armed bands, who, under the specious pretext of keeping the peace, prevented by disorder and ruffianism the organization or the proper holding of such meetings.

The Attorney-General's Office is not provided with the means of any general system of investigation of infractions of the laws. It depends mainly upon the reports of facts in individual cases made by the officers of the department upon the ground, and on their requests for instructions in regard thereto. Availing myself of these, as well as of information from those public sources which are common to all, it is apparent that in various parts of the Union (especially in certain portions of the States of Louisiana, South Carolina, Texas, and Virginia) instances of unlawful combination and violence, intended to prevent a free and peaceful advocacy of

Source: *Annual Report of the Attorney-General*, 1878 (Washington, D.C.: 1878), pp. 18–19.

candidates for Congress, occurred previous to the day of election, and upon the day of election deliberate frauds were resorted to in voting and canvassing the votes, often accompanied by threats and intimidation.

A frequent outrage upon the purity of the ballot was in what is familiarly known as "ballot-box stuffing," and consisted in preparing the boxes by depositing therein before the voting commenced or after it was concluded large numbers of fraudulent ballots, and also by folding smaller ballots within a larger one in such a way that they could be shaken out by the voter as he deposited his ballot or afterward by those who had the custody of the box. This fraud was accomplished by the use of small ballots printed upon tissue-paper, and was perpetrated in so many different places and with tickets so carefully prepared and of such similarity that it cannot be doubted that it was the result of an organized conspiracy of some central directing agency to defeat the will of the people and falsify the true result of the election.

The canvass and election were accompanied in the State of Louisiana by a series of cowardly and cruel murders, the only apparent motive for which was to prevent the colored people from exercising their right of suffrage. These murders occurred in Caddo, Tensas, Natchitoches, and other parishes.

It has been my duty to advise the proper subordinate officers of the department, in such manner as seemed best calculated to secure the ends of justice, to promptly assert and enforce the authority of the laws of the United States in order to bring to justice those who have violated them.

I have seen no reason to believe that any arrests which they have caused to be made have not been fully justified, or that they have acted otherwise than as their duty plainly demanded. The attempt to bring to justice the violators of the law has, however, been followed by a system of persecution of United States officers, and of witnesses who have been called to testify in regard to the transactions complained of, which cannot be too severely condemned. This resistance to the laws of the United States has in some instances taken the form of brutal violence, but more generally that of complaints and prosecutions under the State laws for alleged offenses. In such proceedings bail has sometimes been refused, or fixed at amounts so exorbitant that the accused could not be expected to be able to obtain it. The character of these prosecutions may perhaps be better understood when it is observed that large numbers of them are for alleged perjuries committed before United States commissioners or the courts of the United States— offenses of which it is entirely clear that the States have no jurisdiction.

It will be my effort fairly but decidedly to do all in my power to execute the laws of the United States regarding the purity of elections in the same way as all its other laws and to bring to justice those who have violated them. Some addition to the anticipated expenses of this department for the current year may be occasioned by doing this thoroughly, and the means for meeting these should be provided by Congress.

I respectfully submit to the consideration of Congress whether additional provisions may not be made more effectively to protect officers of the United States and witnesses summoned on its behalf against causeless prosecutions, and to enable them to transfer the examination of them to the courts of the United States.

From Veto Message, April 29, 1879

I have maturely considered the important questions presented by the bill entitled "An act making appropriations for the support of the Army for the fiscal year ending June 30, 1880, and for other purposes," and I now return it to the House of Representatives, in which it originated, with my objections to its approval. . . . The intent and effect of the sixth section of this bill is to prohibit all the civil officers of the United States, under penalty of fine and imprisonment, from employing any adequate civil force for this purpose at the place where their enforcement is most necessary, namely, at the places where the Congressional elections are held. Among the most valuable enactments to which I have referred are those which protect the supervisors of Federal elections in the discharge of their duties at the polls. If the proposed legislation should become the law, there will be no power vested in any officer of the Government to protect from violence the officers of the United States engaged in the discharge of their duties. Their rights and duties under the law will remain, but the National Government will be powerless to enforce its own statutes. The States may employ both military and civil power to keep the peace and to enforce the laws at State elections. It is now proposed to deny to

SOURCE: Richardson, *Messages of the Presidents*, VII:523, 527–528.

the United States even the necessary civil authority to protect the national elections. . . . It is the right and duty of the National Government to enact and enforce laws which will secure free and fair Congressional elections. The laws now in force should not be repealed except in connection with the enactment of measures which will better accomplish that important end. Believing that section 6 of the bill before me will weaken, if it does not altogether take away, the power of the National Government to protect the Federal elections by the civil authorities, I am forced to the conclusion that it ought not to receive my approval. . . .

From Fourth Annual Message, December 6, 1880

I congratulate you on the continued and increasing prosperity of our country. . . .

Continued opposition to the full and free enjoyment of the rights of citizenship conferred upon the colored people by the recent amendments to the Constitution still prevails in several of the late slaveholding States. It has, perhaps, not been manifested in the recent election to any large extent in acts of violence or intimidation. It has, however, by fraudulent practices in connection with the ballots, with the regulations as to the places and manner of voting, and with counting, returning, and canvassing the votes cast, been successful in defeating the exercise of the right preservative of all rights—the right of suffrage—which the Constitution expressly confers upon our enfranchised citizens.

It is the desire of the good people of the whole country that sectionalism as a factor in our politics should disappear. They prefer that no section of the country should be united in solid opposition to any other section. The disposition to refuse a prompt and hearty obedience to the equal-rights amendments to the Constitution is all that now stands in the way of a complete obliteration of sectional lines in our political contests. As long as either of these amendments is flagrantly violated or disregarded, it is safe to assume that the people who placed them in the Constitution, as embodying the legitimate results of the war for the Union, and who believe them to be wise and necessary, will continue to act together and to insist that they shall be obeyed. . . .

I trust the House of Representatives and the Senate, which have the right to judge of the elections, returns, and qualifications of

Source: Richardson, *Messages of the Presidents*, VII:601–603.

their own members, will see to it that every case of violation of the letter or spirit of the fifteenth amendment is thoroughly investigated, and that no benefit from such violation shall accrue to any person or party. It will be the duty of the Executive, with sufficient appropriations for the purpose, to prosecute unsparingly all who have been engaged in depriving citizens of the rights guaranteed to them by the Constitution.

It is not, however, to be forgotten that the best and surest guaranty of the primary rights of citizenship is to be found in that capacity for self-protection which can belong only to a people whose right to universal suffrage is supported by universal education. The means at the command of the local and State authorities are in many cases wholly inadequate to furnish free instruction to all who need it. This is especially true where before emancipation the education of the people was neglected or prevented, in the interest of slavery. Firmly convinced that the subject of popular education deserves the earnest attention of the people of the whole country, with a view to wise and comprehensive action by the Government of the United States, I respectfully recommend that Congress, by suitable legislation and with proper safeguards, supplement the local educational funds in the several States where the grave duties and responsibilities of citizenship have been devolved on uneducated people by devoting to the purpose grants of the public lands and, if necessary, by appropriations from the Treasury of the United States. Whatever Government can fairly do to promote free popular education ought to be done. Wherever general education is found, peace, virtue, and social order prevail and civil and religious liberty are secure. . . .

20. Frederick Douglass Protests the Civil Rights Decision, October 22, 1883

IN THE 1880s Douglass still overshadowed any other leader as spokesman for his people. His speech at a mass protest meeting in Washington, just a week after Justice Bradley delivered the majority opinion in

SOURCE: *Proceedings of the Civil Rights Mass-Meeting Held at Lincoln Hall, October 22, 1883* (pamphlet, Washington, D.C., 1883), pp. 4–14.

the civil rights cases, was both moderate and eloquent. It was also an incisive criticism of the decision and a warning of danger to the nation in the denial of civil rights on the basis of color. Douglass' view of the intent of the Fourteenth Amendment is historically accurate. For the role of the Supreme Court, see the introduction, pp. 88, 121, 126.

FRIENDS AND FELLOW-CITIZENS:

I have only a very few words to say to you this evening, and in order that those few words shall be well-chosen, and not liable to be misunderstood, distorted, or misrepresented, I have been at the pains of writing them out in full. It may be, after all, that the hour calls more loudly for silence than for speech. Later on in this discussion, when we shall have the full text of the recent decision of the Supreme Court before us, and the dissenting opinion of Judge Harlan, who must have weighty reasons for separating from all his associates, and incurring thereby, as he must, an amount of criticism from which even the bravest man might shrink, we may be in better frame of mind, better supplied with facts, and better prepared to speak calmly, correctly, and wisely, than now. The temptation at this time is, of course, to speak more from feeling than reason, more from impulse than reflection. . . .

The cause which has brought us here to-night is neither common nor trivial. Few events in our national history have surpassed it in magnitude, importance and significance. It has swept over the land like a moral cyclone, leaving moral desolation in its track.

We feel it, as we felt the furious attempt, years ago, to force the accursed system of slavery upon the soil of Kansas, the enactment of the Fugitive Slave Bill, the repeal of the Missouri Compromise, the Dred Scott decision. I look upon it as one more shocking development of that moral weakness in high places which has attended the conflict between the spirit of liberty and the spirit of slavery from the beginning, and I venture to predict that it will be so regarded by after-coming generations.

Far down the ages, when men shall wish to inform themselves as to the real state of liberty, law, religion and civilization in the United States at this juncture of our history, they will overhaul the proceedings of the Supreme Court, and read the decision declaring the Civil Rights Bill unconstitutional and void.

From this they will learn more than from many volumes, how far we have advanced, in this year of grace, from barbarism toward civilization.

Fellow-citizens: Among the great evils which now stalk abroad in our land, the one, I think, which most threatens to undermine and destroy the foundations of our free institutions, is the great and apparently increasing want of respect entertained for those to whom are committed the responsibility and the duty of administering our government. On this point, I think all good men must agree, and against this evil I trust you feel, and we all feel, the deepest repugnance, and that we will, neither here nor elsewhere, give it the least breath of sympathy or encouragement. We should never forget, that, whatever may be the incidental mistakes or misconduct of rulers, government is better than anarchy, and patient reform is better than violent revolution.

But while I would increase this feeling, and give it the emphasis of a voice from heaven, it must not be allowed to interfere with free speech, honest expression, and fair criticism. To give up this would be to give up liberty, to give up progress, and to consign the nation to moral stagnation, putrefaction, and death.

In the matter of respect for dignitaries, it should never be forgotten, however, that duties are reciprocal, and while the people should frown down every manifestation of levity and contempt for those in power, it is the duty of the possessors of power so to use it as to deserve and to insure respect and reverence.

To come a little nearer to the case now before us. The Supreme Court of the United States, in the exercise of its high and vast constitutional power, has suddenly and unexpectedly decided that the law intended to secure to colored people the civil rights guaranteed to them by the following provision of the Constitution of the United States, is unconstitutional and void. Here it is:

"No State," says the 14th Amendment, "shall make or enforce any law which shall abridge the privileges or immunities of citizens of the United States; nor shall any State deprive any person of life, liberty, or property without due process of law; nor deny any person within its jurisdiction the equal protection of the laws." . . .

Inasmuch as the law in question is a law in favor of liberty and justice, it ought to have had the benefit of any doubt which could arise as to its strict constitutionality. This, I believe, will be the view taken of it, not only by laymen like myself, but by eminent lawyers as well. . . .

Now let me say here, before I go on a step further in this discussion, if any man has come here to-night with his breast heaving with passion, his heart flooded with acrimony, wishing and expecting to hear violent denunciation of the Supreme Court, on account of this decision, he has mistaken the object of this meeting, and the character of the men by whom it is called. . . .

What will be said here to-night, will be spoken, I trust, more in sorrow than in anger, more in a tone of regret than of bitterness.

We cannot, however, overlook the fact that though not so intended, this decision has inflicted a heavy calamity upon seven millions of the people of this country, and left them naked and defenceless against the action of a malignant, vulgar, and pitiless prejudice.

It presents the United States before the world as a Nation utterly destitute of power to protect the rights of its own citizens upon its own soil.

It can claim service and allegiance, loyalty and life, of them, but it cannot protect them against the most palpable violation of the rights of human nature, rights to secure which, governments are established. It can tax their bread and tax their blood, but has no protecting power for their persons. Its National power extends only to the District of Columbia, and the Territories—where the people have no votes—and where the land has no people. All else is subject to the States. In the name of common sense, I ask, what right have we to call ourselves a Nation, in view of this decision, and this utter destitution of power?

In humiliating the colored people of this country, this decision has humbled the Nation. It gives to a South Carolina, or a Mississippi, Rail-Road Conductor, more power than it gives to the National Government. . . .

The lesson of all the ages on this point is, that a wrong done to one man, is a wrong done to all men. It may not be felt at the moment, and the evil day may be long delayed, but so sure as there is a moral government of the universe, so sure will the harvest of evil come. . . .

To-day, our Republic sits as a Queen among the nations of the earth. Peace is within her walls and plenteousness within her palaces, but he is a bolder and a far more hopeful man than I am, who will affirm that this peace and prosperity will always last. History repeats itself. What has happened once may happen again.

The negro, in the Revolution, fought for us and with us. In the war of 1812 Gen. Jackson, at New Orleans, found it necessary to call upon the colored people to assist in its defence against England. Abraham Lincoln found it necessary to call upon the negro to defend the Union against rebellion, and the negro responded gallantly in all cases.

Our legislators, our Presidents, and our judges should have a care, lest, by forcing these people, outside of law, they destroy that love of country which is needful to the Nation's defence in the day of trouble.

I am not here, in this presence, to discuss the constitutionality or unconstitutionality of this decision of the Supreme Court. The decision may or may not be constitutional. That is a question for lawyers, and not for laymen, and there are lawyers on this platform as learned, able, and eloquent as any who have appeared in this case before the Supreme Court, or as any in the land. To these I leave the exposition of the Constitution; but I claim the right to remark upon a strange and glaring inconsistency with former decisions, in the action of the court on this Civil Rights Bill. It is a new departure, entirely out of the line of the precedents and decisions of the Supreme Court at other times and in other directions where the rights of colored men were concerned. It has utterly ignored and rejected the force and application of object and intention as a rule of interpretation. It has construed the Constitution in defiant disregard of what was the object and intention of the adoption of the Fourteenth Amendment. It has made no account whatever of the intention and purpose of Congress and the President in putting the Civil Rights Bill upon the Statute Book of the Nation. It has seen fit in this case, affecting a weak and much-persecuted people, to be guided by the narrowest and most restricted rules of legal interpretation. It has viewed both the Constitution and the law with a strict regard to their letter, but without any generous recognition of their broad and liberal spirit. Upon those narrow principles the decision is logical and legal, of course. But what I complain of, and what every lover of liberty in the United States has a right to complain of, is this sudden and causeless reversal of all the great rules of legal interpretation by which this Court was governed in other days, in the construction of the Constitution and of laws respecting colored people. . . .

Fellow-citizens! while slavery was the base line of American society, while it ruled the church and the state, while it was the interpreter of our law and the exponent of our religion, it admitted no quibbling, no narrow rules of legal or scriptural interpretations of Bible or Constitution. It sternly demanded its pound of flesh, no matter how much blood was shed in the taking of it. It was enough for it to be able to show the *intention* to get all it asked in the Courts or out of the Courts. But now slavery is abolished. Its reign was long, dark and bloody. Liberty *now*, is the base line of the Republic. Liberty has supplanted slavery, but I fear it has not supplanted the spirit or power of slavery. Where slavery was strong, liberty is now weak.

O for a Supreme Court of the United States which shall be as true to the claims of humanity, as the Supreme Court formerly was to the demands of slavery! When that day comes, as come it will, a Civil Rights Bill will not be declared unconstitutional and void, in utter and flagrant disregard of the objects and *intentions* of the National legislature by which it was enacted, and of the rights plainly secured by the Constitution.

This decision of the Supreme Court admits that the Fourteenth Amendment is a prohibition of the States. It admits that a State shall not abridge the privileges or immunities of citizens of the United States, but commits the seeming absurdity of allowing the people of a State to do what it prohibits the State itself from doing.

It used to be thought that the whole was more than a part; that the greater included the less, and that what was unconstitutional for a State to do was equally unconstitutional for an individual member of a State to do. What is a State, in the absence of the people who compose it? Land, air and water. That is all. As individuals, the people of the State of South Carolina may stamp out the rights of the negro wherever they please, so long as they do not do so as a State. All the parts can violate the Constitution, but the whole cannot. It is not the act itself, according to this decision, that is unconstitutional. The unconstitutionality of the case depends wholly upon the party committing the act. If the State commits it, it is wrong, if the citizen of the State commits it, it is right.

O consistency, thou art indeed a jewel! What does it matter to a colored citizen that a State may not insult and outrage him, if a citizen of a State may? The effect upon him is the same, and it was just this effect that the framers of the Fourteenth Amendment plainly intended by that article to prevent.

It was the act, not the instrument, which was prohibited. It meant to protect the newly enfranchised citizen from injustice and wrong, not merely from a State, but from the individual members of a State. It meant to give him the protection to which his citizenship, his loyalty, his allegiance, and his services entitled him; and this meaning, and this purpose, and this intention, is now declared unconstitutional and void, by the Supreme Court of the United States.

I say again, fellow-citizens, O for a Supreme Court which shall be as true, as vigilant, as active, and exacting in maintaining laws enacted for the protection of human rights, as in other days was that Court for the destruction of human rights!

It is said that this decision will make no difference in the treatment of colored people; that the Civil Rights Bill was a dead letter, and could not be enforced. There is some truth in all this, but it is not the whole truth. That bill, like all advance legislation, was a banner on the outer wall of American liberty, a noble moral standard, uplifted for the education of the American people. There are tongues in trees, books, in the running brooks—sermons in stones. This law, though dead, did speak. It expressed the sentiment of justice and fair play, common to every honest heart. Its voice was against popular prejudice and meanness. It appealed to all the noble and patriotic instincts of the American people. It told the American people that they were all equal before the law; that they belonged to a common country and were equal citizens. The Supreme Court has hauled down this flag of liberty in open day, and before all the people, and has thereby given joy to the heart of every man in the land who wishes to deny to others what he claims for himself. It is a concession to race pride, selfishness and meanness, and will be received with joy by every upholder of caste in the land, and for this I deplore and denounce that decision. . . .

Another illustration of this tendency to put opponents in a false position, is seen in the persistent effort to stigmatize the "Civil Rights Bill" as a "Social Rights Bill." Now, nowhere under the whole heavens, outside of the United States, could any such perversion of truth have any chance of success. No man in Europe would ever dream that because he has a right to ride on a railway, or stop at a hotel, he therefore has the right to enter into social relations with anybody. No one has a right to speak to another without that other's permission. Social equality and civil equality rest upon an entirely different basis, and well enough the American people know it; yet to inflame a popular prejudice, respectable papers like the New York Times and the Chicago Tribune, persist in describing the Civil Rights Bill as a Social Rights Bill.

When a colored man is in the same room or in the same carriage with white people, as a servant, there is no talk of social equality, but if he is there as a man and a gentleman, he is an offence. What makes the difference? It is not color, for his color is unchanged. The whole essence of the thing is a studied purpose to degrade and stamp out the liberties of a race. It is the old spirit of slavery, and nothing else. To say that because a man rides in the same car with another, he is therefore socially equal, is one of the wildest absurdities. . . .

If it is a Bill for social equality, so is the Declaration of Independence, which declares that all men have equal rights; so is the Sermon on the Mount, so is the Golden Rule, that commands us to do to others as we would that others should do to us; so is the Apostolic teaching, that of one blood God has made all nations to dwell on all the face of the earth; so is the Constitution of the United States, and so are the laws and customs of every civilized country in the world; for no where, outside of the United States, is any man denied civil rights on account of his color.

21. Spokesman for Segregation: Henry W. Grady, April 1885

BY THE 1880s the South had developed a leadership and a rationale which looked to the economic development of the section with the sympathetic cooperation of Northern men of substance. The most persuasive spokesman for the "New South" was a young Georgian journalist, who became editor and part-owner of the influential Atlanta Constitution. Although his most widely acclaimed appeal to the North for understanding was an address before the New England Society of New York City in December 1886, the article reprinted below deals more centrally with the "negro question." Notice the link between Grady's forthright defense of segregation and the civil rights decision two years earlier. Also significant is his position in respect to Negro suffrage, which

SOURCE: Century Magazine, XXIX (April 1885):909–917.

should be compared with that of Southern spokesmen just a few years later (doc. 22a and c), when Republicans had at long last regained suf-ficient power to present a clear and present danger to Southern self-determination of racial policy.

In Plain Black and White
a Reply to Mr. Cable

It is strange that during the discussion of the negro question, which has been wide and pertinent, no one has stood up to speak the mind of the South. In this discussion there has been much of truth and more of error—something of perverseness, but more of misapprehension—not a little of injustice, but perhaps less of mean intention.

Amid it all, the South has been silent.

There has been, perhaps, good reason for this silence. The problem under debate is a tremendous one. Its right solution means peace, prosperity, and happiness to the South. A mistake, even in the temper in which it is approached or the theory upon which its solution is attempted, would mean detriment, that at best would be serious, and might easily be worse. Hence the South has pondered over this problem, earnestly seeking with all her might the honest and the safe way out of its entanglements, and saying little because there was but little to which she felt safe in committing herself. Indeed, there was another reason why she did not feel called upon to obtrude her opinions. The people of the North proceeding by the right of victorious arms, had themselves undertaken to settle the negro question. From the Emancipation Proclamation to the Civil Rights Bill they hurried with little let or hindrance, holding the negro in the meanwhile under a sort of tutelage, from part in which his former masters were practically excluded. Under this state of things the South had little to do but watch and learn.

We have now passed fifteen years of experiment. Certain broad principles have been established as wise and just. The South has something to say which she can say with confidence. There is no longer impropriety in her speaking or lack of weight in her words. The people of the United States have, by their suffrages, remitted to the Southern people, temporarily at least, control of the race question. The decision of the Supreme Court on the Civil Rights Bill leaves practically to their adjustment important issues that were, until that decision was rendered, covered by straight and severe enactment. These things deepen the responsibility of the South, increase its concern, and confront it with a problem to which it must address itself promptly and frankly. Where it has been silent, it now should speak. The interest of every American in the honorable and equitable settlement of this question is second only to the interest of those specially—and fortunately, we believe —charged with its adjustment. "What will you do with it?" is a question any man may now ask the South, and to which the South should make frank and full reply.

It is important that this reply shall be plain and straightforward. Above all things it must carry the genuine convictions of the people it represents. On this subject and at this time the South cannot afford to be misunderstood. Upon the clear and general apprehension of her position and of her motives and purpose everything depends. She cannot let pass unchallenged a single utterance that, spoken in her name, misstates her case or her intention. It is to protest against just such injustice that this article is written.

In a lately printed article, Mr. George W. Cable, writing in the name of the Southern people, confesses judgment on points that they still defend, and commits them to a line of thought from which they must forever dissent. In this article, as in his works, the singular tenderness and beauty of which have justly made him famous, Mr. Cable is sentimental rather than practical. But the reader, enchained by the picturesque style and misled by the engaging candor with which the author admits the shortcomings of "We of the South," and the kindling enthusiasm with which he tells how "We of the South" must make reparation, is apt to assume that it is really the soul of the South that breathes through Mr. Cable's repentant sentences. It is not my purpose to discuss Mr. Cable's relations to the people for whom he claims to speak. Born in the South, of Northern parents, he appears to have had little sympathy with his Southern environment, as in 1882 he wrote, "To be in New England would be enough for me. I was there once,—a year ago,—and it seemed as if I had never been home till then." It will be suggested that a man so out of harmony with his neighbors as to say, even after he had fought side by side with them on the battle-field, that he never felt at home until he had left them, cannot speak understandingly of their views on so vital a subject as that under discussion. But it is with his statement rather than his personality that we have to deal. Does he truly represent the South? We reply that he does not! There may be here and there in the South a dreaming theorist who subscribes to Mr. Cable's teachings. We have seen no signs of one. Among the thoughtful men of the South,—the men who felt that all brave men might quit fighting when General Lee surrendered,—who, enshrining in their hearts the heroic memories of the cause they had lost, in good faith accepted the arbitrament of the sword to which they had appealed,—who bestirred themselves cheerfully amid the ruins of their homes, and set about the work of rehabilitation,—who have patched and mended and builded anew, and fashioned out of pitiful resource a larger prosperity than they ever knew before,—who have set their homes on the old red hills, and staked their honor and prosperity and the peace and well-being of the children who shall come after them on the clear and equitable solution of every social, industrial, or political problem that concerns the South,— among these men, who control and will continue to control, I do know, there is general protest against Mr. Cable's statement of the case, and universal protest against his suggestions for the future. The mind of these men I shall attempt to speak, maintaining my right to speak for them with the pledge that, having exceptional means for knowing their views on this subject, and having spared no pains to keep fully informed thereof, I shall write down nothing in their name on which I have found even a fractional difference of opinion.

A careful reading of Mr. Cable's article discloses the following argument: The Southern people have deliberately and persistently evaded the laws forced on them for the protection of the freedman; this evasion has been the result of prejudices born of and surviving the institution of slavery, the only way to remove which is to break down every distinction between the races; and now the best thought of the South, alarmed at the withdrawal of the political machinery that forced the passage of the protective laws, which withdrawal tempts further and more intolerable evasions, is moving to forbid all further assortment of the races and insist on their intermingling in all places and in all relations. The first part of this argument is a matter of record, and, from the Southern standpoint, mainly a matter of reputation. It can bide its time. The suggestion held in its conclusion is so impossible, so mischievous, and, in certain aspects, so monstrous, that it must be met at once.

It is hard to think about the negro with exactness. His helplessness, his generations of enslavement, his unique position among
the peoples of the earth, his distinctive color, his simple, lovable
traits,—all these combine to hasten opinion into conviction where
he is the subject of discussion. Three times has this tendency
brought about epochal results in his history. First, it abolished slavery. For this all men are thankful, even those who, because of the
personal injustice and violence of the means by which it was
brought about, opposed its accomplishment. Second, it made him
a voter. This, done more in a sense of reparation than in judgment,
is as final as the other. The North demanded it; the South expected
it; all acquiesced in it, and, wise or unwise, it will stand. Third, it
fixed by enactment his social and civil rights. And here for the first
time the revolution faltered. Up to this point the way had been
plain, the light clear, and the march at quick-step. Here the line
halted. The way was lost; there was hesitation, division, and uncertainty. Knowing not which way to turn, and enveloped in doubt,
the revolutionists heard the retreat sounded by the Supreme Court
with small reluctance, and, to use Mr. Cable's words, "bewildered
by complication, vexed by many a blunder," retired from the field.
See, then, the progress of this work. The first step, right by universal agreement, would stand if the law that made it were withdrawn.
The second step, though irrevocable, raises doubts as to its wisdom.
The third, wrong in purpose, has failed in execution. It stands
denounced as null by the highest court, as inoperative by general
confession, and as unwise by popular verdict. Let us take advantage
of this halt in the too rapid revolution, and see exactly where we
stand and what is best for us to do. The situation is critical. The
next moment may formulate the work of the next twenty years.
The tremendous forces of the revolution, unspent and still terrible,
are but held in arrest. Launch them mistakenly, chaos may come.
Wrong-headedness may be as fatal now as wrong-heartedness.
Clear views, clear statement, and clear understanding are the
demands of the hour. Given these, the common sense and courage
of the American people will make the rest easy.

Let it be understood in the beginning, then, that the South will
never adopt Mr. Cable's suggestion of the social intermingling of
the races. It can never be driven into accepting it. So far from there
being a growing sentiment in the South in favor of the indiscriminate mixing of the races, the intelligence of both races is moving

farther from that proposition day by day. It is more impossible (if I may shade a superlative) now than it was ten years ago; it will be less possible ten years hence. Neither race wants it. The interest, as the inclination, of both races is against it. Here the issue with Mr. Cable is made up. He denounces any assortment of the races as unjust, and demands that white and black shall intermingle everywhere. The South replies that the assortment of the races is wise and proper, and stands on the platform of equal accommodation for each race, but separate.

The difference is an essential one. Deplore or defend it as we may, an antagonism is bred between the races when they are forced into mixed assemblages. This sinks out of sight, if not out of existence, when each race moves in its own sphere. Mr. Cable admits this feeling, but doubts that it is instinctive. In my opinion it is instinctive—deeper than prejudice or pride, and bred in the bone and blood. It would make itself felt even in sections where popular prejudice runs counter to its manifestation. If in any town in Wisconsin or Vermont there was equal population of whites and blacks, and schools, churches, hotels, and theaters were in common, this instinct would assuredly develop; the races would separate, and each race would hasten the separation. Let me give an example that touches this supposition closely. Bishop Gilbert Haven, of the Methodist Episcopal Church, many years ago came to the South earnestly, and honestly, we may believe, devoted to breaking up the assortment of the races. He was backed by powerful influences in the North. He was welcomed by resident Northerners in the South (then in control of Southern affairs) as an able and eloquent exponent of their views. His first experiment toward mixing the races was made in the church—surely the most propitious field. Here the fraternal influence of religion emphasized his appeals for the brotherhood of the races. What was the result? After the first month his church was decimated. The Northern whites and the Southern blacks left it in squads. The dividing influences were mutual. The stout bishop contended with prayer and argument and threat against the inevitable, but finally succumbed. Two separate churches were established, and each race worshiped to itself. There had been no collision, no harsh words, no discussion even. Each race simply obeyed its instinct, that spoke above the appeal of the bishop and dominated the divine influences that pulsed from pew to pew. Time and again did the bishop force the experiment. Time and again he failed. At last he was driven to the confession that but one thing could effect what he had tried so hard to bring about, and that was miscegenation. A few years of experiment would force Mr. Cable to the same conclusion.

The same experiment was tried on a larger scale by the Methodist Episcopal Church (North) when it established its churches in the South after the war. It essayed to bring the races together, and in its conferences and its churches there was no color line. Prejudice certainly did not operate to make a division here. On the contrary, the whites and blacks of this church were knit together by prejudice, pride, sentiment, political and even social policy. Underneath all this was a race instinct, obeying which, silently, they drifted swiftly apart. While white Methodists of the church North and of the church South, distant from each other in all but the kinship of race and worship, were struggling to effect once more a union of the churches that had been torn apart by a quarrel over slavery, so that in every white conference and every white church on all this continent white Methodists could stand in restored brotherhood, the Methodist Church (North) agreed, without serious protest, to a separation of its Southern branch into two conferences of whites and of blacks, and into separate congregations where the proportion of either race was considerable. Was it without reason—it certainly was not through prejudice—that this church, while seeking anew fusion with its late enemies, consented to separate from its new friends?

It was the race instinct that spoke there. It spoke not with prejudice, but against it. It spoke there as it speaks always and everywhere—as it has spoken for two thousand years. And it spoke to the reason of each race. Millaud, in voting in the French Convention for the beheading of Louis XVI., said: "If death did not exist, it would be necessary to-day to invent it." So of this instinct. It is the pledge of the integrity of each race, and of peace between the races. Without it, there might be a breaking down of all lines of division and a thorough intermingling of whites and blacks. This once accomplished, the lower and the weaker elements of the races would begin to fuse and the process of amalgamation would have begun. This would mean the disorganization of society. An internecine war would be precipitated. The whites, at any cost and at any hazard, would maintain the clear integrity and dominance of the Anglo-Saxon blood. They understand perfectly that the debasement of their own race would not profit the humble and sincere race with which their lot is cast, and that the hybrid would not gain what either race lost. Even if the vigor and the volume of the Anglo-Saxon blood would enable it to absorb the African current, and after many generations recover its own strength and purity, not all the powers of earth could control the unspeakable horrors that would wait upon the slow process of clarification. Easier far it would be to take the population of central New York, intermingle with it an equal percentage of Indians, and force amalgamation between the two. Let us review the argument. If Mr. Cable is correct in assuming that there is no instinct that keeps the two races separate in the South, then there is no reason for doubting that if intermingled they would fuse. Mere prejudice would not long survive perfect equality and social intermingling; and the prejudice once gone, intermarrying would begin. Then, if there is a race instinct in either race that resents intimate association with the other, it would be unwise to force such association when there are easy and just alternatives. If there is no such instinct, the mixing of the races would mean amalgamation, to which the whites will never submit, and to which neither race should submit. So that in either case, whether the race feeling is instinct or prejudice, we come to but one conclusion: The white and black races in the South must walk apart. Concurrent their courses may go—ought to go—will go—but separate. If instinct did not make this plain in a flash, reason would spell it out letter by letter.

Now, let us see. We hold that there is an instinct, ineradicable and positive, that will keep the races apart, that would keep the races apart if the problem were transferred to Illinois or to Maine, and that will resist every effort of appeal, argument, or force to bring them together. We add in perfect frankness, however, that if no such instinct existed, or if the South had reasonable doubt of its existence, it would, by every means in its power, so strengthen the race prejudice that it would do the work and hold the stubbornness and strength of instinct. The question that confronts us at this point is: Admitted this instinct, that gathers each race to itself. Then, do you believe it possible to carry forward on the same soil and under the same laws two races equally free, practically equal in numbers, and yet entirely distinct and separate? This is a momentous question. It involves a problem that, all things considered, is without a precedent or parallel. Can the South carry this problem in honor and in peace to an equitable solution? We reply that for ten years the South has been doing this very thing, and with at least apparent success. No impartial and observant man can say that in the present aspect of things there is cause for alarm, or even for doubt. In the experience of the past few years there is assuredly reason for encouragement. There may be those who discern danger in the distant future. We do not. Beyond the apprehensions which must for a long time attend a matter so serious, we see nothing but cause for congratulation. In the common sense and the sincerity of the negro, no less than in the intelligence and earnestness of the whites, we find the problem simplifying. So far from the future bringing trouble, we feel confident that another decade or so, confirming the experience of the past ten years, will furnish the solution to be accepted of all men.

Let us examine briefly what the South has been doing, and study the attitude of the races towards each other. Let us do this, not so much to vindicate the past as to clear the way for the future. Let us see what the situation teaches. There must be in the experience of fifteen years something definite and suggestive. We begin with the schools and school management, as the basis of the rest.

Every Southern State has a common-school system, and in every State separate schools are provided for the races. Almost every city of more than five thousand inhabitants has a public-school system, and in every city the schools for whites and blacks are separate. There is no exception to this rule that I can find. In many cases the law creating this system requires that separate schools shall be provided for the races. This plan works admirably. There is no friction in the administration of the schools, and no suspicion as to the ultimate tendency of the system. The road to school is clear, and both races walk therein with confidence. The whites, assured that the school will not be made the hot-bed of false and pernicious ideas, or the scene of unwise associations, support the system cordially, and insist on perfect equality in grade and efficiency. The blacks, asking no more than this, fill the schools with alert and eager children. So far from feeling debased by the separate-school system, they insist that the separation shall be carried further, and the few white teachers yet presiding over negro schools supplanted by negro teachers. The appropriations for public schools are increased year after year, and free education grows constantly in strength and popularity. Cities that were afraid to commit themselves to free schools while mixed schools were a possibility commenced building school-houses as soon as separate schools were assured. In 1870 the late Benjamin H. Hill found his matchless eloquence unable to carry the suggestion of negro education into popular tolerance. Ten years later nearly one million black children attended free schools, supported by general taxation. Though the whites pay nineteen-twentieths of the tax, they insist that the blacks shall share its advantages equally. The schools for each race are opened on the same day and closed on the same day. Neither is run a single day at the expense of the other. The negroes are satisfied with the situation. I am aware that some of the Northern teachers of negro high-schools and universities will controvert this. Touching their opinion, I have only to say that it can hardly be considered fair or conservative. Under the forcing influence of social ostracism, they have reasoned impatiently and have been helped to conclusions by quick sympathies or resentments. Driven back upon themselves and hedged in by suspicion or hostility, their service has become a sort of martyrdom, which has swiftly stimulated opinion into conviction and conviction into fanaticism. I read in a late issue of "Zion's Herald" a letter from one of these teachers, who declined, on the conductor's request, to leave the car in which she was riding, and which was set apart exclusively for negroes. The conductor, therefore, presumed she was a quadroon, and stated his presumption in answer to inquiry of a young negro man who was with her. She says of this:

> Truly, a glad thrill went through my heart—a thrill of pride. This great autocrat had pronounced me as not only in sympathy, but also one in blood, with the truest, tenderest, and noblest race that dwells on earth.

If this quotation, which is now before me over the writer's name, suggests that she and those of her colleagues who agree with her have narrowed within their narrowing environment, and acquired artificial enthusiasm under their unnatural conditions, so that they must be unsafe as advisers and unfair as witnesses, the sole purpose for which it is introduced will have been served. This suggestion does not reach all Northern teachers of negro schools. Some have taken broader counsels, awakened wider sympathies, and, as a natural result, hold more moderate views. The influence of the extremer faction is steadily diminishing. Set apart, as small and curious communities are set here and there in populous States, stubborn and stiff for a while, but overwhelmed at last and lost in the mingling currents, these dissenting spots will be ere long blotted out and forgotten. The educational problem, which is their special care, has already been settled, and the settlement accepted with a heartiness that precludes the possibility of its disturbance. From the stand-point of either race the experiment of distinct but equal schools for the white and black children of the South has demonstrated its wisdom, its policy, and its justice, if any experiment every made plain its wisdom in the hands of finite man.

I quote on this subject Gustavus J. Orr, one of the wisest and best of men, and lately elected, by spontaneous movement, president of the National Educational Association. He says: "The race question in the schools is already settled. We give the negroes equal advantages, but separate schools. This plan meets the reason and satisfies the instinct of both races. Under it we have spent over five million dollars in Georgia, and the system grows in strength constantly." I asked if the negroes wanted mixed schools. His reply was prompt: "They do not. I have questioned them carefully on this point, and they make but one reply: They want their children in their own schools and under their own teachers." I asked what would be the effect of mixed schools. "I could not maintain the Georgia system one year. Both races would protest against it. My record as a public-school man is known. I have devoted my life to the work of education. But I am so sure of the evils that would come from mixed schools that, even if they were possible, I would see the whole educational system swept away before I would see them established. There is an instinct that gathers each race about itself. It is as strong in the blacks as in the whites, though it has not asserted itself so strongly. It is making itself manifest, since the blacks are organizing a social system of their own. It has long controlled them in their churches, and it is now doing so in their schools."

In churches, as in schools, the separation is perfect. The negroes, in all denominations in which their membership is an appreciable percentage of the whole, have their own churches, congregations, pastors, conferences, and bishops, their own missionaries. There is not the slightest antagonism between them and the white churches of the same denomination. On the contrary, there is sympathetic interest and the utmost friendliness. The separation is recognized as not only instinctive but wise. There is no disposition to disturb it, and least of all on the part of the negro. The church is with him the center of social life, and there he wants to find his own people and no others. . . .

In their social institutions, as in their churches and schools, the negroes have obeyed their instinct and kept apart from the whites. They have their own social and benevolent societies, their own military companies, their own orders of Masons and Odd-fellows. They rally about these organizations with the greatest enthusiasm and support them with the greatest liberality. If it were proposed to merge them with white organizations of the same character, with equal rights guaranteed in all, the negroes would interpose the stoutest objection. Their tastes, associations, and inclinations— their instincts—lead them to gather their race about social centers of its own. I am tempted into trying to explain here what I have never yet seen a stranger to the South able to understand. The feeling that, by mutual action, separates whites and blacks when they are thrown together in social intercourse is not a repellent influence in the harsh sense of that word. It is centripetal rather than centrifugal. It is attractive about separate centers rather than expulsive from a common center. There is no antagonism, for example, between white and black military companies. On occasions they parade in the same street, and have none of the feeling that exists between Orangemen and Catholics. Of course the good sense of each race and the mutual recognition of the possible dangers of the situation have much to do with maintaining the good-will between the distinct races. The fact that in his own church or society the negro has more freedom, more chance for leadership and for individual development, than he could have in association with the whites, has more to do with it. But beyond all this is the fact that, in the segregation of the races, blacks as well as whites obey a natural instinct, which, always granting that they get equal justice and equal advantages, they obey without the slightest ill-nature or without any sense of disgrace. They meet the white people in all the avenues of business. They work side by side with the white bricklayer or carpenter in perfect accord and friendliness. When the trowel or the hammer is laid aside, the laborers part, each going his own way. Any attempt to carry the comradeship of the day into private life would be sternly resisted by both parties in interest.

We have seen that in churches, schools, and social organizations the whites and blacks are moving along separately but harmoniously, and that the "assortment of the races," which has been described as shameful and unjust, is in most part made by the instinct of each race, and commands the hearty assent of both. Let us now consider the question of public carriers. On this point the South has been sharply criticised, and not always without reason. It is manifestly wrong to make a negro pay as much for a railroad ticket as a white man pays, and then force him to accept inferior accommodations. It is equally wrong to force a decent negro into an indecent car, when there is room for him or for her elsewhere. Public sentiment in the South has long recognized this, and has persistently demanded that the railroad managers should provide cars for the negroes equal in every respect to those set apart for the whites, and that these cars should be kept clean and orderly. In Georgia a State law requires all public roads or carriers to provide equal accommodation for each race, and failure to do so is made a penal offense. In Tennessee a negro woman lately gained damages by proving that she had been forced to take inferior accommodation on a train. The railroads have, with few exceptions, come up to the requirements of the law. Where they fail, they quickly feel the weight of public opinion, and shock the sense of public justice. This very discussion, I am bound to say, will lessen such failures in the future. On four roads, in my knowledge, even better has been done than the law requires. The car set apart for the negroes is made exclusive. No whites are permitted to occupy it. A white man who strays into this car is politely told that it is reserved for the negroes. He has the information repeated two or three times, smiles, and retreats. This rule works admirably and will win general favor. There are a few roads that make no separate provision for the races, but announce that any passenger can ride on any car. Here the "assortment" of the races is done away with, and here it is that most of the outrages of which we hear occur. On these roads the negro has no place set apart for him. As a rule, he is shy about asserting himself, and he usually finds himself in the meanest corners of the train. If he forces himself into the ladies' car, he is apt to provoke a collision. It is on just one of these trains where the assortment of the passengers is left to chance that a respectable negro woman is apt to be forced to ride in a car crowded with negro convicts. Such a thing would be impossible where the issue is fairly met, and a car, clean, orderly, and exclusive, is provided for each race. The case could not be met by grading the tickets and the accommodations. Such a plan would bring together in the second or third class car just the element of both races between whom prejudice runs highest, and from whom the least of tact or restraint might be expected. On the railroads, as elsewhere, the solution of the race problem is, equal advantages for the same money,—equal in comfort, safety, and exclusiveness,—but separate.

There remains but one thing further to consider—the negro in the jury-box. It is assumed generally that the negro has no representation in the courts. This is a false assumption. In the United States courts he usually makes more than half the jury. As to the State courts, I can speak particularly as to Georgia. I assume that she does not materially differ from the other States. In Georgia the law requires that commissioners shall prepare the jury-list for each county by selection from the upright, intelligent, and experienced citizens of the county. This provision was put into the Constitution by the negro convention of reconstruction days. Under its terms no reasonable man would have expected to see the list made up of equal percentage of the races. Indeed, the fewest number of negroes were qualified under the law. Consequently, but few appeared on the lists. The number, as was to be expected, is steadily increasing. In Fulton County there are seventy-four negroes whose names are on the lists, and the commissioners, I am informed, have about doubled this number for the present year. These negroes make good jurymen, and are rarely struck by attorneys, no matter what the client or cause may be. About the worst that can be charged against the jury system in Georgia is that the commissioners have made jurors of negroes only when they had qualified themselves to intelligently discharge a juror's duties. In few quarters of the South, however, is the negro unable to get full and exact justice in the courts, whether the jury be white or black. Immediately after the war, when there was general alarm and irritation, there may have been undue severity in sentences and extreme rigor of prosecution. But the charge that the people of the South have, in their deliberate and later moments, prostituted justice to the oppression of this dependent people, is as false as it is infamous. There is abundant belief that the very helplessness of the negro in court has touched the heart and conscience of many a jury, when the facts should have held them impervious. In the city in which this is written a negro, at midnight, on an unfrequented

street, murdered a popular young fellow, over whose grave a monu-
ment was placed by popular subscription. The only witnesses of the
killing were the friends of the murdered boy. Had the murderer
been a white man, it is believed he would have been convicted. He
was acquitted by the white jury, and has since been convicted of a
murderous assault on a person of his own color. Similarly, a young
white man, belonging to one of the leading families of the State,
was hanged for the murder of a negro. Insanity was pleaded in his
defense, and so plausibly that it is believed he would have escaped
had his victim been a white man.

I quote on this point Mr. Benjamin H. Hill, who has been prosecuting attorney of the Atlanta, Ga., circuit for twelve years. He
says: "In cities and towns the negro gets equal and exact justice
before the courts. It is possible that, in remote counties, where the
question is one of a fight between a white man and a negro, there
may be a lingering prejudice that causes occasional injustice. The
judge, however, may be relied on to correct this. As to negro jurors,
I have never known a negro to allow his lawyer to accept a negro
juror. For the State I have accepted a black juror fifty times, to
have him rejected by the opposing lawyer by order of his negro
client. This has occurred so invariably that I have accepted it as a
rule. Irrespective of that, the negro gets justice in the courts, and
the last remaining prejudice against him in the jurybox has passed
away. I convicted a white man for voluntary manslaughter under
peculiar circumstances. A negro met him on the street and cursed
him. The white man ordered him off and started home. The negro
followed him to his house and cursed him until he entered the
door. When he came out, the negro was still waiting. He renewed
the abuse, followed him to his store, and there struck him with his
fist. In the struggle that followed, the negro was shot and killed.
The jury promptly convicted the slayer."

So much for the relation between the races in the South, in
churches, schools, social organizations, on the railroad, and in
theaters. Everything is placed on the basis of equal accommodations, but separate. In the courts the blacks are admitted to the
jury-box as they lift themselves into the limit of qualification.
Mistakes have been made and injustice has been worked here
and there. This was to have been expected, and it has been less
than might have been expected. But there can be no mistake
about the progress the South is making in the equitable ad-

justment of the relations between the races. Ten years ago nothing was settled. There were frequent collisions and constant apprehensions. The whites were suspicious and the blacks were restless. So simple a thing as a negro taking an hour's ride on the cars, or going to see a play, was fraught with possible danger. The larger affairs—school, church, and court—were held in abeyance. Now all this is changed. The era of doubt and mistrust is succeeded by the era of confidence and good-will. The races meet in the exchange of labor in perfect amity and understanding. Together they carry on the concerns of the day, knowing little or nothing of the fierce hostility that divides labor and capital in other sections. When they turn to social life they separate. Each race obeys its instinct and congregates about its own centers. At the theater they sit in opposite sections of the same gallery. On the trains they ride each in his own car. Each worships in his own church, and educates his children in his schools. Each has his place and fills it, and is satisfied. Each gets the same accommodation for the same money. There is no collision. There is no irritation or suspicion. Nowhere on earth is there kindlier feeling, closer sympathy, or less friction between two classes of society than between the whites and blacks of the South to-day. This is due to the fact that in the adjustment of their relations they have been practical and sensible. They have wisely recognized what was essential, and have not sought to change what was unchangeable. They have yielded neither to the fanatic nor the demagogue, refusing to be misled by the one or misused by the other. While the world has been clamoring over their differences they have been quietly taking counsel with each other, in the field, the shop, the street and cabin, and settling things for themselves. That the result has not astonished the world in the speediness and the facility with which it has been reached, and the beneficence that has come with it, is due to the fact that the result has not been freely proclaimed. It has been a deplorable condition of our politics that the North has been misinformed as to the true condition of things in the South. Political greed and passion conjured pestilential mists to becloud what the lifting smoke of battle left clear. It has exaggerated where there was a grain of fact, and invented where there was none. It has sought to establish the most casual occurrences as the settled habit of the section, and has sprung endless jeremiads from one single disorder, as Jenkins filled the courts of Christendom with lamentations over his dissevered ear. These misrepresentations will pass away with the occasion that provoked them, and when the truth is known it will come with the force of a revelation to vindicate those who have bespoken for the South a fair trial, and to confound those who have borne false witness against her.

One thing further need be said, in perfect frankness. The South must be allowed to settle the social relations of the races according to her own views of what is right and best. There has never been a moment when she could have submitted to have the social status of her citizens fixed by an outside power. She accepted the emancipation and the enfranchisement of her slaves as the legitimate results of war that had been fought to a conclusion. These once accomplished, nothing more was possible. "Thus far and no farther," she said to her neighbors, in no spirit of defiance, but with quiet determination. In her weakest moments, when her helpless people were hedged about by the unthinking bayonets of her conquerors, she gathered them for resistance at this point. Here she defended everything that a people should hold dear. There was little proclamation of her purpose. Barely did the whispered word that bespoke her resolution catch the listening ears of her sons; but, for all this, the victorious armies of the North, had they been rallied again from their homes, could not have enforced and maintained among this disarmed people the policy indicated in the Civil Rights bill. Had she found herself unable to defend her social integrity against the arms that were invincible on the fields where she staked the sovereignty of her States, her people would have abandoned their homes and betaken themselves into exile. Now, as then, the South is determined that, come what may, she must control the social relations of the two races whose lots are cast within her limits. It is right that she should have this control. The problem is hers, whether or not of her seeking, and her very existence depends on its proper solution. Her responsibility is greater, her knowledge of the case more thorough than that of others can be. The question touches her at every point; it presses on her from every side; it commands her constant attention. Every consideration of policy, of honor, of pride, of common sense impels her to the exactest justice and the fullest equity. She lacks the ignorance or misapprehension that might lead others into mistakes; all others lack the appalling alternative that, all else failing, would force her to use her knowledge wisely. For these reasons she has reserved to herself the right to settle the still unsettled element of the race problem, and this right she can never yield.

As a matter of course, this implies the clear and unmistakable domination of the white race in the South. The assertion of that is simply the assertion of the right of character, intelligence, and property to rule. It is simply saying that the responsible and steadfast element in the community shall control, rather than the irresponsible and the migratory. It is the reassertion of the moral power that overthrew the scandalous reconstruction governments, even though, to the shame of the republic be it said, they were supported by the bayonets of the General Government. Even the race issue is lost at this point. If the blacks of the South wore white skins, and were leagued together in the same ignorance and irresponsibility under any other distinctive mark than their color, they would progress not one step farther toward the control of affairs. Or if they were transported as they are to Ohio, and there placed in numerical majority of two to one, they would find the white minority there asserting and maintaining control, with less patience, perhaps, than many a Southern State has shown. Everywhere, with such temporary exceptions as afford demonstration of the rule, intelligence, character, and property will dominate in spite of numerical differences. These qualities are lodged with the white race in the South, and will assuredly remain there for many generations at least; so that the white race will continue to dominate the colored, even if the percentages of race increase deduced from the comparison of a lame census with a perfect one, and the omission of other considerations, should hold good and the present race majority be reversed.

Let no one imagine, from what is here said, that the South is careless of the opinion or regardless of the counsel of the outside world. On the contrary, while maintaining firmly a position she believes to be essential, she appreciates heartily the value of general sympathy and confidence. With an earnestness that is little less than pathetic she bespeaks the patience and the impartial judgment of all concerned. Surely her situation should command this, rather than indifference or antagonism. In poverty and defeat,— with her cities destroyed, her fields desolated, her labor disorganized, her homes in ruins, her families scattered, and the ranks of her sons decimated,—in the face of universal prejudice, fanned by the storm of war into hostility and hatred,—under the shadow of this sorrow and this disadvantage, she turned bravely to confront a problem that would have taxed to the utmost every resource of a rich and powerful and victorious people. Every inch of her progress has been beset with sore difficulties; and if the way is now clearing, it only reveals more clearly the tremendous import of the work to which her hands are given. It must be understood that she desires to silence no criticism, evade no issue, and lessen no responsibility. She recognizes that the negro is here to stay. She knows that her honor, her dear name, and her fame, no less than her prosperity, will be measured by the fullness of the justice she gives and guarantees to this kindly and dependent race. She knows that every mistake made and every error fallen into, no matter how innocently, endanger her peace and her reputation. In this full knowledge she accepts the issue without fear or evasion. She says, not boldly, but conscious of the honesty and the wisdom of her convictions: "Leave this problem to my working out. I will solve it in calmness and deliberation, without passion or prejudice, and with full regard for the unspeakable equities it holds. Judge me rigidly, but judge me by my works." And with the South the matter may be left—must be left. There it can be left with the fullest confidence that the honor of the republic will be maintained, the rights of humanity guarded, and the problem worked out in such exact justice as the finite mind can measure or finite agencies administer.

HENRY W. GRADY.

22. Equal Suffrage and White Racism: The Public Controversy, 1889–1890

THE SOUTHERN APPEAL to Northern race prejudice and Northern economic self-interest, the former equated with a recognition of scientific fact, accelerated as Southerners sought to offset any possibility of national interference with "home rule" following Republican victories in the 1888 elections. The first and third selections below are influential examples of Southern salesmanship. Note that the false stereotype of Republican Reconstruction as one of unrelieved corruption, inefficiency, and Negro domination had become an important weapon in the defense of Southern white supremacy. John T. Morgan was senator from Alabama from 1877 until his death in 1907, and Hilary A. Herbert, who later served in Cleveland's cabinet, was a member of Congress from the same state when he published Why the Solid South. Of the fourteen contributors to that volume, all Southerners, three were senators, five were congressmen, and one was a former congressman.

White supremacists commanded a national audience in the 1880s, but it was not theirs alone. Two effective publicists for equal rights were celebrated novelists of their day, George W. Cable, a recently transplanted Southerner (see doc. 35), and Albion W. Tourgée a former carpetbagger (see doc. 17b). It was Tourgée, a lawyer and former judge as well as a man of letters, who responded to an appeal from Negro leaders in New Orleans to develop a test case against enforced segregation. The result was Plessy v. Ferguson in which Tourgée served as chief counsel without fee. His brief provided some of the arguments used by Justice Harlan in his resounding dissent.

a. John T. Morgan: "Shall Negro Majorities Rule?"

THE population of the United States is made up, mainly, of two races of men, the Caucasian and the African, more than one-seventh being of the latter. In thirteen contiguous States nearly 40 per cent. of the inhabitants are Negroes. In three States the Negroes outnumber the whites. In all political matters the law declares these races to be equal, and secures to men of each all the rights, privileges, and immunities of citizenship that belong to men of the other. In the relations of these races, so different from each other in mental, moral, and physical characteristics, is the "Negro question," which is now receiving, and will hereafter demand in greater degree, the most serious consideration of thinking men of every class and of all sections of the country. . . .

It is a question of race conflict. In whatever connection it is considered, whether in church or social relations, in business, professional, or industrial employments, or in politics, it is a matter of race. Every result that we have reached, or that we can reach, whether it has been worked out by the Negroes in their natural progress, or by the whites in their endeavors to elevate the Negroes, is a consequence of race conflict. Neither race is responsible for the conditions that make this conflict instinctive and irreconcilable, and neither can avoid the issue or its consequences under the circumstances in which both are placed.

These races, brought together here on terms of political equality, are not equal or homogeneous. Their amalgamation is impossible, because it is forbidden by the instincts of both. The whites of the

SOURCE: John T. Morgan, "Shall Negro Majorities Rule?" *Forum*, VI (February 1889):586–599.

United States have been remarkably firm and persistent in their insistence upon the maintenance of race distinctions in everything that relates to social existence and progress, and the Negroes have as distinctly shown their aversion to any relaxation of race ties and exclusiveness. The aversion is mutual, and, in a general sense, fixed. . . .

Between the African and the white race the bar to union is still more absolute. To remove it, if it could be removed, would be to lower the whites to the level of the intellectual, moral, and social condition of the Negroes. It would be to destroy the white race. One drop of Negro blood known to exist in the veins of a woman in this country draws her down to the social status of the Negro, and impresses upon her whole life the stamp of the fateful Negro caste, though she may rival the Easter lily in the whiteness of her skin. The Negroes, though they may accept almost any form of association with the whites, are never satisfied with any admixture of the blood of the races. It relaxes the hold of their own race upon their affections. Negroes of mixed blood are inferior among the race to which they belong.

It is irrational to attribute these race antipathies and aversions to the laws of this country or to anything in the manner of their administration and enforcement. They rest upon foundations that men have not built, and are supported by ordinances that human power can neither enact nor amend nor repeal. After we have done all that we can to abolish or to neutralize these race distinctions and the feelings that grow out of them—attempting to set aside the eternal laws of nature—we shall find that we have only marked more plainly the differences between the races, and that we have rooted race prejudices more deeply in the hearts of the inferior races and the whites, at least so far as the Chinese and Negroes are concerned. The Negro question is not, therefore, a southern question, but a race question, that appears in every phase of human existence as distinctly in the North, wherever a considerable number of Negroes is found, as in the South.

The personal relations between the Negroes and the white people are more friendly in the South than in the North, because in the South they are based upon the recognition, by both races, of the leadership and superiority of the white race. This recognition of a natural and obvious fact is not offensive to the Negroes, and the relations that accord with it are not constrained or disagreeable to either race.

The southern white man, from long association with the Negroes as a dependent and inferior race, can afford to indulge for them an honest and cordial regard; while the white man in the North feels that, in any exhibition of regard for the Negro, he is sacrificing the dignity of his race and making a personal condescension. He is willing to punish himself with a certain self-abasement to prove to the Negro that he is no more than his equal, while the Negro is compelled to lower his opinion of the white man in order to believe what he says.

If these race instincts and proclivities are wrong, and appeal to humanity for their correction, it by no means follows that the remedy is to be found within the domain of the legislative power, either State or federal. . . . When we come to make laws for the regulation of the political powers accorded to the African race, this important factor—public opinion—cannot be disregarded. Without its support such laws will fail of their purpose, however they may be sustained by force. Public opinion, in any part of the United States, will ultimately neutralize statutes that violate the instincts of the white race. . . .

It is certain that no law can long be enforced among a people as free as ours when their opposition to it is sincere. This is especially true when such laws demand the humiliation of the white race, or the admission of the Negroes to a dangerous participation, as a race, in the affairs of our government. . . .

The laws that give the ballot to one-fifth of the Negro race appeal to the race prejudice which incites them to persistent effort to accomplish the impossible result of race equality. "Equality before the law" is the phrase in which this demand is expressed, but this condition is impossible without equality in the opinion and conscience of the white race. The question is the same in every State, North or South, where any considerable body of Negroes is found, and the decree of public opinion is the same.

The Negroes are no more capable than we are of setting aside the natural influence of race. The honest Negro will vote with his race at every opportunity, just as the honest white man will vote with his. Every sentiment and affection of the human heart is engaged in behalf of the race to which the voter belongs. It is impossible that any man can vote impartially when a question is presented in which his race is believed to be vitally concerned, and it is folly to expect such a vote. The sentiment or public opinion of his race will control him beyond his power of resistance. Education, refinement, wealth, and the consciousness of personal merit add a stronger jealousy to the power of race, and continually widen the separation between the white and Negro races. This effect is more decided with the Negro than it is with the white race. It has increased every day since the Negroes were emancipated. They demand, with greater earnestness than ever before, that their representatives shall be Negroes, and not white men. No solidity of political affiliation can resist this burrowing suspicion of the Negro race that a white man is the natural enemy of the Negro power in government.

We have not accomplished any good to either race by conferring upon 1,500,000 Negroes the privilege of voting. Its effect is only to neutralize the same number of white votes that would otherwise be cast with reference to the general welfare and prosperity of the country. It is needless to recall the history of the race contests that have pervaded the ballot-box under this mistaken policy. The facts are present, in every election, to establish the existence of this national misfortune. Unless the voter can sink his race proclivities and aversions in his sense of duty to his country, it is in vain that we endeavor to compel by law the harmonious action of the white and Negro races, either in voting or in conducting the government. This impossible condition is hidden in the core of the Negro question, and neither law-makers, judges, nor executive officers can remove it. . . .

Outside pressure from people who are in no immediate danger and have nothing at stake but their sentiments of justice or philanthropy, cannot change the conduct or modify the opinions of those who have at risk and in charge, as a trust imposed upon them by the blood of kindred, all that is sacred in society and in family. Such pressure must result in permanent harm to the Negro race, while it may also seriously injure the white race temporarily. If the laws of the States in reference to elections, of which no complaint is made, are evaded, or if they are not enforced, it is because public opinion sets too strongly against them. Laws of Congress which can be executed only through the assistance of the people of the States would meet a similar fate. . . .

The southern people are not mistaken as to the dangers of the ballot in the hands of the Negro race. Twenty years of experience, beginning with eight years of the horrors of enforced Negro rule, has demonstrated to them that a relapse into that condition would be the worst form of destruction. They are no more amenable to moral censure for attempting to avoid that desperate fate than are the people who, in all parts of our country, punish with instant death the Indian or Chinaman or Negro who inflicts a worse fate than death upon an innocent woman. Congress can do nothing to prevent such violations of the laws, even in the Territories and against its wards the Indians and Negroes, or its protégés the Chinamen. . . .

If this is a race question that the existing amendments of the Constitution could not settle or suppress, and if it must be solved at last by the will of the people as it shall be expressed either in support of or against the safety of entrusting political power, under our system of government, to the inferior Negro race, the question will be whether the public sentiment, or public opinion, or the laws, which shall furnish the ultimate solution of the problem, shall be those of the people of the States respectively which have this trouble to meet, or whether other States must interfere, through the action of Congress, to settle the matter in all its details.

In support of the proposition that the people of the States respectively should be left free, under the Constitution, to deal with this difficult problem without the interference of other States, it is first assumed, with evident reason, that Congress cannot successfully control the suffrage of the people in the States by any means. Military coercion would only increase the difficulties, and that resort may be dismissed as impossible. Whatever is done to secure to the Negroes the full use of the ballot must be done through State laws and through public opinion in the States. If the belief of the white race is that the enforcement of these laws will destroy their civilization, the laws will not be executed, though the refusal to execute them should cost the States their representation in Congress.

It must be remembered that it was an entire race of people that we enfranchised with the ballot, and not the individuals of that race who may have been personally competent to use it with judgment for the general good of the people. Our process of enfranchising the Indians is just the reverse of this. We make citizens of them, man by man, and upon the condition of their proving their capacity for citizenship by dissolving their tribal relations and taking lands in severalty. A plan looking to some personal fitness of the Negro for the high duties and corresponding powers of citizenship would not have shocked the common sense of the people, and would have collected into the body of voters in the States those Negroes who had at least some idea of the uses and value of the ballot. The plan we adopted, of transferring the whole of this inferior race into the body of our citizenship, with the powers of government, was a rash experiment, that has not succeeded in accomplishing any good to either race. . . .

Protestations of good will for the Negro race, when made by southern people, are not accepted as being sincere by those who believe that the ex-slaveholder and his posterity are incapable of sympathy or regard for that race of men. The argument, if applied to the ex-slave-catcher and his posterity, would carry with it much more logical strength. If we compare the condition of the Negro, caught in his native land and enslaved, with that of his posterity in the South as it was at the date of the 13th Amendment, simple justice cannot deny to the former slaveholding South the credit of having dealt far more generously with the Negroes than those who caught them in Africa or bought them from the slave ships.

The southern people do not desire to deprive the Negro race of any power or facility that will make freedom a blessing to them. What they seek to avoid is the consolidation of power in the hands of the Negro race that will be used, through the incentives of race aversion, to put them in control of the government of the white race.

Agitation in Congress and in political clubs will keep the prospect of such ascendency ever before the Negroes, and will create opposition to the Negro voter that, otherwise, would be of little effect in any respect, and would never endanger the personal rights of that race. If these questions are permitted to await the solution that experience alone can provide, through the conduct of the people who have befriended this race when they had no other counselors or guides than the slave-hunters, and who have developed this class into a condition that no African Negro ever aspired to, the solution will not, at least, cost us the shame of surrendering Anglo-Saxon civilization to the rule of ignorance and race prejudice. If they are forced into such shape as Negro instincts and the greed for power, common to them and their white leaders, shall compel them to assume, the world cannot censure the southern people if they do not welcome such a solution of the questions as will degrade the race to which we belong from its traditional prestige and wipe out the memory of its former grand achievements. This will not be expected of the South; neither will it be done.

The safe, benevolent, and wise solution of the Negro question can be left to the people of the States respectively, under the Constitution, with far greater security for every right now accorded to the Negroes, and for every blessing that may follow, than it can be to the politicians and agitators in other States.

JOHN T. MORGAN.

b. Albion W. Tourgée:
"Shall White Minorities Rule?"

The "Negro question" is unquestionably the most momentous problem of our civilization. Considered with regard either to its scope or character it is almost unprecedented in importance, difficulty, and the possible peril involved in its solution. It is not a new question. Slavery and the slave trade were only its earlier phases. Rebellion, reconstruction, and ku-kluxism were incidents attending its partial solution. For a hundred years it has almost constantly threatened the life of the republic. . . .

The present phase of the question is a controversy touching the Negro's right to exercise freely, peacefully, and effectually the elective franchise, and to enjoy without hinderance its resulting incidents. It is not fairly presented by the inquiry, "Shall black majorities rule?" The rule of the majority is the fundamental principle of our government. It is one of the incidents of the right to exercise the elective franchise, of which no individual or class can lawfully be deprived while that right remains unrestricted. Some confusion has been produced in the discussion of this question by attempting to treat the elective franchise as a privilege instead of a right. Until duly conferred it is a privilege—a privilege which no individual or class has any legal right to demand. Once granted, however, the exercise and enjoyment of it and of all its natural

SOURCE: Albion W. Tourgée, "Shall White Minorities Rule?" *Forum*, VII (April 1889):143–155.

incidents becomes a right which the sovereign must maintain and enforce, or submit to nullification of the law. The particular point in controversy is not whether the colored man shall be allowed a new privilege, but whether he shall be permitted to exercise a right already guaranteed by law. The proper form of inquiry, therefore, is, "Shall white minorities rule?"

The arguments advanced in support of this monstrous proposition thus far are identical with those adduced in favor of slavery and the slave trade, nullification, secession, rebellion, ku-kluxism— all varying phases, let us not forget, of the same idea. They are urged by the same class of our people, with the same unanimity, the same positiveness, and the same arrogant assumption of infallibility as of old. They not only boastfully admit that for a decade and a half they have nullified the law and defied the national power, but boldly proclaim their determination to continue to do so as long as they may see fit. . . .

In its present phase, the Negro question is not one of sentiment, so far as the colored man is concerned. He asks nothing as a Negro. On the score of "race, color, or previous condition of servitude" he makes no demand, asks no favors. It is as a citizen merely that we are called on to consider what rights and privileges he is entitled to exercise, and how far and in what manner it is just, politic, and safe to permit them to be restricted, abridged, or revoked. Like most political questions, it presents a mixed issue of policy and principle. What is best to be done must depend to a great extent upon what we have the right to do. These elements cannot be separated, and must both be allowed due weight in the final decision.

Even if the claim of inherent superiority of the white race be admitted, it does not follow that it constitutes a sufficient ground for the disfranchisement of the inferior race. The world has moved since it was recognized as a fundamental principle that a divine right to rule inhered in particular classes. The chief function of government at the present time is to protect the weak against the strong. . . .

"Ignorance may struggle up to enlightenment," says Mr. Henry W. Grady, in a recent self-reported speech; "out of corruption may come the incorruptible; but the supremacy of the white race at the South must be maintained forever, simply because it is the white race and is the superior race!" There is no doubt that in this he expresses the conviction of the majority of the white race of the

South; and a people who within thirty years punished as a felon the man who uttered the name of liberty in the slave's hearing or taught him to spell it out himself, would not hesitate to destroy the Negro's opportunity for development in order to keep him weak, dependent, and manageable. Not because the Negro is ignorant or incapable do they object to his exercise of the right of suffrage, but because he is a Negro, and as such they will spare no pains to keep him weak.

But even if the inherent superiority of the white race is admitted, and a consequent right to rule not denied, the means by which alone the rule of white minorities can be secured must make the proposition a most serious one. There are but three methods by which it may be accomplished. Two of them would require an appeal at least to the forms of law; the other pre-supposes a steady and persistent defiance of law. The most direct method would be to restore the term "white" as an essential qualification for citizenship in the State constitutions. . . . Another method in which the derived result might be temporarily attained by apparently legal means, is by imposing an educational qualification upon the voter. Such a course would probably command the approval of a majority of the people of the North. They would no doubt be willing to punish the Negro still further for the crime of having been kept in compulsory ignorance by his white Christian brethren for two centuries and a half, in order to conciliate the white people of the South, and get rid, for a time at least, of the unpleasant and annoying Negro question. There is one difficulty in the way of adopting this plan, to wit: forty-five per cent. of the voters of the eight States in which the matter is most pressing are unable to read their ballots. . . .

There remains only the alternative of deterrent violence or neutralizing fraud, which is frankly admitted to have been in operation for a dozen years or more, and which, it is unmistakably intimated by such men as Mr. Watterson, Senator Eustis, Senator Morgan, and Mr. Grady, is to be indefinitely continued as a means of perpetuating the rule of white minorities. This answers all the required conditions. It saves the Negro as a constituent and neutralizes him as a factor in government. This is what southern writers mean when they insist that white minorities at the South shall be left to deal with the Negro question in their own way. . . .

Another difficulty in the way of this indefinite continuance of unlawful usurpation, is the uncertainty that exists as to the course the Negro himself will pursue in regard to the matter. Thus far the Negro has been counted only a silent factor in the problem to which he has given a name. Slavery no more thought of asking him how he enjoyed his condition than the owner does of inquiring whether his horse prefers to go on the road or disport himself in the pasture.

The discussion of the present phase of the problem was started by the grave inquiry of an eminent ecclesiastic, "What shall we do with the Negro?" Is it not about time that we asked ourselves, What will the Negro permit us to do with him? To this inquiry the advocate of the inherent right of white minorities to rule responds with his usual confidence in his own infallibility: "Just let us alone; we will take care of him; we understand the Negro; leave us to manage him." This confidence is very largely based on the docility and submissiveness of the colored race in the past. The man who advocates continued unlawful repression, seems not to realize that a race which has been a perfect type of humility for centuries when in a position of abject servitude, invariably shows altogether different qualities when once it has set its foot upon the lower rung of the ladder of opportunity. . . .

In view of this, it is well to consider briefly who and what the American Negro is. In the first place, he is an American. Since 1802, when the slave trade was abolished, very few African Negroes have entered the United States. In the second place, he is not a heathen. A larger proportion of the colored people of the United States than of any equal body of whites in the country are actual members of a Christian church. It may be well to remember, too, that very few of them are pure Negroes. . . .

There are other qualities which the colored man has displayed that should incline the enthusiastic advocates of the supremacy of white minorities to pause and think very seriously before they decide upon an indefinite perpetuation of this policy of unlawful and defiant despoliation of political rights. Twenty-four years ago the five millions of newly-enfranchised freemen were not worth all together five million cents. They were naked, helpless, inept. They had hands, and a sort of dull, incomprehensible power to endure; that was all. Within a decade they had $12,000,000 in the savings banks alone. They lived on wages and flourished on conditions that would have exterminated the northern white laborer in a generation. To-day they claim a valuation in the southern States alone of $100,000,000. In Georgia they own nearly a million acres of land. . . .

We often hear the idea advanced that what is termed the "race question" will disappear from politics just as soon as a proper issue is presented. No race can separate into parties or factions while its rights and liberties are assailed by another on the ground of race alone. Their rights must be freely admitted before they will dare to surrender whatever power there may be in cohesion. To do otherwise would be an act of stupendous and incredible folly. One might as well expect a herd of sheep to separate in the presence of wolves. Their only hope is in union. So, too, we hear it said that when the present generation dies off slavery will be only a dream to the colored man. Such is not the lesson of history. The farther a people recede from bondage, the keener is their appreciation of the wrong and the more intense their hate of the oppressor. The horror which the American Negro feels for the institution of slavery will become greater rather than less for several generations at least. When did the Jewish prophets cease to anathematize the Egyptian oppressor? Such antipathies were curable only by continued and undeniable recognition of the right.

"But what can they do?" is the triumphant inquiry which greets the objector who calls attention to these things. "We have the arms, the skill, the experience, the wealth; what can they do?" Truly, the question is not an idle one, yet history clearly teaches that whenever an inferior class, intimately intermingled with a dominant and oppressive caste, becomes both intelligent enough to organize and desperate enough to resist, it is sure to overwhelm the arrogant and better-equipped minority. No man can say when the limit of endurance will be reached if this policy is continued, but that it will be reached in the near future is just as certain as that a boiler will explode if the safety valve is fastened down and the fire kept up. When that day shall come, the advocates of a policy of forcible repression and unlawful subjection will find that the battle is not always to the strong.

Should a conflict arise to-morrow, the odds would by no means be entirely with the white race. Their very wealth might constitute a source of weakness. Black eyes and black ears would take note of every white man's movements. In every camp there would be spies; in every household informers. While the Negro has not so heroic a record as the southern white man, it should not be forgotten that there are 50,000 still living who wore the federal blue and fought for the freedom of their race. Besides that, in a strife such as must result if the occasion for it is not carefully and wisely avoided, it is not valor alone that counts, nor excellence of equipment that assures victory. In such a conflict a box of matches is equal to a hundred Winchester rifles!

In the meantime, neither the nation nor the world would sit still and witness the *auto da fé* of a race. Eight millions of people cannot very long be kept in a subordinate position and despoiled of their guaranteed rights by a minority, however superior and arrogant, through the instrumentality of the shot-gun, the cow-hide, the falsified return, or perjured election officials. It is quite probable that the North might not awake to its duty in the prevention of evil until blood had been shed. Thus far it has entirely failed to realize its responsibility. It has left the Negro to his fate, in seeming unconsciousness that the wrongs of the past must be atoned for either by justice or by disaster. The solution of the Negro question is of all the problems of civilization the simplest and yet the most difficult. The trouble is not with the Negro, who has always been content with half a chance in the world's scramble, but with the southern white man, who is not willing that any one should differ with him in opinion or dissent from him in practice; who is the traditional if not inveterate enemy of free thought and free speech, and is so confident of his own infallibility that he would rather appeal to arms or become a cowardly and disguised murderer, than submit to the control of a lawfully-ascertained majority of legal voters. There cannot be any security for our institutions or any guarantee of our domestic peace, so long as the question of depriving a majority of the qualified electors of any State of the rights which they are solemnly guaranteed by law through any unlawful means is coolly discussed as a living issue in the great organs through which popular thought finds expression. The remedy is a simple one—justice and knowledge. These are all the Negro asks. The superior white race should be ashamed to grant him less. It is not a question of sentiment, nor entirely one of right. As a matter of policy, it resolves itself into an inquiry as to what the American people can afford to do or leave undone—whether we can afford even negatively to admit that white minorities have the right not only to rule, but to nullify and subvert the law of the land, boldly, defiantly, and persistently, in order to bar a lawful majority from the exercises of political power, merely because the minority demand it.

ALBION W. TOURGÉE.

c. Hilary A. Herbert, from Why the Solid South

SUNRISE

PROSPERITY FOLLOWS THE RESTORATION OF GOOD GOVERNMENT.

The days during which the reconstruction governments ruled in the several Southern states were the darkest that ever shrouded any portion of our country.

The slaughter and the sacrifices during our great civil war were terrible indeed, but those dark days were lighted by the shining valor of the patriot soldier; the storm clouds were gilded with glory. . . .

The facts stated in the preceding portions of this book and those shown by these figures present, it is believed, the most startling contrast between the results of good government and bad that can be found in the history of mankind. . . .

The political earthquake that convulsed the Southern States for years, some of them from 1865 to 1876, of course left great fissures, some of which are not yet closed; but the kindly processes of nature are carrying on the work of restoration.

It was and is the misfortune of the Southern people to have to deal with the problems arising out of race prejudices.

The negro had neither the will nor the power to resist the forces which arrayed him against his late master, and the solidification of his vote, by those who were to profit by it, meant, of course, a black man's party; for its majority sentiment determines the complexion of every political party. The domination of the black man's party, officered as it was, meant ruin. To avert ruin white men united; and then came a struggle, the issue of which was in all the States the same. It could not anywhere be doubtful. The race against which the negro had allowed himself to be arrayed has never yet met its master. It could not go down before the African.

SOURCE: Hilary A. Herbert et al, *Why the Solid South? or Reconstruction and its Results* (Baltimore, Md.: 1890), pp. 430–443. The selection is from a chapter written by Herbert; the entire volume is dedicated "TO THE BUSINESS MEN OF THE NORTH."

No true friend of the colored man would, except in ignorance, precipitate such a conflict.

But victor though the white man was, no one could regret the enforced conflict more than did the people of the South. And they set to work at once to make a kindly use of their victories. Under the laws passed by Southern white men the negroes in every Southern State are far more prosperous than they ever were under the rule of those who claimed to be their especial friends.

There is no large body of men of African descent anywhere in the world superior in morals, equal in industry and intelligence, or as well to do as the negroes in the Southern States of this Union. In everything going to make up a prosperous and happy career their condition is infinitely better than that of their brethren in such countries as Hayti, where the colored man reigns supreme. And yet there are those who seem to think it an especial duty to foment among these colored people a spirit of strife and discontent. There is none of this spirit among the masses of their white fellow-citizens in the South. They understand well enough that the one condition upon which prosperity can be hoped for is peace and not strife between the races. They know full well, too, that the laborer will not be valuable either as a citizen or a worker unless he is contented, and that he will not be content unless he is fairly treated. So in every State in the South the effort is being made, and successfully, too, to better the condition of the negro, to train him in the duties of citizenship. These States are expending many millions per annum for educational purposes. . . .

When the negro was a slave the white men of the South made it unlawful to teach him to read. This was to prevent his learning the lesson of insurrection which certain writers in the abolition press were seeking to instil into his mind. The Southern whites then desired to keep the negro in slavery. Now that he is free these same whites are taxing themselves to fit him for freedom.

Let the reader ponder this fact and then answer to himself the question whether the Congress of the United States can wisely enact any law that would tend to revive the conflict of races in the South. Is not the problem of the hour being worked out by the people most interested in its correct solution? Are they not proceeding in the only possible manner? No such problem can be solved at once. Time, and patience, and tact, and experience, gathered on the spot and applied to legislation by those most interested, all these are necessary to its solution.

Any legislation at Washington, based upon the assumption that the negro is wronged and having for its object the ostensible purpose of righting the assumed wrongs by arraying the negro again in solid phalanx against the white man in a contest for supremacy in governmental affairs may result in a catastrophe more appalling than misgovernment, for it would tend towards a conflict of races in the South.

When the reconstruction laws gave the negro the ballot the party that passed these laws claimed of the colored man his vote and secured it. The negroes went to the polls in solid masses for that party. We have seen the results. Wherever they got power their leaders robbed and plundered. Wherever the negro majorities were greatest the degradation of society was most complete and despoliation the most absolute—as in South Carolina and Louisiana. If Congress shall again take control of suffrage the negro will be again appealed to. The party that interferes in his behalf will again claim title to all his ballots, will again urge that he muster all his forces under its banner. The theory upon which these laws are urged undoubtedly must be that this appeal would again succeed; and if it should, then negro majorities would again dominate South Carolina, Mississippi and Louisiana, as well as also many of the richest counties in each of the former slave states.

To the people whose lives and fortunes would thus be imperiled, how appalling the prospect! And not only the properties of Southern, but of Northern men also—railroad stocks, state bonds, city bonds, county bonds, mining and manufacturing interests—all would be in peril. Nay, if the program should be carried out, as it is claimed it would be, with the United States army to enforce the law, and negro domination should again be forced at the South, many a princely fortune would vanish into air. It is amazing that capitalists, proverbially sagacious in their forecasts, should be so quiescent and complacent in view of this threatened legislation. The Southern people themselves look on with the profoundest concern. They judge the future by the past. They themselves passed through the scenes that are only faintly pictured in the preceding pages. Experience has demonstrated to them, what reason itself would teach, that Federal control over election laws and election methods, interference by the General Government, expressly in favor of the blacks and against the whites, would tend to array one race against the other in bitter hostility, that such hostility in a contest for supremacy in affairs of government would engender race conflicts and that race conflicts would furnish an excuse for military interference.

It will not answer to say that conditions have changed. There will be Northern adventurers and native whites in great plenty to lead the negroes. No mass of voters able to put men in power have ever yet lacked for leaders, and it matters not what prejudices the voters have, they will find men to pander to them, and, how great soever their cupidity may be, their chosen representatives will answer to the demands that may be made upon them. No section of our country can impute to any other the exclusive possession of bad men. The North never showed an adventurer who could over-match Moses or Crews of South Carolina and every other Southern state can point to similar examples.

As to whether the attempt to put the South under the dominion of the negro again would succeed, the history of the past may furnish an instructive lesson. Would the army be used more freely than it was in South Carolina, Mississippi or Louisiana, and would the results now be different?

There was a time, just after the close of our Civil War, when Northern capitalists began to look upon the South as a field for investments, but after the carpet-bag governments had had opportunity fully to demonstrate their capacity for evil not a single dollar for investment went into that region for years. Years had elapsed even after the overthrow of these governments, before confidence was restored. Southern men they were, who, with their own capital, demonstrated to the world the resources of the South. At last the North has ceased to doubt either the stability of state governments or the values of Southern properties; and now Northern capital is flowing southward in a steady stream. It is said that to one town in Alabama—now not more than eighteen months old—investors have come from thirty-two of the states of the Union. The flow has only fairly begun. If not checked by some untoward movement it will steadily increase in volume. There is no finer field for investing the surplus capital of the North. There is no better customer for the Northern merchant than the Southerner. There is no more steady demand for the products of the Northwest than comes from the South; and no one can deny that the continued prosperity of that section is necessary to the prosperity of the North and West.

How shall Southern prosperity be continued except by continuing the conditions which brought it about? The chiefest of these are honest, economical state governments. These secure to labor its reward, and to capital its profit.

Our ancestors believed that local self-government was the greatest of blessings. That was the foundation stone upon which was builded all our institutions of government. The unwisdom and peril of departing from this theory has never had a more convincing illustration than in the reconstruction laws of Congress and the results which followed.

Certainly the masses of the people of the distant North, if they had understood the situation at the South as the people there did, and if they could have foreseen the consequences of the reconstruction laws, would not have sanctioned their passage as they did. Intelligent Americans cannot be misled as to facts transpiring in their midst. On these their judgment is always to be trusted; but there is always danger of mistake when voters in any one part of the Union undertake to pass upon questions peculiar to a far-distant section of the country. Herein lies the distinguishing excellence of our complex form of government. Local questions are left to be determined by those most interested in correct conclusions and best acquainted with the facts out of which the questions arise.

It is sincerely to be hoped that the American people may not need to take another lesson in the school of Reconstruction.

HILARY A. HERBERT.

23. Last Republican Battle for Equal Suffrage: The Federal Elections Bill, 1890–1891

LONG PRESENTED as an indefensible "bloody shirt" measure to secure partisan advantage, the Federal Elections Bill of 1890—mislabeled the "Force Bill" by its opponents—is now recognized as a moderate and reasonable proposal, thanks to the careful study made by Richard E. Welch, Jr.[1] Upon the petition of one hundred citizens in a congressional district, federal circuit courts would have been authorized to appoint federal supervisors to watch and report on registration and election pro-

1.   Richard E. Welch, Jr., "The Federal Elections Bill of 1890: Postscript & Prelude," Journal of American History, LII (December 1965):511–526.

cedure; and they would also have been empowered to determine the candidate-elect in case of a disputed election and to initiate investigation of alleged election bribery, intimidation, or fraud. The senators who fought for the measure, headed by George Frisbie Hoar, were determined to redeem their party's pledge to the Negro. Other Republicans may have been more concerned to garner Negro votes in the South, though it is suggestive that the most practical of "politicos," Senators Matthew Quay and James D. Cameron, were either lukewarm or obstructionist.

First passed in the House in July by a majority of six on a strictly partisan vote with only two Republicans breaking ranks, in the Senate the bill was in jeopardy from the start not only from the opposition but also from Republicans eager to pass tariff and silver legislation. Senator Hoar agreed to delay consideration of the measure until after the November elections, thereby giving way to tariff legislation, but only in return for a written pledge signed by every Republican senator save one. The agreement was that in the next session the elections bill would be given undisputed and continuing priority. Early in December, on the opening of the new session, Hoar brought the measure before the Senate and was at once met by Democratic obstruction and filibuster, which provoked him to make the rejoiner reprinted below (doc. a).

A few days later a group of Silver Republicans, in violation of their written commitment, acted with the Democrats to set aside the bill in favor of silver legislation. The first newspaper selection (doc. b), a letter to the editor, was printed in this interim period. Senator Hoar and his supporters rallied and, with a tie vote broken by the vice president on January 14, 1891, again brought the bill before the Senate. Its consideration continued, with even an all-night session, but efforts to close debate failed. On January 26 the bill was finally put aside by a vote of thirty-five to thirty-four, with a handful of Republicans, mostly Silver men, again bearing responsibility. The failure to enact a Federal Elections law has been viewed as a reflection of Northern apathy toward the Negro's civil rights. There can be no doubt but that the status of the Negro by 1890 was no longer the central theme of American politics as it had been in the 1860s, nor that the climate of race prejudice apparent then had continued and intensified. On the other hand the closeness of victory, the slender margin of defeat, and the passionate indignation of a Senator Hoar suggest a surprising tenacity of commitment within the Republican party despite the changing times. The vitality of that commitment, however, was not to survive this major defeat in the battle for justice irrespective of race.

The Mississippi constitution of 1890, to which the Senate debate directed considerable attention, served as a model for other Southern states. Supplementing it by the use of the "grandfather clause" and other devices, they succeeded through "legal" disfranchisement in practically eliminating the Negro as voter in the South by the early twentieth century. Whether the 1890 Federal Elections Bill, if passed, could have reversed this trend is not at all clear. In debate Senator Hoar himself acknowledged that the new "legal" devices for disfranchisement would require additional legislation. Note that he cited the unanimous decision in the Yarbrough case (1884) as ample authority for congressional power to protect the vote. Congressional action was not forthcoming, and the Supreme Court in fact upheld the Mississippi literacy test before the turn of the century. By that time the court had also legitimatized segregation by the "separate but equal" doctrine of the Plessy decision.

a. Senate Debate: Frisbie Hoar, December 29–30, 1890

MR. HOAR [Rep. Mass]. There have been some criticisms on the phraseology of the bill. Some of them are easy to be answered. Some of them are just and are to be met by amendments of phraseology. But, in the main, the attack on this bill, from the other side of the Chamber, except so far as it has been mere railing and reviling, has been but a repetition of outgrown theories, overrated arguments, discarded policies, and vanished dreams. . . .

The fact that there is a Constitution, that there is a fifteenth amendment, that there is a duty to enforce it, that there is an oath to support and defend it, that there are lawful rights of citizens under it, that there is a Government created by it, finds no place in Democratic reflections.

It will be seen, also, that the bitterness of Democratic attack has been almost entirely against the existing law. Nearly all the provisions which are subject of criticism have been law in this country for twenty years.

It is curious to see whence comes the outcry against this measure, so moderate, so just, so beneficent. Arkansas, where the blood of Clayton still cries, unavenged, from the ground, lifts up her hands in holy horror that election inquiries are to be made hereafter under the peaceful shadow of the courthouse. The Democratic riders of Copiah County, Mississippi, who murdered and scourged unoffending Republicans in their dwellings at midnight, are shocked at the suggestion of domiciliary visits. The constituents of the great tariff reformer at Washington, Tex., who raided the ballot boxes and hung the election officers so that they should not bear testimony to the fact, are overcome with emotion that the processes which

SOURCE: U.S., *Congressional Record*, 51 Cong., 2d sess. (December 29–30, 1890), pp. 859–872.

have answered so well for a hundred years should even be witnessed by an officer of the court. . . .

The red shirts of South Carolina are afraid they will have to turn out again, and that the eight-ballot-box device will no longer serve its purpose. Louisiana, where, if her Senators tell me correctly, the Democratic governor appoints every election officer throughout the State—I have not been able to find the law to examine it—is afraid that the will of the people shall be interfered with. The Senator who represents Danville is afraid that the race issue will be raised again. Baltimore, where the governor, always a partisan leader, even when himself a candidate, appoints the board who select every precinct officer, and where the armed police are authorized, if they see fit, to turn out every officer and conduct the election themselves, shudders at the thought that local election officers shall not be appointed by the localities.

This is, as I said, a very simple bill to accomplish a very simple purpose. Its friends suppose:

First. That every citizen of the United States is entitled to demand from Congress all legislation which is necessary to protect him in the rights which the Constitution of the United States confers upon him.

Second. It is the duty of Congress to make all laws necessary and proper to carry into execution the powers therein conferred, and among them the power to elect, by the fair choice of the persons entitled to vote, a national House of Representatives.

Third. They find in the Constitution an express declaration that Congress may at any time make regulations as to the manner of holding elections for Representatives in Congress, or alter those made by the States.

Fourth. They find that the authors and advocates of this clause of the Constitution of the United States declared that it was inserted to meet such a state of things as has now actually arisen.

I have here the statements which have already been read in the debate. I wish to read a line or two from each of them, from Mr. Madison, Mr. Rufus King, and Mr. Gouverneur Morris, in order to show how completely they anticipate and overthrow the criticisms which have been made by the Senators on the other side of the Chamber upon the constitutional power. . . .

Mr. Hamilton goes on to say, speaking of the power of Congress to regulate in the last resort the election of its own members:

I am greatly mistaken if there be any article in the whole plan more completely defensible than this. Its propriety rests upon the evidence of this plain propostion, that every government ought to contain in itself the means of its own preservation.

Mr. President, we find that the Supreme Court of the United States have in a recent most solemn and unanimous judgment made a like declaration, and the court go on to declare that it is the duty of Congress—

to provide in an election held under its own authority for security of life and limb to the voter while in the exercise of this function. Can it be doubted that Congress can by law protect the act of voting, the place where it is done, and the man who votes from personal violence or intimidation and the election itself from corruption and fraud?

In the latter of these two judgments of the Supreme Court it is not only declared to be the unanimous judgment of the court, but Justice Miller states these propositions as propositions in regard to which there is no doubt.

MR. REAGAN. [Dem., Texas] May I ask the Senator what opinion he quotes from?

MR. HOAR. I am reading from the opinion of *Ex parte* Siebold, and from the latter opinion I will, with the leave of the Senate, print the extracts in full. I have omitted some of the language of it. Here is the sentence in *Ex parte* Yarbrough to which the judge applies his statement that there is no doubt about the proposition:

It is indispensable to the proper discharge of the great function of legislating for that Government that those who are to control that legislation shall not owe their election to bribery or violence.

MR. REAGAN. Does the Senator understand that in that opinion and that class of opinions the court were unanimous?

MR. HOAR. In the first opinion Justices Clifford and Field dissented. The second opinion was not only the unanimous judgment of the court, but the court say, "These propositions are propositions of which there can be no doubt." . . .

Now, Mr. President, having settled these propositions, we further think that the right of the American citizen to cast his vote in safety and in honor is the most precious right he can enjoy under the Constitution. Is not a citizen deprived of his right under the

Constitution of his country entitled to look to the Legislature of his country for a remedy? . . .

Now, what have the Senators on the other side to answer? Some of them seem to think that their best answer is in railing and reviling at the Senator who has charge of the bill. Their abuse does me an honor to which I should not otherwise have thought of laying claim. Their abuse brings me into a company with which I should otherwise be far too modest to seek admission. How the Democracy of their day reviled Adams and Sumner and Seward and Lincoln. The Senators from Virginia and West Virginia are but repeating with far less capacity what their predecessors who defended the barbarism of their day did to men the latchet of whose shoes I am not worthy to unloose.

In reporting this bill, I but discharge a duty which devolves on me as chairman of the committee of the Senate to which that class of subjects belongs. It is in full accord with my own opinions. But how idle, how unjust, how wicked is it to impute these opinions to prejudice or hatred against any section of my country or any portion of my countrymen. They are opinions which I share with Grant, whose tenderness and kindness toward all his countrymen is now everywhere confessed, whose last recommendation before the Republicans went out of power in the House in 1875 was the force bill of that winter. The little finger of that bill was heavier than the loins of this.

That bill authorized the President to suspend the habeas corpus and declare martial law in four great States for offenses far less than those which have given occasion to this. Numerous national election laws were introduced by Senators in this Chamber at the last session, among them the Senator from Ohio, the Senator from Wisconsin, and the Senator from New Hampshire. This bill came over from the House of Representatives. My function in regard to them has been to soften and mitigate the severity of every one of them. Even the Senator from Nevada, who spoke on Friday, declared his support of the old force bill, and declared his readiness, even now, to establish martial law and to make use of military force if such should be the opinion of his Republican associates.

In reporting and in supporting this measure I am but keeping the pledges made by Grant, and Hayes, and Garfield, and Logan, and Harrison, made by every Republican national convention and by the Republican conventions in nearly every State, by Massachusetts by Maine, by New York, by Nebraska, by Pennsylvania, by Alabama, by Missouri, by Mississippi. If I err, I err in good company and in obedience to voices I am bound to respect.

Mr. President, it will not be expected that I should take up the numerous and elaborate speeches on the other side in all their detail. I think I shall have done my full duty if I examine what has been said by four Senators, who, between them, seem to me to have covered the whole ground. Each of these Senators stated the case on his side clearly and powerfully. Each of them maintained the decencies of debate. While neither of them forgot that he was a Democrat, neither forgot that he was a Senator. I refer to the junior Senator from Alabama, the Senator from Delaware, the junior Senator from Mississippi, and the junior Senator from Tennessee.

It is not difficult to extract from the speeches of these Senators evidence in abundance both of the necessity for this bill and the righteousness of this bill. The junior Senator from Alabama, usually so calm and temperate, uses the following language. He uses it, be it remembered, in reply to complaints of citizens disfranchised, of seats usurped, of lawful majorities overthrown, of the will of the American people frustrated, of the Presidency itself made the prize of violence and false counting and ballot-box-stuffing. This is his language:

They—

The whites—

are the governing race in this and all free countries, and can not be forced into partnership with the negro on terms of political equality in the Federal or State governments of this country.

He goes on—I omit some sentences now:

That indefensible political crime—

The giving of suffrage to the blacks—

is the fountain whence all our bitter waters flow. Here we find the fatal mixture of black and white suffrage.
It must therefore be conceded—

Says the Senator further—

that all the troubles and dangers and complications confronting this country on account of race conflicts and irreconcilable antagonisms grow out of the stupendous blunder of the fifteenth amendment.

The Senator is not speaking of social equality. He is answering the charge that the Republican vote in the South is unlawfully suppressed. He answers it by asserting that "the white is the governing race," that "they can not be forced into partnership with the negro on terms of political equality in the Federal or State governments of this country." He goes on to denounce the Constitution in this part of it as "an indefensible political crime," as "the fountain from which all our bitter waters flow," as "a stupendous blunder," and says that its mixture of black and white suffrage is "fatal." I know that the Senator in another part of his speech uses language inconsistent with this conclusion. I shall quote that presently.

The number of the two races in Alabama is not far from equal. I think under the census of 1880 the whites had a majority of a few thousand. It is probable that the present census will show that both races there are on a substantial equality in numbers. I do not know how that may be. Yet her honored Senator declares, as his answer to a complaint that the Republicans can not vote freely at the South, that the white people "can not be forced into partnership with the negro on terms of political equality" and that the Constitution of his country is an "indefensible political crime" and a "stupendous blunder."

I can see but one meaning to these utterances. That meaning is that the Constitution shall not be obeyed. The Constitution of this country is an infamous crime and the men of whom the Senator is speaking will not obey it. . . .

"Fatal mixture of black and white suffrage," says the Senator from Alabama. "Will not be forced into partnership on terms of political equality!" We are dealing wholly with securing an honest vote for members of Congress. There never were in the times of which you so much complain, when, as you say, the negro ruled the whole South, more than seven or eight members of that race in Congress at one time. Is it asking too much in a Republic that the creators of three thousand millions of your wealth, that the preservers of your country against financial disaster, that the laborers who, as the Senator from Florida [Mr. CALL] told us the other day, live on their own real estate, which they manage, and get a dollar and a half a day on the average, should at least have their votes counted when they content themselves with sending this small number of their own race to the House of Representatives?

There is another very interesting statement which comes as a contribution to this debate. It comes both from the Senator from Tennessee and the Senator from Mississippi. The Senator from Tennessee says (page 674) that he lives in a city of seventy-five or eighty thousand inhabitants, where the Republican party, mostly colored, has been predominant, and that there has been no trouble of late years. He says, too, that they have a modified Australian ballot law; that the saloons are closed election day and the police on guard; that it is like Sunday. Men go to the polls as quietly as to church, notwithstanding there is a Republican majority and five out of six of that majority are colored voters.

Pretty good political partners, it seems to me, these colored voters make in the city of my honored friend, the junior Senator from Tennessee [Mr. BATE]. They compare very well with the white Democrats of New York or Chicago, or, if the Senator from New Jersey [Mr. McPHERSON] be right, the white Republicans of Philadelphia.

MR. BATE. [Dem.] I know the Senator from Massachusetts will not take it as an interruption when I simply state to him that the peaceful condition of affairs to which I alluded grows out of the fact that the whites do not disturb the negroes, who vote as they please, and there is no necessity for a change.

MR. HOAR. That is what we want to make the law, and that is a stupendous political blunder and an infamous political crime, according to the Senator from Alabama.

MR. BATE. That peaceful condition exists now, and therefore there is no reason for changing the law.

MR. HOAR. There is no harm in having the votes counted then.

The honorable Senator from Mississippi [Mr. WALTHALL] told us the other day of county after county in his State where he says the negro is in the majority, where a large proportion of the public officers there are colored people, and where a state of things similar to that described by the Senator from Tennessee exists. . . .

Where, then, is the mighty harm? Where is the danger to civilization? What is the terror in letting this race have their votes honestly counted? Why do you not let them even elect a dozen of their own race to the House if they like, the race who by your own confession have manifested the most sublime example of patience and forgiveness known to history, the creators of your new wealth, the shield of the country from financial disaster, and who in the cities and counties where they have unquestioned sway, according to these Senators, show you communities which are models of order and peace?

But the Senator from Alabama says in another part of his speech:

It can not be denied that each State has exercised the power judiciously and in good faith, so as to secure free and fair elections.

It can not be denied! But it is denied. It is denied in the platforms of a great national party. It is denied in the messages of Presidents. It is denied in the complaints of millions of injured citizens. It is denied by the reports of investigating committees. It is denied in many a solemn judgment of the House of Representatives. It is denied by his associate, the Senator from New Jersey, who asserts that free and fair elections do not exist in the chief city of the great State of Pennsylvania. It is denied by the Southern Democratic press, by the official utterances of Democratic governors, and the confessions of Democratic statesmen. It is denied by the logic of the Senator's own speech and by the history of his own State.

Has the Senator read the history of the more than two hundred contested-election cases in the House? Has he forgotten the history of the Fourth district of Alabama? Does not he know that Shelley, the Democrat, was three times certified by the Alabama election officers, though in a minority of thousands? The case was so gross that even the Democratic House was compelled to seat the Republican contestant, although they put off the act of justice until late in the second session. Five times have the Republicans, as I claim and as I firmly believe, carried that district by large majorities.

Five times have they been counted out by the local election officers. Three times have the House done a tardy justice to the man really elected. I remember the Republican member, Mr. Craig, calling upon me at the end of the Congress of 1885, in which though really elected he had filled his seat for about five weeks only, to ask me whether I thought it his duty to waste his life in contesting a district where he could always be elected, but never be returned. . . .

MR. HOAR. Mr. President, just before the adjournment yesterday I had cited a good deal of testimony, which I think would be enough to convince even the honorable Senator from Alabama that it is denied that the States of the South have made legal provision to secure free and fair elections; that it is not only denied in the national platforms of a great party, denied by the representatives of many States, denied by many solemn judgments of the House of Representatives, but that it is denied also by great authorities from his own State, from his own party, and from his own section of the country. I had just read the statement of perhaps the principal editor in the northwestern portion of what is called the South, who says that if he did not deny it he should be entitled to no respect whatever. Let me read a corresponding testimony from the principal paper in the southeastern portion of the South, the Charleston News and Courier, speaking of the device enacted into law by the Legislature of that State known as the eight-ballot-box law, under which there being eight boxes at each poll it is contrived that the Republican or the colored man, if he be ignorant, shall be unable to tell into which of the eight his ballot for a member of Congress ought to go, and thereby the whole vote is lost.

In regard to the eight-box law I have already read a statement of the governor of South Carolina.

> The eight-box law, though it has served its purpose well, is an evasion after all. It would be far better and far manlier—

Says the Charleston News and Courier—

> to grasp the difficulty squarely at once and amend the constitution of the State so as to impose an educational qualification upon the voters. It is beneath the dignity of the State to admit that there is no statesmanship in South Carolina to face the consequences of ignorant suffrage and overcome them without political trick or subterfuge.—Charleston News and Courier, December 5, 1888.

That is what the leading Democratic paper of the State and the South says. What is the political trick and subterfuge? Gentlemen speak sometimes as if we were harsh in our judgment or in our expression about our Southern brethren. The great Democratic paper of the State is speaking of the action of the State itself, of its solemnly enacted law, of the result of the deliberations of its statesmen and the will of its people so far as that people have expressed their will in the ballot-box law. Has anything ever been uttered by the wildest radical, by the most extreme fanatic, by the bitterest opponent of slavery or of Southern methods, on this floor or elsewhere, importing a tenth part of the severity of the statement of a great leading Democratic newspaper, a guide of public sentiment, that that State, so renowned for its chivalry and its honor and its courage, is resorting to a political trick and subterfuge to get rid of the constitutional rights of a majorty of its citizens? . . .

Why, Mr. President, the Democratic party of the United States in the year 1876, repeating in substance what it had affirmed in 1872, unanimously, the representatives of Mississippi joining with their brethren throughout the country, made this statement in regard to the fifteenth amendment:

> For the Democracy of the whole country, we do here affirm our faith in the permanence of the Federal Union, our devotion to the Constitution of the United States, with its amendments universally accepted, as a final settlement of the controversies that engendered civil war.

The Democratic party of the United States, then as now controlled by the Democracy of the South, solemnly promised, not merely acquiescence, but devotion to this "stupendous crime and blunder," as the Senators on the other side now call it. Is it we who are to be reproached with this thing when you made the bargain with us and pledged not merely your official oaths, but your honor as men and gentlemen that you would give your devotion to this constitutional amendment if you only were to be brought back into your old condition in the Union and freed from the consequences of rebellion? Here is an extract from the Greenville Times, another leading Mississippi paper:

> Our side may no more be maintained by evasions of the fact of the nullification of these negro majorities. We doubt if these ever deceived anybody, and now they would be traversed by a thousand authoritative contradictions. We had just as well accept the state of facts presented by the Republican leaders, and make our defense accordingly.

That is the Greenville Times.

But, Mr. President, what necessity for citing local newspapers, however eminent, or public men, however distinguished, in the face of the recent action of the people of Mississippi in adopting the constitution which has been so well discussed and stated by my eloquent friend from Wisconsin [Mr. Spooner]? Nobody, I suppose, will deny that that constitution was adopted and framed for the purpose of overthrowing the government by a majority in the State of Mississippi. The old constitution of the State of Mississippi contained, as I understand, a clause for its amendment, which was not observed.

The Legislature provided for the calling of a constitutional convention without submitting that request to the people, and the constitutional [convention] itself enacted the constitution, and it has been or is to be put in force without any submission of the constitution itself to the people. That convention contained, if I am rightly informed, but a single person belonging to the race which constitutes a large majority of the people of that State. The county after county which the distinguished Senator from Mississippi [Mr. Walthall] spoke of as peaceful and quiet and flourishing and prosperous, administered by the colored people there, with colored judges, colored treasurers, and colored county officers, were not permitted to send a single man of these admirable governors and excellent citizens who had created the cotton crop of the South and restored its prosperity, according to the statement of the Senator from Tennessee [Mr. Bate], which I quoted yesterday. Now what is it proposed to do?

> On and after the 1st day of January, 1896, the following qualifications are added to the foregoing—

Which are the ordinary qualifications of residence and age.

> Every qualified elector shall be able to read any portion of the constitution of this State, or he shall be able to understand the same when read to him, or give a reasonable interpretation thereof. A new registration shall be made before the next ensuing election after these qualifications are established.

In other words, the election officers of the State of Mississippi (whether they are appointed by the governor or by a board appointed by the governor, or elected by the people of localities, I have not looked to see), however chosen, are to pass upon the question, in the first place, in regard to the capacity of a man to read and write. Then you come to the men who can not read and write, who were I do not know what per cent of the people of Mississippi by the last census, but I suppose from 40 to 50 per cent, counting the colored people and the white; perhaps that is too much, and Senators will correct me if they remember the exact percentage. But, however it may be, it is an enormous percentage of the population of Mississippi, and when the Democratic white man, who can not read the constitution, and the Republican black man, or the Republican white, who can not read the constitution of the State, present themselves to those local election officers, they are to be accepted or rejected according as that election officer shall think their interpretation of the constitution of Mississippi is reasonable or not.

MR. SPOONER. [Rep., Wisc.]. Whether their interpretation is right or his is wrong.

MR. HOAR. Yes, whether their interpretation is right or his is wrong. No other authority is to judge. Mr. President, the American people are not blind—. . . .

MR. HOAR. Mr. President, as I was saying, if anybody's eyes are blind on this subject I think they would be opened by the declaration of Judge Calhoun, the president of that convention. Here is what he said:

> If asked by anybody if it was the purpose of the convention to restrict negro suffrage he would frankly answer: "Yes; that is what we are here for." The fiat had gone forth that fraud, force, and intimidation must cease.

I take it that Judge Calhoun is speaking not of the negro now, but of the white Democrats of Mississippi, and it is their fraud and force and intimidation that must cease.

> And if the convention failed to insure white supremacy by peaceful methods, he would, in case a negro were hereafter killed in a political riot, regard himself and every member as accessory to the murder.

That was an open secret all over the United States, as my friend on my right [Mr. SPOONER] suggests. . . .

MR. GRAY. [Dem., Del.]. Will the Senator from Massachusetts allow me to ask him a question?

MR. HOAR. Certainly.

MR. GRAY. I do not wish to interfere with or to intrude myself in any discussion in relation to the constitution of Mississippi, that State being represented here by Senators who can at all times defend her institutions and her constitution; but I wish to inquire in all good faith in what respect that provision of the constitution which the Senator has just read contravenes the inhibition of the Constitution of the United States against a discrimination on account of color in conferring the elective franchise.

MR. HOAR. Not in the least as far as I know. What the Mississippi Democratic authorities, whom we have quoted and of whom quite a number more will be quoted before we get through with this debate, say of it is not that it undertakes to do that on its face and by its terms, but that it provides an artifice, a fraud, a trick, that it puts it into the power of election officers who are all white men to hold that a Republican does not understand the constitution of the State or does not give a reasonable interpretation of it, and that a white Democrat does. That is the point. . . .

But, Mr. President, the single function of passing on a *prima facie* title and witnessing and reporting facts, intrusted to the judges and not to local election officers, is a very different thing from the right of any human being to pass on my title to be a voter according as he shall think I understand the Constitution or give a reasonable interpretion of it, or passing, if not on my right, on the right of any man to vote.

I do not wish to take up time unnecessarily, but I am going to say something about this matter when I come to deal with the argument of the honorable Senator from Delaware. What I am talking about now is that the Mississippi Democrats of high authority, the president of that convention and others, have declared that this provision was inserted in the constitution of that State as a fraudulent method of getting rid of the Republican vote of Mississippi, the negro vote, for the sake of saving themselves from what that South Carolina paper called the terrible stain of murder and fraud and outrages by which it had previously been done, and that is what Judge Calhoun said, as I understand it.

MR. TELLER. [Rep., Cal.]. Will the Senator allow me to ask him a question?

MR. HOAR. Certainly.

MR. TELLER. There has been a good deal of discussion as to this Mississippi constitution, which probably means just what the Senator says it does. I want to ask the Senator if there is anything in this bill which touches that wrong of which he complains.

MR. HOAR. No, I do not suppose there is.

MR. TELLER. I wish to ask the Senator whether in his judgment there is any power in Congress to touch that wrong.

MR. HOAR. I think there is. . . .

MR. MORGAN. [Dem., Ala.]. I desire to ask the Senator from Massachusetts a question for information merely. Under the constitution of Massachusetts, which requires that the voter shall be able to read a designated section in the Constitution of the United States, what is the practice there? Under the law who decides whether or not a man reads and reads correctly the designated section of the Constitution of the United States?

MR. HOAR. It is done by the mayor and aldermen in the cities and by the selectmen in the towns.

MR. MORGAN. Is that before the election takes place?

MR. HOAR. Yes.

MR. MORGAN. A question of registration?

MR. HOAR. Yes, a question of registration.

MR. MORGAN. There is no appeal from their decision?

MR. HOAR. There is no appeal from their decision. In Massachusetts it is not a question of reasonable interpretation, of construction, but it is a question of fact whether a person can read and write his name, and that is all the constitution of Massachusetts requires. . . .

MR. MORGAN. I will state to the Senator from Massachusetts that it seems to me, if he will allow me to say it, that the doctrine he is now arguing and advocating, of the right of a State to exclude everybody from suffrage upon any ground except race, color, or previous condition, it seems to me, applies very pointedly to the case of the South Carolina law providing eight ballot boxes—

MR. HOAR. I think that is hardly within the ordinary limit of interruption.

MR. MORGAN. I was just going to say that if a man did not have sense enough to find a ballot box he would scarcely have sense enough to put a ballot in the box.

MR. SPOONER. But sometimes they shift the ballot boxes.

MR. HOAR. The ballot boxes are shifted from place to place.

MR. MORGAN. They are all marked.

MR. HOAR. They are marked so that they can not be understood. The Senator from Alabama and the Senator from Delaware and the Senator from Mississippi, all are answering not me, as far as they answer anything or anybody, but the Democrats of the South who confess this thing. I have made very little comment on the South Carolina eight-ballot-box law. I said that the Charleston

News and Courier says that it is a shame to the manhood of the State to resort to his fraud and subterfuge. . . .

It may be hard for two populations differing in race and color, in political opinion, yet locally intermingled, to dwell together in amity under republican government, but in the present case the crime, the blame, the barbarism, have been on the side of the superior race. Out of the thousands of outrages on black and white Republicans which have been committed in Mississippi in the interest of the Democratic party the Senator has not pointed to one that was ever punished. I believe one poor dog of a white man has been hanged for a nonpolitical murder of a negro, but the countless election outrages have gone on without punishment and without rebuke. The murder of Print Matthews, the kindly citizen and excellent neighbor, in the act of casting his ballot and in the hearing of his wife and daughter, by the Democratic city marshal, whom he had received as a guest in his house within a week, was approved by the Democrats of Copiah County. The district attorney wrote the resolutions. The superior race in Mississippi marked their dread of being reduced to barbarism by Republican policies by burning the house of his widow shortly afterwards. Within the Christmas season of this very year, the time of peace upon earth and good will to men, that widow's son, the Republican postmaster, a young man of twenty-one, has been shot down in the streets of Carrollton, the home of the Senator's colleague. How long, oh God, shall the blood of these martyrs cry for vengeance from the ground? How long shall the murder of men because they are Republicans be the only crime to which Republicans are indifferent?

The Senator thinks that the era of these things is passing by in Mississippi. Let us hope so; let us hope so. Let us hope that when its dark and bloody history is written it may be recorded that there was at least one manly voice in all her chivalry to utter the indignation of an American freeman at the outrage on Americanism and on freedom. . . .

The Senator from Delaware says that this bill takes the conduct of elections from the people of the local precincts and transfers it to partisan officers. On the contrary, this bill does not touch the conduct of elections—and that can not be repeated too often—except where the State officials refuse to appear and proceed to perform their duties. It leaves the officers appointed by the State to conduct, as now, both the registration and the election. It only transfers the witnesses and the recording of what has happened from partisan leaders to officers appointed by the judiciary, subject to the direction and final control of the judiciary itself. . . .

Mr. President, Senators now clamor and say that we are interfering with the authority of the people of the precinct to elect their own election officers, when many of them represent communities which have taken the control away from the people of the precincts and put it into the power of the great partisan leader of the State, the governor, for the very purpose and with the very effect of suppressing and overcoming Republican majorities in the localities.

Here is extending through many States an ingenious, deliberate, and settled policy to take the control of elections out of the hands of local officers and place it in the hands of a central power in order that elections may be manipulated for partisan purposes.

The Senator from Indiana says these two races can not live together except on the terms that one shall command and the other obey. That proposition I deny. They can live together, neither, as a race, commanding, neither, as a race, obeying. They can live together obeying nothing but the law, framed by lawmakers whom every citizen shall have his equal share in choosing.

It would be something if Senators who ask us to refrain from using the powers the Constitution has placed in our hands to protect the suffrage, and to leave to them and to their States to cure this evil in their own way, could point to a single act or utterance of their own or to a single law of their States, in all these years, designed to end this wrong and to secure justice to these American citizens. They expend all their ingenuity to find constitutional objections to any remedy we propose. They enact in their State Legislatures cunning devices to prevent the lawful expression of the will of the majority. They retain the increased representation which the population whose votes they suppress gives them. They cast the votes which they get by these unlawful practices in opposition to our dearest interests, and yet they expect us to remain quiet. They affect to dread the rule of negro barbarism, but they expect us tamely to submit that a power gained by a worse barbarism shall rule us.

The error, the fundamental error, of the Democratic party of the South, in dealing with this problem, is in their assumption that race hatred is the dominant passion of the human soul; that it is

stronger than love of country, stronger than the principle of equality, stronger than Christianity, stronger than justice. To that passion, and to that alone, do they make their appeal. They make it
not so much, in my judgment, for the sake of race supremacy as for
the sake of party supremacy. Out of that appeal came the black
codes of the period which followed the war. From that came the
Mississippi plan of 1875. From that came the thousands of election
crimes and the overthrow of the rule of the majority in many States
and in the other House of Congress. From that has come the
Mississippi constitution of 1890.

If the Democratic party of the South had shown one-tenth of
the energy in raising up and fitting for citizenship their colored
fellow citizen, in improving his condition, in guiding him in honest
paths, in gaining his confidence, in securing him justice, that they
have put into rebellion, or into wresting their States from the rule
of the majority, or into contrivances like the new Mississippi constitution, the two races would to-day be dwelling together under
the flag in freedom and in honor, in peace, in prosperity, and in
mutual regard. You have tried everything else, try justice. . . .

b. Comment from the Negro Press, January 1891

THE FEDERAL ELECTIONS BILL
AN APPEAL TO THE PRESS

Gentlemen:

The hope of fair elections is fading. The friends that once
pledged themselves at a hundred altars now stand perjured. The
friend that may prevent the blood from flowing afresh from the
healing wounds of the race. The Federal Elections Bill, that oft
pledged boone to secure which we have lost a thousand martyred
negroes every year since the war, now lies upon the marble cooling
boards in the Senate of the United States. Eight Republican
daggers are sticking in its heart; twenty Democrats have shrouded
it for the tomb, its grave is dug. Do you propose to allow it to be
buried?

There is still a spark of life in it but it is only a spark. Can you
not forge electri[city enough] and revive it? Is there not fire
enough in the burning hearts of eight million indignant people to

SOURCE: Washington Bee, January 10, 1891.

warm it into life? Is there not power enough in a hundred throated press speaking for one million voters to make it a living, vital absorbing issue, commanding unwillingly attention forcing immediate action?

Do you propose to allow that little spartan band of true blue republicans that have gathered about the dauntless leadership of Hoar to fight this battle alone? Do you propose to allow them to forge all their own arguments, facing a powerful and relentless opposition fighting our battle without a blow from the iron arm of negro journalism? Are you content to drape your papers in mourning and acknowledge that the great battle for human rights have been fought and lost?

This is not the time for a hopeless chorus of I told you so's; not the time for gloomy forebodings and melancholy predictions, now is the time for action. We are not whipped until we concede it. The reason the white people of the south are always victorious, is because they will never concede defeat. The men to demand rights are the men to whom they are denied; and the time to do it, is when they are denied. The sentiment of the world is that a man who wont fight for himself is not worth being fought for.

We are past the time of nice distinctions, of arguments, of expediency. We are now where we must commend them or denounce threaten and destroy—we must either take sides with the eight in their mean, cowardly, treacherous and abject surrender or we must wage a fierce unflinching warfare against them, a battle without quit or quarter.

Having been introduced by republicans, it has been endorsed by four-fifths of our race, our papers are committed to it. Wherever three or four of our people were assembled, it has been endorsed. Having cause[d] all the bitter turgid vituperation that has been cast upon us while it was pending. Having aroused all the strongest and worst passions that slumber in the rebellious hearts of the south, we are now turned loose naked and defenceless. Wolves have been prodded and starved until their fury rages and now without a weapon and without a friend they are to be turned loose on us. Are you content to see your recommendation treated with impunity, your appeal ignored, and the welfare of the race disregarded by men who have bought their seats in the Senate and now sell so many ounces of blood for so many nuggets of silver. The impression has gone abroad that we are not strongly in favor of this bill—and it is asserted that we would as soon see it die as live. Gentlemen, if you are in favor of it at all, you must be strongly in favor of it—it is a bill that makes strong partizans. You can write strong and able articles in favor of protecting industries from which a black man is shut out as if he were a leper. Have you nothing to say upon this measure except a few gloomy quibs to the effect that the Senate is too cowardly to pass the bill?

If we would have a safe smooth road to the ballot we must blast our way through a solid rock of democratic opposition.

CHARLES S. MORRIS

They Are Traitors

About the time we had begun to hope—for a second time—that the Federal Elections bill would be passed in the Senate, it was side-tracked again by the Democratic minority, led by Senator *Wolcott* and his silver Republican (?) colleagues, *Stewart, Teller, Jones, Washburn* and *Cameron*. Senator *Ingalls* should be included, for he was paired with Senator Allison or some other *Republican* favorable to the bill, thus showing his opposition to a measure he advocated in a speech in the Senate but a short time ago, and depriving the Republican majority of the one vote needed to prevent the side-tracking of the bill. One thing is sure and that is, Afro-Americans will not waste any sympathy on him over his defeat by a Farmers' Alliance Republican who comes out boldly, like a *man,* and *says* he is opposed to it and does not try to *sneak* out of doing what he feels to be his duty. Congressman Robert Kennedy, of this State, an old soldier, was justified in circulating in the House, Monday, that telegram to the Republicans in the Kansas Legislature, asking them to defeat Ingalls, and there is no doubt but that it had effect upon some. As for the recently re-elected Senator, Mr. Cameron, of Pennsylvania, whose staunchest friend, Chris Magee, proprietor of the stalwart Republican Pittsburgh Times, calls on him "to resign"—we can not find words to express our estimate of him. He ought to resign, and, with Senators *Stewart, Teller, Wolcott, Washburn* and *Jones,* throw off their masks and *remain* in the ranks of Democracy. They can't do this

SOURCE: Editorial in the Cleveland *Gazette,* January 31, 1891.

too quickly for the good of the Republican party, for they are seriously crippling it daily. A dispatch from Pittsburgh Tuesday night read: "At Wood's Run, this county, to-night Senator Cameron was burned in effigy by a company of indignant Republicans, a brass band playing a dirge during the ceremony."

PART TWO
Flawed Freedom:
The Southern Experience,
1868–1900

A. Blacks Share Power
in the South

24. Legal Foundations and Legislation

THE MAJOR CONCERNS of Southern Negroes are highlighted below in the convention debates and in the Reconstruction constitutions and laws which they helped to frame. In Louisiana, South Carolina, Alabama, Florida, and Mississippi they had constituted a majority of the voters registered in 1867 under the congressional Reconstruction laws; but South Carolina and Louisiana were exceptional in that the former returned an overwhelming majority of Negro convention delegates and the latter, by prearrangement, an equal number of whites and blacks.

The extent of white disenfranchisement during Reconstruction is an illusive problem, with suffrage restrictions set by Congress (but variously interpreted by local administrators) until readmission of the states and thereafter by provisions of the new state constitutions. Of the states readmitted in 1868 or later, only Arkansas' constitution contained sweeping disfranchisement clauses. Those of Louisiana and Alabama, the former abstracted below (doc. a), have also been characterized as severe. Undoubtedly they were an affront to whites; their practical effect, however, is not clear and their duration was very brief for Republicans in both states quickly initiated steps to remove the disabilities (cf. doc. e). The recognition of civil equality mandated by the Louisiana constitution as part of the oath of office, a requirement generally offensive to Southern whites, was identical with a section of the oath required as a prerequisite to voter registration by Alabama and Arkansas in constitutions adopted some months earlier. Historians have considered generous the suffrage provisions of South Carolina's constitution (doc. b: art. 8, sec. 2), the bitter complaint of the state's conservatives notwithstanding (doc. c). Disfranchising clauses framed by Republican-dominated conventions in Virginia and Mississippi were voted down by the congressionally-delimited electorate. In general modern scholarship in explanation of the weak showing of conservative whites during the beginnings of Republican Reconstruction has emphasized their failure to register, or if registered to vote, rather than proscription.

*The racial and political complexion of the speakers in the South
Carolina debates (doc. b) is often evident in the course of their remarks,
but the reader should find useful the following identification of speakers:*

Richard H. Cain, Northern Negro minister
Francis L. Cardozo, native Negro, educated University of Glasgow
Robert C. DeLarge, native Negro
B. O. Duncan, native white Republican
Charles P. Leslie, white New Yorker
Niles G. Parker, Northern white
Benjamin F. Randolph, Northern Negro minister
Alonzo J. Ransier, native Negro
Benjamin F. Whittemore, white Massachusetts minister
Jonathan J. Wright, Pennsylvania Negro lawyer

a. Abstract of Louisiana Constitution, March 2, 1868

CONSTITUTION OF LOUISIANA

Adopted by Convention March 2, 1868, and ratified by the
people April 18, 1868. Provides, among other things, that slavery
shall not exist.

All persons, without regard to race, color, or previous condition,
born or naturalized in the United States, and subject to the jurisdiction thereof, and residents of this State for one year, are citizens
of this State. The citizens of this State owe allegiance to the
United States; and this allegiance is paramount to that which they
owe to the State. They shall enjoy the same civil, political, and
public rights and privileges, and be subject to the same pains and
penalties.

All persons shall enjoy equal rights and privileges, upon any
conveyance of a public character, and all places of business, or of
public resort, or for which a license is required by either State,
parish, or municipal authority, shall be deemed places of a public
character, and shall be opened to the accommodation and patronage of all persons, without distinction or discrimination on account
of race or color. Every elector shall be eligible to a seat in the
House of Representatives and to the Senate, if twenty-five years
old; and he shall be eligible to any municipal office.

Every male person, of the age of twenty-one years or upwards,

SOURCE: McPherson, *Handbook for 1868*, pp. 329–330.

born or naturalized in the United States, and subject to the jurisdiction thereof, and a resident of this State one year next preceding
an election, and the last ten days within the parish in which he
offers to vote, shall be deemed an elector, except those disfranchised by this constitution, and persons under interdiction.

The following persons shall be prohibited from voting and
holding any office: All persons who shall have been convicted of
treason, perjury, forgery, bribery, or other crime punishable in the
penitentiary, and persons under interdiction.

All persons who are estopped from claiming the right of suffrage
by abjuring their allegiance to the United States Government, or by
notoriously levying war against it, or adhering to its enemies, giving
them aid or comfort, but who have not expatriated themselves, nor
have been convicted of any of the crimes mentioned in the first
paragraph of this article, are hereby restored to the said right,
except the following: Those who held office, civil or military, for
one year or more, under the organization styled "the Confederate
States of America;" those who registered themselves as enemies of
the United States; those who acted as leaders of guerrilla bands
during the late rebellion; those who, in the advocacy of treason,
wrote or published newspaper articles or preached sermons during
the late rebellion; and those who voted for and signed an ordinance
of secession in any State. No person included in these exceptions
shall either vote or hold office until he shall have relieved himself
by voluntarily writing and signing a certificate setting forth that he
acknowledges the late rebellion to have been morally and politically wrong, and that he regrets any aid and comfort he may have
given it; and he shall file the certificate in the office of the secretary
of State, and it shall be published in the official journal: *Provided,*
That no person who, prior to the 1st of January, 1868, favored the
execution of the laws of the United States popularly known as the
reconstruction acts of Congress, and openly and actively assisted
the loyal men of the State in their efforts to restore Louisiana to
her position in the Union, shall be held to be included among
those herein excepted. Registrars of voters shall take the oath of
any such person as *prima facie* evidence of the fact that he is
entitled to the benefit of this proviso.

Members of the General Assembly and all other officers, before
they enter upon the duties of their offices, shall take the following
oath or affirmation:

I, (A. B.) do solemnly swear (or affirm) that I accept the civil and political equality of all men, and agree not to attempt to deprive any person or persons, on account of race, color, or previous condition, of any political or civil right, privilege, or immunity enjoyed by any other class of men; that I will support the constitution and laws of the United States, and the constitution and laws of this State, and that I will faithfully and impartially discharge and perform all the duties incumbent on me as————according to the best of my ability and understanding: so help me God.

No liability, either State, parochial, or municipal, shall exist for any debts contracted for or in the interest of the rebellion against the United States Government.

There shall be no property qualification for office.

All agreements, the consideration of which was Confederate money, notes, or bonds, are null and void, and shall not be enforced by the courts of this State.

Contracts for the sale of persons are null and void.

The State of Louisiana shall never assume nor pay any debt or obligation contracted or incurred in aid of the rebellion; nor shall this State ever, in any manner, claim from the United States, or make any allowance or compensation for slaves emancipated or liberated in any way whatever.

All contracts by which children were bound out without the knowledge or consent of their parents are null and void.

There shall be at least one free public school in each parish, for children between six and twenty-one, who shall be admitted to the public schools or other institutions of learning sustained or established by the State in common, without distinction of race, color, or previous condition. And no municipal corporation shall make rules contrary to the spirit and intention of this article. Public school fund provided for, of which one half of the poll-tax is a part.

The militia are all able-bodied male citizens, between eighteen and forty-five.

The ordinance of secession of the State of Louisiana, passed 26th of January, 1861, is hereby declared to be null and void. The constitution adopted in 1864, and all previous constitutions in the State of Louisiana, are declared to be superseded by this constitution.

An election for State officers provided for April 17 and 18, at the same time with the vote on the constitution. All civil officers thus

elected shall enter upon the discharge of their duties on the second
Monday after the return of their election shall have been officially
promulgated, or as soon as qualified according to law, and shall
continue in office for the terms of their respective offices herein
prescribed, said terms to date from the first Monday in November
following the election. The Legislature shall meet in New Orleans
on the third Monday after the promulgation aforesaid, and proceed, after organization, to vote upon the adoption of the XIVth
Amendment to the Constitution of the United States.

b. Proceedings of the 1868 Constitutional Convention of South Carolina
[DECLARATION OF RIGHTS]

Mr. B. F. Randolph offered the following amendment: "Distinction on account of race or color in any case whatever shall be
prohibited, and all classes of citizens, irrespective of race and color,
shall enjoy all common, equal and political privileges."

It is, doubtless, the impression of the members of the Convention that the Bill of Rights as it stands, secures perfect political and
legal equality to all the people of South Carolina. It is a fact,
however, that no where is it laid down in the instrument, emphatically and definitely, that all the people of the State, irrespective of
race and color, shall enjoy equal privileges. Our forefathers were no
doubt anti-slavery men, and they intended that slavery should die
out. Consequently the word color is not to be found in the Constitution or Declaration of Independence. On the contrary, it is
stated distinctly "all men are created free and equal." But that was
too general, too comprehensive, and our forefathers made a mistake, the result of which was that the land has been drenched in
blood to perpetuate slavery. The Constitution of the United States
was too vague; it was misinterpreted. On the one hand, the ablest

SOURCE: *Proceedings of the Constitutional Convention of South Carolina held at Charleston, beginning January 14th and ending March
17th, 1868* (Charleston, S.C., 1868), I: 353–355, 454–457, 824–826,
830–831, 890–894. For the selected articles of the constitution as
adopted, which are in brackets, *The Constitution of the State of
South Carolina with the Ordinances Thereunto Appended*, Adopted
by the Constitutional Convention, which was held at Charleston, and
Adjourned on the 17th March, 1868 (pamphlet, Charleston, S.C.,
1868).

statesmen of England and America had pronounced it anti-slavery; on the other, equally able minds regarded it as pro-slavery in its character.

In our Bill of Rights, I want to settle the question forever by making the meaning so plain that a "wayfaring man, though a fool," cannot misunderstand it. The majority of the people of South Carolina, who are rapidly becoming property holders, are colored citizens—the descendants of the African race—who have been ground down by three hundred years of degradation, and now that the opportunity is afforded, let them be protected in their political rights. The words proposed as an amendment were not calculated to create distinction, but to destroy distinction; and since the Bill of Rights did not declare equality, irrespective of race or color, it was important that they should be inserted. Here I would say that all of my radicalism consists in believing one thing, namely, that all men are created of one blood; that "God created all nations to dwell upon the earth."

MR. C. P. LESLIE. I would ask the delegate if it would not have been a little better for his theory if the Scriptures had added "without distinction of race or color."

MR. B. F. RANDOLPH. If the gentleman will tell me why Congress saw fit to say "all men are born free and equal," I may answer his question.

MR. C. P. LESLIE. I can't tell why Congress did this or that. They do a great many curious things, but it does strike me that God in his infinite wisdom knew fully as much about this business as Congress.

MR. B. F. RANDOLPH. I will say to the gentleman that if God did not see fit to prepare such laws as we may adapt to the present condition of society, it becomes us to add to God's laws in such a manner as to suit circumstances, and yet not conflict with them.

MR. A. J. RANSIER. I favor the spirit of the amendment, but wish to see the clause inserted in some other portion of the Bill of Rights.

MR. B. F. WHITTEMORE. This whole subject is covered by previous sections, and it is unnecessary to be more explicit. We discussed this matter in Committee, and the determination arrived at was not to introduce the word color in the Bill of Rights. All citizens duly qualified are entitled to equal privileges, and it is unnecessary to draw lines of distinction. The colored man was a citizen, his rights had been declared, and I propose to defend those rights wherever called upon, whether it be in the halls of legislation or upon the field of contest.

MR. A. J. RANSIER. While I want the principle laid down clearly, that in all matters my race are civilly and politically equal with, and entitled to all the privileges of other men, I am not in favor of employing the words "race and color" in the Constitution.

MR. F. L. CARDOZO. It is a patent fact that, as colored men, we have been cheated out of our rights for two centuries, and now that we have the opportunity, I want to fix them in the Constitution in such a way that no lawyer, however cunning or astute, can possibly misinterpret the meaning. If we do not do so, we deserve to be, and will be, cheated again. Nearly all the white inhabitants of the State are ready at any moment to deprive us of these rights, and not a loop-hole should be left that would permit them to do it constitutionally. Not one of them scarcely were in favor of this Convention, and just so soon as they had the power, whether by the election of a Democratic President, or by an increase of emigration, they would endeavor to overthrow the Constitution. Hence, while they (the Convention) had a chance to do it, by all means let them insert the words "without distinction of race or color," wherever it was necessary to give force and clearness to their purpose. . . .

[ARTICLE I: Section 12. No person shall be disqualified as a witness, or be prevented from acquiring, holding and transmitting property, or be hindered in acquiring education, or be liable to any other punishment for any offence, or be subjected in law to any other restraints or disqualifications in regard to any personal rights than such as are laid upon others under like circumstances.

Section 39. No title of nobility or hereditary emolument shall ever be granted in this State. Distinction on account of race or color, in any case whatever, shall be prohibited, and all classes of citizens shall enjoy equally all common, public, legal and political privileges.]

[HOMESTEAD EXEMPTION]

MR. N. G. PARKER. . . . It has been said that to secure the present landholders in the possession of a homestead will prevent the sale of lands; consequently none will be put on the market, and the colored man will get no land. Why, sir, this bill provides for a homestead of only one hundred acres; few of the landholders of this State who own one hundred acres of land own less than five hundred acres, and from that to ten thousand, and even more. It is not proposed to make a homestead exemption for the very rich man of ten thousand acres, and for the rich man of five hundred acres, and for the man of moderate means of one hundred acres, and for the poor man of one acre, but sir, taking all things into account in this State in the present condition, it is a broad and liberal proposition of exempting one hundred acres of land to every man the head of a family who has already, or may hereafter acquire the same, as a homestead, which shall forever be inviolate and exempt from all claims, and be forever the property of the family who acquired it.

I am aware that the amount or value of the exemption named in this ordinance is larger than the average of such exemptions; but, sir, I do not consider this an objection to it; on the contrary, for several reasons, it is one of its principal merits.

I have said, on a former occasion, that I would have this Convention offer a Constitution to the people of this State which would stand forth pre-eminent among the Constitutions of the States of our national Government for humanity, justice and liberality. To pass this section of the Constitution will be to go far to establish its merits for these great qualities. I desire to remove every obstacle that stands in the way of the prosperity of this State. Circumstances over which the great majority of our people had no control, has brought them into this suffering condition. I desire to show that the great war through which we have passed was not a curse but a blessing, not only to the colored man, but to the whites. That the emancipation of slavery was not the only emancipation that was effected by it. The emancipation of the mind of the great mass of my brother whites was quite as great an event to them as the emancipation of slavery was to the colored race. It is not yet comprehended by all our people, but that is no sign that it will not be; it is our duty as legislators, as representatives of the people, to force this conclusion home upon our constituents. And, sir, in my opinion there is no way in which we can do so much by any one act as to pass this homestead exemption. We can afford to be generous, and we must be both generous and just.

The tables have turned; for the first time in the history of this State, a race hitherto denied not only the right to sit in assemblies like this, but the right to have any voice whatever in the election of any one to sit here, are now not a mere minority, but a clear majority. Being clearly in the majority, it is doubtless the belief of nearly all of our white brethren throughout the State that you will imitate their example, and legislate exclusively for your own benefit and not for all.

We, the few white Republicans in the State, are satisfied that no such thing is contemplated, nor ever was. We have all along been satisfied on this point, but it is incumbent on us all to satisfy all persons of the fact and pass this homestead exemption, and all doubts will be expelled. I have heard it said that the colored man would get no land if this bill was passed, that it would keep all lands out of the market, and this was what the landholders wanted; but, sir, this will not follow, it is not true, and I will show it. This exemption, as I have before repeated, exempts only one hundred acres. There are plenty of debts hanging over the heads of the great majority of landholders, in my opinion, and within my positive knowledge, to show the utter falsity of this presumption. It is to be deplored that there are so many debts hanging over our people that must be paid if they have the property to pay it with, for it cripples their means, destroys to a great extent their hopes and energies, and retards not only their prosperity but the prosperity of all. Those who own land cannot prosper unless those who do not own prosper. No one can dispute this, hence you desire, we all desire the prosperity of the present landholders. I do not, however, desire any man to hold ten thousand acres of land, nor five thousand, nor hardly in any instance one thousand acres. I hope to live to see the time when there will not be a large plantation in the State; but to see those that now exist cut up into one hundred thousand farms, and all of them prospering.

But, sir, this exemption does not provide for any person retaining a large plantation; it is only for one hundred acres. Now, I would ask, if this bill is passed would the colored men be injured by it? Supposing all the land of the State to pass under the auctioneers hammer to-day for debt, or to-morrow, or next month, or next spring, or next year, at any time, would the colored man get much of it? Have they the means to purchase now? I do not believe it. And precious little would they be able to purchase at any price. I verily believe, and I say it in no disparagement to them, that if it was sold to-day for one dollar per acre, there is not one in a hundred throughout the State who could purchase a single acre.

They are not ready to purchase lands yet, and I fear that unless more prosperity is established among the present landholders that they never will be ready to purchase. Pass this homestead exemption, and one step will be taken in the right direction; do not be afraid of it because it seems to please many of the whites. There may be some white men who take the view of the case that I have endeavored to overthrow; they may believe that they can keep you out of land if such an act is passed, but they are really mistaken. They will be glad enough to sell it, they cannot afford to keep it, it will ruin them if they do; they cannot work it profitably in such large tracts, and they will be ruined if they persist in the attempt. It may be the motive of some for wishing this exemption passed; but never mind that, we must pass it if at all upon its merits alone, regardless of any ones opinions. . . . It is a mistaken idea that to pass this homestead exemption will keep land out of the market; it will do no such thing, there will be plenty of it on the market at all times in our day for all who want it, and I believe at a reasonable price. There are debts due from the landholders that must be paid, and their land must pay them; they have nothing else wherewithal to pay them; they can sell their surplus lands, pay their debts, and be better off. Taxes are always (at least in hard times) a burden, will be assessed yearly upon all lands, and they must be paid. The expenses of the State (constantly increasing, will be a continual drag upon those who attempt to carry on large landed estates with a small amount of money,) will alone force sufficient lands upon the market at all times to meet the wants of all the landless. This Convention will cost the State quite a large sum of money. A Legislature will soon assemble, and that will cost money. Education, once limited, is to be general, and that will be expensive; and, to keep up with the age, it is fair to presume that the State tax will be greater next year than this, and increase yearly; this will be felt, and will be the stimulus to many for owning less land, and cause them to see the necessity of disposing of their surplus. . . .

[ARTICLE III: Section 32. The family homestead of the head of each family, residing in this State, such homestead consisting of dwelling house, out-buildings and lands appurtenant, not to exceed the value of one thousand dollars, and yearly product thereof, shall be exempt from attachment, levy or sale on any mesne or final process issued from any court. To secure the full enjoyment of said homestead exemption to the person entitled thereto, or to the head of any family, the personal property of such person, of the following character, to wit: household furniture, beds and bedding, family library, arms, carts, wagons, farming implements, tools, neat cattle, work animals, swine, goats and sheep, not to exceed in value in the aggregate the sum of five hundred dollars, shall be subject to like exemption as said homestead, and there shall be exempt in addition thereto all necessary wearing apparel: *Provided*, That no property shall be exempt from attachment, levy or sale, for taxes, or for payment of obligations contracted for the purchase of said homestead, or the erection of improvements thereon: *Provided further*, That the yearly products of said homestead shall not be exempt from attachment, levy or sale, for the payment of obligations contracted in the production of the same. It shall be the duty of the General Assembly at their first session to enforce the provisions of this Section by suitable legislation.]

[SUFFRAGE]

The Convention re-assembled at three P. M., and resumed the consideration of the report of the Committee on Franchise and Elections.

Section two was taken up as follows:

Section 2. Every male citizen of the United States, of the age of twenty-one years and upwards, not laboring under the disabilities named in this Constitution, without distinction of race, color, or former condition, who shall be a resident of this State at the time of the adoption of this Constitution, or who shall thereafter reside in this State one year, and in the county sixty days next preceding any election, and every male inhabitant of foreign birth of the age aforesaid, who shall have resided in this State one year, and in the county sixty days immediately preceding such election, and shall have declared his intention to become a citizen of the United States, conformably to the laws of the United States on the subject of naturalization, shall be entitled to vote for all officers that are now, or hereafter may be, elected by the people, and upon all questions submitted to the electors at any elections; *Provided*, That every person coming of age after the year 1875, to be entitled to the privilege of an elector, shall be able to read and write; but this qualification shall not apply to any person prevented by physical disability from complying therewith; *Provided, further,*

That no person shall be allowed to vote or hold office who is now, or hereafter may be, disqualified therefor by the Constitution of the United States; but the General Assembly shall have power to remove such disability by a two-thirds vote; *Provided, further,* That no person, while kept in any alms house or asylum, or of unsound mind, or confined in any public prison, shall be allowed to vote or hold office.

MR. F. L. CARDOZO. Every person now fourteen years of age, who cannot read at the time fixed in this section, cannot vote on coming of age. I say it will take ten years to establish a school system in the State. There is but one place in the State where there is a system of common schools, that is in Charleston; and yet there are seven hundred thousand people in the State. I would not be surprised if it takes twenty years to establish a thorough system of common schools. It will take several millions to erect school houses. Where are we to get the money? I hope the amendment of the gentleman from Edgefield (MR. R. B. ELLIOTT), to strike out altogether the reading and writing qualification of a voter, will be adopted. I think it would come with bad grace from any individual in this State, who has helped to deprive men for two centuries, of the means of education, to demand that in seven years all unable to read should not be allowed to vote. It not only comes with bad grace from those opposed to us, but it is extremely ridiculous, coming from ourselves. We scarcely know what we are doing. The adoption of this section would be fatal to our success. I am convinced, if gentlemen allow this section to pass, with the reading and writing qualification proviso, before two months have passed over their heads, they will repent of their action. They will desire that that section should be reconsidered and struck out altogether. I hope gentlemen will exercise now that "ounce of prevention" which is so much "better than a pound of cure," by striking out the section altogether, or putting the time to such a distance that every one will have a fair chance to vote. It will take to 1875 to establish our system of schools. If you fix it at 1890, that will be fifteen years; then every child six or seven years of age will have fifteen years. At fourteen, parents generally demand the services of their children. I hope we will not, by our action here to-day, deprive a poor man of the only means to protect himself. I feel sure no further argument is needed. I call the attention of members to this important matter. I hope the period will be stricken out, or fixed at 1890. . . .

MR. R. H. CAIN. The right of suffrage ought not to be abridged under any circumstances, and under no provision of our Constitution ought any citizen of the State to be deprived of the enjoyment of that right, which is his by virtue of his creation, by virtue of the act of Congress, and by virtue of that justice which is due to all men. Why should we place any restriction whatever upon a vote? It is said that man must learn to read. Why, if you go into New York city, or among those States where the Democratic party have the strongest power, and muster their cohorts in double file, you will find that probably not one-tenth of them can read and write.

MR. S. A. SWAILS. Are they white or colored voters?

MR. R. H. CAIN. They are white voters; but, as Burns says, "a man's a man for a' that." A man may not be able to educate himself. The circumstances of his childhood may possibly have prevented the acquisition of knowledge, but for all that he is a man, the noblest work of God; and I would not deprive any being rich or poor, of the enjoyment of that franchise, by which alone he can protect himself as a citizen. Whether learned or ignorant, he is subject to government, and he has an inalienable right to say who shall govern him; to say what shall be the character of that government. He may not understand a great deal of the knowledge that is derived from books; he may not be generally familiar with the ways of the world; but he can, nevertheless, judge between right and wrong, and to this extent he has as much ability to cast his vote and declare his opinion as any other man, no matter what may be his situation in life. It has too long been the right of tyrants to rule over man and prescribe for him a line of action, and never again will this right be conceded to any class, especially in South Carolina, where, as I believe, we have entered upon a new era, and obliterated those peculiar distinctions which made the ruling class the tyrants of those held in subjection. For two hundred years it has been the curse of the slave States, that a certain class of men have dictated the laws that guided the multitude, and have deprived the majority of their God-given right to express their will in the creation of those laws, in which they themselves were most interested. In remodelling the institutions of this country, we propose to establish them upon a broad basis, so that the halo of liberty may overshadow every class of men, and no right, however small, shall be withheld from those entitled to enjoy it. I am surprised to find gentlemen who, through life and amid all its fortuitous circumstances, have been permitted to enjoy the blessings of education, are not willing to confer the same blessings upon the poorer classes by whom they have been surrounded. One of the greatest reasons why I feel thankful to my Maker for the present condition of things, is that it has opened to us an age of progress, in which mankind will take a forward bound towards humanity, developing its purest principles and bringing out its greatest results. Hence it is that in this Constitution we do not wish to leave a jot or tittle upon which anything can be built to remind our children of their former state of slavery. On the contrary, I would have this instrument so comprehensive as to embrace all classes, and hold up to every man an inducement to become, in mind and estate, an honest, educated and efficient citizen of the country.

But it is said that a certain class of citizens are not qualified to vote: be that as it may, I desire to state here especially, that, for my part, I will never, never, give my influence to establish one barrier against any class of men. I care not whether they be white or black, rich or poor, I shall never interfere with their possession of this sacred right. Now, I propose to strike out this article entirely, and, in doing so, believe I shall be doing justice to ourselves, to posterity, to the coming generation, and, at the same time, we shall lay the foundation of a career in which equity, and every principle of right will be possessed, and the prosperity of man advanced. . . .

[ARTICLE VIII: Section 2. Every male citizen of the United States, of the age of twenty-one years and upwards, not laboring under the disabilities named in this Constitution, without distinction of race, color, or former condition, who shall be a resident of this State at the time of the adoption of this Constitution, or who shall thereafter reside in this State one year, and in the County in which he offers to vote, sixty days next preceding any election, shall be entitled to vote for all officers that are now, or hereafter may be, elected by the people, and upon all questions submitted to the electors at any elections; *Provided*, That no person shall be allowed to vote or hold office who is now or hereafter may be disqualified therefor by the Constitution of the United States, until such disqualification shall be removed by the Congress of the United

States; *Provided further,* That no person, while kept in any alms house or asylum, or of unsound mind, or confined in any public prison, shall be allowed to vote or hold office.]

[EDUCATION]

MR. B. O. DUNCAN . . . Now, what is likely to be the result of retaining this section, and thereby opening the public schools to all? Simply, that they would be attended only by the colored children. If the attempt is made to enforce a mixture in this way, I have no idea that fifty white children in the State would attend the public schools. The freedmen's schools are now, if I mistake not, open to all; and yet I believe not one white pupil in the State attends them. The result would be exactly the same with our public schools. This is a state of affairs that we should certainly desire to avoid. In the first place, the poor white children would be deprived of any chance of education. They would continue ignorant and degraded and prejudiced. The whites who have means would send their children to private schools, but the poor whites would be as heretofore, unable to do so. You would also have the strange condition of affairs, of the whites paying probably nine-tenths of the expenses of institutions, which, by their organization, they would regard themselves as shut out from using. This would be a continual barrier in the way of peaceable and friendly relations existing between the two races all over the country. It would, I fear, have a most injurious effect on the ratification of this Constitution, and go far towards counteracting the good impressions made by our moderation thus far.

Again, in attempting to enforce mixed schools, you bring trouble, quarrelling and wrangling, into every neighborhood; and that too among those who are not directly responsible to the law, and who are more likely to be governed by prejudice and passion than by reason. You come in contact with the women and children, who are more prejudiced and more difficult to control. Suppose the case that it were possible to force the whites to send to mixed schools; and let a white boy and a colored boy have a little "pass at arms," as would continually occur, and at once you have a row between the mothers, which will frequently involve the fathers. In this way every neighborhood all over the State would be kept in a continual state of turmoil and strife. In this way passion and prejudice of race will be continually nurtured, and peace and quiet will not be allowed to prevail in any portion of the country. Both races, the colored as well as the white, would have good reason to complain of our inconsiderate action in bringing about such a state of affairs. . . .

Now, how are we to avoid these dangers? This does not seem to me so difficult. Let us simply strike out this section, and leave the whole matter to the Legislature. If that body determines that the schools shall be mixed, and it is found after a year or two that the plan does not work well, it can easily be changed, but if we retain this section, no matter how injurious it may be found; no matter how dangerous to the welfare of the country, and to the cause of education, it cannot be removed. It does seem to me that we should leave a question so untried, so delicate, and yet of such paramount importance, where it may be changed, if it is found that the first experiments do not work well. I believe we have everything to gain and nothing to lose by such a course. We would certainly gain among the whites, and I believe we would lose nothing among the colored people. Our colored people want schools to send their children to. That is a universal desire, and certainly a most praise-worthy one. But I do not believe they would prefer or even desire to have white children attending the same schools with their own. If they can have well organized schools under competent and kind teachers, sustained by the public, I believe they will be perfectly satisfied.

Now, would it not be far better to have schools entirely impartial in their organization, but separate, and all classes attending them, and acquiring an education, and everything working harmoniously together, than for us to introduce a measure here that would very likely prove injurious to the cause of education, but which we could not change, because it is in the Constitution? It seems to me there should be no doubt on this point among intelligent, reasonable men. . . . The future welfare of our State, and of our people, individually and collectively, depends upon our success in this cause. I do most sincerely trust and entreat that this all-important question may receive the calm and careful consideration it merits; and that we will not adopt a section so sure to injure the cause of education in our State, as this most certainly would.

MR. J. J. WRIGHT. I did not suppose that this section would elicit any discussion whatever. The gentleman who last resumed his seat has referred to the impropriety of allowing the children of the two races to attend school together. If I read the section aright, it contemplates no such thing. It simply says, "all schools, colleges, etc., supported by public funds, shall be open to all classes, without regard to race, color or previous condition." The gentleman said such a state of things would not be allowed even in Massachusetts. I must say I have read the laws of that State, and know of no such provision. The school law of Massachusetts is that all persons, without discrimination, are allowed to attend all schools, colleges or public institutions, supported by public funds. I have had the pleasure of visiting the schools in Massachusetts, New York, New Hampshire, and a large number of States, and all children can attend school in these States without regard to color. If they do not want to go, they can remain at home. I know, however, there are but few schools where white and colored children mingle together, and the same arrangements could be carried out in South Carolina. This provision leaves it so that white and colored children can attend school together, if they desire to do so; but I do not believe the colored children will want to go to the white schools, or vice versa. I think there will be separate schools established, and there is no clause in our Constitution that prevents it; therefore I hope this clause will be adopted exactly as it is. One thing I would have understood, the colored people do not want to force what is called social equality; that is a matter which will regulate itself. No law we can pass can compel associations that are distasteful to anybody. It is useless to attempt it, and when the idea is held up before you, it is only a bugbear, with which some persons would frighten you from the performance of your duty. All you have to do is to stand up, face the music for a while, and I tell you that every man, white and black, in South Carolina will come to time. This prejudice will be broken down. We are not framing a Constitution for to-day, but for years, and we should be careful how we execute that task. Let us so enact laws that all children will have the benefit of all schools for which the public pay. We cannot leave this matter wholly to the General Assembly. We must not falter or shrink one inch, or pause in the work of doing all classes justice. Time will prove our work.

MR. R. C. DELARGE. I wish to know if the gentleman is in favor of compelling the children of the two races to go to school together?

MR. J. J. WRIGHT. I am not. The gentleman knows that no person in this Convention has raised his voice louder against the compulsory attendance of children than I have done. . . .

[ARTICLE X: SECTION 10. All the public schools, colleges, and universities of this State supported in whole or in part by the public funds, shall be free and open to all the children and youths of the State, without regard to race or color.]

c. South Carolina: Democratic Party
Appeal to Congress, 1868

THE RESPECTFUL REMONSTRANCE,
ON BEHALF OF
THE WHITE PEOPLE OF SOUTH CAROLINA,
AGAINST THE CONSTITUTION OF THE LATE CONVENTION
OF THAT STATE, NOW SUBMITTED
TO CONGRESS FOR RATIFICATION.

To the Honorable the Senate and House of Representatives of the United States, in Congress assembled:
The undersigned respectfully sheweth, that a Constitution fraught with evil to the State, and to all classes of the people thereof, is about to be submitted to your honorable body for ratification. Before your honorable body shall set upon that instrument the seal of your approval, and thus consummate upon a proud and faithful people a great and irreparable wrong, we respectfully ask a hearing at your hands, whilst with a due sense of our responsibility to God and to truth, we submit for your consideration the grave objections that may be urged against the proposed fundamental law for this State. And first, permit us to lay before your honorable body the following analysis of the said Constitution, prepared by the Hon. B. F. Perry, of this State—a pure man, an able lawyer, and a life-long, bold and out-spoken Unionist. As a man who opposed nullification and secession you will, perhaps, not regard him as one whose views on the Constitution are apt to be pervaded by that disunion spirit, which many members of your honorable body might deem sufficient to prejudice any paper emanating from

SOURCE: *The Respectful Remonstrance* . . . (pamphlet, Columbia, S.C., 1868).

South Carolina. Mr. Perry thus states the most prominent objections to be urged against the Constitution of the Reconstruction Convention of this State:

"ARTICLE I.—SECTION 19—Of the Declaration of Rights, gives Justices of Peace jurisdiction of all offences, less than felony, and in which the punishment does not exceed a fine of $100, or imprisonment for thirty days. This is a gross invasion of that boast and bulwark of Anglo-Saxon liberty, the trial by jury. Any one may be arrested and 'tried summarily,' before a Justice of the Peace, or other officer, authorized by law, on information under oath, without indictment or intervention of a Grand Jury." Can anything be more despotic or alarming, than the power of an ignorant, vicious negro Justice to fine and imprison any and every man in the State?

"SEC. 24—Enables the Legislature to authorize and empower any one, a police or military officer, to suspend the laws of the State, or the execution of the laws! The Constitution of the United States limits the suspension of the writ of *habeas corpus* by Congress, even to cases of rebellion or invasion. But here the whole laws of the State, in time of peace, may be suspended by some worthless minion, authorized by the Legislature.

"SEC. 25—Authorizes the General Assembly to subject any one to martial law, or to the pains and penalties of martial law, whenever they think proper. This infamous power is given the Legislature under the guise, too, of protecting personal rights. It seems to have been suggested by the minority of the Supreme Court's dissenting opinion in Milligan's case. They held that Congress could authorize the trial of a citizen by a military court. The framers of this Constitution did not intend to leave the legislative power doubtful in this particular.

"SEC. 28—Clearly and distinctly empowers and authorizes the Legislature to keep up and maintain a standing army in time of peace! This alarming power is given, too, most adroitly, under the pretence, that armies being dangerous to liberty, ought not to be maintained in time of peace 'without the consent of the General Assembly!' The purpose of this section is to enable the Legislature to keep up a regular force of five or ten thousand negro soldiers, to suppress and keep in subjection the white race, after the United States forces are removed from South Carolina! The Constitution of the United States especially prohibits any State 'keeping troops or ships of war in time of peace.' But this Constitution declares it may be done with the consent of the Legislature! . . .

"SEC. 2 of ART. 8—Enfranchises every male negro over the age of twenty-one, whether a convict, felon or a pauper, and disfranchises every white man who has held office in South Carolina. Intelligence, virtue and patriotism are to give place, in all elections, to ignorance, stupidity and vice. The superior race is to be made subservient to the inferior. Taxation and representation are no longer to be united. They who own no property are to levy taxes, and make all appropriations. The property holders have to pay these taxes, without having any voice in levying them! The consequences will be, in effect, confiscation. The appropriations to support free schools for the education of negro children, for the support of old negroes in the poor houses, and the vicious in jails and penitentiary, together with a standing army of negro soldiers, will be crushing and utterly ruinous to the State. Every man's property will have to be sold to pay his taxes.

"SEC. 8—Expressly prohibits the Legislature passing any law depriving a convict of larceny of the right of suffrage. It was apprehended that in a few years a large proportion of the negro voters might be convicted of larceny, and the radical party thereby shorn of their strength in all elections. But is it not most shameful, that in forming a Constitution, care should be taken to prevent rogues from being disfranchised, whilst the same caution is exercised to exclude the most intelligent, virtuous and patriotic from the right of suffrage! It would seem that the purpose of the framers of this Constitution was to found a community of rogues and paupers in South Carolina! And so astute have they been in carrying out their purpose, that they provide in section 12, that all who have already been convicted of felony shall be allowed to vote.

"SEC. 2 of ART. 9—Prohibits the Legislature from levying a poll tax of more than one dollar on each person, and declares that this tax shall be applied exclusively to the public school fund! And no additional poll tax shall be levied by any municipal corporation. In other words, the property must pay all the taxes of the Government, and persons shall pay nothing for their protection of life and liberty. The idea is that vagrants and rogues are to be a sort of *noblesse*, exempt from taxation, as was the case of the aristocracy in France previous to the French Revolution. . . .

"SEC. 3 of ART. 10—Establishes a uniform system of free public schools throughout the State, and provides for the division of the State into school districts. This will do very well in New England, where they have a dense population, but is wholly unsuited to the sparse population of South Carolina. In many of the school districts, four miles square, there will not be a child to be educated. In a majority of them there will not be children enough to make a respectable school. The expense of such a system will be at least $1,000,000. It contemplates and forces the education of the white and black children in the same school. This, no one, who has any regard for the morals, manners and future respectability of his children, will tolerate. They who are able may employ private tutors for their sons and daughters; but the poor children will have no alternative but to go to these schools, or be uneducated. . . .

"SEC. 8—Provides for the establishment of State reform schools for juvenile offenders. This is a new system to be introduced in South Carolina, and of very doubtful policy. It will certainly add hundreds of thousands of dollars to our taxation. All the public schools, colleges and universities in the State are, by section 10, to be free and open to all the children, without regard to race or color. There seems to be a studied desire throughout all the provisions of this most infamous Constitution, to degrade the white race and elevate the black race, to force upon us social as well as political equality, and bring about an amalgamation of races.

"SEC. 5 of ART. 11—Forces each County to provide for the support of the aged, infirm and unfortunate. It does not require children to support their aged, infirm or unfortunate parents, nor parents to provide for their children; but this heavy and most enormous burden is to be thrown on the public and provided for by taxation.

"Heretofore South Carolina has pursued a wise policy in refusing all divorces. The marriage contract is not like that of any other, which the parties may rescind at pleasure, without injury to society. There is a third party—innocent and helpless children—who are deeply interested in all divorces. Moreover, it tends to demoralize every community where it is allowed or tolerated. But section 4 gives the courts power to grant divorces. This section was intended, perhaps, for the especial benefit of the negroes. It ought also to have legalized polygamy, which has likewise great favor with this class of people.

"The settlement of a wife's property, provided for in section 8, might have been left to the discretion and wisdom of the Legislature. It is an experiment, and if found mischievous or unwise, the Legislature ought to have the power of changing or altering the law. But this ordinary act of legislation has been incorporated in the Constitution as a fundamental law, not to be repealed. . . .

"The ordinance to create a Board of Land Commissioners, authorizes the purchase of lands for the purpose of selling them out in small tracts to purchasers on credit. This wild and ruinous scheme is, likewise, for the negroes, and is likely to benefit no one, except the land commissioners and their friends. State stocks are to be issued for the purpose of purchasing these lands. They may be sold, but the purchasers will never pay for them, and the loss will ultimately fall upon the State. Did any one ever before hear of so many effective provisions for squandering public money, when the whole State, and all the people in it, are reduced to bankruptcy and poverty?"

Thus has it been shown, in the above analysis, how injuriously this Constitution must affect the interests of the white man, and how inconsistent it must prove with the peace and prosperity of the State. But, in addition to this, the Committee believe that it can be shown that the said Constitution is not the less injurious to the very class—to wit: the black people—whom it seemed most especially to have been designed to benefit. On this point, the Committee ask leave to invite attention to the comments of the Hon. A. Burt, one of the ablest lawyers of the State, and a man of the highest character, and of well known political conservatism. The following is his language on the subject of the provisions of the new Constitution which confer the power of taxation:

An analysis of the provisions of the new Constitution, which confer the power of taxation, I have not a doubt, will assure any candid mind that no people on this continent can endure the burdens which it imposes. The principle which pervades that entire instrument is that all taxation, except for a single purpose, shall be imposed upon real estate and upon the income from the sale of merchandize. In estimating the inequality of taxation, we cannot omit the fact of the great diversity between the two races which inhabit the State. At this moment the taxable property is held by one race, and under that Constitution the political power is vested exclusively in the other. Not only are the ordinary appropriations for the civil service of the State imposed upon the property held by the smaller number, but the other race, as a race, is at the present moment entirely exempt from any taxation, except for the support of public schools. A very large number of the race which own the taxable property are disfranchised—cannot vote, and cannot even hold the humblest office created by that Constitution; while all others, without reference to property, to educational qualification, to past citizenship, or any other qualification, are allowed to vote. Need I say that this is a condition of things which the world never before witnessed! . . . I say that a more arrant and infamous spoliation of a class was never designed by any country on the face of the earth.

Now, what must be the consequences? Property under forms of law, in the guise of taxation, will be transferred from the hands of those who now possess it to others. It is inevitable. The holders of taxable property in South Carolina cannot to-day, and will not hereafter, be able to pay the taxes imposed upon them. . . .

If there be any colored man who intends to be industrious, frugal and moral—to elevate himself and family—to that man I desire to say one word: Let him acquire real estate and learn to read and write, so that he may be placed in the category of the white man who owns taxable property, and if I am not totally mistaken in the opinion I have derived from successful and critical examination of the new Constitution, he will be unable to retain his property three years. It will be taken from him by those of his own race who are idle, thriftless, and do not mean to work. Hence it is that I call upon all respectable colored men, who entertain hopes of future prosperity, to denounce that Constitution and join his natural, ancient and true friends in opposing its ratification. . . .

We have thus suggested to your honorable body some of the prominent objections to your adoption of this Constitution. We waive all argument upon the subject of its validity. It is a Constitution *de facto*, and that is the ground upon which we approach your honorable body in the spirit of earnest remonstrance. That Constitution was the work of Northern adventurers, Southern renegades and ignorant negroes. Not one per centum of the white population of the State approves it, and not two per centum of the negroes who voted for its adoption know any more than a dog, horse, or cat, what his act of voting implied. That Constitution enfranchises every male negro over the age of twenty-one, and disfranchises many of the purest and best white men of the State. The negro being in a large numerical majority, as compared with the whites, the effect is that the new Constitution establishes in this State negro supremacy, with all its train of countless evils. A superior race—a portion, Senators and Representatives, of the same proud race to which it is your pride to belong—is put under the rule of an inferior race—the abject slaves of yesterday, the flushed freedmen of to-day. And think you that there can be any just, lasting reconstruction on this basis? The Committee respectfully reply, in behalf of their white fellow-citizens, that this cannot be. We do not mean to threaten resistance by arms. But the white people of our State will never quietly submit to negro rule. We may have to pass under the yoke you have authorized, but by moral agencies, by political organization, by every peaceful means left us, we will keep up this contest until we have regained the heritage of political control handed down to us by an honored ancestry. This is a duty we owe to the land that is ours, to the graves that it contains, and to the race of which you and we are alike members—the proud Caucasian race, whose sovereignty on earth God has ordained, and they themselves have illustrated on the most brilliant pages of the world's history.

Nor, Senators and Representatives, does the State of South Carolina merit, at your hands, the political treatment that has been meted out to her without stint.

It is true, South Carolina took the field promptly, in the late war between the States. Her people embarked their all in the struggle, because the sovereignty of the State demanded this of them. But when the war ended, and the arbitrament to which they resorted was adverse to their cause, no people ever yielded more gracefully to the decree of Providence. Quietly they laid down their arms, and, in peace, they became law-abiding, as, in war, they had been faithful to their flag. They accepted the legitimate results of the war. They were ready to abandon the claim of the right of their State peaceably to secede from the Union, and they assented, in Convention assembled, to the emancipation of their slaves. And now, were the State admitted into the Union, on a just and reasonable basis, we hesitate not to declare that again would our people greet the starry banner of the Union, and unite with their fellow-citizens of the whole country in the effort to promote the glory, wealth and prosperity of our common land.

In our relations, as proposed by us, with the black people of this State, we are not disposed to exact anything that just men may deny or Heaven disapprove.

When South Carolina assented to the act of Federal emancipation, we hold that the freed people became members of the body politic, and, as such, entitled to all the civil rights that are enjoyed alike by all classes of the people. They became entitled to "life, liberty and the pursuit of happiness"—to all that the Declaration of American Independence and the English *Magna Charta* claim for man as his inalienable rights. But as it regards suffrage, we hold that this is not a political right nor a civil one for man, either white or black, but it is a *trust*, a delicate trust, to be conferred by the State upon the people thereof, according to considerations of expediency, and agreeably to the sound political doctrine of the greatest good to the greatest number.

With respect, now, to the extension of this trust to the colored people, we believe that nine-tenths of our people are willing to concede it to them, duly qualified. We cannot admit universal suffrage, because the great body of the colored people are utterly unfitted to exercise it with intelligence and discretion; and because it would make the negro dominant, and thus bring about a fatal antagonism between the races. We cannot deny it altogether to the black man, because that would be neither right nor politic. Hence the policy of the mean between the two extremes, which has met with general favor in this State. The conservative party of South Carolina now stands and gathers strength, day after day, upon this proposition. The Convention of the party lately passed the following resolution:

"*Resolved*, That under the action of the State of South Carolina, heretofore taken, we recognize the colored population of the State as an integral element of the body politic; and, as such, in person and property, entitled to a full and equal protection under the State Constitution and laws. And that as citizens of South Carolina, we declare our willingness, when we have the power, to grant them, under proper qualifications as to property and intelligence, the right of suffrage."

In behalf at least of the Democratic party of South Carolina, which embraces nearly every white inhabitant, and many of the colored people, the Committee declare that this policy represents the political sentiment of the State. We offer this in good faith, as the basis of a true, a genuine and lasting reconstruction. This, we earnestly believe, is the peaceful solution of the great question of white man and black man in the South. This solution we offer to the conservatism of the country, as one alike advantageous to both races. Let this be accepted; let the vexed question of the black man be removed from the high court of the land, and let all of our people North, South, East and West, be permitted harmoniously and earnestly to address themselves to the great work of individual improvement and national aggrandizement—then again may we expect a return of the better days of the Republic, and a restoration of the Union in fact as well as in name.

WADE HAMPTON,
JOHN P. THOMAS,
JOSEPH DANIEL POPE,
F. W. MCMASTER,
SAMUEL MCGOWAN,
W. M. SHANNON,
State Central Executive Committee.

d. South Carolina Selected Laws, 1868–1871

STATUTES AT LARGE OF SOUTH CAROLINA

AN ACT TO PROVIDE FOR THE RECORDING OF CERTIFICATES OF SALE ISSUED TO PURCHASERS OF LANDS SOLD UNDER DIRECTION AND AUTHORITY OF THE UNITED STATES DIRECT TAX COMMISSIONERS IN BEAUFORT COUNTY, SOUTH CAROLINA.

Whereas, a large number of land titles in the form of certificates of sale, issued by the United States Direct Tax Commissioners for South Carolina, have been created in the County of Beaufort, in said State, during and since the close of the late rebellion:

Be it enacted by the Senate and House of Representatives of the State of South Carolina, now met and sitting in General Assembly, and by the authority of the same, That the holders of all certificates or titles, issued by or under the authority of the United States Direct Tax Commissioners for South Carolina, shall be allowed to record the same in the office of the Register of Mesne Conveyance for the County aforesaid; and that when such certificates shall have been so recorded, such recording shall be deemed to be a legal notice of title to the land described in the same.

[August 20, 1868]

SOURCE: Acts and Joint Resolutions of the General Assembly of the State of South Carolina, 1868–1871 (Columbia, S.C., 1868–1871).

AN ACT to determine the manner of disposing
of lands purchased by the state for taxes

SECTION 1. *Be it enacted* by the Senate and House of Representatives of the State of South Carolina, now met and sitting in General Assembly, and by the authority of the same, In the case of all lands purchased on behalf of the State, under the provisions of Section 108 of an Act entitled "An Act to provide for the assessment and taxation of property," the County Treasurer shall, in the name of the State, enter upon and take possession of the same, and may lease the same in parcels not exceeding forty acres each, to any person or persons who are citizens of the State, and who may desire to cultivate the same; said leases to be in such form as shall be prescribed by the Attorney-General, and subject to all the rights of redemption in such case provided for by law. Said lands may be leased for a sum certain, not less than ten per cent. of the cost thereof, or for such share of the crops as shall be reasonable and just.

SEC. 2. Any person who shall have rented lands under the provisions of the foregoing Section, entered upon and fulfilled the conditions of the lease, shall, at the expiration of the time during which said lands were redeemable by the original owner, be deemed to have acquired a right of pre-emption in the same.

SEC. 3. After the time allowed for the redemption of any lands purchased by the County Treasurer, on behalf of the State on account of taxes, shall have passed, the said Treasurer shall cause the same, or any portion thereof, to be sub-divided and sold, in parcels not exceeding forty acres each, at public sale, after giving sixty days' notice thereof, and issue a certificate therefor. Said lands shall be sold to the highest bidder, and on terms most advantageous to the revenue of the State: *Provided*, The party or parties who may have gained a right of pre-emption shall have the right to purchase the same at a sum not less than the cost thereof to the State, one-fourth of the purchase money to be paid down, and the balance, with interest, in three annual instalments.

SEC. 4. After the purchase money shall have been fully paid, together with the interest thereon, the Governor is authorized and required to cause a patent or patents to be issued to any such person as may be the *bona fide* purchaser, owner, assignee or transferee of such lands or tenements, under and by virtue of any certificates of sale, or under and by virtue of any assignment or transfer of such certificate: *Provided*, That in case of an assignment or transfer of a certificate of sale, the person applying for such patent shall give satisfactory proof to the County Treasurer of the preceding transfers and assignments.

SEC. 5. The County Treasurer shall, on or before the first day of November in each year, report to the State Treasurer all lands leased under this Act, giving the names of the lessees and the terms of each lease, and the names of the original owners of such lands. Also, a report of all lands sold, and of the certificates of sale issued, and the terms of each sale. All moneys accruing to the State under the provisions of this Act shall be paid over and accounted for in the same manner as money received for taxes.

[September 23, 1868]

AN ACT TO PUNISH DISCRIMINATION IN THE TREATMENT OF PRISONERS BY JAILERS AND SHERIFFS

SECTION 1. *Be it enacted* by the Senate and House of Representatives of the State of South Carolina, now met and sitting in General Assembly, and by the authority of the same, That from and after the passage of this Act it shall be unlawful for Sheriffs or Jailers to make any discrimination in the treatment of prisoners placed in their custody.

SEC. 2. Every violation of this Act shall be a misdemeanor, and upon conviction thereof the party convicted shall be fined not less than twenty-five dollars, and imprisoned for not less than one month, nor more than twelve months.

[September 25, 1868]

AN ACT TO ESTABLISH A BUREAU OF AGRICULTURAL STATISTICS FOR THE ENCOURAGEMENT OF INDUSTRIAL ENTERPRISES, AND TO INVITE CAPITAL TO SOUTH CAROLINA, FOR THE DEVELOPMENT OF THE RESOURCES OF THE STATE

SECTION 1. *Be it enacted* by the Senate and House of Representatives of the State of South Carolina, now met and sitting in General Assembly, and by the authority of the same, That for the purpose of encouraging, promoting and protecting industrial enterprises in this State, and of supplying truthful information to the people of the United States, and inducing them to bring hither

their capital and aid in the development of the resources of South
Carolina, the Governor is hereby authorized to establish a Bureau
of Agricultural Statistics, and to appoint a Commissioner thereof
to perform such duties as may appertain to the office.

Sec. 2. It shall be the duty of the said Commissioner to collect
all the information practicable concerning lands, crops, climate,
railroads, telegraphs, manufactories, water powers, schools,
churches, and other institutions in the several Counties of the
State, and preserve a record of the same, in such manner that the
facts relating to any locality may be promptly communicated to the
inquirer.

Sec. 3. That the said Commissioner shall be specially charged to
ascertain, by advertisement or otherwise, the location of lands for
sale, and to cause said lands, after having been duly laid off and
described, to be registered, together with the price demanded and
the conditions of payment.

Sec. 4. That the said Commissioner shall, by official publications
in the journals of the North and West, by correspondence and
pamphlets, convey this information, describe the lands thus offered
for sale, and the advantages which this State offers in soil, climate,
productions, and so forth, to the industrious and frugal citizen, and
at the same time invite him to bring hither his means, and aid in
the promotion of general prosperity. . . .

[September 26, 1868]

AN ACT to regulate the manner of drawing juries

Section 1. *Be it enacted* by the Senate and House of Representatives of the State of South Carolina, now met and sitting in
General Assembly, and by the authority of the same, All persons
who are qualified to vote in the choice of Representatives in the
General Assembly shall be liable to be drawn and serve as jurors,
except as hereinafter provided.

Sec. 2. The following persons shall be exempt from serving as
jurors, to wit: . . .

[Secs. 3 through 42 follow, with detailed provisions for drawing
and empanelling jurors, &c.]

[September 26, 1868]

AN ACT to enforce the provisions of the civil rights bill
OF THE UNITED STATES CONGRESS

Section 1. *Be it enacted* by the Senate and House of Representatives of the State of South Carolina, now met and sitting in

General Assembly, and by the authority of the same, That from and after the passage of this Act it shall not be lawful for common carriers, or any party or parties engaged in any business, calling or pursuit, for the carrying on of which a license or charter is required by law, municipal, State, Federal or otherwise, to discriminate between persons on account of race, color or previous condition, who shall make lawful application for the benefit of such business, calling or pursuit.

SEC. 2. Any party so discriminating shall be considered as having violated this Act, and, upon conviction, shall be punished by a fine of not less than two hundred dollars, or imprisonment for not less than six months in the Penitentiary.

SEC. 3. No Act of incorporation shall be conferred upon any organization, the rules and regulations of which contain features not compatible with the provisions of this Act.

SEC. 4. All Acts or parts of Acts inconsistent with this Act are hereby repealed.

Approved February 13, 1869.

AN ACT FURTHER TO AMEND THE ACTS
INCORPORATING THE UNIVERSITY OF SOUTH CAROLINA.

SECTION 1. *Be it enacted* by the Senate and House of Representatives of the State of South Carolina, now met and sitting in General Assembly, and by the authority of the same, The Board of Trustees of the University of South Carolina shall hereafter consist of seven members, who shall be elected on joint ballot by the General Assembly, and shall hold their offices for the term of four years and until their successors shall be appointed, no one of whom, during his continuance in office, shall be in any other manner connected with the University. Neither the said Board of Trustees, nor the Faculty of the University, shall make any distinction in the admission of students or the management of the University on account of race, color or creed. . . .

SEC. 7. There shall be admitted to the University one student annually from each County in the State, who shall be entitled to entrance into as many as three of the schools, not including either the school of law or medicine, without the payment of tuition fees. Such student shall be appointed by the Governor, on the nomination of the delegation in the General Assembly from the County in which the students shall respectively reside; the nomination to be made by the delegation in accordance with such regulations as the Governor may prescribe: *Provided,* That every student thus appointed shall show, upon examination before the Faculty, the degree of proficiency required of other students for admission into the University, and shall be otherwise admissible, according to the regulations governing the University. . . .

Approved March 3, 1869

AN ACT TO PROTECT LABORERS AND PERSONS WORKING UNDER CONTRACT ON SHARES OF CROPS.

SECTION 1. *Be it enacted* by the Senate and House of Representatives of the State of South Carolina, now met and sitting in General Assembly, and by the authority of the same, That all contracts made between owners of land, their agents, administrators or executors, and laborers, shall be witnessed by one or more disinterested persons, and, at the request of either party, be duly executed before a Justice of the Peace or Magistrate, whose duty it shall be to read and explain the same to the parties. Such contracts shall clearly set forth the conditions upon which the laborer or laborers engaged to work, embracing the length of time, the amount of money to be paid, and when; if it be on shares of crops, what portion of the crop or crops.

SEC. 2. That whenever labor is performed under contract on shares of crop or crops, such crop or crops shall be gathered and divided off before it is removed from the place where it was planted, harvested or gathered. Such division to be made by a disinterested person, when desired by either party to the contract. . . . When such division has been made, each party shall be free to dispose of their several portions as to him or her or them may seem fitting: *Provided,* That if either party be in debt to the other for any obligation incurred under contract, the amount of said indebtedness may be then and there settled and paid by such portion of the share or shares of the party so indebted as may be agreed upon by the parties themselves, or set apart by the Justice of the Peace or Magistrate, or any party chosen to divide said crop or crops.

SEC. 3. That whenever laborers are working on shares of crop or crops, or for wages in money or other valuable consideration, they shall have a prior lien upon said crop or crops, in whosesoever hands it may be. Such portion of the crop or crops to them belonging, or such amount of money or other valuable consideration due, shall be recoverable by an action in any Court of competent jurisdiction.

SEC. 4. That whenever such contract or contracts are violated, or attempted to be violated or broken, or whenever fraud is practiced, or attempted to be practiced, by either party to such contract or contracts, at any time before the conditions of the same are fulfilled and the parties released therefrom, complaint may be made before a Justice of the Peace or Magistrate, or may be carried before any Court having jurisdiction in such cases, where the extent and character of the offence shall be determined. If the offending party be the land owner or owners. . . . upon proof to conviction, such offender or offenders shall forfeit and pay a fine, not less than fifty (50) dollars, nor more than five hundred (500) dollars; or if it be a disinterested party chosen to make a division or divisions of crops hereinbefore provided, he, she, or they, shall be liable to an action of trespass, and shall be tried in any Court of competent jurisdiction, and on proof to conviction, be fined in a sum not less than fifty nor more than five hundred dollars, or be imprisoned for a period not less than one month nor more than one year, at the discretion of the Court. If the offending party be a laborer or laborers, and the offence consist either in failing wilfully and without just cause to give the labor reasonably required of him, her, or them, by the terms of such contract, or in other respects shall refuse to comply with the conditions of such contract or contracts, or shall fraudulently make use of or carry away from the place where the crop or crops he, she, or they, may be working are planted, any portion of said crop or crops, or anything connected therewith or belonging thereto, such person or persons so offending shall be liable to fine or imprisonment, according to the gravity of the offence, and upon proof to conviction before a Justice of the Peace or a Court of competent jurisdiction.

SEC. 5. Any Justice of the Peace or other officer before whom complaint is made, and whose duty it is to try such cases as is hereinbefore provided, who shall offend against the true intent and meaning of this Act, or shall refuse to hear and determine, impartially, all cases that may be brought before him, under the provisions of this Act, and all peace officers, whose duty it is to apprehend all offenders against the laws of the State, who shall refuse to perform their duty in bringing to justice any and all offenders against this Act, shall be liable to a charge of malfeasance in office, and upon proof to conviction shall be forthwith removed from office, and fined in a sum not less than fifty nor more than one hundred dollars.

SEC. 6. All Acts and parts of Acts in any way conflicting with the provisions of this Act are hereby repealed.

SEC. 7. This Act shall take effect and have full force of law from and after its passage.

Approved March 19, 1869.

AN ACT TO AMEND AN ACT ENTITLED "AN ACT TO REGULATE THE MANNER OF DRAWING JURORS."

SECTION 1. *Be it enacted* by the Senate and House of Representatives of the State of South Carolina, now met and sitting in General Assembly, and by the authority of the same, That Section 5 of the Act entitled "An Act to regulate the manner of drawing juries," ratified the 25th day of September, Anno Domini 1868, be, and the same is hereby, amended by the addition of the following at the end of the Section: "*Provided, always*, That the list, when completed, shall be such that the number of names of white voters thereon shall bear, to the number of names of colored voters, as near as may be, the same proportion as the whole number of white voters bears to the whole number of colored voters in the township, city or County, as the case may be." . . .

Approved March 23, 1869.

JOINT RESOLUTION AUTHORIZING THE GOVERNOR TO EMPLOY AN ARMED FORCE FOR THE PRESERVATION OF THE PEACE

SECTION 1. *Be it resolved* by the Senate and House of Representatives of the State of South Carolina, now met and sitting in General Assembly, and by the authority of the same, That the Governor of the State, with the assistance of the Adjutant-General, be, and he is hereby, authorized to enlist a company of one hundred men, or more, if in his opinion more be needed, who shall be fully armed and equipped, and, if necessary, be mounted, and that when in any County in this State it shall become impossible, from any cause, to enforce the laws and keep the peace by the ordinary civil processes, the Governor shall have, and is hereby given, authority to send as many of the aforesaid armed and equipped men into said County as, in his judgment, may be necessary to quell such disturbance and arrest the guilty parties; and that, in order to carry out the intent of this resolution, the Governor is hereby authorized to exercise any or all of the powers conferred upon him by an Act entitled "An Act to suppress insurrection and rebellion," passed on the twenty-second day of September, 1868. . . .

Sec. 4. This resolution shall remain of full force and effect until the militia of the State is organized and ready for service.

Approved February 8, 1869.

AN ACT to provide for the protection of persons, property and the public peace

Whereas threatenings, intimidation and violence are used in portions of this State against the peace of the same; and whereas the laws are set at defiance, and the officers of the law hindered, prevented and obstructed in the discharge of their duties; and whereas armed, disguised and lawless persons are threatening, maltreating and assassinating peaceable and defenceless citizens; therefore,

Section 1. *Be it enacted* by the Senate and House of Representatives of the State of South Carolina, now met and sitting in General Assembly, and by the authority of the same, That if any person shall assault or intimidate any citizen because of political opinions or the exercise of political rights and privileges guaranteed to every citizen of the United States by the Constitution and laws thereof, or by the Constitution and laws of this State, or, for such reason, discharge such citizen from employment or occupation, or eject such citizen from rented house or land or other property, such person shall be deemed guilty of a misdemeanor, and, on conviction thereof, be fined not less than fifty or more than one thousand dollars, or be imprisoned not less than three months or more than one year, or both, at the discretion of the Court.

Sec. 2. That if any two or more persons shall band or conspire together, or go in disguise upon the public highway or upon the premises of another, with intent to injure, oppress, or violate the person or property of any citizen, because of his political opinion or his expression or exercise of the same, or shall attempt, by any means, measures or acts, to hinder, prevent or obstruct any citizen in the free exercise and enjoyment of any right or privilege secured to him by the Constitution and laws of the United States, or by the Constitution and laws of this State, such persons shall be deemed guilty of a felony, and, on conviction thereof, be fined not less than one hundred or more than two thousand dollars, or be imprisoned not less than six months or more than three years, or both, at the discretion of the Court; and shall thereafter be ineligible to and disabled from holding any office of honor, trust or profit in this State.

SEC 3. That if, in violating any of the provisions of this Act, any other crime, misdemeanor or felony shall be committed, the offender or offenders shall, on conviction thereof, be subjected to such punishment for the same as is attached to such crime, misdemeanor and felony by the existing laws of this State.

[SECS. 4–6. Detailed enforcement provisions]

[SEC. 7. Penalties for hindering enforcement of the law]

SEC. 8. That any citizen who shall be hindered, prevented or obstructed in the exercise of the rights and privileges secured to him by the Constitution and laws of the United States, or by the Constitution and laws of this State, or shall be injured in his person or property because of his exercise of the same, may claim and prosecute the County in which the offence shall be committed for any damages he shall sustain thereby, and the said County shall be responsible for the payment of such damages as the Court may award. . . .

SEC. 9. In all cases where any dwelling house, building, or any property, real or personal, shall be destroyed in consequence of any mob or riot, it shall be lawful for the person or persons owning or interested in such property to bring suits against the County in which such property was situated and being, for the recovery of such damages as he or they may have sustained by reason of the destruction thereof; and the amount which shall be recovered in said action shall be paid in the manner provided by Section 8 of this Act.

[SEC. 10. If person damaged had foreknowledge of intent must have given notice to authorities; latter liable for damages if fail to protect]

[SEC. 11. Persons injured may sue participators in mob or riot]

[SEC. 12. County Commissioners may sue offenders for recovery of costs to county]
Approved March 1, 1871.

e. General Summary of Southern Election Laws, 1872

ELECTION LAWS OF THE LATE INSURRECTIONARY STATES

We have examined the election laws of the late insurrectionary States, and communications, documents, and testimony relating to their operation, in order to ascertain what changes have been made since the war, and how far they have contributed to lawlessness and violence. Important changes are common to all the States.

We give them in general terms, omitting minor matters, such as qualifications of residence, sanity, &c., and disqualifications for crimes other than those committed in rebellion.

1. Before the war only white males of twenty-one years and over were voters.

Now all male citizens of twenty-one years and over, having the qualifications of residence, sanity, &c., have the right of suffrage. The only exception to this rule is in Arkansas, and the governor of that State recommends the removal.

2. Before the war voting was *viva voce*; now it is by ballot.

3. Before the war there was no registry of voters; now all electors are required to register before voting.

4. Before the war the returning officers and those issuing commissions were bound by the arithmetical results of the polls, and required to give the commission or certificate of election to the person having the highest number of votes. Now there are boards of canvassers, who, in several of the States, are required not only to count the returns, but to pass upon questions of violence and fraud, and to exclude returns from precincts where they find the elections to have been controlled by such means.

5. Before the war the basis of representation was, property or property and slaves; or slaves, by enumerating three-fifths or all. Now it is all *inhabitants*.

6. Before the war white male citizens only, and, in some of the

SOURCE: Report on the Condition of Affairs in the Late Insurrectionary States, 42d Cong., 2d sess., Senate Report no. 41, pt. 1 (Washington, D.C., 1872), I:245–246 (cited hereafter as K.K.K. Report).

States, property-holders only were eligible to office. Now all male citizens having general qualification, save those under disabilities by the Constitution of the United States or disfranchised in Arkansas, are eligible.

These changes were made against the will of the old ruling class. The most important—that securing impartial suffrage without regard to race, color, or previous condition—was proposed by the national Government, and accepted by the States as a condition of their readmission to the Union. The other changes were consequent upon and deemed requisite to protect impartial suffrage, though some of them may have been carried further than was necessary.

Complaints have been made by people, who have not become reconciled to the results of the war, against all these changes. They complain of equal suffrage because it elevates the freedmen, their former slaves, to equality with themselves, and enables a few of the poorer classes of white citizens, and citizens from the North, to combine with the enfranchised freedmen electors, and thus form a majority over the greater number of old white citizens of the State; and thus the control of the State is taken from the class who have been accustomed to rule, and given to those whom they ruled over. This complaint goes to the foundation of reconstruction and of republican government. It is that the minority, differing in opinion from the majority, are not permitted, on questions affecting the majority, to govern according to their own will. Such an objection may seem strange to those used to the rule of majorities; but we should not be surprised to hear it from those who have been accustomed to govern by minority.

It was not expected that the old ruling class would be soon reconciled to the loss of power they had so long enjoyed, nor to the transfer of that power to classes whom they hate as enemies and despise as slaves. This complaint seems, to those who make it, strengthened by the fact that they hold nearly all the property in the State, and are the majority of citizens of intelligence and of experience in public affairs. They do not appear to consider that the abandonment and loss of their rights by rebellion should have shaken their prestige, or diminished their weight; nor do they admit that their influence as property holders should be affected by the fact that their titles were lost by treason and restored by the Government.

25. The Functioning of "Negro Government": Testimony of James L. Orr, 1871

JAMES L. ORR was a prominent, respected South Carolinian with a distinguished public career before, during, and after the Civil War. Democratic speaker of the House of Representatives (1857–1859), Confederate senator and the first postwar, elected governor of the state, Orr was willing to concede more in respect to the status of the freedmen than most of the state's white leaders. During his governorship, he became politically isolated and in 1868 joined his fortunes with those of the Republicans, being elected a circuit judge by the General Assembly. Orr died in St. Petersburg in 1873 shortly after Grant had appointed him United States minister to Russia.

CONDITION OF AFFAIRS IN THE SOUTHERN STATES

SOUTH CAROLINA.

WASHINGTON, D.C., June 6, 1871.

Hon. JAMES L. ORR sworn and examined.

By the CHAIRMAN:

Question. Have your public duties brought you into contact with people from various parts of the State; and from that contact and the knowledge so derived, can you inform us of the condition of the State, so far as it relates to the execution of the laws, and the security of life, person, and property? The general nature of the question will indicate to you what we desire, and you can make your statement in your own way.

Answer. I have, of course, been brought into close personal contact with the people of the counties constituting my judicial circuit. The law requires the circuit to be rode in each county three times during each year, and that has brought me in contact, very intimately, with the population of those counties. My other duties occasionally carried me to Columbia, and to some other portions of the State. So far as the administration of the law is concerned, in my section of the State, I do not think there is any fault to be found with it. We have gone through the experiment there of

SOURCE: K.K.K. Report, III:1, 9–15.

having mixed juries, and, so far as my experience has gone, I have had no occasion to find fault with it. In one instance where a colored man was on trial, and the jury was made up entirely of colored men, they convicted him in twenty-five minutes' absence from the jury box. In another instance, of the trial of a colored man, where the jury was composed of eleven colored men and one white man, I suppose the conviction took place in less than thirty minutes after the jury retired. The counties to which I refer more especially now, where I think the law is administered, are Greenville, Oconee, Pickens, Anderson, and Abbeville. In the fall of 1868 there were allegations of violence and intimidation of voters in the presidential and congressional elections. Abbeville was not at that time, however, a part of my judicial district; it has been added to my circuit since then. I think there has been comparative quiet there since then. I happened to be in that county holding court at the time of the election of 1870, and the election was conducted very quietly; I think there was not even a riot in the entire county. In that county the colored element largely preponderates, in about the proportion of two to one. In the other counties the proportion of white and colored population is, in Greenville, about two to one, in Anderson two to one, in Pickens four to one, and in Oconee about five to one.

By MR. VAN TRUMP:
Question. The whites preponderating?
Answer. Yes, sir. . . .
Question. After the facts and data which you have given, it is hardly necessary for me to ask the question; still, I want your opinion. I will ask you whether, at this time, the State of South Carolina is not absolutely and essentially under a negro government?
Answer. A majority of those who have control of it are negroes; that is, there is a majority of negroes in the house of representatives, while in the senate the majority are white men. The governor is a white man; the lieutenant governor is a colored man; the secretary of state is a colored man; the treasurer, the comptroller general, the attorney general, and the adjutant general are white men. Of the supreme court judges one is a colored man; all the eight circuit judges are white men.

Question. How in the counties; are the county officers, commissioners, clerks, &c., especially in the negro counties, colored men?

Answer. The auditors and treasurers are not elected by the people, but are appointed by the governor; the trial justices are appointed by the governor; the county commissioners are elected by the people. I would say that in the counties where the negro race is in the majority, a majority of the county commissioners are colored.

Question. That is the important office of the county, so far as taxes are concerned?

Answer. Yes, sir; so far as taxation and the general police of the county are concerned.

Question. How is it with regard to these negro officers in South Carolina; are they selected from the better educated negroes, negroes from the North, or have they generally been taken from those who were slaves before the war?

Answer. The negroes who have had most influence and control of the organization of the republican party, from 1865 to the present time, are men from the North.

Question. Those are the orators and politicians; I speak now of the office-holders.

Answer. They are of the 400,000 blacks in the State, and their standard of intelligence is a little higher than that of one-half or two-thirds of the 400,000. As a general rule, in their selections, they have taken about the best they could get among their own people, restricting their choice among themselves. In the legislature, a very large proportion of the eighty colored members of the house of representatives were formerly slaves, I suppose, and at the time of manumission I presume two-thirds if not three-fourths of them could not read. Now most of them are able to read; most of them have learned to write their names, and some of them have made more progress than that; very considerable progress, the younger portion of them. But of course there are a great many who are still ignorant.

Question. In regard to those eighty colored members of the house of representatives, if I understood correctly your answers to some of General Blair's questions, you have some fears that there is some truth in the charges of bribery?

Answer. I think they are true as to some of them.

Question. Is it not the fact in regard to negroes of that character, (uneducated and who have been slaves,) that wily white men, approaching them with money, can seduce them into violating their official obligations?

Answer. I think that is according to our experience and knowledge of men of all classes; it would apply as well to whites as to blacks. I have no doubt they are more susceptible to such influences than if they had a high moral training and good intellectual culture.

Question. You say that the law, so far as your region of the State is concerned—I suppose you speak of your judicial circuit—is fully administered?

Answer. Yes, sir.

Question. In regard to the violations of law, of which you have spoken, could not the State power control them without asking for or resorting to the Federal power to come there and subdue them?

Answer. That is one of the difficult questions I had in my mind when I replied to a question of the chairman, as to how those disturbances could be best suppressed. If there was, in those localities, a healthy public opinion among the substantial men of the country, if they were determined to put down these disorders, I think the law there is abundantly sufficient to put them down.

Question. The law, without resort to armed force?

Answer. Yes, sir. You could not very well resort to State militia, because there is no system that I know of by which you mingle the two races together in a military organization without running a greater hazard than even to allow marauding to go on. If you were to attempt to unite the two races in a military company, you could not get it done by volunteering, and you would fail if you attempted to do it by compulsion.

Question. Then you think that the attempt at a half-white and a half-negro government is a failure?

Answer. I think it has been a very difficult experiment.

By MR. BLAIR:

Question. You say that all persons in the State, of adult age and of sufficient residence, are now entitled to the right of suffrage?

Answer. Yes, sir.

Question. Will you give us a general idea how their suffrages are collected; what is the machinery by which it is done?

Answer. Do you mean the machinery for collecting the votes on the day of the elections?

Question. Yes, sir.

Answer. Well, sir, the existing law provides that the governor shall appoint three commissioners of election for each county. Those county commissioners are charged with the duty of selecting managers of elections for the different polling precincts in the county. There is no registration now required; that has been done away with since the election of 1868, which, I suppose, is a very great mistake. The present election law provides that the polls shall be opened at 6 o'clock in the morning and closed at 6 o'clock in the evening, and that there shall be but one day set apart for each election. The county commissioners designate as many polling places in each county, city, and town as the convenience of the voters may require.

Question. And the county commissioners appoint the managers of election?

Answer. Yes, sir. Under the present law those managers are permitted to retain the ballot-boxes, which are required to be sealed up at the close of the election, for five days; or rather, they are required within five days to turn them over to the commissioners of elections, and the commissioners of elections have five days within which to count the votes. . . . I think it was very improper for any such election law to have been passed. If I had been framing an election law, I would have required that the votes should be counted on the evening of election and the returns made the next day. The present law certainly gives to persons who are so disposed an opportunity to commit fraud. And in one of the counties, in regard to the congressional election, two of the commissioners have been convicted, before Judge Bond's court, within the last six weeks, of stuffing the ballot-box.

By MR. VAN TRUMP:

Question. Were they white or black men?

Answer. One was a white man and one was a black man. It was in regard to the election between Mr. Bowen and Mr. De Large.

By MR. COBURN:

Question. You have said in substance that the State authorities can do nothing to suppress these outrages, for the reason that public opinion is in an unhealthy condition, and that the State militia, composed of whites and blacks, would not be of any service. Now, under the circumstances, what authority should be used to restore order?

Answer. That is a hard question to answer. I examined carefully the provisions of the bill passed by Congress at its late session, in the hope that I might there find something that would give the proper authority. But I apprehend that the same difficulty will exist in connection with the military forces of the United States. As an illustration, let me say that there has not been a more quiet community than that of Laurens County since the United States troops went back there. And yet if the troops were to leave there today, there is no telling but what by the day after to-morrow this thing would be just as rampant as ever. If you undertake to enforce the law by troops, according to our experience, and we have had a pretty large experience since 1865, and especially if you undertook to do so by troops who are not familiar with the country, and where there is not among the people much sympathy with the troops, you would find this difficulty: those who commit these offenses are familiar with the country, with every by-way, every hedge, every swamp, stream, and road, and they will have it in their power to make their escape in spite of officers and men, let them be ever so vigilant. They will select portions of the county remote from the troops to commit their offenses, and then they will get such a start in their flight as to prevent the officers and soldiers from capturing them. That is the difficulty, I apprehend, in the United States authorities enforcing the law. . . .

By the CHAIRMAN:

Question. Assuming that these organizations exist, and that the persons who ride in armed bands are members of them for the purpose of inflicting these injuries upon citizens, is not the plain way of looking at the matter to treat them as a public enemy in armed resistance to the State and General Government?

Answer. I would be prepared to go to that extent. But then you have the very same difficulty; you have to find out who these parties are before you can inflict any punishment upon them.

By MR. STEVENSON:

Question. Unless you find them in arms?

Answer. How would you find them in arms? They would take very especial pains that the gaps should all be let down, so that they could make their escape. And if the matter looked threatening on account of the presence of marshals and troops, the probability is that they would keep very quiet.

By the CHAIRMAN:
Question. It amounts, then, to predatory or guerrilla warfare?
Answer. It will have to cure itself. I am very nervous, occasionally, about its leading to retaliation and violence.

By MR. STEVENSON:
Question. You have spoken of corruption in the legislature. Do you mean to say that it was confined to colored men?
Answer. I do not think it was, from what I heard. I have no positive information upon the subject; I have been very little in Columbia, but I have heard a great deal. I think in all probability a portion of the whites are just as culpable as the colored men; whites in the legislature and also whites outside of the legislature.
Question. Lobbyists?
Answer. Lobbyists are more responsible, perhaps, than anybody else, as is generally the case.
Question. Is it your opinion that this corruption, of which you have heard, is confined exclusively to either party?
Answer. No, sir; I am sorry to say that it is not.
Question. A majority of the people of South Carolina are colored men, are they not?
Answer. Yes, sir; about 120,000 majority colored population.
Question. Yet I infer from what you say that a majority of office-holders, taking the importance of the office also into consideration, are white.
Answer. Yes, sir. . . .
Question. Speaking in regard to the disposition of the negroes in South Carolina, I would like to ask you whether, in your opinion, if the old white citizens had taken part in reconstruction and had manifested a disposition to accept the situation, as the phrase is, to take part in administering the government of the State under the reconstruction acts, would the negroes have been willing to support them and elect them to office?
Answer. My answer to that would be this: Freedom was considered by the negro a great boon, and he naturally felt very grateful to that particular party that he supposed had given him his

freedom. From the very outset he was made to believe that the republican party, as a party, had done that for him; that Mr. Lincoln, in September, 1862, issued the proclamation providing for their freedom on the 1st of January, 1863. Then there was the legislation of Congress afterwards, the civil rights bill and the Freedmen's Bureau bill; then the constitutional amendments, &c., &c. That was all explained to him; and it required a very short argument to be addressed to the most ignorant negro in the State to satisfy him that his attachment to the republican party should be greater than to the democratic party. It was charged publicly by his orators, those whom he had confidence in, that the democratic party had resisted all that legislation; that the democratic party had declared that reconstruction was unconstitutional, revolutionary, and void; and that if the democrats were reinstated in power very many of these privileges would be taken away from the colored people. I thought at the time that it was very unreasonable to imagine for a moment that the colored population could be induced to vote for a party from whom they apprehended such results, and against a party that had done them such service. I have no doubt in the world that if the white element of the South would turn republican, would consent to support the republican party instead of the democratic party—although in the republican party there has been a very pernicious element, there is no doubt of it—I have no doubt if they should support the republican party instead of the democratic party, then the white population of the South would obtain absolute control of affairs there. In the contest of 1870, and it will be the same thing in 1872, the great bulk of the whites thought the democratic party was the party nearest to them. The colored men think the republican party the party nearest to them. . . .

By MR. STEVENSON:
Question. As I understand you, the reason the colored men in a body have gone for the republican party is not their antagonism to the old white citizens as such, but their opposition to the democratic party?
Answer. The very moment that the colored man could have been satisfied that it was not the purpose of his old master to put him back into slavery, the old master would have obtained influence over him. And as conclusive proof of the correctness of my

statement, I think if you will deem it worth while to put the question to every gentleman of the South who may come before you, you will be told that in everything outside of politics the white population, the democratic population, the old slaveholders, the men of most intelligence in the community, have just as much influence over the negro and his conduct, and the management of him, as they ever had. He goes to them for advice, and takes their advice on everything except on the subject of voting. . . .

Question. According to your knowledge of the negro race, is it not the most docile of all races?

Answer. I cannot tell about some of the Eastern races. I think the negro race is a very controllable and manageable race. While they have not a very high sense of right of property, (and that could not be expected of them,) yet I do not think they are wanting in gratitude upon all proper occasions. But when you consider the sudden change wrought in the condition of the slave from 1865 to the present time, the matter of surprise is that the negro has not become much more insulting, exacting, and domineering than he has. . . .

Question. I would like to have your opinion on a question that has been somewhat mooted, and that is, why, in a State like South Carolina, where the negroes are largely in the majority, they have not resisted and retaliated when outraged? Why have they not done somewhat as the white race would do if attacked in the same way?

Answer. I think the moral power of the white race over the colored race, which was acquired during two hundred years of slavery, exists to a very great extent yet. I think you may take colored men and train them and make good soldiers of them, if you have officers who will lead them. But if you trust to their individuality in resisting aggression and outrage upon them, it would be an exceptional case where the white race would be resisted.

Question. Do you believe that, having the numerical majority, as they have there, if they would make an organized and determined effort at resistance and retaliation, they would be successful?

Answer. No, sir; I do not.

Question. Why not?

Answer. For the very reasons that I have assigned to you. Nearly all the white element of South Carolina, from twenty to sixty years of age, was, more or less, during the war, trained to bear arms; they are familiar with the use of arms and have always been. And when you put what would practically be an organized mass against an unorganized mob you will at once perceive what the result would be. I have no doubt that great damage would be done by them.

Question. You mean the whites would be organized and the negroes unorganized?

Answer. Yes, sir; and they could not be organized to such an extent as to accomplish the end you seem to indicate. . . .

Question. Do you know whether any and what advice has been given by the leaders of the republican party, white and black, on that question generally?

Answer. No, sir, I do not.

Question. Have you any knowledge that they have ever advised retaliation?

Answer. No, sir; I do not think they have as a general rule. I have heard it charged against one republican, the only one I know of.

Question. You have heard it charged against only one?

Answer. He was one of the men I had reference to in the county of Laurens. I saw a speech it was alleged he had made, in which he advised the colored organization there that if further aggression was perpetrated upon them, why, a box of matches would cost only five cents, rather intimating that they should resort to the torch. I have heard that he denied it, but I am prepared to believe it.

Question. What class of colored men have been leaders among themselves?

Answer. In my portion of the State the native leaders constitute the leaders of the colored race; generally the best and most intelligent of the former slaves and the issue of the old free negroes. Most of the negroes born there have some intelligence and some education. Then a great many slaves were mechanics and house servants; and although the law prohibited the teaching of those people to read and write, yet in almost every gentleman's house there was more or less of that thing done. They would pick it up, you could hardly tell how; little negro children, by the side of white children when they were learning their lessons, would pick it up. I think as a general rule in those counties the leaders have been very good men. I think that, perhaps, has been one reason why we have had as little trouble as any portion of the State.

26. A Short-Lived Resurgence:
Danville, Virginia, 1883

FOR A FEW short years Conservative Redeemer rule in Virginia was successfully challenged by the Readjusters under the leadership of the controversial William Mahone, Confederate general and postwar railroad entrepreneur. Representing primarily the less affluent whites, the party actively sought Negro support not only through campaign appeals but through legislative action which included laws that abolished the whipping post and the poll tax and that established an institution of higher learning for Negroes. The Readjuster legislature also granted Danville, a town where Negroes constituted a majority, a new town charter which made it possible for them to obtain a significant number of town offices, though the mayor and several other important officials remained white. The Democratic political circular reprinted below appeared shortly before the general state elections of 1883, and by its distortions raised the issue of "negro rule," and helped create local tensions that erupted in the so-called Danville riot. Arising from a minor street incident, the encounter left five dead and ten wounded, two-thirds of whom were Negroes. Readjusters charged that the violence had been instigated by Democrats in order to intimidate Negro voters. However the affair began, Democrats capitalized on the incident and through aroused white fears, intimidation of blacks, and election frauds swept the Readjusters from power. The ensuing Democratic legislature took care to amend Danville's town charter with a view to ensuring white control.

COALITION RULE
IN DANVILLE

To the Citizens of the Southwest and Valley of Virginia:

We, the undersigned, of the merchants and manufacturers and mechanics of the town of Danville, Va., earnestly request that you will permit us to lay before you a few facts from which you can form some idea of the injustice and humiliation to which our white people have been subjected and are daily undergoing by the domination and misrule of the radical or negro party, now in absolute

SOURCE: Pamphlet, Mahone Papers, Duke University Library, Durham, N.C.

power in our town, and under the leadership of William Mahone, seeking to extend and perpetuate its power all over the Common-wealth.

By the census of 1880, Danville contained 7,526 persons, of whom 4,397 were colored, and 3,129 were white. The population of the town has increased greatly since that time, and the propor-tion between the numbers of whites and blacks has also increased, there being a much larger proportion of blacks now than in the year 1880.

The taxes actually paid by the inhabitants of the town for the year 1882, upon property exclusive of license taxes for its corpo-rate uses, exclusive of taxes paid to the State, amounted to over $40,000 in round numbers, of which only $1,206.63 were paid by the blacks, making $38,894.00 more of money paid for the support of the town by the white people than was paid by the negroes. Out of the total sum derived from taxation upon property, $2,000 were appropriated to the education of the negro children of the town—a sum, it will be seen, $794 more than the entire amount of tax paid by the whole negro population. So it appears that the negroes of the town do not contribute one single dollar to the use of the town, towards paying the interest upon its corporate debt, the improve-ments of its streets, the maintenance of its public works, the pay of its officers, and its incidental expenses of government. But on the contrary, every dollar, and much more besides, paid by the mem-bers of that race in the nature of taxes, is returned to them and applied to the education of their children.

Up to the session of the last Legislature the town was not divided into wards, but voted as a single precinct; and in that way the council was generally kept in the hands of the white people. But the negro party, desiring to get complete possession of the town government that they might share in the offices as well as levy upon the treasury of the whites whatever they thought proper, applied to the Legislature and obtained an amendment to the town charter requiring that the town should be divided into three wards, and that four councilmen and one justice of the peace should be elected from each ward. From the localities in which the negroes had herded themselves, it was totally impracticable to so run the ward lines without creating two wards in which the negroes had a large majority, and this they and their white leaders knew. The result was that they elected seven out of twelve of their candidates for the council and their candidates for justice of the peace from each ward.

Then began the deeds which have so humiliated us in our own estimation, and made our town, once so noted for wealth and enterprise, a by-word for shame and reproach from one end of this land to the other. Wherever it was possible for anything to be done by the council or its magistrates that would irritate and wound the pride of the whites, it was executed with the keenest relish. Out of nine policemen—four *negroes* were chosen—something before that time unknown to the history of the town—two of them acting not only as *policemen*, but one *as a health officer* and *the other as weighmaster at the public scales and clerk of the market*. Out of the 24 stalls and stands at the market place, 20 are *rented out by the council to the negroes*. The scenes about this important and attractive institution (attractive in all cities) will give any person visiting the town a fair idea of the general state of the government under the negro rule. The market, once occupied in all its stalls by polite white gentlemen, with their clean, white aprons, and the most enticing meats and vegetables upon their boards, is now the scene of filth, stench, crowds of loitering and idle negroes, drunkenness, obscene language, and pettit thieves. The white men have been driven out and forced to take up private places for vending their meats and vegetables, and the public market, erected by the money of the white people and intended to be occupied by men at least courteous and cleanly, has been converted to the use of squalid negro hucksters, and presents a spectacle of loathsomeness positively repulsive to any person who has the least idea of how a market should be kept.

The whites of the town are powerless to prevent this outrage upon their rights. In fact, it is believed that their well-known objection to such an indignity is the principal cause of its infliction. The council, which has the power of regulating the conduct of the market, is presided over by a carpet-bagger—J. B. Raulston—Mahone's collector of internal revenue for the Danville district, and the patronage of his Federal office enables him to control the council with the same undisputed power that the General does his party. Raulston is exceedingly offensive to the white people and it is well known he takes no pains to carry out any of their wishes. Two of the negro members of the council hold positions under him at the custom-house, and they are as obedient to his will in the council as they are in the revenue office.

It is seen, therefore, that our town is practically in the hands of and actually controlled by the officers and slaves of the Federal government, not one of whom has a dollar's worth of visible property within its limits, and this too by the most shameless usurpation; for the Constitution and law of the State and the Presidential order by which the Norfolk postmaster was removed, all declare that such officials shall hold no office under the government of this commonwealth. The Federal government, through its internal revenue collector and the negro councilmen hired by him to scrub the floor of the custom-house and make incendiary speeches against the white people of the town, make our town laws, lay and collect our taxes, distribute our money, and elect *negro policemen* to watch our town while its inhabitants are asleep. This revenue collector declared, when he was elected president of the town council, that it was his intention to use the patronage of the council to build up the radical negro party.

The police-court of the town is another scene of perpetual mockery and disgrace. There the most active justice is a young negro named Jones, who first became famous by seducing a girl under promise of marriage, and was only saved from conviction upon indictment, by the evidence of his partner in a junkshop, who swore that he had had criminal intercourse with her before Jones. This court which, before the negro *regime* came into power, was only open a few hours every morning, is now practically open from morning till night, and nothing but actual observation can convey the least idea of the travesty of its transactions. Malice and partiality, whenever there is a motive, and ignorance, in its absence, are the rules of decision. The officials of the court, justices and policemen, co-operate in the work to make fees, and every act of word or deed of the citizen, whether atrocious in its character or too frivolous for the law to take notice of, is brought before a justice, and the party, if not fined, is required to pay the costs; and if there is more than one party, the cost is doubled, and both parties made to pay costs. White men are arrested for the most frivolous acts by negro policemen and borne along to the Mayor's office followed by swarms of jeering and hooting and mocking negroes, and tried, fined and lectured and imprisoned by a *negro* justice and then followed to the jail by the same insulting rabble.

At the October Court of this year two of the party magistrates were removed from office by the judge of the Hustings Court, one for embezzling the money of the Commonwealth, the other for "causes sufficient to the court," and one of them has fled the town to avoid indictment.

The notoriety which this state of things in our town has produced, has attracted to the town large numbers of idle and filthy negroes, from the border counties of North Carolina, and from Halifax, Mecklenburg, and Charlotte, Va. Although there is a law against vagrants, they are never disturbed. They infest the streets and sidewalks in squads, hover about public houses, and sleep on the doorsteps of storehouses and the benches of the market place. They impede the travel of ladies and gentlemen, very frequently forcing them from the sidewalk into the street. Negro women have been known to *force ladies from the pavement, and remind them that they will "learn to step aside the next time." In several instances white children have been struck by grown negroes.* We know of several cases where the *lie has been given to a white lady to her face by a negro.* It is a very common practice for the negroes who are employed about our houses to allude to white ladies and gentlemen as *men* and *women*, and to negroes as *ladies* and *gentlemen.* This is a practice almost without exception with the negro women. They do it to irritate and throw contempt upon the white race. A short time since, when the town was in great excitement over the murder of a respectable gentlemen and farmer of Pittsylvania county, in his wagon, while on his way home from Danville, by *three negro highwaymen,* a negro man in the town stood in the centre of a crowd of his friends, with a pistol exhibited on his person, and with threatening gestures and loud oaths, declared that he wanted to "start a row with some d——d son of a b——h of a whiteman" that he might kill him.

A few nights ago the negroes were very indignant because they heard of the earnest work that was going on by the whites to register all of their voting strength, and called a meeting which was addressed by an incendiary negro, named Pleasants, a postal agent, and one of the town councilmen, hired at the Custom-house, and they passed a resolution requesting the Governor to have Federal troops sent to our town on election day, to intimidate the white people at the polls.

They have also a scheme to amend the town charter, if they elect the Legislature this fall, and take into the town a large negro settlement, outside of the town limits, called *Jacksonville,* by which they will get several hundred more black voters, *and then it will be impossible for any white man to hold office in the town. We knew this is their plan.*

It is well known that hundreds of the North Carolina tobacco raisers who live within a few miles of Danville, and used to sell their tobacco in our market, now go five times as far to a market in their own State, *on account of the negro rule in our town.* At the negro meeting, referred to above, one of their speakers said they did not want the people of North Carolina to come here any way.

Now fellow citizens of the Valley and Southwest we cry out to you in our affliction to deliver us from this awful State *of humiliation and wretchedness.* We know that as a rule the cries of the wretched make but little interruption of the general progress of things. The Sun rises and sets all the same, and the work of the Government, and the work of the feast and the torture goes on with exactness and tranquility. But we appeal to you by that sympathy which constitutes the bond of union between honorable men struggling in the cause of freedom, to help us throttle this viper of Negroism that is stinging us to madness and to death, *by voting against the Coalition-Radical candidates who are yelling and screaming with delight at the prospect of fastening its fangs into us forever.*

We appeal to you to say, do you think it is just that we should contribute *every cent* to the maintenance of our town, pay our town *debt, and appropriate not only all the negro pays in the ways of tax, but much more besides,* of our own money, to the *education of his children, whom he raises upon our money to be our bitterest enemies,* and then let him have possession of our town government too? Is it that right the negro should have all this given him and then be allowed to control our offices and plunder our treasury besides?

It is an injustice at which we know your humanity will revolt.

It is the injustice of the frozen serpent, which after being warmed into life by its benefactor, stings him to death.

Help us, fellow citizens, by voting for the Conservative-Democratic candidates for the Legislature, for *unless they are elected we are doomed.*

[There were twenty-eight signatures of which one was a real estate agency, one a manufacturing company, three were individuals whose occupation was not indicated, six were identified as merchants, six as tobacconists, four as warehousemen, three as builders or contractor, two as foundrymen, and one each as grocer and tanner.]

B. The Process of "Redemption"

27. Georgia

REPUBLICANS NEVER ACHIEVED secure control in Georgia although they dominated the constitutional convention in the winter of 1867–1868 and in the following spring won the governorship and the upper house of the state legislature. Whether most members elected to the lower house were Republicans is a matter of dispute but one of little practical importance since Negro members were expelled only two months after the legislature convened, an action that destroyed any possibility of Republican control. This victory for racism was followed by violence in the fall elections of 1868 and the defeat of Grant electors, with many counties that had gone Republican in the spring returning Democratic majorities. These developments placed Georgia in an ambiguous position, led to a brief reassertion of military control, and delayed readmission until mid-1870. The elections that followed in December 1870 resulted in a decisive victory for the Democrats, and the "redemption" of the state by white supremacists is usually dated from 1871. In October of that year the Republican governor resigned, in November the new Democratic legislature assembled, and in December without contest the Democrats won the governorship.

Reports of local agents of the Freedmen's Bureau presented below (doc. a) provide an intimate glimpse of the day-by-day intimidation and terror upon which Democrats relied heavily in their struggle for political power. The reports came from the southwest corner of the Georgia black belt where the so-called Camilla riot exploded in Mitchell county during mid-September 1868, gaining national attention. The violence they reveal was not limited either to the southwest area or to the year 1868. In respect to Georgia a recent detailed examination of white terrorism has focused attention upon 1869–1870 and upon the counties in the north and east of the state. Its author has concluded that "terror probably accomplished more in Georgia than in any other state to subvert the Republican party and Reconstruction."[1]

1. Allen W. Trelease, White Terror: Ku Klux Klan Conspiracy and Southern Reconstruction (New York: Harper & Row, 1971), p. 236.

Henry M. Turner, who testified before congressional investigators of the Klan (doc. b), was an outstanding Negro leader in Georgia during Reconstruction. His background and political role are revealed in his testimony. George W. Ashburn, whose name appears in Turner's statement and in the questioning, was murdered in Columbus shortly before the spring elections of 1868; a Northerner, active in Republican politics, he died apparently as the result of a deliberate attempt by Democrats to intimidate their opponents. Military authorities intervened to obtain arrests and began a military trial, but when civil authority in the state was restored, the military released the suspects, and no civil trial followed.

a. Reports of Freedmen's Bureau Agents, August–November 1868

Bureau R. F. & A. L.
Office Sub Asst. Com'r
Columbus, Ga. August 26th 1868.

Col. J. R. Lewis
A. A. I. General
Atlanta, Ga.
Colonel

I have the honor to report that I have been to Butler, and find about one hundred complaints made by freedmen on file in the office of Mr. Pokorney, all of these cases are for wages or a portion of the crops, in many cases the only reason assigned by they employers for discharging Freedmen is that they are Radicals and Radicals cannot live on their plantations, and others assigne equally frivolous charges for discharging freedmen. Thus the freedmen are swindled out of their wages or their lawful portion of the crop, and their lives threatened should they dare to return. I am informed that no freedman living in Taylor or Macon counties dare to attend a political (Republican) meeting without incuring the penalty of being discharged.

I have advised the freedmen to avoid any neglect of duty, or breach of contract, in attending political meetings and not to give their employers any excuse to discharge them; with your permission I would like to visit the civil officers in some of the adjoining counties and confer with them. I think I might accomplish some good results;

SOURCE: Freedmen's Bureau Records for Georgia, National Archives.

Mr. Pokorney appears to do the best he can but he appears not to have much influence with white or colored people.

I am Colonel
Very Respectfully
Your obdt Servt
John Leonard
Bvt. Maj. U.S.A. &c.

Personal

Hawkinsville Ga Aug 28th/68

Major J R Lewis
A I Gen. Bureau R F & A L
Atlanta Ga
Dr Sir

Through my brother in law I learn that you desire me to write to you. I suppose he informed you that I intended resigning my position and will now state the causes that have induced me to this. This country is rather remote in civilization & the man that can best flourish the knife or pistol is a *gentleman*, while the military had control of the courts &c, these men out of fear held their peace & treated me civily, but since the State is back into the Union military power withdrawn, they have abused and insulted me, trying to draw me into quarrels fights &c but I heed them not. Political excitement is raging high here and you are aware that as soon as excitement gets to a certain pitch judgment looses its virtue. I assure you Major that I live in continual fear. I have made friends here, but in a case of emergency I could not rely on them. I differ with them in politics, therefore the hate they bear me. Some three weeks ago I was ordered by a certain party to leave. Robt. Anderson preacher was treated likewise, but we still remain. Anderson was brutally beaten on the streets yesterday. On Saturdays large crowds of people collect here to hold Democratic meetings. There is a good deal of drinking & carousing going on, and I generally keep in the house during this time. Now Major you have my reasons for wishing to get away from here. I could say more, but do not wish to bother your mind with unnecessary remarks. I am sorry that the military withdrew. I fear it was the worst thing that could be done. Shall send up my resignation in a few days, hope the same will be received. I would be under many obligations to you Major if you could secure me transportation to Atlanta, if such

is consistent with orders. Our school gets along very well considering the times &c. Our great drawback the whites are unfavorable to
it, yet the school will thrive. I hope Major that I may have the
pleasure of hearing from you soon and when I get back to Atlanta I
want to have a good talk with you.

Very Respectfully
Your Obedient Servant
L. Lieberman
Agt &c

P.S.

I forgot to mention that the town was thrown into quite an uproar
last Saturday. A col'd man & a white man got into an altercation,
when the col'd started away led by some of his friends, he had just
got to my door, when up came a large body of whites armed with
guns & pistols & commenced firing on him. The col'd man fled the
whites after him. They did not catch him. I learn that he was not
hurt. This is a sample of doing things in this country. Law, order &
justice are things of the past.

L L

Bureau R. F. & A. L.,
Bainbridge, Geo.,
Sept. 1, 1868.

Bt. Brig. Gen'l Sibley,
Asst. Comr.,
Atlanta,
Geo.

I have the honor to transmit herewith the substance of the statement of a freedman from the lower part of this county, who has
been severely whipped. His name is Adam Garney. He is about 35
years of age, and a very ordinary negro in every respect.

On Thursday night, the 27th inst., or rather Friday morning
between 1 and 2 o'clock, a band of men, (6 or 7, he judges), came
to his house and called him out. They wanted to talk to him. As
soon as he opened the door two fastened onto him: He was
blinded, led away into the woods and tied to a tree. His pants were
dropped to his feet, his shirt caught up over his head, and the
whipping administered. He thinks the whip was a piece of stout
leather or gear. He did not count, but supposes he was struck 50 or

60 times. Was then untied, the blinder was removed and he was told to march away without looking back, on pain of being shot. Was told to leave the neighborhood in three days.

He cannot identify any of those engaged. One only did the speaking and in a disguised voice; the others when anything was said went to a distance.

They gave no reason for what they did. When asked by the freedman, one replied that *he* (the freedman) knew well enough.

The man thinks it was done for political reasons. Attempts have been made to form Democratic Clubs in the vicinity without success. Meetings would be appointed, and not a dozen negroes would attend. This may have been done, he says, to frighten others into joining them. It has been said by some of the whites there that the freedman "should sign their papers" or leave.

Adam also testifies that another colored man named Henry McNair, was taken out the same way two nights before and received 20 or 30 lashes.

I could really *do* nothing for the complainant. Gave him the best advice I could, and report the matter to you.

Probably his family can remain to look after the crop, and he can for the present, get plenty to do else where.

Very Respectfully,
Your ob't serv't,
W. L. Clark,
Agent.

Bureau of Refugees Freedom and Abandoned Lands.
Office Agent Division of America;
(Sumter, Schley and Webster Counties)
Americus, Ga., Sept 30th 1868.

Bt Maj O H Howard
Sub Asst Comr
Albany Ga
Major;

In accordance with instructions in Circular No 4 dated Office Asst Comr Atlanta Ga Aug 3d 1868 I have the honor to report that during the past month the relation between the employer & employee has been more or less disturbed in this division by the intense political excitement existing particularly among the white population. Many cases have been reported of freedmen being turned off from their work ostensibly for violating their contract, (in attending any republican meetings) by leaving their work without permission, but in reality because the freedman belongs to the republican organization. There seems to be a determination to control, or let starve, the colored people. From the present standpoint I fear serious disturbances on the plantations between this time & that for elections of Pres't. Nothing but a decided republican victory in the great states that vote on the 13th Oct will have any effect upon the determination of the whites to make the freedman do as he desires in politics as well as labor. I can but reiterate my former expressed opinion regarding the material condition of the freedmen should there be no serious disturbance between the two parties. Generally the crop is about an average and cotton bringing a good price while the corn crop is this section is excellent—of which the laborer has ⅓. The political feeling before alluded to has operated against the schools sought to be established. Any one assisting to ameliorate the condition of the freedmen being considered guilty of treason to the lost cause—

Very respectfully
Your obt Svt
W. C. Morrill
Agt &c

Bureau Refugee, Freedmen and Abandoned Lands
Office Agent Division of Cuthbert;
(Randolph, Stewart, and Calhoun Counties)
Cuthbert, Ga., Aug. 13th 1868.

Personal
Bv't Maj. O. H. Howard,
Albany, Ga.
Dear Sir:

I am in receipt of a communication from Rev. Jno. T. Gibson (Colored), of Blakely Early Co. setting forth the following facts,

On Saturday Aug't 8th the freedmen of Early Co. held a political meeting at Blakely. This meeting was disturbed by one of their own members called "Billy McDonly" who being intoxicated, threatened to shoot sundry persons with a revolver, which he held in his hand. This pistol was taken from McDonly, by two freedmen called Wilson & Fryer, & was handed by Fryer to one Steven Craft (freed) for safe keeping until McDonly was sober.

Monday morning, being sober McDonly enquired for his pistol, & was told that Fryer took it from him; he then went to Fryer & asked for it; but Fryer having forgotten who he had handed it to, asked McDonly to wait a short time & he would hunt it up & return it. McDonly agreed, but instead of waiting got out a warrant, (signed by one *Rowland* J.P.) and had Fryer arrested & confined in jail, for stealing his pistol; within four hours the pistol was brot to Rowland, by Craft, (it having been in Crafts hands for safe keeping) and Fryers release requested; Rowland refused to release him, and said that he would not accept bail for him, unless a bond was signed by some one worth $3000 in gold, clear of all encumbrance, that these niggers had made this infernal Constitution & now they might suffer for it. Rowland also stated that he should keep Fryer in jail until the next term of Court and R. Holmes Powell, Atty at Law stated that he should "do his best to convict Fryer and to send him to the penetentiary for four years."

Seven (7) freedmen offered to give bonds for Fryers appearance at Court if they would release him, but this was refused and he is now incarcerated and held for no other reason, but being a radical.

Two freedmen who were cognisant of all the facts in this case, bro't the letter of Mr Gibson to me, and gave some facts in addition to those contained in that letter, but which are set forth in the preceding statement.

These freedmen stated also that the whites had shot at them & endeavored to break up their meetings, and have refused to allow them (the freedmen) to enter the town of Blakely, or to pass through it, when returning from their meetings.

They also stated that that they, the freedmen, have borne all that they can, or will, and if interfered with by the whites, without cause, that they are determined to protect themselves to the last extremity.

I counseled extreme moderation and advised them to bear with & overlook all that they could; but told them they had an undoubted right to hold their meetings after giving the Aut'ys due notice; and also, that the law did not require that they should tamely submit to personal violence, or to attacks or impositions from anyone;

Can anything be done for Fryer, the freedman confined in jail? &

had *anyone* authority to arrest & confine him at that time, Augt 10 '68?

Please advise me by return of mail.

With much Respect
Truly Yours
Geo R Ballou

Bureau Refugees, Freedmen and Abandoned Lands
Office Agent Division of Cuthbert;
(Randolph, Stewart, and Calhoun Counties)
Cuthbert, Ga. Aug. 22, 1868

Personal
Major O. H. Howard,
Albany, Ga.
Dear Sir:

Affairs in my division are rapidly assuming an alarming phase, and unless prompt and decisive measures are taken to bring about a better state of feeling, I have every reason to apprehend serious and perhaps bloody collisions at an early day.

Both freedmen and whites are making extensive preparations of a hostile nature, gunsmiths are working night & day, ammunition is being bought in large quantities, and both white and black speak openly of war.

In Stewart Co. the freedmen are organized and to a great extent armed and drilled, and have already by threats of tearing down the Court house and burning the town of Lumpkin, compelled the authorities to release a prisoner (arrested by the Marshall & confined) on bail, the bond being signed by freedmen.

The streets of that town are now, I am informed, nightly guarded by an armed patrol.

Randolph Co. is at present quiet, but there is an organization of over 1000 freedmen here.

Quitman and Clay counties are quiet, as yet although in each of these counties the freedmen are rapidly organizing and for the same purpose avowed by all, mutual protection by force of arms against the merciless assaults of the whites, assaults which are becoming of daily occurence and which are entirely overlooked by the Civil Aut'ys.

The condition of affairs in Early County is truely deplorable; the whites at Blakely have disarmed all freedmen that they could, freedmen have been shot, and some, nearly killed by being beaten with gun stocks.

All the roads leading into Blakely, are guarded nightly by armed men and no freedman not living in the town is allowed to pass these guards, under penalty of death. This prevents the holding of meetings by the freedmen.

These facts are reported to me by the Rev. Jno. T. Gibson, (Col'd) who has been driven from his home by these fellows who twice shot at him while lying in his bed at dead of night with his wife & child in the same bed; he was fired upon thru the windows of his house & barely escaped with his life, the bullets missing him by only a few inches. He states that before making his escape, he passed several nights under his house gun in hand, and that his home was watched nightly by armed men seeking to take his life.

Mr Gibson is now here and does not dare to return to his home, as they are sworn to kill him, and as he states all radicals.

Mr Gibson also states that the freedmen of Early County are "completely cowed" by the whites, as their organization was very imperfect and the whites were disarming the freed who possessed weapons; deadly assaults are being daily committed there upon freedmen and there is no punishment for the whites.

Subsequent to Mr Gibsons report I was informed that a large armed body from the organization here was about to proceed to Blakely to as they expressed it "Clean out the rebels," but by using my influence I prevented this movement for the time being, but I doubt my ability to restrain them for any great length of time.

Couriers are being sent off to all the counties, and the preparations for an uprising are being rapidly pushed forward.

The freedmen are fully conscious of the fact that they have in many ways the advantage of the whites. One told me yesterday that he "very well knew what would be the result of trouble between the white & black races." Said he, "the whiteman has got his all to lose," and then said he "they can't quit their homes & get together like we can."

I am using all my influence to prevent overt acts of violence, advising moderation and a strict compliance with the requirements of the law; but advice and persuasion has but little effect now; they say, "why don't you protect us as you used to do? If you can't do it we must take care of ourselves for the courts wont do it, they wont punish a whiteman for killing us," and it is almost, it not utterly, impossible to convince them that it is not so.

I most earnestly request that you will advise me how to act, and particularly in the case of Early Co.

I propose to visit Blakely next week, to be there on Thursday the 27th inst.

Again, I will say Sir, that unless some measures be devised for quieting the apprehensions of the freedpeople, something more tangible than mere words, the most serious and disastrous collisions must be feared as they seem almost inevitable.

I am Sir
With much Respect
Very Truly Yours
Geo. R. Ballou

Bureau R. F. & A. L
Div. of Cuthbert
Cuthbert, Ga. Sept 1st 1868

Bv't Maj. O. H. Howard
5th U.S. Arty and S. A. Com'r
Albany Ga.
Major:

In compliance with instructions contained in Circular No 4 Bureau R. F. & A. L. dated at Atlanta Ga. Aug 3d 1868, and in connection with my report of contracts approved during the month of August ultimo, I have the honor to report that my time has been employed during the past month chiefly in securing wages for freedmen who had been driven from the plantations where they had been employed, in bringing cases of assault and maltreatment before the civil authorities, and in settling many minor cases between freedmen and whites, and adjusting difficulties occurring among the freedmen, cases in which advice and instruction only was required.

The general state of affairs in this division is not such as I could desire. The transition from military to civil government, combined with the excitement and high party feeling incident to a political campaign and the strong opposition of the people generally to this Bureau, and to the organizations in existence among the freedmen, known as "Grant Clubs," have all tended to engender and foster a spirit of animosity and hatred between the white and black citizens, and to render still more complicated the general derangement of judicial affairs.

These irregularities and disorders are more marked in the counties of Stewart and Early, where the opposition of the white citizens, has led to violent outbreaks and riotous assemblages, but as these difficulties originate entirely from political prejudices and the attempts of the whites to suppress what are known as "radical" organizations, it is to be hoped that these hostile demonstrations will cease with the political campaign, although pending that time it is possible, and even probable, that serious collisions may occur.

In a portion of the counties composing this division, the civil authorities evince a willingness to cooperate with the Agent of this Bureau in preserving order and in securing justice to aggrieved parties, while in other counties the magistrates pursue an entirely different course.

Under existing circumstances, the freedmen have little or no protection and it is to be desired by all friends of their race that a reform may be speedily effected.

I am Major
Very Respectfully,
Your Ob't Serv't
Geo. R. Ballou Agent

Bureau of Refugees, Freedman and Abandoned Lands,
Office Agent Division of Cuthbert;
(Stewart, Quitman, Randolph, Clay and Early Counties)
Cuthbert, Ga. Oct. 31st, 1868

Bv't Maj. O. H. Howard
5th U.S. Arty and S. A. Com'r
Albany, Ga.
Major:

In compliance with instructions contained in "Circular No. 4" Bureau R. F. & A. L. dated at Atlanta Ga. Augt 3d 1868, and in connection with my report of contracts for the month ending October 31st 1868, I have the honor to report as follows, viz.

During the past month I have been engaged in bringing cases of assault upon freedmen, before the civil courts in securing the arrest, so far as practical, of guilty parties and in making settlements for freedmen, who have been driven from their employment, by threats of violence or actual assaults (usually the latter) made by the planters employing them, when the consent of the interested parties could be obtained. I have made these settlements myself, but whenever the planter has refused to acquiesce in my decision, I have taken steps looking to a recovery of the claims at as early a date as is possible under existing laws although I have every reason to believe that the ultimate benefit to be derived by the freedman from claims thus prosecuted will be very small, if not of an entirely negative character as a "lawsuit" is calculated to unsettle the minds of the freedmen, and the prosecuting attorney usually gauges his fees to suit the amount collected.

I have visited every point in the different counties, under my supervision where business required my presence including Lumpkin, Florence, Georgetown, and Fort Gaines, and have found the general condition of affairs to be such as to render nugatory my efforts, in many instances, to secure to the freedmen reparation for the injuries, personal and pecuniary, inflicted upon them by the white planters, although I have succeeded in amicably adjusting many cases and, by the cooperation of local magistrates, in recovering amounts due to the freedmen where my personal efforts deprived of all authority as I am, had proven futile.

Randolph County is by far the least turbulent in this Division, the civil authorities evince a willingness to render impartial justice in cases brought to their notice at the instance of the Agent; this statement however, must be qualified by saying that as yet only justices courts can be included in the above remarks, the higher courts in this county not having been tested; and even these lower courts are much less prompt than could be desired as in the instance of a case, freedmen vs one Dozier (white) who has for some time effectively baffled all attempts made by Agents of this Bureau to bring him to justice for assaults with intent to kill certain freedpeople; two warrants were issued for his arrest by the magistrate at Cuthbert, at the instance of the Agent, of which one was for an assault with intent to kill, both these warrants were placed in the hands of an officer for immediate execution, but up to the present time nothing has been done by this officer, although the guilty party resides at present in Cuthbert.

In connection with the above mentioned case, I would respectfully state that great difficulty is experienced by me in securing the attendance of freedmen at the time they are most needed to testify, as they often come many miles to report a case to me and after a warrant is issued for the arrest of offending parties, they (the freedmen) are compelled to return to their work, as a matter of course no day can be fixed for the trial of the case, as the time of arrest is uncertain, consequently when the arrest is finally made, the guilty party is discharged for want of any prosecution, and this evil I am unable to obviate as I have no means of securing the attendance of either witness or prosecutor.

In Stewart County much ill feeling exists among the whites against all political organizations or meetings of the so called "Radical" party, and violent measures have been resorted to by these people to effectually break up and destroy the efficiency of all such organizations.

Many freedmen have been driven from their homes by the planters and are compelled to abandon, not only the fruits of a year of toil, but often their personal effects, these last however, I have been enabled to recover in a great measure by civil processes.

Quitman County has the same types of disadvantages, outrages and impositions as the preceding counties mentioned, and the apathy, or direct connivance, of the civil authorities, with the whites in the outrages perpetrated by them, is strongly marked.

Early County is at present "quiet," the freedmen having been brought into complete subjection by the whites, as to be in a condition little if any less servile than that of actual slavery, and the same may be said, with certain limitations of every county under my supervision.

In each of these counties there is in existence a deep and settled determination to make Georgia, so far as in them lies, emphatically a "whitemans State," hence the merciless persecution of all prominent leaders of the negroes, who profess political opinion at variance with the tenets held by the whites. The killing of W. T. Walker (colored), in Early County exemplifies this, as also the trial and conviction of Jno T. Gibson (the leading freedman in that county) for an "attempt to incite insurrection."

Affairs in Clay County do not materially differ from other counties in their general aspect, each and all, present a long list of lawless and high-handed proceedings, which this Bureau is powerless to correct or remedy, and which the civil authorities will not take cognizance of; the natural consequence being the increased boldness of the planter in his fraudulent and violent proceedings, and the gradual but sure breaking down of that buoyant and enthusiastic spirit which has inspired the freedman up to the time when protection was withdrawn from him.

It cannot be denied that the freedman is often guilty of criminal acts particularly of theft, but this spirit of lawlessness so rapidly developing itself among them may almost wholly be ascribed to the unchecked system of fraud and outrage practiced by the whites; for example, a freedman labors faithfully for 10 months, has perhaps in his desire to accumulate something for himself deprived himself and family of many necessaries (I know instances of their going without food even) and after the crops are made and nearly gathered, the freedman is driven away, with his family upon some slight pretext (or none at all) and loses all; he becomes discouraged, disheartened and to a certain extent desperate; he has no tribunal to which he may appeal for justice, and his only resort, to prevent actual starvation, is to steal and to kill the stock of the planter who defrauds him.

Nearly all freedmen who report cases of assault to me evince an utter unwillingness to return to the place they have left and invariably because they have been threatened with death in case they "report to the Bureau," and for the same reason it is extremely difficult to obtain witnesses to attest the truth of the complaints of freedmen, and if these witnesses are compelled to give evidence in a case between a white man & a freedman, they will in nearly all cases sustain the whiteman; such has been my experience.

I would respectfully state in closing my report that many of the lawyers in this Division use their utmost skill in placing obstacles in the way of the freedman's obtaining justice thru any intervention of the Bureau, thus rendering the duties of an Agent far more arduous and difficult.

The freedmen as a class are now completely controlled by the whites and I would respectfully state that my obervation will warrant me in saying that the freedman cannot except in isolated cases obtain justice in the civil courts.

I am Major
Very Respectfully
Your Ob't Serv't
G. Ballou
Agent Etc.

b. *Testimony of Henry M. Turner, November 3, 1871*

ATLANTA, GEORGIA, November 3, 1871.

HENRY M. TURNER (colored) sworn and examined.

By the CHAIRMAN:

Question. State your age, where you were born, where you now live, and what is your present occupation.

Answer. I will be thirty-eight years old on the 1st day of next February; I was born in Newberry, South Carolina, and now live in Macon, Bibb County, Georgia; I am a minister of the gospel and a kind of politician—both; I am presiding elder of a district, and a member elect of the legislature; I was to-day ejected from my seat, and the opposing party seated in it.

Question. Your connection with politics is thereby ended?

Answer. For the time being.

Question. How long have you been living in Bibb County?

Answer. Six years.

Question. Did you go there directly from South Carolina?

Answer. No, sir; I left South Carolina in 1859 and went to Baltimore, where I remained until I was appointed by Mr. Lincoln as a chaplain in the Army. I served nearly three years as a chaplain; that is, I served two years under the appointment of Mr. Lincoln, and then I was reappointed by President Johnson, and sent to Georgia to labor in the Freedmen's Bureau. After remaining here for some time, and not receiving the respect I thought was due me, I resigned, not because of anything I had against the Government, but the officers I had to work with. I was appointed chaplain in the Regular Army the last time.

Question. Have you been living in Macon since?

Answer. Yes, sir; Macon is my home; I am there when I am at home. I travel a great deal all over the State. I am missionary agent and presiding elder of the district, and have taken a leading part in republican politics, so far as colored men are concerned.

Question. What church do you represent?

Answer. The African Methodist Episcopal church.

Question. I wish you would state what knowledge or reliable information you have upon the subject of lawless violence and outrages by those people who are popularly known as Ku-Klux.

SOURCE: *K.K.K. Report*, VII:1034–1042.

Answer. Well, I will state that I cannot say that I have ever seen any Ku-Klux, that is, as a band roaming about at night. I have, however, had my life threatened, and I am satisfied that on two or three occasions, I may say in a dozen instances, if I had not secreted myself in houses at times, in the woods at other times, in a hollow log at another time, I would have been assassinated by a band of night-prowlers, or rovers, I will call them. . . . I may state, however, that a few years ago I made a speech in Columbus, Georgia; I had Mr. Ashburn on the stand with me. About a half an hour after I came out, a band of organized Ku-Klux, or assassins, went to Mr. Ashburn's house and murdered him. I learned from rumor that they would have murdered me had they known where I was; but they did not know at that time at what place I was stopping, and therefore they did not find me.

Question. We have had an opinion expressed here, that Mr. Ashburn was killed by a colored man or by colored men. . . . Another hypothesis that has been suggested, is that he was killed by republicans in order that they might make use of his death for the purpose of political agitation.

Answer. O, not a bit of it. I tell you, as a man who knows as much probably about the city of Columbus as a man can know who goes very frequently there, and who generally goes there to give shape and direction to political matters, for they look to me there as a leader although I do not live there; I say this, that there was not a solitary republican at that time in the city of Columbus, except one colored man, who had the least animosity whatever toward Mr. Ashburn. There was one colored man who was a little sore and aggrieved, because Mr. Ashburn defeated him in a nomination in the legislature. But that colored man, Van Jones, is a good religious man, a class-leader, and a man whose Christian deportment is known to the citizens there, white and black.

Question. Have you known, or have you reliable information, of people who have been otherwise injured by these disguised night marauders?

Answer. I have seen scores of them. I have seen men who had their backs lacerated. I have seen other men who had bullets in them; I have seen others who had their arms shot off, shot so badly that they had to be amputed; I have seen others, with legs shot off. I have heard of any quantity of horrible deeds. . . .

Question. You spoke of having been elected to the lower house of the Georgia legislature. . . . What was the character of the election?

Answer. Do you want me to give you the general character of it?

Question. Yes. . . .

Answer. On the first day that the election was held the colored people had it pretty much their own way; they thronged there in great numbers and voted peaceably and quietly. In the afternoon there was some little bickering, but nothing that amounted to anything. The second day some kind of a little scramble broke out; some colored man voted the democratic ticket, and I think he received a small, insignificant donation for it; I do not know now to what it amounted. As he was coming out the colored republicans hollered, and jeered, and laughed at him, and two or three prominent democrats walked by the side of him; he was walking between them. Finally one of the democrats looking back commenced to curse, and I think eventually pulled out a pistol, but I will not be certain of that. I know they fired first, fired back into the crowd. I was standing about three hundred yards above where that occurred. This caused the crowd to run to a wagon that had brought in a load of wood, and they picked up the wood and commenced heaving it; the owner never saw his wood after that. This produced a considerable amount of confusion. However, in a short time the military were brought down. Several pistols were fired into the air; a great many persons ran away, white and colored, and the excitement was then somewhat quelled. But from that time, a kind of bitterness began to devlop itself. The white people turned out in great numbers; indeed they were on the ground in great numbers. On the third day affairs were in a very bitter state; the whites, the democratic party, turned out and staid around the polls all day. They were pulling, hauling, snatching tickets, and doing a great many things of that sort. Yet I cannot say that any violence was perpetrated upon any person beyond threats, and a little intimidation of that sort. I know I was advised personally to go away, or otherwise I would be killed before night; Mr. Fitzpatrick says he was so advised. All the candidates, I think, were under terror to a greater or less extent, excepting Long; he was running for the short term of Congress, and nobody cared about him; no one was particularly interested about the short term of Congress. There is not half so much interest on the part of democrats in this State about Congress as there is about the legislature, or ordinaries, or sheriffs. They do not care so much about Congress admitting negroes into their halls; they have no special objection to that, but they do not want the negroes over them at home; that is the truth of the matter. Well, in the afternoon, or I may say for the whole of the third day, they voted everything there. A circus came there that day, and they voted the whole circus.

Question. What ticket did they vote?

Answer. They voted the democratic ticket, of course. They got altogether probably about thirty colored democrats. Well, they would carry them into a room and put a cloak on them, bring them out and vote them, and then carry them back again and put a high hat on, and bring them out and vote them again; then carry them back and put on a slouch hat and bring them out and vote them again. In this way repetition after repetition went on. All the wagoners that came in with cotton and other produce, everybody, whether he belonged there or not, was voted. I am satisfied there were seven or eight hundred illegal votes given there. I do not think there are more than sixteen hundred or seventeen hundred democrats in the county of Bibb, yet on that occasion they polled twenty-seven-hundred votes. There may have been some fraudulent votes on our part. We have some twenty-five hundred voters in that county that we know of, and we voted twenty-seven hundred votes at that election. Probably we may have voted some fraudulent votes. There may have been some repeating; they saw the democrats were doing it, and I dare say some of our men did the same. For about three hours before the election closed it was just one repetition, voting everything. I saw seven white men vote twice. They would go up and vote, and then go around and laugh and talk and say that they had voted four times in that way. Long was standing there and witnessing how they were changing the dress of the few democratic negroes they had there; and Fitzpatrick witnessed the same. I could not begin to describe the scene of the last evening for about three hours before the election closed. If we had had a fair election we would have beaten them by five or six hundred votes; but in consequence of not having a fair election we beat them upon the average only about thirty-eight votes. . . .

Question. You have spoken of the crimes in Macon as having no political significance.

Answer. Yes, sir.

Question. In your opinion, do these offenses in the other counties have any significance; and if so, what is it?

Answer. They have this significance with me: I am satisfied, and every man in Georgia who has got any brains must be satisfied, that there are organized bands of night assassins, murderous villains, who have banded themselves together and roam about and kill republicans, kill any man who has got the name of radical attached to him, especially if he is a leader. There is no especial desire to exterminate a man who has not got any influence, but any man who is a leader, who is, I will say, a chairman of a Grant club or a Union League, who is thought to be a center of influence, every such man, in many of the counties, they are determined to kill out. They will kill out all they can kill; they will do like they did in Putnam County a few weeks ago or they will get up some charge against them, and have them tried, convicted, and sent to the penitentiary. Mr. Abram Turner, a man who was elected to the legislature in Putnam County, was shot down in open daylight as he was walking the street. A man rode up to him and shot him dead and then galloped off. The authorities of the county have made no attempt whatever to follow him or arrest him; he is not arrested yet. I am informed that he is in Macon; I do not know him. . . .

Question. Were you in the constitutional convention that framed the present constitution of this State?

Answer. I was.

Question. I see you have a provision in your constitution which requires the pre-payment of taxes as qualification for voting?

Answer. Yes, sir.

Question. How is that going to operate upon the colored people?

Answer. I am fearful it is going to destroy their power of representation in every branch of the government, State and national.

Question. Did you or not see that when your constitution was framed?

Answer. No, sir; I was one of the men who advocated that provision. I was inexperienced at the time; a majority of the republicans were against it. I took the position that the dollar tax was to go to educate our ignorant children; that we needed it, and that every man should be compelled to pay at least one dollar a year for the education of the children; and I advocated it for that reason. I think, however, I made a great blunder in doing so. At the time I advocated it I thought, as did many others, that the law would be so framed that if a man did not pay his taxes he would be arrested and punished for it. We did not think it would be left optional with the citizen to pay it or else be deprived of his vote. We did not think that the tax collectors would sit down and put a little notice in the paper that nine-tenths of the colored people never would hear anything about, in consequence of being unable to read, and therefore they would know nothing about when the tax was to be paid. . . .

Question. What do your people think of doing; what is their outlook for the future?

Answer. At this present time there is quite a feeling in favor of emigrating from the State of Georgia, and going to Florida and Alabama and South Carolina. I suppose that if the leading men were to give any encouragement to it at the present time the colored people would commence a regular exodus, and that thirty thousand people could be got out of Georgia between now and Christmas, if the leading men would give any encouragement to it.

Question. Would their purpose be to go upon Government land and live?

Answer. Not that only, but to get in such States as they hope will be under the control of the republican party, and not subject themselves to what they are in many instances now subjected to, and what they expect to be subjected to before this legislature shall get through with its proceedings. For instance, there was a bill introduced into this legislature the other day to make it a penal offense for a laborer to break his contract, regardless of the treatment to which he may be subjected.

Question. Has such a bill as that been introduced?

Answer. Yes, sir. For instance, a white man writes out a contract; he gives the black man a copy of it, and takes a copy of it himself. He reads the contract to the black man, and of course he reads just what he pleases. When the black man takes it to somebody else and gets him to read it, it reads quite differently. Among other things, there is a provision in the contract that he must not go to any political gathering or meeting, or if he does, he will lose $5 for every day that he is absent, and yet he is to receive only $50 or $75 a year. Every day that he is sick, a dollar or a dollar and a half is to be deducted. Possibly the man may find that under such a contract as that his wife and children are starving, and he may want to quit there and go and work for some person else who will pay him better wages.

Question. The practical effect of the proposed legislation would be to render the laborer practically a slave during the period of his contract?

Answer. A slave, or else he would be liable to punishment by imprisonment. . . .

28. Mississippi

REPUBLICAN RULE lasted longer and was more complete in Mississippi than in Georgia, but its path was far from smooth. The opposition succeeded in defeating the Republican constitution in July 1868. The following year under President Grant's leadership, a compromise was arranged by which the proscriptive clauses of the constitution were voted down and the rest accepted. Mississippi was returned to the Union and to civil administration early in 1870 with a Republican governor, James L. Alcorn, a wealthy Mississippi planter who had accepted the new legal status of the Negro, and an overwhelmingly Republican legislature. Meanwhile, General Adelbert Ames, a New Englander with a Civil War record that won him a Medal of Honor, had been appointed first to act in place of the obstructionist civilian governor in 1868 and then to take command of the military district. As military commander and governor he won the respect of whites and the confidence of Negroes, whose rights he vigorously protected, with the result that the new Republican legislature chose him to fill one of two unexpired terms as United States senator. Before long his fellow senator from Mississippi was Alcorn, who had resigned the governorship to accept the more prestigious post. The two men were soon locked in battle with Ames supporting and Alcorn opposing the Third Enforcement Act (doc. 15b). In 1873 when they were rival candidates for governor, Ames received the regular Republican nomination with three Negro running mates, and Alcorn challenged him as a dissident Republican with Democratic support. The division among Mississippi Republicans was important to the events leading to the state's "redemption," for Ames' difficulty in obtaining military support from the Grant administration arose in part from the Alcorn faction whose opposition to Ames' request seemed to confirm the assurances of Democrats that federal troops were not needed.

By 1875 the Democratic party was dominated by "white-liners" who used the race issue and a new technique of open intimidation with semi-military organizations marching in uniform with cannon and pistol. The overturn of Republican control in Mississippi was referred to at the time as war and revolution. The family letters of Governor Ames and his wife Blanche (the daughter of Benjamin F. Butler), whom he courted and wed while senator, provide a poignant account of the one-sided battle.

Adelbert Ames was a man of integrity as well as of conscience, and his administration of the state had not been marred by corruption or extravagance. The impeachment charges brought against him by his political opponents were totally lacking in substance. In a retrospective letter at the turn of the century written in reply to a young historian engaged in research for a volume on Reconstruction in Mississippi, Ames explained that his reason for taking political office might appear ludicrous in 1900, but "then, it seemed to me that I had a Mission with a large M."[1]

Thomas S. G. Dabney, whose letters together with the comments of his son and daughter represent the view of Ames' adversaries (doc. b), was a Virginia planter who had moved his family and slaves to Mississippi in 1835; he had been known as a benevolent and considerate slave master.

a. Correspondence of Governor Adelbert Ames, September 1875–March 1876

JACKSON, MISS., September 5, 1875

DEAR BLANCHE: I had finished my letter to you yesterday and was looking for George to mail it when Capt. Fisher came to me out of breath and out of heart to tell me of a riot which had just taken place at Clinton (a village ten miles west of here) and from which he had just escaped, with his wife. He was speaking when the riot began. It was a premeditated riot on the part of the Democracy which resulted in the death of some four white men and about the same number of Negroes and quite a large number of Negroes wounded. There were present at a Republican barbecue about fifteen hundred colored people, men, women and children. Seeking the opportunity white men, fully prepared, fired into this crowd. Two women were reported killed, also two children. As the firing continued, the women ran away with the men in many instances, leaving their children on the ground. Today there are some forty carriages, wagons and carts which were abandoned by

1. Ames to James W. Garner, Jan. 17, 1900, in Blanche Ames Ames, *Adelbert Ames, 1835–1933: General, Senator, Governor* (London: Macdonald & Co., 1964), pp. 573–577.

SOURCE: The family letters are from *Chronicles from the Nineteenth Century: Family Letters of Blanche Butler and Adelbert Ames Married July 21st, 1870*, compiled by Blanche Butler Ames (Clinton, Mass., 1957), II:163–164, 166–167, 169–170, 183, 195–196, 199–200, 212, 215–218, 248, 249–250, 310–311, reprinted by courtesy of Jessie Marshall Williams.

the colored people in their flight. Last night, this morning and today squads of white men are scouring the county killing Negroes. Three were killed at Clinton this morning—one of whom was an old man, nearly one hundred years old—defenseless and helpless. Yesterday the Negroes, though unarmed and unprepared, fought bravely and killed four of the ringleaders, but had to flee before the muskets which were at once brought onto the field of battle. This is but in keeping with the programme of the Democracy at this time. They know we have a majority of some thirty thousand and to overcome it they are resorting to intimidation and murder. It is cold-blooded murder on the part of the "white liners"—but there are other cases exactly like this in other parts of the state. You ask what are we to do. That is a question I find it difficult to answer. I told you a day or two ago that the whole party has been opposed to organizing the militia and furthermore I have been unable to find anyone who was willing to take militia appointments.

The Mansion has been crowded all day long with Republican friends and Negroes from the field of battle. I have run off to the northwest chamber for my daily chat with you, leaving a crowd in the other rooms. There has also been a crowd at the front gate all day long. The town is full of Negroes from the country who come to escape harm. The whites here are afraid of the Negroes who have come in. A committee of white men have just waited on me and offer to keep the peace so far as may be in their power. The Sheriff has selected a number of them to act as a posse to go out into the country and arrest those who are murdering Negroes. This last step has caused a subsidence of the excitement felt by the whites as well as blacks.

I anticipate no further trouble here at this time. The "white liners" have gained their point—they have, by killing and wounding, so intimidated the poor Negroes that they can in all human probability prevail over them at the election. I shall at once try to get troops from the general government. Of course it will be a difficult thing to do.

I send a world of love.

ADELBERT

JACKSON, MISS., September 7, 1875

DEAR BLANCHE: Today I issued a proclamation commanding the illegal military companies to disband: and I also telegraphed the President to make an inquiry before formally making a requisition for troops. I asked him if his proclamation of last December was still in force, and state that if he does not so regard it I will at once make a requisition as required by the Constitution of the U.S. The excitement in this vicinity is abating, but there is enough and more throughout the state. As I have already stated, the Democracy seek by violence to defeat the purpose of the Constitutional amendments and deprive the colored men of their political rights, to do which they do not hesitate to murder. Lamar and Gordon of Georgia are in the state making, it is reported, most incendiary speeches. The language they use is not of itself violent, but the conclusions they reach are that this election must be carried, even if violence be resorted to.

So much for politics. You may read to your Father such portions of my letters as touch on the political situation. Tell him that in '60 and '61 there were not such unity and such preparation against the government of the U.S. as now exist against the colored men and the government their votes have established. Gibbs and Raymond report that Gen. Augur is ready to act but that he requires authority from the President. He holds, as I have told you our party generally does, that the organizing of the militia of colored men precipitates a war of races and one to be felt over the entire South. He says thousands in Louisiana are ready to come here to fight the Negro. As it is, the power of the U.S. alone can give the security our citizens are entitled to. If it is not given, then no effort will be made by Republicans to carry the election.

I send you love.

ADELBERT

JACKSON, MISS., *September 9, 1875*

DEAR BLANCHE: Yesterday I wrote you I applied to the national government for aid to maintain order, etc. but have not as yet received any reply. I presume, however, the President will act at once even if he does not notify me of his action. I am fully alive to the fact that my action will be like an exploding shell in the political canvass at the North. It may injure Republicanism there, but I had but one course open for me to take—and that I have taken. I anxiously await the action of the President. There is no special news. The Democracy are beginning to deny my statements and will by their lies attempt to deceive the North as they did last winter relative to the murders in Warren Co. . . . .

I am always glad to hear of the babies—none of your letters are more interesting than those which tell of yourself and them—for is not a man's heart where his treasures are? To you all I send a world of love.

ADELBERT

THE ATTORNEY-GENERAL TO GOV. AMES.

DEPARTMENT OF JUSTICE,
WASHINGTON, Sept. 14, 1875.

To Governor AMES, Jackson, Miss.:

This hour I have had dispatches from the PRESIDENT. I can best convey to you his ideas by extracts from his dispatch.

"The whole public are tired out with these annual autumnal outbreaks in the South, and the great majority are ready now to condemn any interference on the part of the Government. I heartily wish that peace and good order may be restored without issuing the proclamation. But if it is not, the proclamation must be issued, and if it is, I shall instruct the commander of the forces to have no child's play.

"If there is a necessity for military interference, there is justice in such interference as to deter evil doers. I would suggest the sending of a dispatch (or better by private messenger) to Gov. Ames, urging him to strengthen his own position by exhausting his own resources in restoring order, before he receives government aid. He might accept the assistance offered by the citizens of Jackson and elsewhere. Gov. Ames and his advisers can be made perfectly secure.

"As many of the troops now in Mississippi as he deems necessary may be sent to Jackson. If he is betrayed by those who offer assistance, he will be in a position to defeat their ends and punish them."

You see by this the mind of the President, with which I and every member of the Cabinet who has been consulted are in full accord. You see the difficulties; you see the responsibilities which you assume.

We cannot understand why you do not strengthen yourself in the way the President suggests; nor do we see why you do not call the Legislature together, and obtain from them whatever powers

SOURCE: McPherson, Handbook for 1876, pp. 42–43.

and money and arms you need. The Constitution is explicit that the executive of the State can call upon the President for aid in suppressing *"domestic violence"* only *"when the Legislature cannot be convened."* And the law expressly says: *"In case of an insurrection in any State against the government thereof, it shall be lawful for the President, on application of the Legislature of such State, or of the Executive when the Legislature cannot be convened, to call, etc."* It is the plain meaning of the constitution and the laws, when taken together, that the executive of the State may call upon the President for military aid to quell "domestic violence" only in case of an insurrection in any State against the government thereof, when the Legislature cannot be called together. You make no suggestion even that there is any insurrection against the government of the State, or that the Legislature would not support you in any measures you might propose to preserve the public order.

I suggest that you take all lawful means and all needed measures to preserve the peace by the forces in your own State, and let the country see that the citizens of Mississippi, who are largely favorable to good order, and who are largely Republican, have the courage and the manhood to *fight* for their rights, and to destroy the bloody ruffians who murder the innocent and unoffending freedmen.

Everything is in readiness. Be careful to bring yourself strictly within the Constitution and the laws; and if there *is such resistance to your State authorities as you cannot by all the means at your command suppress,* the President will swiftly aid you in crushing these lawless traitors to human rights.

Telegraph me on receipt of this, and state *explicitly* what you need.

Yours very respectfully,
EDWARDS PIERREPONT, Attorney-General.

JACKSON, MISS., *September 17, 1875*

DEAR BLANCHE: I have been nearly all the afternoon engaged in replying to a telegram from Atty. Genl. Pierrepont, relative to affairs. His telegram is rather severe on us and our party, simply because we have taken no action to protect ourselves. The fact is, however, that I have endeavored time and again to organize militia and have utterly failed. You will see my letter by and by, when you can judge of its merits. I have been heretofore disgusted at the condition of affairs, but Pierrepont's telegram has quite exasperated me. Perhaps, however, my own helplessness to protect has had its effect of laying the foundation of both my disgust and exasperation.

I shall turn to something else now. I never give you more than a page or a page and a half of politics in my daily letters. . . .

I am a great deal preoccupied now-a-days, and find much difficulty in driving my more serious affairs out of my head, even when writing to you, my Love. I am such a serious fellow—when I am serious—and take my duties so seriously that it is uncomfortable to myself—however, I believe I hide it from all the rest of the world—at least I try to.

Love,

ADELBERT

JACKSON, MISS., *September 24, 1875*

DEAR BLANCHE: I have no news for you today, except that I am organizing my militia and preparing for an emergency by and by. The programme of the Democracy now is to remain passive till two or three days of the election, when it will be too brief a time for Grant to issue his proclamation—he needs five days—at least that seems to be the minimum time to make his proclamation generally known—and on the day of election or two or three days preceding—bring forth their guns, rifles and pistols for slaughter. I will try to meet such demonstrations, but even now there are no Republicans in the eastern part of the state who will consent to the organization of the militia there. Such is the report I get from there today.

Carrying the election by violence and murder, the Democracy intend, so they say among themselves, to impeach me and turn the state over to the president of the Senate, one of their own men.

You ask what is to be done with Lt. Gov. Davis. This,—The charge against him of receiving a bribe for the pardon of young Barratine will be sustained (information received by me convinces me beyond a doubt of this fact). The charge sustained disqualified him and at the same time displaces him. A jury might disagree, to be sure,—but such a legislature as the Democracy expect would impeach him. In fact, the Democracy at the last extra session in July introduced resolutions of condemnation of his act, and would have tried to present articles had there been any hope.

You may feel astonished at what I say and ask what under the sun they can impeach me on. To which I reply I cannot conceive of anything done by me that a single charge against me can attach to. But a party that will take innocent blood for success will not hesitate at anything else. While they will have the will to do anything to advance their own interests I do not imagine they will have the power to impeach anyone. They may however, get control of the lower house. Time flies, and will solve these problems.

I had no letter from you yesterday nor any today. It is unusual that two days in succession should pass without word from you. I hope you have not started on a journey to me. No, I cannot believe it. The mails are somewhat irregular here anyhow, and your letters could well have been delayed.

We are having delightful weather—cold enough for a fire if you want—and warm enough without one if you be so minded.

I send you, Beloved, much love.

ADELBERT

JACKSON, MISS., *September 27, 1875*

DEAR BLANCHE: I received from you by today's mail two letters and the Treasurer's bond. I was glad to see that the style of paper is changed, for now I shall be almost sure of having a reasonably long letter. Why do the young ladies, who as a class are not renowned for much learning (slander of course), submit to a fashion which demands much ink or a glaring blank of fancy paper? I hope you will buy so large a stock that it will last long after the next new fashion which may revert to the pigmy sheets which have been so familiar to the world of late.

It is not because I would not like to have you near me that I telegraphed the "no"; but because you had better be with the babies and out of this tumult which envelops us. Like all who have to *endure* I get disgusted, but believe it is all making me a better man and preparing me for a quiet happy life (D.V.) with my Beloved Ones so far away.

What hurts me most is that the cowardice of our party since its organization is now visited on my head, and there seems no escape from it. Also all the sins and iniquities of Republican rule in South Carolina, Louisiana, and other Southern states are weighed against me in judgment of the country. Also—this—I am fighting for the Negro; and to the whole country a white man is better than a "Nigger."

Gen'l. Warner, Gibbs, Raymond and others have been playing croquet this evening. Judge E. Hill has just come in. He has interrupted me for some time and is now talking. He wishes to be remembered to you. Love,

ADELBERT

JACKSON, MISS., *October* 10, 1875

DEAR BLANCHE: I have nothing new to tell you today—except perhaps that our friends are very much dispirited and seem almost ready to abandon the contest. In fact, many have lost all hope of success unless aided by the national government. Consequently they are very persistent in urging me to make a call. Even in counties where there is no actual killing, the Republicans are paralyzed through fear, and will not act. They refuse to accept arms, and organize militia. As this feeling is general, you can well understand what little hope we have of success. The company I sent out to Edwards Depot has not been disturbed as I understand. The result will be that the colored man ceases to be a free man—serfdom awaits him as certain as fate.

Your letter telling of your Father's visit to Washington was received today. I do not know that he can accomplish much when the administration will not even make a change in the U.S. Marshal here, which is a necessity, and which was asked by our committee which went to W———n and also by myself. By what I have written, you will perceive I see nothing very flattering ahead.

This is Sunday—hardly a day of rest. Yet, I have read a good deal of my history of England. Love and kisses.

ADELBERT

JACKSON, MISS., *October* 12, 1875

DEAR BLANCHE: I had thought I would not be at liberty long enough to write you today, but just at this moment I have dismissed visitors till a later hour, and write you just one word while George is arranging my supper on the table in the center of the room.

Caldwell's company (colored) has returned from Edward's Depot, not having been interfered with. But the excitement occasioned by his march is very great. The Democracy say they see in it an effort to intimidate the white people. It is strange that they should assume the position they do while at the same time they assert the superiority of the whites over the blacks, and that the former should rule. Asserting substantially that the Negro shall be disfranchised, notwithstanding the constitutional amendments, they pretend they will secure him in his rights if I will call off my militia. They began this campaign with the assertion that they would win if they had to wade in blood—they now are on the eve of other outbreaks. Each of these days is important. Tomorrow the election will be held in Ohio. I hope it will go Republican, and yet I fear it will go Democratic. Today I understand the Supreme Court of the U.S. delivers an opinion on the Enforcement Act— We look for a favorable decision—yet, it may be against us.

While I have been scrawling the above, my supper has been getting cold. I think I will stop a moment to make (pour out) my cup of tea and when my first visitor comes I will take a moment of his time to close—I have had half of my supper.

I enjoy your accounts of yourself and the babies. Kiss Butler and Edith and the baby for me, and keep many kisses from me for yourself.

ADELBERT

JACKSON, MISS., *October 12, 1875*
DEAR BLANCHE: This has been another busy day for me. The militia question is agitating the "white-liners" very much. They are prepared for another New Orleans affair if need be, so they say. The leaders have asked me for an interview, which will take place tomorrow. I think, among other things, they really fear the militia will disturb their families in case of a disturbance. We began too late to organize and have too little means to accomplish much with the militia. Inasmuch as peace exists—or rather as there is no open violence—the militia cannot be called out. I understand they are willing to promise almost anything if I will cease with my militia movements.

Through the terror caused by murders and threats, the colored people are thoroughly intimidated. They cannot be rallied unless we have U.S. troops and it is now too late for that. It is too late for this reason. My demand must be made in writing—not by telegraph— Four days will be thus consumed. A number of days will be taken by the President for consideration, and when he decides to act, five days must be given. I do not believe a call at this time would be heeded. Ten days at most would be all the time allowed in which the troops could act. Of course they would have to be moved from where they now are to points of action. The result would be that hardly a day would be left for them to act in.

Yes, a *revolution* has taken place—by force of arms—and a race are disfranchised—they are to be returned to a condition of serfdom—an era of second slavery. It is their fault (not mine, personally) that this fate is before them. They refused to prepare for war when in time of peace, when they could have done so. Now it is too late. The nation should have acted but *it* was "tired of the annual autumnal outbreaks in the South"—see Grant's and Pierrepont's letter to me. The political death of the Negro will forever release the nation from the weariness from such "political outbreaks." You may think I exaggerate. Time will show you how accurate my statements are. In fact, look at other Southern states.

Last night I made up my mind to resign after the election when this revolution shall have been completed. Why should I fight on a hopeless battle for two years more, when no possible good to the Negro or anybody else would result? Why?

After all this I turn from myself to you, Beautiful—the bright, happy dwelling place of my thoughts, and send forth to you a world of love without end.

ADELBERT

JACKSON, MISS., October 14, 1875

DEAR BLANCHE: This is the first opportunity I have had during the past forty-eight hours to have a chat with you. I doubt if I, even now, have an opportunity to say what I have to communicate to you. The telegraphic dispatches have doubtless informed you of a "compromise" here. They have said perhaps—I have not seen them—that I have disbanded and disarmed my militia and that the opposition was to cease its lawlessness. The facts are, in brief, these. Yesterday a committee of the leading citizens of the state— at least this part of it—waited on me, and proposed that they would do all in their power to preserve the peace and secure a fair election if I would disband my militia. I refused to disband or disarm the militia or in any way impair its efficiency.

But I did agree to do just what I had intended to do, even before the interview; which was to order the companies (two) on active service, to their homes to await orders. I had brought here two companies to aid in re-instating Sheriff Morgan of Yazoo County.

Morgan, fearing assassination, would not go. I had nothing to do but dismiss my militia, to be called upon whenever new troubles occur. I also agreed that the arms should be kept in armories instead of in the hands of the members of the companies. This also I had previously intended. The reasons of the opposition for asking this was to keep them (the arms) from the Negroes and by me and also by the Negroes that the "white-liners" should not take them. Thus far I have agreed to do nothing I had not intended to do. That the arms should be safe I agreed that guards of U.S. soldiers should guard them if they could be had—always subject to my orders. The militia is to be ordered out at any and all times when necessity may demand. Thus my power through the militia is not curtailed in the least. I also agreed to stop organizing more militia. Here I yielded little as I had organized about all the militia I could organize. Since I began I have been able to organize only in this one county and all the rest of the state is militia-less, because in other counties they would not organize—one or two counties excepted.

The opposition were content that I should do what I have told you—in fact it constitutes all they asked except that they wanted me to disband and disarm, which I could not and would not do. They were moved by at least two reasons—first they and their families *feared harm* from the Negroes.—Second the planters wanted this movement stopped on account of their cotton still unpicked in the fields. They began to carry the election by violence but the consequences of the attempt grew to be more portentous than anticipated and they, at least the leaders, have not withdrawn. I believe them honest in their promises, and believe much good will result. Some doubt their sincerity, but be that as it may, all of my means to protect had been exhausted.—The U.S. had substantially refused to aid us.

While I have not departed from principle or yielded a single right or duty, I believe the compromise has saved many lives. The facts which prove it I will give you at some other time.

This has been written hurriedly.—George has come with my supper. Love,

ADELBERT

JACKSON, MISS., *November 1, 1875*
DEAR BLANCHE: The canvass is at an end, and tomorrow the

voting will take place. The reports which come to me almost hourly are truly sickening. Violence, threats of murder, and consequent intimidation are co-extensive with the limits of the state. Republican leaders in many localities are hiding in the swamps or have sought refuge beyond the borders of their own counties. The government of the U.S. does not interfere, and will not, unless to prevent actual bloodshed. But no preparations have been made by a proper disposition of troops to meet the murderous designs of the white-liners. I have copies of the orders to the troops. They are to be used to "prevent bloodshed in case of disorders." Observe, they cannot be used to prevent *disorders* nor to prevent intimidation nor to secure to all men their political rights—only where disorders may occur are they to stop the flow of blood. What a mockery are such orders, when as the troops are now disposed, there are but three points where they can act and at those points no disturbances are anticipated.

Warner has gone up to his county to vote. His wife is almost distracted, as she fears he will be assassinated, and the government detective reports to us that the probabilities are that he will be. Mr. Chase [the representative of Attorney-General Pierrepont] has gone to see the chairman of the Democratic state committee to get protection papers for Warner! You can thus surmise what my power, or the power of the civil authorities, is. I am glad this state of affairs is drawing to an end. I begin to speak of the situation in a fair frame of mind, but before I close I lose all patience. Today— now—I have held out longer than usual.

I send you love—for yourself, Beautiful, and for the babies.

ADELBERT

JACKSON, MISS., November 4, 1875

DEAR BLANCHE: I did not write you last night, not being in a writing humor. The reports of disasters which came to us then were mild as compared to those of today. So complete and thorough was the intimidation of Republican voters that we have yet to hear of the first county which has gone Republican. There may be a few counties on the river which have been neglected by the murderous white leaguers that have maintained their virtue, but of such we have no word. The legislature will be nearly unanimous in both branches and will be able to do anything it may incline to do. The election has been a farce—worse than a farce. . . .

My visitors are increasing, and I must stop. Mr. Chase starts for the North tonight. I expect to leave for Minn. next Saturday.
Love,

ADELBERT

JACKSON, *March* 1, 1876

DEAR MOTHER: You have heard that the legislature has brought articles of impeachment against Gen'l. Ames. Your letter received a day or two ago intimating that we might expect other action, owing to promises made by members of the Democratic Party, caused a smile of derision. Will the people of the North never learn that truth, honor and virtue do not and can not belong to Democratic ci-devant slave holders, that while those at Washington speak soft cooing words, make kindly promises and prate of peace and good fellowship, their hearts are full of gall and bitterness, and they are the fitting representatives of constituents who, with none of the virtues of human nature, have all the vices, and have perpetrated every crime forbidden in the Decalogue. Hill, Toombs and Davis are entitled to some respect as compared with those who, while wearing cloaks of hypocrisy in Washington, go home and expose their hate and ferocity to such an extent that no reports are allowed of their utterances, lest Northern men may discover the wolves in sheeps' clothing.

Of the principal men in Jackson, there is hardly one who has not, by counsel or action, taken some part in the Negro murders. These murderers, and I use the term advisedly, thinking that Father ought to be or might be interested in Gen'l. Ames' case and come here to lend assistance, have arranged a plan to assassinate him. No doubt you will think I am carried away by indignation; on the contrary, although I deplore impeachment because I fear some good men of the North may be deceived into believing that it is merited, yet as far as my personal preference goes you know I have never been contented with this country, and I hail with pleasure anything which will shorten our sojourn here. Nature has made it the garden of the earth. But with that law of compensation by which the gorgeous perfumed flowers of the tropics live side by side with poisonous reptiles and deadly seeds of miasma, so this lovely climate and fertile country is inhabited by a race which seems to have lost all the heavenly fire of noble purpose. There is hardly a spark left for rejuvenation.

I think I hear you say "But Blanche many of these Southern men are from the North, they are our kinfolk, our brothers." When I spoke of ci-devant slave holders, it was with meaning. There has been a leveling process in this country, by which in proportion as the Negro acquired under the lash docility, humility, and subservience to authority, the master gained ferocity, arrogance and resistance to all law, human and Divine. I believe it impossible for any nature, however perfect and refined, to have lived with slaves and not to have suffered deterioration.

I have written rather more freely than usual, and given you my opinion of the South, and I venture to say if Mr. Spofford would live here three years, and take part in politics, he would go home to Newburyport and feel ashamed to acknowledge himself a Democrat. Do not think that we are wanting in appreciation of the kindness which prompted the efforts in Gen'l. Ames behalf. We are not, but recognize their utter futility, owing to the class of men with whom we have to deal.

[Blanche]

b. A Planter's Version, August–October 1875

T. S. D. TO HIS SON-IN-LAW B. H. GREENE

"BURLEIGH, 29th August, 1875.

. . . "WE are having lively times in the political way. I have seen nothing like it since 1840,—those days of 'hard cider,' 'log cabins,' ' 'coon skins,' and what-not, by means of which the Whigs gave Van Buren and the Democrats so signal an overthrow. I believe the impulse under which the outraged white race of the South are now being urged on will be equally irresistible. At a mass-meeting held in Raymond on the 18th instant, falling in with T. J. Wharton, I remarked to him that such an uprising was wonderful! 'Uprising?' replied he. 'It is no uprising. It is an insurrection!' To give you some notion of the enthusiasm of the people, I only have to say that they do not straggle in to such meetings, but go in clubs, each club with its band of music, flags, and regalia, and a cannon in many instances, and these cannon they make roar from every hill-top on the road. The procession of cavalry from Edwards

SOURCE: Susan Dabney Smedes, Memorials of a Southern Planter (Baltimore, Md.: 1887), pp. 258–261.

Dépôt (some other clubs having joined the Edwards Club) reached from the court-house far beyond John Shelton's house,— the length of the column being two miles, as one of the number told me. That from Utica, taking in my club and one other, was a great deal longer. The thing to be appreciated had to be seen. The 'carpet-baggers' and negroes are evidently staggered. We have been carrying on this thing for a month without their having moved a peg. They do not know where to begin. I suppose something will be hatched up in Washington after a while, and the cue be given to the faithful, and then 'we shall see what we shall see.'

"Among the anomalies of the canvass upon which we have just entered, not the least significant is that we have not a single candidate in the field who, for himself, sought office; whereas every 'carpet-bagger' and a large percentage of the negroes are clamorous for some place or other. All of our candidates have been brought out by nominating conventions; many of these against their wish,—for these conventions pick out our best men. For example, we are running John Shelton for supervisor, A. R. Johnston for the State senate, Daniel Williams for magistrate at Dry Grove, etc. None of these desire the positions proposed for them, but it would be considered in very bad taste in either to refuse.

"The upshot of the whole is that I am kept on the 'pad,'—being president of the Dry Grove Club, that has to march, or *be marched to*, at every whip-stitch. We held two club meetings last week, and I have ordered one for this week. Next week, on the 11th of September, we go in a body to Edwards Dépôt, where preparations will be made for ten thousand people. I suppose Jackson will respond, as I know other places will, and so many barbecues will be given by the clubs, to each of which the others must march in a body, and in military order, that I will esteem myself lucky if I get through alive. But I expect to be lucky to that extent, as my whole soul is in it."

It was early in 1875 that the citizens of Mississippi, believing that it was unmanly and stupid to submit longer without protest against ruinous misrule of "carpet-baggers," backed by negro voters, determined to lay aside all minor interests and make an organized effort to throw off the incubus which was rapidly involving the whole State in financial bankruptcy and social degradation and misery. Hence the formation of Democratic clubs.

From 1865 to 1875,—ten long, weary years,—tenfold harder to endure than the four years immediately preceding 1865, the State had been under military rule, our last governor from Washington being Adelbert Ames (a man honest and brave, but narrow and puritanical), who seems to have hated the Aryan race of the South. In proof of this I merely cite the fact that he was impeached by the State Legislature for fomenting race strife, but, by advice of counsel, he wisely or unwisely evaded the issue of trial, and fled away to his own.

During the years 1870–74 the taxes, imposed by aliens and the misguided African element, in many cases exceeded the incomes derived from the plantations; and it was then that men, nerved with a courage born of despair, cast about them for suitable leaders (men of unquestioned integrity, cool judgment, and dauntless resolution) under whose guidance relief might be attempted. Intuitively all eyes were turned to Thomas Dabney, and he was chosen president of the Democratic club of his neighborhood.

[Written by Edward.]

T. S. D. to His Son Thomas

"BURLEIGH, 15th October, 1875.

. . . "I will have my house as full as it can hold tomorrow night, as Utica, Raymond, Clinton, Boltons, Edwards, etc., will send their clubs here in force. You will perceive that a great many will have come long distances. I must take as many as I can accommodate reasonably, having already invited a number. It will put your sisters to much trouble, but as it is unavoidable, they undertake it with great cheerfulness."

The daughters worked by day and night on the uniforms for Thomas and his friends. Some of the negroes joined the club, and uniforms must be made for them too, and it was the patriotic thing for the ladies in the house to make these also. Besides, an immense United States flag was called for by the club, and was made by us in those hot July days and nights.

Thomas was as ready to extend the simple hospitality of his house in helping on this movement as he had been in former times to render more extensive aid. His life-long friend, Mr. John Shelton, in writing of this side of his character, says,—

"We were both Henry Clay men while he lived, and Whigs of

the straitest and strictest type. . . . A most zealous Whig before the civil war, the leaders and candidates of that party were often the recipients of his unbounded and princely hospitality, and, as a zealous party man, he took a great interest in whatever elections were pending, and shared his means with an unsparing and free hand for the advancement of party ends."

T. S. D. to His Daughter Emmy

"Burleigh, 20th October, 1875.
. . . "We are in a very hot political contest just now, and with a good prospect of turning out the carpet-bag thieves by whom we have been robbed for the past six to ten years. They commenced at Clinton on their old game of getting up riots and then calling on Grant for troops to suppress them,—these troops to be used afterwards to control elections. They succeeded in getting up their riot, which was put down by our own people after so sanguinary a fashion as to strike them with a terror not easily described."

29. South Carolina

The campaign plans printed below (doc. a) inspired by the success of the Mississippi "white-liners" the previous year, were formulated by Martin W. Gary of Edgefield county, leader of the "straightout" or anti-fusionist Democrats, who opposed working with the reform Republicans. Items numbered 3, 8, 16, 21 in Plan No. 1 were marked for omission in copies to be circulated throughout the state, but they as well as the others indicate the spirit that prevailed during the summer and fall of 1876 despite efforts at restraint by party members fearful of federal intervention and by the openly moderate and prestigious Wade Hampton, Democratic candidate for governor. About 300 Democratic rifle clubs were organized throughout the state intent on intimidating Republicans. Widespread election frauds supplemented the threat of violence, with a narrow victory resulting for the Democrats. The election returns were contested by the Republicans, and for a time South Carolina experienced the chaos of two governors and two houses of the legislature. When President Hayes withdrew federal troops from the state house in April 1877, Republican resistance collapsed, and Democrats were left in full control. (For the background of national action, see introductions to documents 16 and 19.) Once in power they relied increasingly upon refined methods of election fraud rather than upon overt intimidation and violence. This is evident from Sir George Campbell's account of the elections of 1878 (doc. b).

A member of Parliament with considerable experience as colonial administrator in India, Campbell visited the United States in the fall of 1878, showing particular interest in what he called the "Black question." There are interesting parallels between his contemporary judgment and the conclusions of modern revisionist historians for he commended the laws passed by blacks and carpetbaggers, pointed out that corruption and accusations of corruption were general in American politics, and viewed the official state investigations of deposed Republican administrations as neither impartial nor conclusive.

a. Red Shirt Campaign Strategy, 1876

No 1 "PLAN OF THE CAMPAIGN" 1876

1. That every Democrat in the Townships must be put upon the Roll of the Democratic Clubs. Nolens Volens.
2. That a Roster must be made of every *White* and of *every negro* voter in the Townships and returned *immediately* to the County Executive Committee.
3. That the Democratic Military Clubs are to be armed with Rifles and pistols and such other arms as they may command. They are to be divided into two companies, one of the old men—the other of the young; an experienced captain or Commander to be placed over each of them. That each Company is to have a 1st and 2nd Lieutenent. That the number of ten privates is to be the unit of organization. That each Captain is to see that his men are well armed and provided with at least thirty round of ammunition. That the Captain of the young men is to provide a Baggage wagon, in which three days rations for the horses and three days rations for the men are to be Stored on the day before the Election in order that they may be prepared at a moments notice to move to any point in the County when ordered by the Chairman of the Executive Committee.

ELECTION

4. We must get the three Commissioners of Election, who are appointed by the Governor, as favorable to us as possible, and we must demand that at least one reliable Democrat is on the

SOURCE: Martin W. Gary Papers, South Carolinian Library, University of South Carolina, Columbia, S.C.

Commission and he must endevor to get to be the Chairman of the Commission, and the Clerk that is allowed them must be a Democrat if we can possibly bring it about.

5. We must have at least one half of the managers of Election Democrats and as many more as we can get. We must have the Chairman of the Board of Managers a Democrat by all means, also all the clerks to the managers of the Precincts must be Democrats.

6. We must have a duplicate of the result of the Election made out for the benefit of the Executive Committee, so soon as the ballots are counted and forwarded at once by a courier, on the night of the Election. There must be a committee who shall keep watch and guard over the ballot boxes to prevent the Radicals from tampering with them in any way.

7. We must send a committee with a duplicate of the Election to Columbia in order to see to it that the State Canvassers do not perpetrate any fraud upon us after the Election is held, and see also that the Clerk of the Court files a copy of the returns of Election in accordance with Law.

8. There must be at least Two Hundred Selectmen, chosen from the different clubs, to go to Columbia in the event of a refusal to seat the Democratic members elected, to compel and enforce their rights to be seated at all hazzards.

9. Every Democrat must be at the polls by five o'clock on the morning of the Election, carry his dinner with him and stay there until the votes are counted unless the exegencies require him else where.

10. It shall be the duty of each club to provide transportation to old and helpless voters and assist them to the Polls; and at the same time see to it that all Democrats turn out and vote.

11. Every Democrat must be on the alert on the day of Election to see that negroes under age do not vote and that those who are properly entitled to vote do not repeat, and if they should discover that squads should leave the precincts and go in the direction of another precinct, they must follow them and challenge their role at the next precinct.

12. Every Democrat must feel honor bound to control the vote of at least one negro, by intimidation, purchase, keeping him away or as each individual may determine, how he may best accomplish it.

13. We must attend every Radical meeting that we hear of whether

they meet at night or in the day time. Democrats must go in as large numbers as they can get together, and well armed, behave at *first* with great courtesy and assure the ignorant negroes that you mean them no harm and so soon as their *leaders* or speakers begin to speak and make false statement of facts, tell them *then* and *there* to their faces, that they are liars, thieves and Rascals, and are only trying to mislead the ignorant negroes and if you get a chance get upon the Platform and address the negroes.

14. In speaches to negroes you must remember that *argument* has no effect upon them: they can only be influenced by their *fears*, superstition and cupidity. Do not attempt to flatter and persuade them. Tell them plainly of our wrongs and grievances, perpetrated upon us by their rascally leaders. Prove to them that we can carry the election without them and if they cooperate with us, it will benefit them more than it will us. Treat them so as to show them you are the superior race, and that their natural position is that of subordination to the white man.

15. Let it be generally known that if any blood is shed, houses burnt, votes repeated, ballot boxes stuffed, false counting of votes, or any acts on their part that are in violation of *Law* and *Order*: that we will hold the leaders of the *Radical Party Personally Responsible*, whether they were present at the time of the commission of the offense or crime or not, beginning *first* with the white men, second the Mulatto men and third and last with the Black leaders. This should be proclaimed from one end of the county to the other, so that *Every Radical* may know it, as the *certain, fixed* and *unalterable determination* of every Democrat in this county.

16. "Never threaten a man individually, if he deserves to be threatened, the necessities of the times require that he *should die*. A dead Radical is very harmless—a threatened Radical or one driven off by threats from the scene of his operations is often very troublesome, sometimes dangerous always vindictive."

17. Members of the Executive Committee and the leading members of the Party should visit the various clubs and explain the Plan of the Campaign and such facts as are necessarily of such a nature as are not to be reduced to writing.

18. There should be at least five mass meetings in the County, during the Canvass, and the last one should be held at Edgefield C.H. on or about the middle of October.

19. The months of July and August ought to be devoted to speaches at the Club meetings or Township meetings, and speaches should then be made by the canidates and such other speakers as we can obtain.

20. At our Mass Meetings we should invite distinguished men of this and other states to address our people.

21. In the month of September we ought to begin to organize negro clubs, or pretend that we have organized them and write letters from different parts of the County giving the facts of organization but from prudential reasons the names of the negroes are to be withheld. Those who join are to be taken on probation and are not to be taken into full fellowship, until they have proven their sincerity by voting our ticket.

22. In the nomination of canidates we should nominate those who will give their time—their money—their brains, their energies and if necessary lay down their lives to carry this election. Any attempt to run independent canidates must be prevented at any risk.

23. There should not be any assessment for money to carry on the Campaign, before the month of October, when the cotton crop begins to mature and our people have an opportunity of raising money by its sale.

24. In voting for or nominating canidates, for County, State or Federal offices, we must give the preference to Native born *White South Carolinians* over Carpetbaggers.

25. The watchword of our Campaign should be, "fight the Devil with fire." That we are in favor of Local Self government— Home Rule by Home Folks and that we are determined to drive the Carpetbaggers from this state at all hazzards.

26. That we must make the Campaign an aggressive one and prosecute it with great vigor and try and get up all the enthusiasm we can among the masses.

27. That harmony, and concord should be preserved in our ranks. Personal considerations must be given up for the good of the County. Success must be achieved at the sacrifice of everything except the *principles* of our Great Party.

28. The boys from 16 upwards are to be enrolled on the lists of our clubs. In all processions the clubs must parade with banners, mottoes &c and keep together so as to make an imposing spectacle.

29. Every club must be uniformed in a red shirt, and they must be sure and wear it upon all public meetings, and particularly on the day of election.
30. Secrecy should shroud all of our transactions. Let not your left hand know what your right does.
31. Whenever there are two election precincts at the Court House the Democracy should remain mounted in order to move at once from one box to the other in case of any disturbances.
32. When the negroes are largely in the majority a corps of challengers should be organized, with appropriate questions. You gain time by this.
33. Any member of the party who fails to vote the ticket nominated must be read out of the party.

PLAN OF CAMPAIGN

May be divided into Preparation action and Real action.
Preparation action may be subdivided into
    Preparing the Public mind for Democratic Success
    Preparing the minds of the Negroes to accept the results of the Election as a matter of course,
    Preparing the Democrats to use to the fullest extent their powers, influence, and time.

Real action may be divided into General action, or a certain general plan upon which the Democrats must all agree, and to which they must adhere under any exegencies, and Experimental action, or such sub-plans as Individuals may upon the spur of the moment adopt, but which would be impracticable for general use.

Now under the Preparation action the first thing to be done is to prepare the Public mind.

This can be done by attacking the Leaders of the Opposition fiercely through the press, showing up in strong light their rascalities and their faithlessness to their constituents. By talking freely to Negroes upon the subject, and every one who agrees with you & professes to see things in the true light; take his name down and through the press announce how gratifying it is to see that the Negroes are at last awake & frequently predict a brilliant Democratic Negro vote. State too that you can give names, but from prudential motives with hold them, as intimidation of the Radicals is carried to such an extent that a Democratic Negro would not be safe if he were known as such.

State also & state positively that the majority of the Radicals is only nominal, that it has been obtained by the Negroes repeating & the lukewarmness of the Whites, that at this Election the Whites are determined that the Negro shall have a showing for once, and that after the Election the names of the Democratic Negroes will be made public if desired, (& if we carry the Election the trouble will be to find a Negro who dident vote our ticket).

Under the second head of Preparation action, we must prepare the minds of the Negroes by showing our ability to prevent a thorough organization of their party.

By meeting their Leaders before their faces and hacking them publicly. By swinging their most active Leaders up, if they become offensive. By telling them that their party has gone to pieces—their bell-wether has jumped the fence—and the friends who accomplished their emancipation have turned against them on account of the Rascality of their Representatives, &c. That we are *determined* to see that they vote as they please, but that we dont care a picaune how they vote as so many have left the County that we are now in the majority. That we are not talking to gain their votes but on account of kind feelings &c we are simply telling them how things are &c., assure them of kind treatment after our success if they behave &c.

Tell the Negroes that if they will put up good men who can give good security for faithful performance of duty, we will give them a fair fight at the Ballot Box & beat them too as we have the majority.

Under the 3d head of preparatory action, we must prepare the Democrats, so that they can use to advantage their powers influence & time.

We must be thoroughly organized, so that at short notice we can throw a given body of men in any given position.

We must rouse them if possible to the fullest appreciation of our position.

Every man must know his duty and be willing to do it.

We must have plenty of tickets judiciously distributed, so that we can use them freely.

Those who are to remain at the Boxes must be selected, & those who are to visit (just to see how things are going on) neighboring precincts, must also be selected & have their programs prepared for them.

We must prepare to mass our men at weak boxes, & post our

managers so that when a stranger rides up he may vote and ride on.

Our execution Committee must see every White man in their respective Townships & urge him to vote at home if no more & if he is slow to agree come out, he must be looked after, & talked to by his neighbors. We must be prepared to do our level best or die day of election. This exhausts the Preparitory action.

Under the head of Real action only a few General ideas can be laid down, & from these such subplans may be deduced as meet the exegencies of the case and suit the capacity or genius of the Individual.

First every strange Negro must be challenged—& in fact every Negro should be challenged—kill time should be our motto when the Negroes are voting.

It is not yet too late to hack the Leaders if opportunity occurs.

Assure the Mass that they shall have a fair showing but that they *must* vote according to law.

Vote every white man who is willing to vote.

These suggestion form the basis of a general plan.

Under the Experimental head so much can be said, & so many different plans successfully carried out by enterprising and fearless men that I will only touch on it briefly. We must have some one for clerk who can cook the record make no distinction between white & black voters but put them all down indiscriminately. Have a private clerk to check off the votes of the party & if towards the close of day you find that they have the majority stuff the box. Take away the votes from the Distributors if possible, but so manage it that no box shall be broken. We want every box if they are manipulated correctly. If they are very much in majority make two boy load their pistols with blank cartridges & get up a fight at the box, shoot in good earnest if a Negro is impertinent, but shoot straight & hit a leader & if once hit be sure to finish him &c.

b. Consolidation of Redeemer Control, 1878

To return to the history of South Carolina. After the withdrawal of the United States troops the Carpetbaggers were entirely routed and put to flight, and Wade Hampton assumed the undisputed government. He has certainly had much success. His party claim (I

SOURCE: Sir George Campbell, *White and Black: The Outcome of a Visit to the United States* (New York, 1879), pp. 180–187.

believe with justice) that he has done much to restore the finances, promote education, and protect blacks and whites in the exercise of peaceful callings. As regards political matters, his policy amounts, I think, to this;—it is in effect said to the blacks: "If you will accept the present régime, follow us, and vote Democratic; we will receive you, cherish you, and give you a reasonable share of representation, local office, &c.; but there shall be nothing for those who persist in voting Republican." Some of them accept these terms, but to vote Democratic is the one thing which the great majority will not do. They may be on excellent terms with white men with whom they have relations, will follow them and be guided by them in everything else, but they have sufficient independence to hold out on that point of voting, even when they have lost their white leaders and are quite left to themselves. They know that they owe their freedom to the Republicans, and it is to them a sort of religion to vote Republican. I think it was in Georgia (where they have not held out so stoutly) that, talking to a small black farmer, an ex-slave, as to the situation, I asked him about the black vote. "Well," he said, "some wote straight, and some don't; some is 'suaded and some is paid, but I wote according to my principles, and my principles is Republican." In South Carolina that is the view of the great body of the blacks, as the Democrats fully admit. Stories are told of personal dependants of the present Governor who owe everything to him and would do anything else in the world for him, but who will yet openly vote against him. Such, then, was the state of things when the elections of November 1878 came on.

It seemed to be well known beforehand that the Democrats were determined to win everything in the South. It was said to be a necessity finally to emancipate all the States from the scandal of black and Carpet-bag rule, and so far one could not but sympathise with the feeling; but so much had been already achieved, and there was not the least risk of a reaction. On the contrary, the power of the native whites was thoroughly re-established. In South Carolina Wade Hampton's re-election was not opposed, and there was no question whatever that by moderate means the Democrats could retain a very decided majority in the State Legislature. But they were not content with this; they aimed at an absolute possession of everything, leaving no representation to their opponents at all, and especially at a "solid South," in the United States Congress. "They are determined to win," I was told. "They will get the votes by fair

means, if they can; and if not I am sorry to say they will steal 'em."
And that is just what was done in South Carolina.

To understand what took place we must look at the election law
prevailing in the United States. It seems to me that if the law had
been designed to facilitate fraud, make detection difficult, and
render the settlement of disputed elections impossible, it could not
have been more skilfully devised. There is something to be said for
open voting and something for a well-managed ballot, but the
pretended ballot of the United States seems to combine all the
evils of both systems. It may be just possible for an independent
man connected with no party, who manages the thing skilfully, to
conceal his vote; but if he consents to make it known, there can be,
and in practice there is, no secrecy whatever. There are no official
ballotpapers, numbered and checked, so as to be afterwards traced,
as with us; every man may deposit in the box any ballot-paper he
chooses, written or printed in whatever form he chooses. In practice voters use papers in a particular form supplied by their own
party, so that there can be no mistake which way they vote. There
being no means of identifying the papers so cast, everything depends on the honesty and fair dealing of those who have the official
management of the polls. In all things the executive Government
has much greater power in America than with us, and the party
which has the executive power has also the control of the ballot-
boxes. They appoint returning boards and election managers at
each polling-place, who, when party spirit runs high, are in the
interest of the dominant majority. This was carried to an excess in
South Carolina during the recent elections. The United States
officers are entitled to take certain precautions to see that the
United States election law is fairly carried out, but they could only
be present at the principal places, and sent very subordinate agents
to the other polling places, where they were hustled and treated
with no respect whatever. Under these conditions the elections
were held in South Carolina.

There is a remarkable frankness and openness in speaking of the
way in which things were managed, and I believe I violate no
confidences, because there was no whispering or confidence about
it. There was not a very great amount of violence or intimidation.
Some Republican meetings were violently interfered with before
the election, and on the day of the election there was at some
places a certain amount of galloping about, firing guns, and such-

like demonstration by men in red shirts; but any intimidation used was rather moral than physical. In all districts where the parties in any degree approach equality perhaps there would be no very strong grounds for disputing the victory of the Democrats. It is in the lower districts, where the Republicans are admittedly in an immense majority, that great Democratic majorities were obtained by the simple process of what is called "stuffing the ballot-boxes." For this purpose the Democrats used ballot-papers of the thinnest possible tissue-paper, such that a number of them can be packed inside of one larger paper and shaken out as they are dropped into the box. These papers were freely handed about; they were shown to me, and I brought away specimens of them. I never heard a suggestion that these extraordinary little gossamer-web things were designed for any other purpose than that of fraud. Of course the result of such a system was that there were many more ballot-papers in the box than voters. At one place in the Charleston district, where not above one thousand persons voted, there were found, I believe, three thousand five hundred papers in the box. In such case the practice (whether justified by law or not, I know not) is that the election managers blindfold a man, who draws out and destroys the number of papers in excess of the voters. Of course he takes care to draw out the thick papers of the opposite party, and to leave in the thin papers of his own party; so when the process is completed the Democrats are found to be in a great majority, and the return is so made by the returning board. There are some other grounds of complaint. In some of the black districts the number of polling-places has been so reduced that it is impossible for all who wish to poll to do so in the time allowed. At one or two places the ballot-boxes were stolen and carried off. At one place of which I have personal knowledge the appointed election managers simply kept out of the way, and had no poll at all. Hundreds of blacks who came to vote were told they must go elsewhere, when it was too late to do so. In short, I have no hesitation in saying, as matter within my own knowledge, that, if these elections had taken place in England, there were irregularities which must have vitiated them before an election judge a hundred times over.

The result of these elections was that, except in the single county of Beaufort, not one Republican or Independent was returned to the State Legislature; nor, I believe, was a single office-bearer of those persuasions elected. The dominant party took everything, and the Republican members of Congress were all ejected. South Carolina returns a solid Democratic representation to the next Congress.

I have throughout, on the spot, as I do now, expressed the opinion that there is no excuse whatever for the lengths to which the triumph of the Democrats has been pushed. Granting that they were fairly justified in vigorous measures to give them the control of the Government and Legislature, and that they were in a position thus to obtain a good working majority, there could be no reason for unfairly depriving their opponents of a certain representation. It was bad policy, too, for the things that have been done have roused the indignation of the North, and it is believed that the somewhat unexpected Republican successes in the North were in great degree due to the feeling excited by unfair attempts to make a solid South. Perhaps, for the time, it may not be a matter of the very first importance whether the Democrats have only a good majority in the Southern State Legislatures, or almost the whole representation; but in the present state of parties in Congress two or three seats, or say, including Louisiana and Florida, half a dozen seats, won by extreme and palpable irregularities and fraud, make a great difference; and the question of these elections raises very large and difficult issues. Not only are nearly-balanced parties very much affected, but, in case of a struggle over the next Presidential election, these votes might just turn the scale; and the question whether there is any remedy practically available to redress wrongs which are, I may almost say, admitted, puts in issue the wider question whether the 15th Amendment of the United States Constitution, securing equal electoral rights to the blacks, is really to be enforced, or whether it may be set aside in practice by the action of individual States. Is, in fact, the settlement at the end of the war to be maintained or surrendered? The excuse made by the Southern whites for their proceedings is, that throughout the United States elections are not pure and free from fraud; that there has been as much of it in New York as in the South; that the laws admitting of such things were made by their enemies to crush them; that the Presidency was "stolen" from them by fraud; and that they are justified in reprisals. I have no doubt that it is an absolute necessity that the election laws should be improved. But besides this there is need of a final laying of the issue between North and South, depending on a due execution of the war settlement.

C. The Condition of the Negro

30. No Land for the Freedman

EVEN THE restrained official communications give evidence of the conflict in purpose between the commissioner of the Freedmen's Bureau and the president in respect to freedmen and the land. They do not, of course, present a full, explicit account of General Howard's losing battle for a land program, but they document major developments. In July 1865, a few weeks after the agents of the Treasury were directed to turn over abandoned land to the bureau, General Howard issued an order that the lands be set apart and divided into lots for the freedmen. President Johnson, in effect, countermanded the directive by ordering immediate restoration of lands to their former owners when pardoned. Howard then tried to retain control of lands for which confiscation proceedings had already begun but was again overruled, Johnson insisting that even lands legally condemned be returned unless they had actually been sold. The commissioner was particularly concerned to salvage land ownership for those Negroes on the Sea Islands, largely in South Carolina, who were in possession of tracts under General Sherman's order of January 1865. When Johnson supported the planters in their insistence upon restoration but was willing to have special agreements worked out with these freedmen, Howard with the tacit encouragement of Secretary of War Stanton came close to insubordination in approving delaying tactics and asking congressional leaders to make special provision for the black Sea Island settlers. In fact Howard helped frame the Freedmen's Bureau Bill of February 1866 vetoed by the president, including both its general and special land provisions. The original draft had gone even further than the measure sent the president for it would have confirmed freedmen's possessory titles in the Sea Islands (cf. doc. 6c, sec. 5). After the veto and before another Bureau bill (doc. 6d) could be passed, the military, acting independently of Howard largely effected the president's purpose, leaving only a minority of the Sherman settlers in possession of land. Meanwhile, the president had also been responsible for the removal of the freedmen's advocate, General Rufus Saxton, as assistant commissioner for South Carolina and of Captain Alexander P. Ketchum, the officer Howard had trusted to safeguard the interests of the freedmen in the restoration of the Sea Island plantations. Reference is made to both men *in the exchange of letters between Howard and William H. Trescot, a distinguished man-of-letters and an effective lobbyist at Washington for South Carolina.*

Two years later, as the conflict between Congress and President Johnson approached its climax, a federally financed land program (which Howard had recommended and Congress had accepted in the winter of 1865–1866) presented too vulnerable a political issue for sponsorship by embattled Republican leaders. This is made clear in the extracts from debates on the land resolution passed by the South Carolina convention asking Congress to appropriate $1 million to purchase lands for resale through the Freedmen's Bureau as homesteads of ten to 100 acres (doc. b). The debates also speak eloquently to the justice and statesmanship of the proposals. For identification of the speakers, see introduction to doc. 24; on the question of land, see the introduction, pp. xxviii–xxx.

a. Report and Correspondence of O. O. Howard, September 1865–February 1866

REPORT OF THE COMMISSIONER OF THE BUREAU OF REFUGEES, FREEDMEN, AND ABANDONED LANDS

WAR DEPARTMENT,
BUREAU OF REFUGEES, FREEDMEN, AND ABANDONED LANDS,
Washington, December—, 1865.

SIR: I have the honor to submit, for the consideration of his excellency the President of the United States, the following report, called for by an act of Congress approved March 3, 1865:

In compliance with General Orders No. 91, current series, Adjutant General's office, I relinquished command of the army of the Tennessee, and assumed, as Commissioner, the direction and organization of this bureau.

The act of Congress above referred to charges me with "the supervision and management of all subjects relating to refugees and freedmen from rebel States, or from any district or territory embraced within the operations of the army, under such regulations as may be prescribed by the head of the bureau and approved by the President."

On entering upon the discharge of these duties, I separated the bureau into four divisions: one of lands, embracing abandoned, confiscated, and those acquired by sale or otherwise; one of records, embracing official acts of the Commissioner, touching labor,

SOURCE: U.S., 39 Cong., 1st sess., House Ex. Doc., no. 11 (Washington, D.C.: 1866).

schools, quartermaster and commissary supplies; another of financial affairs; and the fourth the medical department.

To each of these divisions I assigned an officer, and secured the required number of clerks by appointment and by detail from the ranks of the army. . . .

LAND DIVISION

Under this head I cannot do better than quote from the explicit report of Major Fowler, who has the immediate charge of the land division.

1. *What property is under the control of the bureau.*

The act of Congress approved March 3, 1865, which establishes the bureau, intrusts it with the supervision and management of all abandoned lands, *i.e.*, lands taken by the government while their lawful owner was voluntarily absent from them, engaged in arms, or otherwise in aiding or encouraging the rebellion.

On the 2d of June the President ordered all officers of the government having property of the character specified in this act to turn it over to this bureau. In compliance with this order, the Secretary of the Treasury, on the 27th of June, issued a circular, directing his subordinates who had in their possession or under their control "any abandoned or confiscable lands, houses or tenements," to transfer them to some duly authorized officer of this bureau.

The greater portion of abandoned property in the insurrectionary districts was held by treasury agents, and as the result of this order the bureau came into possession, not only of abandoned lands, but of all abandoned real property, except such as was held by military authority, for strictly military purposes.

2. *Nature of the control of the bureau over abandoned property.*

With respect to abandoned lands, it was the evident intention of the act of March 3 to give the bureau control, solely for the purpose of assigning, leasing or selling them to refugees and freedmen. It was impracticable, however, to divide and assign them immediately. A great proportion of the lands was already under lease, given by the treasury agents, and good policy, as well as the necessities of the bureau, for which no appropriation had been made, demanded that all should be made immediately useful, and that none should remain unused and unproductive. . . .

The leases of town property have, as a rule, been made from month to month. The rents exacted have been moderate, and based generally upon those demanded by agents of the Treasury Department. Farms and plantations are let by the year for a portion of the crop, varying from one-tenth to one-twentieth.

From one to ten thousand acres in each of the several States have been used as colonies for vagrant and destitute freedmen. In South Carolina, Georgia, and Florida some land, the exact amount of which has been reported, has been actually divided and assigned to freedmen as contemplated in the act establishing the bureau. In these States the policy of setting apart lands for freedmen was initiated anterior to the establishment of the bureau, and under Field Orders No. 15, issued by Major General Sherman. A comparatively insignificant amount of town property is used as quarters for teachers and officers connected with the bureau, and as hospitals. With these exceptions, all property in the hands of the bureau is held as a means of revenue.

3. *Restoration of property.*

Shortly after the organization of the bureau parties whose property was held by it commenced to apply for restoration of their former rights. The policy first adopted by the bureau was to return estates to those only who could show constant loyalty, past as well as present—a loyalty which could not be established by the mere production of an oath of allegiance or amnesty. As the bureau held property by authority of an act of Congress for certain definite purposes, it was supposed that this tenure must continue to exist until those purposes were accomplished; that property must be surrendered only when it was evident that the control over it was unauthorized and improper.

This course did not meet with the approval of the President, who gave orders that a pardon, either by special warrant or the provisions of his amnesty proclamation, entitled the party pardoned to demand and receive immediate restoration of all his property, except such as had been actually sold under a decree of confiscation. Shortly after this decision was made known Circular No. 15, dated September 12, 1865, was issued from the bureau, and embodying the provisions of the act of Congress establishing it, promulgated for the first time definite rules regarding the restoration of this property to former owners. . . .

Under the provisions of this circular the work of restoraton has progressed very rapidly, and it is probable that when the year terminates little or no property will remain under control of the bureau. . . .

5. *Result of the plan of restoration.*

The uncertainty of the tenure of the bureau over property which is the immediate result of the policy of restoration adopted, has rendered the division and assignment of land to refugees and freedmen impracticable. Fortunately, experience seems to have shown that it is not a necessity. Difficulty has arisen from disappointing the natural and well-founded expectations of freedmen in this subject, but it has been overcome with comparative ease. Much embarrassment, and in some instances actual suffering, has resulted from the restoration of property in use as offices, colonies of freedmen, and hospitals, and much more will result from the curtailment of the revenue of the bureau.

6. *Amount of property held by the bureau.*

The tabular statement annexed presents all the statistics respecting the quantity of property in possession and the quantity restored, which can be gained from the reports thus far furnished by the Assistant Commissioners of the bureau. About one five-hundredth (.002) only of the entire amount of land in the insurrectionary districts has ever been held, and had the plan of assigning it to freedmen been carried out the bureau would have been unable to furnish an acre per family. . . .

[Following Fowler's report, Commissioner Howard himself continues with reference to lands embraced under General Sherman's Field Orders of January 15, 1865.]

Immediately after returning from Edisto, and before issuing the above orders, I sent a telegram to the honorable Secretary of War, of which the following is an extract:

[Telegram.]

"I met several hundred of the colored people of Edisto island today, and did my utmost to reconcile them to the surrender of the lands to former owners. They will submit, but with evident sorrow, to the breaking of the promise of General Sherman's order. The greatest aversion is exhibited to making contracts, and they beg and plead for the privilege of renting or buying land on the island. My task is a hard one, and I am convinced that something must be done to give these people and others the prospect of homesteads.

"O. O. HOWARD, *Major General.*
"HON. E. M. STANTON, *Secretary of War.*"

I hoped to obtain an answer before leaving Charleston, but did not. I made selection of the most judicious officer [Captain Ketchum] I could find for the work to be done. . . .

Captain Ketchum accompanied me to Savannah, and met several of the planters interested in lands held under General Sherman's order, and was instructed by me to see that the interests of the freedmen were so protected as not to deprive them of homes.

I passed from Georgia to Fernandina, Florida, and thence to Jacksonville, explaining in the best manner I could the object of my mission to both the planters and the freedmen.

Circular 15, from this bureau, approved by the President, had already occasioned the restoration of the great proportion of the lands held as abandoned in different parts of the United States, and as General Sherman's Special Field Orders No. 16, hereto attached, required the confirmation of the President before any show of title could be given to the freedmen, the land-owners claimed the benefits of the same—Circular 15.

On arriving at Mobile, I received the following telegram from yourself:

"WASHINGTON, *October* 25, 1865.
"I do not understand that your orders require you to disturb the freedmen in the possession at present, but only ascertain whether a just, mutual agreement can be made between the pardoned owners and the freedmen: and if it can, then to carry it into effect.

"E. M. STANTON, *Secretary of War.*
"Major General HOWARD."

I at once sent the following despatch to Captain Ketchum:

BUREAU OF REFUGEES, FREEDMEN, AND ABANDONED LANDS,
"*Mobile, Alabama, November* 4, 1865.
"Despatch of Secretary received. Be sure to have the supervising

boards constituted for each locality, before anything else is done. They can aid in making the agreement referred to by Mr. Stanton.

"O. O. HOWARD,
"*Major General, Commissioner.*

In Virginia quite an amount of land was libelled and about to be sold by the marshal just previous to the establishment of the bureau, when the sales were suspended by the Secretary of War, in order that these lands might be turned over to the bureau for the benefit of the freedmen. I claimed that these lands, which had been condemned to sale, though not actually sold, were already the property of the government, and objected to his excellency the President against the insertion of the word "sold" in the definition of confiscated property. The President referred the matter to the Attorney General, whereupon, finally, the word "sold" was inserted.

This decision necessitated the restoration of all the property where the sale had been suspended. I have been very desirous of conforming to the letter of the law in setting apart lands, but was unwilling to do so before it became probable that they could be retained. In this way much disappointment and suffering would be avoided.

The freedmen were so eager for the possession of land, and so likely, without that possession in fact or in prospect, to be obliged to leave their present homes, that I made the following proposition through yourself:

WAR DEPARTMENT,
BUREAU OF REFUGEES, FREEDMEN, AND ABANDONED LANDS.
Washington, September 4, 1865.

SIR: The matter of imposing some conditions in the cases of pardoning those who have lands already under cultivation by freedmen, for the benefit of this class of persons, having been presented to me by the Attorney General, and a plan having been suggested by a distinguished officer of the army, which I heartily indorsed, I deem it best to combine these suggestions in the following proposals, to wit:

1st. That hereafter pardons of the President of the United States, extended to those who have been excepted in his proclamation of May 29, 1865, having more than 20,000 dollars' worth of property, be conditioned by specific stipulation in each individual case: that the land-owner agree to set apart and grant title, in fee-simple, to each head of family of his former slaves, a homestead varying in extent from five to ten acres, to be secured against alienation during the lifetime of the grantee. The location, precise extent, and other details to be determined by three referees, two to be chosen by the interested parties, each selecting one, and the two a third.

2d. That other persons, not land-holders, be conditioned according to their several circumstances by equivalent or proper stipulation, to be determined by a committee of three appointed by the President.

Very respectfully, your obedient servant,

O. O. HOWARD,
Major General, Commissioner.

HON. E. M. STANTON, Secretary of War.

I felt quite sanguine that this course would produce contentment among the freedmen, and afford an example to other land-owners beside those affected by it. My proposition may have come too late for adoption, for already quite a number of land-owners had been pardoned.

Private & Unofficial

Columbia
December 4, 1865

My Dear General

I received your telegram yesterday in reply to mine in reference to Captain Ketchums action and the exchange of General Saxton. I regret very much that the exchange has not been effected and the more as I learn by letters from Charleston today that Captain Ketchum refuses to compel contracts unless the owners are willing to lease or sell to the freedmen. If this is so it is a direct violation of all that I understood from the President's orders and your instructions. I have neither desire nor intention to censure your conduct which I have in all our intercourse found consistent and true but I am forced to infer that you have been overruled and that the experiment which you proposed to make has been abandoned and that a policy of continued spoliation instead of gradual conciliation has been resolved on. I believe the consequences will be miserable. I am sure that if the Bureau had not perseveringly interfered against the planter that this question of labour would have adjusted itself gradually. The planter would have found that free labour has great advantages and once the negro understood that he *must* work, he *would* have worked. Of course for some years there

SOURCE: O. O. Howard Papers, Bowdoin College Library, Brunswick, Me.

would have been difficulties, the negro would not do as much as he could; the planter would expect more than he ought—But it would have come right. A great deal that you do not understand and a great deal that we do not understand would have explained itself to both of us. I had determined to try the experiment fairly even if I leased my lands to my former slaves for the next year without profit. I was willing, perfectly willing to loose a year to ascertain upon what true basis our future relation could rest. But what can we do with this persistent bitter determination to excite and exaggerate the antagonism between the races? I will not stop now to argue the individual injustice or the violation of general right involved in the administration of the Bureau in S.C. but let me ask you—putting as out of the question to consider as a statesman what must be the consequence of giving these lands to the freedmen.

1. You add to the antagonism which recent events have naturally excited but which time will as naturally mitigate, all the bitterness which unjust and tyrannical spoliation must and will provoke. You put the state and the freedman at arms length. And yet in that state he must live and you create a condition of things requiring a perpetual, costly and contentious interference on your part.

2. You willfully destroy the productive energy and capability of the richest portion of the state by leaving laborer without the help of capital for capital will not invest in negro industry or negro enterprise. Either the negro will be supplanted by capital—(the only difference between which and us will be that it is not ours—for in no sense will it be his) or will drag out a bare existence creating barrenness all around him.

3. You place the negro on the sea coast which the interior needs for its commercial developement and from which this necessity will drive him or where he must stand, stopping every railroad, choking up every harbour and neither using the advantages which God has given the country, nor permitting us to use it.

Do you suppose if Hayti was a sea coast county of Massachusetts or New York that its existence would be tolerated for twenty years. Do you not know that the enterprise of these great Commonwealths would sweep such an encumbrance away—and rely upon it that to give the negro possession now will be merely to dispossess us to make way for other white men who will benefit by our loss. If this is what you mean—if this is the mode of punishment—so be it—but say so.

I regret all this for I really thought that your honesty and sincerity would aid us to get through this crisis into better times. I wish the experiment of free black labour to succeed. I have been brought up among negroes, have lived among them, and owe them much of the comfort and pleasure of my life. Their labour has given me wealth, leisure and opportunity. I do not wish to see them perish from the soil to which they are so much attached and for which they have done so much. But if a mistaken policy will have it so, it must be so for yours is the power but so also will yours be the responsibility.

Believe me with all our differences of opinion

Yours respectfully & kindly
Wm Henry Trescot

Major Gen Howard

Washington, Jan. 14th, 1866

Dear Sir:

I received your letter some time since, and wished to reflect upon it a day or two, and then answer it; but unfortunately mislaid it, and think it must have been destroyed. I have read your able letter to the Charleston Daily News, Jan. 6th. I think you have mistaken my spirit. My views with regard to land, are grounded upon the belief, that the former slaves earned something besides a bare subsistence. Further, quite a large number of planters have taken the course I recommended, giving lands as a homestead to heads of families, and I honestly believe this the very best course, as a matter of interest, for the large landed proprietors to pursue. You must recognize the fact, that the freedmen form no inconsiderable part of your people, and had you voluntarily made them free, as wise men, you would have made ample provision for them, not only in point of fundamental rights, but in point of privileges which might have a tendency to elevate them.

You will notice before this that you have a new Asst. Commissioner for South Carolina.

I thank you for the candor of your first article.

Very truly yours,
(Sig.) O. O. Howard, Maj. Genl.

[Feb. 22, 1866]

To the President
Sir

Permit me in delivering the accompanying letter from Gen Howard to ask your attention to the following considerations

1. That the number of estates on the Sea Islands of South Carolina which have not been restored under the provisions of Circular No 15 are few—and have not been restored simply by the delay in the Freedmans Bureau in that state in order to wait for the expected passage of the Freedmans Bureau Bill lately vetoed—and that they stand now in precisely the same position as those already restored and now worked by their owners.

2. That this restoration can work no possible injustice to the freedmen who are occupants under Gen Shermans order because the Order No 1 of Gen Sickles has regulated the whole subject. The old and infirm are to be provided with homes and the able bodied cannot be removed without an opportunity given to make such contracts as the military authorities may approve.

3. That owing to the advance of the planting season it is absolutely necessary that within the next ten days the owners should be able to make definite arrangements for the agricultural labour of the year.

I would most earnestly ask that such instructions may be given to Gen Howard as would effect an immediate restoration of these estates

Very respectfully
Wm Henry Trescot
Executive Agent State So. Ca.

WAR DEPARTMENT
Bureau of Refugees, Freedmen and Abandoned Lands
Washington, Feby 22 1866

His Excellency
Andrew Johnson
President of the United States.
Sir:

The subject of the land set apart by General Sherman's Special

SOURCE: Andrew Johnson Papers, Library of Congress, Washington, D.C.

Field Order No 15, series of 1865, now presses upon me for immediate settlement. The crop for the present year turns upon the decision of the Government.

The orders under which I am now acting, are to make an arrangement mutually satisfactory between the land-owners and the resident freedmen. Many places have been restored under these instructions. In order not to break faith with these freedmen, who had received possessory titles, or who occupied lands under General Sherman's order, I had hoped to render them some equivalent as indemnity; possibly this may yet be afforded them by some future action of Congress.

With a most earnest desire to do everything I can, to promote a satisfactory settlement of all the conflicting claims, I still feel unwilling to make any sweeping restoraton of the lands above named to their former owners without more definite instructions than I have yet received either from yourself or the Secy of War. In your recent message to Congress with reference to this very matter, it is claimed by the agents of these landowners, that your orders are sufficiently clear to require me to make an immediate restoration putting their lands on precisely the same footing as other lands held by the Bureau. I may be mistaken, but I do regard the question as one of the greatest importance, and requiring for the interest of all parties concerned, the most speedy solution.

I am Sir,
Very Respectfully
Your obt Servant
O. O. Howard
Maj. Gen'l, Commissioner

b. Debates in South Carolina on Petition to Congress for land,
February 1868

MR. CAIN. I offer this resolution with good intentions. I believe there is necd of immediate relief to the poor people of the State. I know from my experience among the people, there is pressing need of some measures to meet the wants of the utterly destitute. The gentleman says it will only take money out of the Treasury. Well that is the intention. I do not expect to get it anywhere else. I

SOURCE: *Proceedings of the Constitutional Convention of South Carolina, 1868, 378–381, 385–386, 405–406, 411–414, 422–424.*

expect to get the money, if at all, through the Treasury of the United States, or some other department. It certainly must come out of the Government. I believe such an appropriation would remove a great many of the difficulties now in the State and do a vast amount of good to poor people. It may be that we will not get it, but that will not debar us from asking. It is our privilege and right. Other Conventions have asked from Congress appropriations. Georgia and other States have sent in their petitions. One has asked for $30,000,000 to be appropriated to the Southern States. I do not see any inconsistency in the proposition presented by myself.

MR. C. P. LESLIE. Suppose I should button up my coat and march up to your house and ask you for money or provisions, when you had none to give, what would you think of me.

MR. CAIN. You would do perfectly right to run the chance of getting something to eat. This is a measure of relief to those thousands of freed people who now have no lands of their own. I believe the possession of lands and homesteads is one of the best means by which a people is made industrious, honest and advantageous to the State. I believe it is a fact well known, that over three hundred thousand men, women and children are homeless, landless. The abolition of slavery has thrown these people upon their own resources. How are they to live. I know the philosopher of the New York Tribune says, "root hog or die;" but in the meantime we ought to have some place to root. My proposition is simply to give the hog some place to root. I believe if the proposition is sent to Congress, it will certainly receive the attention of our friends. I believe the whole country is desirous to see that this State shall return to the Union in peace and quiet, and that every inhabitant of the State shall be made industrious and profitable to the State. I am opposed to this Bureau system. I want a system adopted that will do away with the Bureau, but I cannot see how it can be done unless the people have homes. As long as people are working on shares and contracts, and at the end of every year are in debt, so long will they and the country suffer. But give them a chance to buy lands, and they become steady, industrious men. That is the reason I desire to bring this money here and to assist them to buy lands. . . .

I do not desire to have a foot of land in this State confiscated. I want every man to stand upon his own character. I want these lands purchased by the government, and the people afforded an opportunity to buy from the government. I believe every man ought to carve out for himself a character and position in this life. I believe every man ought to be made to work by some means or other, and if he does not, he must go down. . . . I want to have the satisfaction of showing that the freedmen are as capable and willing to work as any men on the face of the earth. This measure will save the State untold expenses. I believe there are hundreds of persons in the jail and penitentiary cracking rock to-day who have all the instincts of honesty, and who, had they an opportunity of making a living, would never have been found in such a place. I think if Congress will accede to our request, we shall be benefited beyond measure, and save the State from taking charge of paupers, made such by not having the means to earn a living for themselves. . . .

MR. C. P. LESLIE. . . . I assert that time will prove that the petition offered, and the addresses made here to-day, were most inopportune. These addresses have been listened to by a large concourse of spectators, and have held out to them that within a very short time they are to get land. We all know that the colored people want land. Night and day they think and dream of it. It is their all in all. As these men retire from the hall and go home, the first thing they do is to announce to the people "joy on earth, and good will to all mankind." We are all going to have a home. . . . And when I know as they know, that without land a race of people, four millions in number, travelling up and down the earth without a home are suffering, I cannot but denounce those who would, for political purposes, add to their misery by raising expectations that could never be realized. . . .

Let us have a little more light upon the subject. Parson French, who, it is well known, has the welfare of the colored people at heart, did go to Washington and portrayed to leading Senators and members of Congress the terrible predicament of the colored people in the State. He said that cotton had sold so low that all the people were poverty stricken. The white people, he told them, were not able to plant, and there being no necessity to employ laborers, the colored people were turned out of house and home, and he begged them to loan the people, or the State, a million of dollars. Their answer was, "Mr. French, for God's sake, send up no petitions for money, for we cannot give one dollar." . . .

MR. F. L. CARDOZO. . . . The poor freedmen were induced, by many Congressmen even, to expect confiscation. They held out the hope of confiscation. General Sherman did confiscate, gave the lands to the freedmen; and if it were not for President Johnson, they would have them now. The hopes of the freedmen have not been realized, and I do not think that asking for a loan of one million, to be paid by a mortgage upon the land, will be half as bad as has been supposed. I have been told by the Assistant Commissioner that he has been doing on a private scale what this petition proposes to do. I say every opportunity for helping the colored man should be seized upon. I think the adoption of this measure will do honor to the Convention. We should certainly vote for some measure of relief for the colored men, as we have to the white men, who mortgaged their property to perpetuate slavery, and whom they have liberated from their bonds.

MR. N. G. PARKER. I am glad that the gentleman who has just taken his seat has distinctly laid down the proposition that any member who votes against this petition votes against the colored man. I am a friend to the colored man, and he knows it. I have a record extending back for twenty years that shows it. . . .

I tell you, Mr. President, that the destitution that prevails this winter in those snow clad [Northern and Western] States is greater than it has ever been before. Thousands, yes millions, are out of employment, and what is the cause of it. I cannot stop now to elaborate the causes, but I will only briefly allude to them. War and its results are directly the cause of it. One of the results of the war, and the principal one, was the overthrow of slavery and tyranny in the Southern States; this was the good result of it; but the expense it caused the nation to do this, and the debt it incurred, and the overthrow of the labor system and consequent disturbance of trade and commerce, was the immediate evils. The burdensome taxation which followed is another principal cause of distress which now prevails in the Northern and Western States. The fact is patent that all the manufacturing States need aid; and let me tell you if the Congress of the United States grants additional aid to any of the unreconstructed States, for anything further than to perfect the reconstruction already half consummated, and the support of the Military and the Freedmen's Bureau, that in my opinion such a howl will go up as never was heard before, and I for one, would despair of success.

Our friends are trembling at Washington to-day, and all over the country, lest New Hampshire should cast a Democratic vote at her approaching election. I am of the opinion that if Congress should pass the appropriation called for just at this particular time, that every State from Maine to California would roll up such a Democratic vote in the coming election that was never heard of, or dreamt of, by the most ardent Democrat in this country. The result of the elections for the last year should not be unheeded.

Where would be our reconstruction if Andrew Johnson and the Democratic party had the handling of us? . . .

The Treasury of the United States has already as many drafts upon it as it can well bear. They have no money to purchase lands in South Carolina to sell on a credit—it is asking too much. Look at the almost overwhelming debt of the nation, and would you colored men, or white men, seek to increase it? For what was it contracted? and what keeps the expenses of Government to-day so large? It was contracted to make you free, and it is continually increased to preserve, protect and defend your freedom.

There never was a more liberal and humane government, nor never one that made such herculian efforts to retrieve the past as she has made and is making. We cannot ask her to do more than she is doing. There is such a thing as disgusting our friends. Do not let us weary them. If she will continue to afford us the protection she has afforded us in the past three years, if she will continue to the end in sustaining the reconstruction she commenced, if she will sustain the Freedmen's Bureau as long as it is a necessity, and give us the military necessary to protect and defend us, in God's name let us be satisfied. . . .

MR. R. H. CAIN. This measure, if carried out, therefore, will meet a want which the Bureau never can meet. A man may have rations to-day and not tomorrow, but when he gets land and a homestead, and is once fixed on that land, he never will want to go to the Commissary again. It is said that I depicted little farms by the roadside, chickens roosting on the fence, and all those poetical beauties. . . . I prefer this to seeing strong men working for the paltry sum of five or ten dollars a month, and some for even three dollars a month. How can a man live at that rate. I hate the contract system as I hate the being of whom my friend from Orangeburg (MR. RANDOLPH) spoke last week (the devil). It has ruined the people. After fifty men have gone on a plantation, worked the whole year at raising twenty thousand bushels of rice, and then go to get their one-third, by the time they get through the division, after being charged by the landlord twenty-five or thirty cents a pound for bacon, two or three dollars for a pair of brogans that costs sixty cents, for living that costs a mere song, two dollars a bushel for corn that can be bought for one dollar; after I say, these people have worked the whole season, and at the end make up their accounts, they find themselves in debt. . . . I want to see a change in this country. Instead of the colored people being always penniless, I want to see them coming in with their mule teams and ox teams. I want to see them come with their corn and potatoes and exchange for silks and satins. I want to see school houses and churches in every parish and township. I want to see children coming forth to enjoy life as it ought to be enjoyed. This people know nothing of what is good and best for mankind until they get homesteads and enjoy them.

With these remarks, I close. I hope the Convention will vote for the proposition. Let us send up our petition. The right to petition is a jealous right. It was a right guaranteed to the Barons of England. The American people have always been jealous of that right, and regarded it as sacred and inviolate. That right we propose to maintain. It is said here that some high officers are opposed to it. I do not care who is opposed to it. It is none of their business. I do not care whether General Scott, General Grant or General anybody else is opposed to it, we will petition in spite of them. I appeal to the delegates to pass this resolution. It will do no harm if it does no good, and I am equally confident that some gentleman will catch what paddy gave the drum when they go back to their constituents.

31. Transition From Slave to Free Labor

WITHOUT EITHER *regular monthly cash wages or possession of the land as protection against the hazards of commercial agriculture, the vicissitudes of crop failures and falling prices fell heavily upon the freedmen. In that respect the first crop years after freedom proved to be little short of disastrous. Although not all aspects of the planter statement printed below (doc. a) can be accepted, the distress as reported was real and widespread. Indeed, it should be difficult to overemphasize the impor-*

tance of the early years to the developing patterns of Southern agriculture. They exhausted local capital and constricted sources of credit, demoralized both laborer and planter, and helped fasten upon the South systems of yearly contracts which friends of the freedmen had regarded as temporary, transitional devices. In such circumstances even the most vigorous efforts of agents of the Freedmen's Bureau could not start their charges up the agricultural ladder; and not all agents were as concerned and able as Raushenberg, who, it will be noted, indirectly criticized his predecessor at Cuthbert, a native white (doc. c). In Georgia until 1867, unlike bureau practice elsewhere, members of the local community had been favored for appointment as agents in a vain effort to build goodwill. Lapses from the standard of performance expected by the bureau chief, whether by native or Northerner, by military or civilian personnel, were not so significant for the future of the Southern Negro as the fact that the bureau itself, with the exception of a few continuing functions, was prematurely terminated at the end of 1868. As the labor contract of that year indicates (doc. b), a wide variety of arrangements were current, all susceptible of abuse; and share payments as wages had not yet congealed into the familiar sharecropping pattern. More often than not shares were paid to a group working the planter's land rather than to a family working its own allotted acres. As suggested by the Mississippi proposals (doc. d), and as selections in document 32b will make even clearer, neither planter nor laborer could be certain from year to year which annual arrangement—wages or shares—would be most economically advantageous. Monthly cash wages were not a viable alternative for the vast majority of planters and laborers. The former would have regarded such payments with suspicion, even if the money to pay had been available, because a stable labor force during "crop time"—a major objective behind annual contracts—was considered essential to cotton production.

a. Agricultural Distress: Mississippi Memorial, December 1867

MASS MEETING of the Citizens of Desoto County, Missi. at Hernando

Pursuant to previous notice the Citizens of Desoto met at Hernando, in front of the Probate Clerk's office, on the 12th December 1867.

On motion—Dr Henry Dockery, was selected President; whereupon he addressed the meeting explanatory of its object.

On motion—Dr E. M. Parks was appointed Secretary. The Late Proclamation of Gov. Humphreys, together with the endorsement of Genl. E. O. C. Ord was read.

Col F. Laubauve, presented the following Memorial

Source: Freedmen's Bureau Records, National Archives.

Memorial

The People of Desoto County, Mississippi in Mass Meeting assembled desire to call the attention of the authorities of the United States Government, both civil & military to the present condition & probable approaching destitution of the poorer classes in said county, and it is believed through the entire state.

The crop of 1866 was made throughout the South almost entirely upon borrowed capital. The impoverished condition of the country rendered this a necessity and the high price of our great staple cotton, rendered such a course comparatively easy. The result of the year's labor in our county was an almost total failure in the corn crop and a very inferior yield in the cotton crop; but, although the price of the latter had considerably declined from the high prices obtained in the fall of 1865, yet it still remained sufficiently high notwithstanding the short yield to enable the bulk of our farmers to pay expenses and to stimulate increased & enlarged exertions to make a still larger crop in 1867.

The crop of the present year like its predecessor has been made almost exclusively upon borrowed *capital*. The result of the year's operations has been a corn crop sufficient perhaps for home consumption and a cotton crop about equal to that of 1866.

But while the yield of the present crop is perhaps equal to that of 1866, which was itself almost a failure, there has been the most tremendous & unprecedented decline in price.

Cotton instead of selling at 40 cents, as in the fall of 1866, now only brings 14 with a prospect of a still further decline.

The result of this most unexpected calamity has been most disastrous.

Our people pressed with an accumulation of old debts and new ones are thoroughly bankrupt & disheartened.

Personal property of all sorts has greatly declined in value while real estate has become almost wholly valueless and lands which twelve months ago would have commanded twenty dollars per acre cannot now be sold for ten. Money is scarcer today in the very midst of the cotton season than it usually is in mid summer—collections are impossible & credit totally destroyed.

Such a condition of affairs can have but one result—widespread suffering & want.

The evil will of course fall heaviest upon that class of the community least able to bear it & perhaps the severest sufferers will be the freedmen to whose condition we ask the special attention of the Government. There are about twelve thousand of this class in our county. The crop of the county is gathered—the share of the freeman as a general rule has been nothing. They have in most cases worked for one half of the crop—the planter supplying all their wants during the year & charging these advances against the laborers' share of the crop.

In a majority of cases the freedman has nothing coming to him at the end of the year & in many instances he is largely indebted to his employer. The end of the year finds him ragged, dirty, hungry & homeless. Several months must elapse before his labor can be made profitable upon the plantation. In addition, the straitened & impoverished condition of the farmer renders it impossible for him to carry on his farm on so large a scale during the succeeding year. Much of his land must lie idle while of that which is tilled, a much larger proportion will be sown in cereals, which require a less number of hands.

The inevitable consequence must be that in a few weeks hundreds of these people must be turned out of doors without a change of clothing or a day's rations. That they must steal or starve is unquestionable.

In this condition of affairs we are forced to look to the General Government for relief. Our state and county treasuries are empty— our own people impoverished, bankrupt, & already ground down with taxes.

We appeal to the Federal Government for relief with less scruples because poor as our people are, they will during the present year pay to that Government a most onerous and excessive tax which is peculiar to the people of the South. In addition to all other taxes our people will this year pay to the General Government a tax of $12.50 per bale upon about fifteen thousand bales of cotton amounting to more than a quarter of a million of dollars.

If one half of this amount could be returned to the county for charitable purposes, it is safe to say that all fears of any suffering among any class of the community might be dismissed, nor does it seem unreasonable to ask this, since it was derived from a tax upon a product of agriculture from which all the other agricultural productions of the nation are free, and a tax which by its recent legislation seems to admit was unwise & unjust.

Should Congress see fit to grant this request, we would respectfully ask that its charity be dispensed, either by our own local commissioners of the poor, or through the U.S. Revenue officers, or through the Military officers of the U.S. Army, and not through the agents of the Freedmen's Bureau. This latter institution though doubtless established for a wise & beneficent purpose has in our humble opinion proven a nuisance both to white and black. Its agencies are the resort, & the loafering places of the idlest & most improvident negroes who seem to think that by hanging around its doors rather than by honest labor a living is to be procured. The only arguments we have ever heard urged in favor of its creation & continuation are, that it rendered justice cheap to the poor freedman, and that it was impossible for him to obtain a fair decision in the civil courts of the country.

To the first of these arguments, we would reply that the average cost of a suit in the magistrates courts is about $5, while in the Freedmen's Bureau the fees of the agent and his employees rarely amount to less than ten dollars and frequently exceed fifteen (15$). This too when the agent is paid a salary in addition, out of the United States' Treasury.

As to the impossibility of the freedmen obtaining justice in the state courts, we would remark that until a very few months ago we had no Bureau Agent in our county, & that before his arrival it was the universal remark of every intelligent observer, that our courts & juries seemed disposed to give the negro more than justice on account of his poor & ignorant condition.

We do not hesitate, therefore, to say, that the best interests of both races, in our county, would be promoted by the removal of the Bureau from among us. Hower this may be determined by those in authority, we would again call the attention of the Major General Commanding this Military District, and through him of Congress, to the necessity of immediate steps being taken to prevent suffering, famine & starvation in our midst.

All of which is respectfully submitted.

After the reading thereof, the President announced that it was now before the meeting for consideration, subject to be amended, adopted or rejected. On motion, the Memorial, was adopted *unanimously* as in bodying the sense of the meeting. Dr E. Bullington, made known his desire, to put it, exclusively to the freedmen present, for adoption or rejection & on his motion, the President put the question and it was adopted without a dissenting voice.

On motion, the President was requested to transmit a copy of these proceedings to Genl. E. O. C. Ord & through him to Congress.

On motion, the "Peoples' Press" was requested to publish the foregoing, and the meeting adjourned.

Henry Dockery
President

E. M. Parks
Secretary

b. Agricultural Labor Contract, Mississippi, 1868

This agreement between John P. Mitchell of Yallabousha County Miss employer and the undersigned laborers witnesseth, that said John P. Mitchell hereby hires said laborers as farm hands from this date until the first day of January 1869 and for faithful services to be rendered in said employment, by said laborers during all that time, the said employer agrees to pay said laborers as specified. Employer furnishes land, stock, and half the feed for stock, all farming implements on hand. Laborers furnish themselves and the other expenses in carrying on farm, the proceeds of farm to be divided equally between employer and laborers. Also agrees to furnish said laborers free of charge during the term of said service with quarters and fuel. Laborers working for wages to be paid as stipulated in margin. And said laborers in consideration thereof, hereby agree to render to said employer or his agent, for and during all of said time due obedience and faithful service, and well and promptly to perform all work in the line of their duty in accordance with the instructions of said employer or his agent and to bestow due care and attention in all things upon all property and interest committed to said laborers charge and keeping and will faithfully account or pay for the same, to be deducted out of said laborers wages so far as the same will pay, and will discharge in all things the duties of a faithful servant. And it is hereby understood and mutually agreed that the wages of the said laborers are to cease during such time as said laborers may be absent without leave, each absence not to count less than one day, and said employer or his agent may at any time discharge said laborers for any such absence

SOURCE: John P. Mitchell Papers. Reprinted by courtesy of the Mississippi Department of Archives and History, Jackson, Mississippi.

or habitual neglect of duty. Also that for time lost by sickness a proportional deduction shall be made in the next succeeding settlement and the said laborers shall also be charged with the actual cost of medical attendance, medicines, and other supplies furnished by employer during such period of sickness. And it is further agreed that the said employer or his agent reserves the right to establish such rules and regulations for the government of his plantation or premises as he may deem proper not inconsistent with his contract and the provisions of an act of the legislature of the State of Mississippi entitled an act to confer civil rights upon Freedmen and for other purposes approved Nov 25th 1865.

Employer agrees to put plows in order to commence with.

Given under our hands in duplicate this first day of January, 1868.

John P. Mitchell

Witness

J. A. Willking

Clerk in Office

S. A. C.

$$\begin{bmatrix} \text{Three two cent U.S.} \\ \text{Internal Revenue} \\ \text{stamps attached} \end{bmatrix}$$

his
Ben X Blanks $6 per month
mark
his
Tom X Mitchell $50 per year
mark
his
George X Mitchell $7 per month
mark
his
Davy X Mitchell $75 per year
mark
his
Job X Mitchell   part crop
mark
her
Hester X Johnson $4 per month
mark

                                    his
                    John X Davis   part crop
                         mark
                                    his
                    Albert X Mitchell   part crop
                         mark
                                    his
                    Jim X Blanks $80 per year
                         mark

                    Puts in Dock $25 per year
                                    his
                    George X Graham   part crop
                         mark
                                    his
                    Lewis X Johnson $75 per year
                         mark
                                    his
                    Simon X Hardy $75 per year
                         mark
                                    his
                    Abram X Blanks   part crop
                         mark
                                    his
                    Allen X Blanks   part crop
                         mark
                                    his
                    Allen X Blanks Sr $5 per month
                         mark
                                    her
    Jan 13   Mary X George $4 per month
                         mark
                                    his
                    Jack X Mitchell $100.00 per year
                         mark
                                    her
    Feb 1st   Fany X Boon $40 per year
                         mark
                                    his
    Feb 12th   George X Blanks $6.00 per month
                         mark
                                    his
    Feb. 17th   Steven X Anderson $6 per month
                         mark
                                    her
    Feb 17th   Lizzy X Anderson $4 per month
                         mark

RULES AND REGULATIONS OF FARM

1st   Signers of this contract are required to do all work required on the farm.
2nd   No stock to had individually except such as allowed.
3rd   All hands must rise by daylight and be at work by sunup.
4th   One hour will be allowed for dinner from date of contract until 15 June, two hours from 15th June until 1st Sept.
5th   One dollar and a half will be charged for every day lost except from sickness during crop time.
6th   Good order must be observed at all times on the place.
7th   No public gatherings will be allowed.
8th   No visitors must be entertained except occassional visit from relativcs.
9th   Prayer mectings will be allowed as usual but must close invariably at ten o'clock.
10th Strangers will not be permitted to attend them.
11th Men will be required to work all day Saturday from 15th Apl until 15th July also throughout the fall in gathering crop.
12th Stock must be attended to Sunday and all times.

c. Labor Relations in Georgia

Office Agent Bur. R. F. A Lds.
Division of Cuthbert
Cuthbert, Ga. Novbr. 14, 1867.

Lieut O. H. Howard,
Sub. Asst Commnr Bur R. F. A. Lds
Albany, Ga.
Sir,

In obedience to the instructions received from you I have the honor to submit this Report on the General Condition of Affairs in my division.

When I entered upon my duties as Agent in this Division the Bureau of R. F. A Lds seemed to be generally considered by the community, a substitute for overseers and drivers and to take up and return run away laborers and to punish them for real or imaginary violations of contract by fines, imprisonment and some times

SOURCE: Freedmen's Bureau Records for Georgia, National Archives.

by corporeal punishment seemed to be the principal occupation of its agents.

The idea that a planter or employer of any kind should in case of dissatisfaction with his freedmen, instead of driving him of often without paying him his wages, first establish a complaint before the Bureau and let that tribunal decide wether a sufficient violation of contract existed to justify the discharge of the laborer or not, was then considered quite unreasonable; while every employer thought it perfectly proper that a Bureau agent, when notified of a freedmans leaving his employment should immediately issue an order for the arrest of the same and have him brought back—in chains if possible. The fairness of the principle that either party must submit its complaints to the Bureau for adjustment and that the white man can not decide the case a priori and only use the agent of the bureau as his executive organ and that employer as well as employee must submit to its decision wether the laborer ought to be discharged or ought to remain is just beginning to gain ground amongst both races and the negroes have ceased to a great extent to leave their employers as they used to do and employers are not as apt to run them off at will as they used to do. The common bulk of the population is just beginning to suspect that nothing else but what is justice and equity to a white man under certain circumstances would be justice and equity to a negro under the same circumstances and while they begin to feel the truth of this fact their moral courage and conscientiousness is generally not sufficient to overcome their prejudices and passions to a sufficient extent to give life and practical execution to this principle in their conduct towards and treatment of the negro in every day life.

The number of complaints made at this office is very large and increasing continually as the time of settlements is drawing nearer. The white man complains generally that the freedman is lazy, impudent and unreliable, that he will not fulfill his contract any further than it suits his convenience, that he claims the right to loose as much time as he pleases and when he pleases but wants full rations all the time, that he owes for goods and provisions more than his wages or his part of the crop amount to and that he wants to quit his employment on account of it; the freedman on the other hand generally complains that the white man has made him sign a contract, which he does not understand to mean what the white man says it does mean, that the white man wants him to do work which he did not contract to do, that the employer does not want to furnish him rations; that he charges him to much for lost time, that he curses him, threatens to whip him or has really struck him or shot at him. This is about the usual purport of the complaints of the two races and these complaints are frequently well established by each party and inevitably lead to the conclusion that a great deal of bad material exists in both races and that both in reality have much cause to complain of each other.

The freedpeople generally have worked better this year then last year and have adhered more faithfully to their contracts by staying out their time and a large number certainly at least one half of them have got along with their employers without serious dissatisfaction and trouble.

The majority of complaints that have been made at this Office by both races have found their origin in contracts, where freedmen received as compensation for their labor a certain share in the crop. The majority of the plantations in my division were worked under such contracts. The freedman claims under such contracts frequently that he has no other work to do but to cultivate and gather the crop, that being a partner in the concern he ought to be allowed to exercise his own judgement in the management of the plantation, that he ought to be permitted to loose time, when it suits his convenience to do so and when according to his judgement his labor is not needed in the field, that he ought to have a voice in the manner of gathering and dividing the corn and cotton and in the ginning, packing and selling of the latter product— while the employer claims that the labor of the employee belongs to him for the whole year, that he must labor for him six days during the week and do all kinds of work required of him wether directly connected with the crop or not, that he must have the sole and exclusive management of the plantation and that the freedman must obey his orders and do all work required as if he was receiving money wages, the part of the crop standing in the place of money, that the laborer must suffer deduction for lost time, that if he does not work all the time for him, he is not bound to furnish him provisions all the time, that the crop must be gathered, divided and housed to suit the convenience and judgement of the employer and that the share of the employee must be held responsible for what he has received in goods & provisions during the year. Taking in consideration that often quite a number of freedmen

342   FLAWED FREEDOM

are employed on one plantation under such a contracts, who frequently not only become discontented with the employer but with each other, accusing each other of loosing time unnecessarily and of not working well enough to be entitled to an equal share in the crop, it is easily understood to what amount of implicated difficulties and vexations questions these contracts furnish the material.

If the freedmen generally were intelligent enough to make contracts of that kind advantageously and to understand their duties and obligations and were disposed to exercise a sufficient degree of energy and good will, if the white people were unselfish, conscientious & patient enough to treat freedpeople with kindness and justice under such contracts they might be made a means of profit and advantage to both parties but as it is I consider them inimical to the maintainance of good order discipline and success on plantations and productive of ill will and hatred between the parties concerned, an impediment to fair and equitable settlements and a fertile source of premeditated difficulties, the laborer when he is in debt seeking for a cause to get out of his contract, the employer, when the maine part of the work is done seeking to get shed of his laborers under some pretext with a hope to appropriate the laborers share.

Only a very small number of parties will get along peaceably and attain success under such contracts and Agents should not approve them unless they contain the most definite and unmistakeable stipulations in relation to all the details of the duties and obligations of each party concerned.

My conviction is that plain labor contracts for wages for the year, one half of the wages paid every month or every quarter, the other half to be forfeited if the freedman fails to comply, are the most practicable contracts that can be made. They cause frequent & therefore fairer settlements, showing the freedman oftener what he consumes and how much is left to him, prompting him to economy on the one hand and cheering him up to increased energy if he finds himself saving money and, giving very little cause for difficulties and troubles. The objection to such contracts that the employers are not able to pay wages monthly or quarterly looses its strength, when it is considered, that two thirds of all freedmen take up more than half their wages during the year any how.

The disposition of the negro generally is to earn his wages as easy as possible, he is not active and energetic but unconcerned even if he workes for a portion of the crop. The pressure of necessity, unfavourable circumstances brought about by the weather, the condition of animals etc are not often taken into consideration by him and he is not inclined to accomodate his action and conduct to what good judgement under these circumstances would dictate; but goes along careless and slotheful never calculating consequences and not very accessible to advice under any circumstances. When he takes a notion to quit work and go to town he is very apt to do so no matter how much his work may be needed and how much he and his employer may loose by it. This spirit is entirely to predominant amongst them and gives rise to much trouble with the employers.

The freedman like other human beings thinks and studies more about his rights and privileges than his duties and obligations and his ignorance and deficient capacity to comprehend and reason cause him to invariably overrate the extent of the former and to underrate that of the latter, hence he often claims an independence and freedom of action, which is justly incompatible with the faithful performance of his duties as a laborer and servant, and which very much impedes his usefulness and his success and which in many instances would test the patience of less passionate & irritable people then the former slaveowners of the south.

While the colored people have thus erred and, as might naturally have been expected of a people brought up in ignorance, have done wrong in many instances, the whites themselves as a mass have fallen far short of realizing a sound perception of their duties towards the freedmen in their new condition.

They have failed to treat them with justice, kindness and forbearance and have not evinced by their conduct towards the freedmen that superiority of intellect and integrity which they so jealously claim over them and which should prompt them to set an example of justice and uprightness for the imitation of the freedmen, who are ignorant and depraved not by their own fault so much as that of their former masters and who, when kindly and justly treated will in the majority of cases yield to all reasonable demands of their employers. Employers generally are exacting and tyrannical not disposed to forbear, to reason or to exhort but require implicit obedience and unconditional submission and try very frequently to accomplish by revolting harshness and unscrupulous overbearance, what a universally mild and kind but firm and just treatment should accomplish. They yet act the masters.—The freedman in his new condition is not willing to bear that kind of treatment, he either becomes sullen and stubborn or he returns it with the same kind of language and conduct and so a large number of difficulties arise which with a little moderation & judgement on the part of the white man might easily have been avoided.

The political excitement and the election troubles between the employer and employee have, I am sorrow to say, perceptibly increased the already existing antagonism between the two races in my division and particularly in Cuthbert. They have no confidence to each other whatever and the freedpeople generally look almost upon every white man here as an enemy, they are defiant & challenging and many really insulting in their language and conduct and I think there is a very reasonable fear to be entertained that, as far as Cuthbert is concerned, a collision might take place most any time. The whites have made threats & have used imprudent language on the streets and every now and then the paper contains an article calculated to hurt feelings. The general voting of the colored people for the colored candidates and their radical ticket has called into existence an association amongst the whites of Randolph undoubtedly for the purpose of controlling hereafter the colored vote. It is impossible for me to find out the full nature of this association but, from all I can learn, they threaten or rather pledge themselves not to employ a colored man, who is not a friend to the white people, which undoubtedly means one that will not vote their way.

The present aspect of the two races in their relations to each other therefore warrants no just expectation that they will get along amically with each other for any length of time but insures the belief that after the removal of the military authority the freedmen when allowed to exercise all the rights & privileges of citizens with their want of knowledge and experience in business and law, will generally fail to obtain justice from the hands of the white race in the daily relations of life as well as in the courts. They would generally come out the loosers, factors liens and mortgages being pushed in before their claims, frequently before they even suspected a danger of any loss, would yearly take away thousands of Dollars of their wages, all kinds of frauds would be practiced on them in making contracts, all kinds of impediments and obstacles would be put in the way of their complaints even reaching the courts and when there they would often fail to receive the necessary attention as the ignorance of the freedmen would often furnish opportunities to take advantage of them and to let them go by default or have them nol' pros.'d etc. This all would exasperate the freedmen more and more he would feel the wrong and still not be able to mend the matter and so, many outbreaks and at least local troubles would certainly take place.

The Judges of the County Courts of my counties have, since I have been in office, promptly acted on all cases referred to them and no palpable act of neglect of duty or injustice has come to my knowledge on the part of the officers of the Courts. The causes, why freedmen fail so often to get redress for wrongs practiced on them and are unjustly found guilty appears to me less owing to the conduct of the officers of the courts, then to the indifference and trickery of lawyers and the partial and prejudiced spirit of Juries. The freedmen need friends, who will espouse their cause and who will show them the way to justice, they need attornies who are not afeared of injuring their popularity by pleading for them and who will conscientiously fulfil their whole duty towards them, when their clients, and they need good and conscientious men of their own race on the Juries. No cases of crimes or cruelties have occurred or come to my knowledge in my division but what have been reported at once.

The prospects of the two races as to success and prosperity in life from the present aspect of affairs are certainly not flattering. The producing capacity of this section has been well tested this year, the weather and circumstances generally having been favourable— and where land has been well worked the crops of cotton and corn are good; still the average amount of cotton raised to the working hand will hardly reach three bales. Cotton at the same time having gone down to from 10 to 12½ cents per pound, where it promises to remain as a normal standard with only moderate fluctuations, the majority of planters will at the end of the year come out even and many in debt and unable to continue their planting operations for an other year. Where one working hand does not realize more to the employer than from $150 to $165.00 per year in cotton and certainly not more than $200.00 at best counting corn and everything else in, he can not afford to pay from $125 to $175.00 and rations per year & the freedman who works for a share of the crop, when he even gets one half of that can not realize any profit at the end of the year. Wages therefore in my division next year will certainly not exceed $100.00 for first rate field hands and many will have to take less to get employment at all. The planting system on a large scale will be abandoned to a very great extent, by many from a want of means, by others from a conviction that it does not pay and I am therefore much inclined to believe that labor will not be so much in demand as it usually has been. I have not yet heard of any body trying to make contracts for an other year. Large numbers of freedmen have been very extravagant this year and many will not have one cent left to go on for an other year and if my fears in relation to labor, which I have just expressed, prove correct I apprehend a good deal of want & suffering for the necessities of life amongst the freedpeople, particularly in the towns, and more in Randolph— and Quitman— then Stewart Co, as lands are generally better in that county and as many freedmen there have made good crops.

The educational progress of the colored people in this division is of late origin but of very fair promise. One educational association exists and is in good working order in each one of my counties at Cuthbert, Lumpkin and Georgetown and the people generally seem to be fully aware of the great importance of this subject and have now for some time been contributing regularly for the maintainance of their schools. Young and old are anxious to learn, in some instances almost to the neglect of other duties.

The American Miss. Association through Mr. Rockwell has furnished two teachers for Cuthbert, who since the first of the month have taught a school here. They are found by the colored people. Rev T. J. Stewart cold teaches a school of sixty odd scholars at Lumpkin principally supported by the patrons. Mrs Holoman white and Mrs Susan Hardy cold teach two smaller schools there supported by the patrons also. G. Chatters cold teaches a school at Florence Stewart Co also maintained by the patrons but not as well as it should be. Encouragement and aid in the building of schoolhouses is much needed at all these places.

If the colored people in the different country settlements could be got together easier so as to establish and keep alive educational associations, such associations for the support of schools ought to be established at Cotton Hill, Benevolence, Wards Station & Colemans Station on the Southwestern Railroad for Randolph, at Bos Ankle, Hardmoney, Green Hill and half way between Lumpkin & Florence for Stewart and the adjoining counties. Each one of these localities could furnish more scholars then one teacher could well attend to, but to establish and keep up educational associations at these points would furnish alone sufficient employment for one man.

I apprehend little danger but what the growing generation of the freedpeople will generally have a common education & will be able to read, write and cypher and to take care of themselves pretty well.

A task of more difficulty and more immediate necessity seems to me to consist in capacitating the already grown up freedmen to the performance of their duties and the exercise and enjoyment of their rights and privileges as citizens and the idea has presented itself to me that a series of readers for their use at night schools and at home, gotten up with the particular view of not only teaching them to read but at the same time to impart to their minds in an easy comprehensible and attractive manner that particular information on their rights and duties and their relations to the white race as is of the most immediate practical value for them, might prove a great ansilliary measure to elevate them to that standard of knowledge as a class, without which they will fail to become good citizens and continue yet for some time the victims of the evil designs of the corrupt and dishonest portion of the white race.

As a mass the freedpeople are easier governed by Bureau authority than any other and the large majority of the freedpeople in my division, I am convinced, look upon the Freedmans Bureau as an institution where they will receive full justice.

There are self conceited and arrogant freedmen particularly about this place who are always finding fault of the Bureau and no agent will ever satisfy them or be able to convince them that he is honestly and conscientiously representing their interests. They are ignorant of law, never listen to anybody but their side, they overrate the power and authority of an agent and want him to do things that he can not do and are naturally disposed to be discontented with any thing that does not exactly carry out their wishes or puts any restraint on their conduct.

I have the honor to remain

> Very respectfully
> Your ob'd't serv't
> Ch. Raushenberg
> Agent etc &

Bureau R. F. A Lds.
Office Agent Division of Albany,
Albany, Ga. November 10, 1868.

Brvt Major O. H. Howard, U.S.A.
2nd Lieut 5th Artillery
Sub. Asst. Commissioner,
Albany, Ga.
Sir.

In compliance with Circular No 4 Office Asst. Comm'r Atlanta, Ga Aug 3, 1868 I have the honor to report:

that no Contracts have been presented at this Office for approval during the month of October.

2, that complaints of arbitrary discharges of laborers without sufficient cause and without compensation for the labor performed, complaints of arbitrary disposals of the freedmens share of the crop by the employer without the laborers consent, reports of assaults of a more or less serious character and often caused by political hatred alone constitute the principal business upon which action is taken at this Office.

I have endeavored to apply the proper legal remedy to the different cases and have succeeded well in some cases while in general I can only deplore the inefficiency of the present Law and present Judiciary system of the State in enabling the laborer to collect his wages by a summary process of law in such a length of time and at such expense as corresponds with his necessities and his pecuniary abilities.

In cases of arbitrary discharges, the most frequent cause of complaint of the freedmen, he has very nearly no remedy. His wages or his share in the crop almost invariably amount to more then one hundred Dollars and he therefore must in the majority of instances sue in the Superior Court. Before he can obtain the services of a lawyer he must pay a fee of from $25.00 to $50.00 or must secure the payment of it by giving a lien on his share of the crop, when in a majority of instances the same man who thus seeks to obtain payment for his labor after having worked perhaps nearly the whole year is driven off often with a family without one cent of money, or one mouthful of provisions while the employer for whom he worked holds the entire proceeds of his labor, claims the right to drive him off any time, but refuses to settle with him until

Christmass. When suit is commenced six or twelve months will elapse until trial term, twelve or eighteen months until judgement term, the colored plaintiff has since had to change homes once or twice his patience in waiting for his money is nearly worn out & he has given up all hope of getting it and has perhaps from carelessness or want of proper information or want of means to travel and live on while at Court or from fear that he will be discharged and loose the present years labor if he stays away at Court several days failed to make his appearance at the proper term or his principal witnesses being colored people have become so scattered that they can not be found and made appear at the proper time—so the case grows old, wears out and with a little management on the part of the employers attorney goes by default or is thrown out of Court or dies some other technical death in due form of law while the freedman at home curses the law and the white man who cheated him out of his honest earnings and instead of improving in industry and diligence as a laborer and in honesty and reliability as a man he true to old habits and old modes of thinking arrives again at the conclusion that he might as well be lazy and take life easy, that he will make about as much as if he works hard and that it is no harm to practice lying and stealing on people who according to his views take so much advantage of him only in a more refined manner.

Or even if the case is tried the white man brings up a Contract in which the freedman, as frequently has been and frequently will be the case, gives him all possible advantages. The Jury does not take the inequity of the Contract in consideration but says he is free let him look out for his own interest if he makes a bad contract it is not our fault and decides according to the Contract and the freedman has the cost to pay in two thirds of the cases that are tried.

In cases of arbitrary disposals of the freedmens portion of the crop by their employers which have been frequent during the past month I have generally succeeded by taking steps towards levying attachments on the cotton in preventing it from being sold or shipped and in causing the employer to make preliminary settlements at this office with a view of ascertaining what amount of the freedmens share of the cotton was required to pay their indebtedness to him and how much of it ought to be retained by them as their own cotton.

In every instance of that kind I have had to encounter the opposition and ill will of the parties concerned and have had to put up with some sneers from warehouse men and plantation managers, the so called overseers of former days, who with very few exceptions under the new regimen are a curse to employers as well as laborers and a nuisance generally as the larger amount of all trouble on plantations is brought on by their over-bearing & tyrannical treatment of laborers and their hatred and opposition to anything in the treatment of a negro that savors of kindness or equity. All cases of assault & batteries or other crimes where the injured party was willing to appear as prosecutor have been referred to Notary Publics for action, but as it is not their duty to issue warrants the freedman generally has to pay five Dollars to some lawyer to write out a warrant before he can accomplish his object, which I think constitutes a very objectionable feature in the manner the law is executed by them. The County Judges used to issue the warrants and charged for them in the cost the legal fee of, I think, $1.25 which the party found at fault had to pay with the cost. I have from all this arrived at the conclusion that the Justices —or Notary Publics Courts unless their jurisdiction in civil cases is extended considerably over $100.00 will generally not answer the purpose for the adjudication of the claims of laborers and that the system of Notary Publics with criminal jurisdiction in all cases less then felony unless it be made their duty to issue the warrants themselves & charge for them in the bill of cost will not answer as good a purpose as County Courts have or District Courts in the sense of the New Constitution would have answered and that the passage of a law establishing a summary process by which the lien given to laborers in the New Constitution on the products of their labor can be enforced is a pressing necessity and should be urgently demanded by the laboring classes from the next Legislature.

A large number of assaults generally with intent to kill committed on freedpeople can not be brought before the civil authorities for trial as each crime has to be tried in the county where it has been committed and as a large number of these assaulted people have just escaped with their lifes they are generally not willing to risk them again by going back to the county from which they were driven to swear out a warrant before a magistrate. Hence no warrants are issued and no commitment trials instituted and the sovereign perpetrators of these crimes remain unchecked in the exercise of their chivalric prowess upon their former slaves.

When I consider in addition to these deficiencies of the Laws &

Judiciary system that it is plainly the aim and object of a majority of the employers to take advantage of the ignorance of the colored people and to allure them by fair promises and liberal potations of whiskey about Christmass times into foolish & inequitable contracts, work them as hard as possible all the year and pay them at their liking at the end and that very few if any of the lawyers will take hold of the cases of colored people without fear or prejudice and apply the proper legal remedy to them with the alacrity with which they serve the white men I can not fail to come to the conclusion that their chances for obtaining justice hereafter in the civil or criminal courts of this section of country will be deplorably poor.

The System of Contracting which has been established, during the few years freedom has existed for the colored men, needs very material changes. Contracts for wages say from $5.00 to $15.00 per month for field laborers one half at least payable every month or every other month and their nonpayment constituting a forfeiture of the Contract are the best and most suitable agreements for the ignorant freedmen. If the laborer neglects his duty let him be discharged and paid up at the end of the month, if the employer fails to pay punctually let the freedmen quit & sue for the amount due him in Justices Court. Monthly settlements are easily made and suit the illiterate freedman, who can not read and write, much the best & offer the unscrupulous or dishonest employer but a poor chance for fraud in comparison to these popular yearley settlements.

Contracts for a part of the crop, where the laborer bears a portion of the expenses or even pays for his provisions at the end of the year should never be made by any freedman. They give rise to innumerable complications, miscomprehensions on the part of the freedmen and all kinds of troubles and offer to unscrupulous employers a wide field to take advantage of the ignorance of the laborer.

If the freedman can not get a Contract for wages let him work for one fourth of the crop, the employer feeding him and paying all expenses, so that no account, if possible, is kept against him at all during the year.

In all contracts for a portion of the crop it should be distinctly mentioned: 1) as what class hands the different freedpeople work, first, second or third and what difference exists in the rate of pay or interest of each class, instead of leaving this point undecided until towards the end of the year as a good pretext to delay all division of crops and all settlements.

2) that each crop, oats, fodder, corn, cotton etc is to be divided at once when housed between employer & freedmen and that each freedman as he receives his share pay it to the employer at current rates in pay for advances made to him. This will lighten his indebtedness & cause him to get his proper share while when it is stored away in a bulk for division at Christmass much of it is fed away by the employer, no correct account is kept, some of it is stolen and matters go wrong.

3) that the freedmens share of the cotton crop should be stored in their own name separately from that of the employer, that the employer bring up each ones account as soon as the hauling of cotton commences and that whenever enough cotton is sold to pay the advances of the employer the balance is stored in their name but not to be sold or shipped until a final & conclusive settlement between them and the employer is made at the end of the year.

4) that a certain amount of lost time say 26 days per year shall be allowed to each laborer free of charge, that other lost time shall be charged to each laborer monthly at a reasonable rate say 50 cts per day, that all extra labor, which the crop might require should be paid out of this fund & the balance divided in proportion between employers and laborers.

In consideration of the fact that these people will have to rely upon themselves alone in making their contracts hereafter I have taken much pains when occasion offered to impress the importance of the above mentioned points & others of minor importance upon their minds.

Very respectfully
Your obd't servant,
Ch Raushenberg
Agent

d. Planter Proposals, Mississippi, December 1867 and December 1870

The Joint Crop–Contract System a Necessity

SOURCE: Hinds County *Gazette*, December 6, 1867 and December 21, 1870.

As the time is near at hand to contract with freedmen for the ensuing year, it is vitally important to the planter, and, indeed, to every interest of the South, that some uniform plan be adopted to secure greater efficiency and permanency of labor than we have experienced for the past two years.—The present depression in the price of our leading staple, and the general distress prevailing throughout the South, are dangerous to all speculative theories, and force us to adopt the severe but practical lesson which misfortune never fails to teach.

The defects of our free labor system are apparent to every intelligent planter, and they can only be partially met and removed by uniformity of action, both as to terms and manner of enforcement.

In the cultivation of an average quantity of land in the South, during the past two years, the results have shown that the money rates which have been paid for labor will ultimately involve the planter in irretrievable ruin; and it is to meet this point that we wish to direct the "crop system" which has been partially and successfully adopted by some, and is now being generally discussed in Southwestern Georgia as to the plans for next year's operations. There are three modes that have been adopted by planters in contracting with freedmen for a portion of the crop:

1st. To furnish land and stock, and provisions for freedmen and stock, and give one-fourth of the crop to the freedmen.

2d. To furnish land and stock, and provisions for stock and give one-third of the crop to the freedmen—freedmen furnishing their own provisions.

3d. To furnish land and stock and one half the provisions for stock, and give one-half of the crop to the freedmen—the freedmen furnishing their own provisions and the other half of the provisions for stock.

In a series of year there will be but little difference in the aggregate paid out, under either of the above contracts, which can be adopted according to the condition of the planter or the necessities of the freedmen. If this uniform plan of hiring should meet general favor, the following would be some of the advantages to both planter and freedmen. To the planter:

1st. With a knowledge of the usual productions of his land, he could approximate an estimate of his annual portion of the crop, as a certain basis of credit, free from any incumberance of lien for labor.

2d. The increasing benefits of a localized labor. There being no difference in the terms of contracts, when the freedmen are once established in comfortable houses and kindly treated, there would be no inducement to change homes at the close of each year.

3d. As a consequence of localized labor, the Conservative sentiment of each neighborhood would be strengthened and stimulated to more enlarged efforts for the moral and educational interests of the freedmen, thereby securing a more peaceable and well ordered system of labor.

To the freedmen: The certainty of receiving their wages at the end of each year. As the crop is gathered, they can separate their portion and have it marked, stored and sold under their direction, and the proceeds applied only to the payment of their debts. This will be appreciated by many who have not yet received their wages for the past two years' labor.—In addition to the above the freedmen will share relatively in the advantages enumerated for the planter.

These points require no elaboration and are submitted to planters for their practical solution. The pressure is too great, and the future is too dark and uncertain, for the trial of doubtful experiments, and nothing is more certain than that inevitable disaster awaits the planter if some plan be not adopted by which freedmen shall share the vicissitudes of the crop and the fluctuations in price.

Very respectfully yours,
A Planter

RESOLUTIONS OF PLANTERS' CONVENTION, JACKSON, MISS., DECEMBER 1, 1870

1st. That it is the deliberate opinion of this Convention, that the policy hitherto pursued by planters and laborers of "farming on shares", as it is called, is false in theory and ruinous in practice, exhaustive of present values and inimical to the improvement and permanent prosperity of the farm, and must eventuate in the utter and hopeless ruin of the landed estates of the country.

2nd. That the system of monied wages based on contracts for general farm work stipulating the hours of labor, (part payable to meet current want and balance on final statement,) constitute the only true and proper relations of landholder and laborer, and furnishes the most certain security and protection to the interests of both parties.

3rd. That without attempting to limit or fix the wages for labor upon any other basis than that of supply and demand to be adjusted by the circumstances of each locality, we hesitate not to affirm as a principle of sound political economy, that the only certain test and measure of the value of labor and land is the market value of its produce, and that the impoverishment and bankruptcy which has thus far attended our experiment with free labor, results from the practical disregard of this common sense maxim, and the ruinous competition for labor to which it has given rise. . . .

32. Cotton Production and Systems of Labor: Tenth Census, 1880

By 1880 family sharecropping in cotton production (a form of wage payment though often mistakenly identified as a form of tenancy) had become a familiar pattern although not to the exclusion of other arrangements. The first selection (doc. a) highlights the problem of maintaining soil fertility under cropping and tenancy. The others (doc. b) are summaries of responses from local correspondents (white) to queries in respect to labor. While there was no consensus as to whether wages or shares were best for the worker, note the general recognition that shares involved greater risk but afforded greater opportunity.

A. Cotton Production in Alabama

We find that over 55 per cent. of the colored population of the entire state is to be found in the central cotton belt, where about 60 per cent. of the cotton is produced. Something over 10 per cent. of the blacks are found in the second cotton area, the Tennessee valley, and about 5 per cent. in the Coosa valley. This accounts for more than 70 per cent. of the colored population, which is thus concentrated in the three large cotton-producing areas of the state, where about 80 per cent. of the cotton crop is produced. . . .

PRODUCT PER ACRE AND ITS RELATION TO POPULATION.–In product per acre Alabama stands No. 13 of the fourteen principal cotton-producing states of the Union. Other things being equal, the product or yield per acre may be taken as an index to the fertility of a

SOURCE: *Report on Cotton Production in the United States*, Tenth Census (1880), VI: 72–74.

soil, and if we apply this test to the several agricultural regions of Alabama they take the following ranks:

1, Coosa valley; 2, Coal Measures; 3, oak, hickory, and short-leaf pine uplands; 4, Tennessee valley; 5, gravelly hills; 6, oak, hickory, and long-leaf pine uplands; 7, long-leaf pine region; 8, metamorphic; and 9, central prairie region.

Putting Chambers and Lee together with the counties which constitute the *prairie reigon*, we have the nucleus of the central cotton belt as above defined. In all these counties the average product per acre is 0.27 of a bale. This somewhat unexpected result cannot be considered as due to the relative infertility of the soils of this belt, for correspondents unite in giving as the average yield on the fresh lands of this region from 700 to 1,600 pounds of seed-cotton, or from one-half a bale to more than a bale to the acre, and the chemical analyses show that these soils in their virgin state are among the very best in the state. We are led, therefore, to the conclusion that the soils of the great cotton belt have been exhausted by improvident culture, and, as a matter of fact, we know that in many parts of this belt cotton is planted year after year upon the same soils without rotation with other crops, and without an attempt at maintaining the fertility by the use of manures. In the other parts of the state where cotton is produced a selection is generally made of the better soils, rotation of crops is more generally practiced, and in some sections fretilizers are in more general use.

That the character of the laborers and the system of farming practiced are largely concerned in determining the yield cannot, on general principles, be denied, and we find ample proof that these two things are responsible in no small degree for the results above shown.

The *central cotton belt* is generally a region of large farms or plantations, in which the laborers are chiefly negroes, as seen in the tables. As a rule, these laborers do not own the land, have no interest in it beyond getting a crop from a portion of it, which they rent either for a sum of money or for a share of the crop, and are not interested in keeping up the fertility, at least not to the extent of being led to make any attempts at the permanent improvement of the same. In the case of the owner of the land, while the conditions are different, the result is the same. He is, of course, interested in the improvement of his land; but to supply the fertilizers for a large plantation, when he cultivates it by hired labor, would cost more than he usually has to expend, and where the share system, or that of renting, prevails he is still further removed from personal care of the land; and thus from all causes there is an exhaustive cultivation of the land, without any attempt at maintenance or restoration of its lost fertility.

In addition to these, the system of advances or credit, so prevalent throughout the cotton-producing parts of the state, is not without its evil influence, for the laborer, and too often the owner of the land, is obliged to get advances of provisions from their merchants, for the payment of which the crop is mortgaged; and as cotton is the only crop which will always bring ready money, its planting is usually insisted on by the merchants making the advances and selected by the farmer as a means of providing for payment. In this way cotton comes to be the paramount crop, and there is little chance for rotation with other things.

In this connection it will be instructive to read the reports given under Part III, treating of cultural details. It will there be seen that the system of credits in the large cotton-producing regions prevails to such an extent that the whole cotton crop is usually mortgaged before it is gathered; and when we consider that the prices charged for provisions, etc., thus advanced are at least 50 per cent. higher than regular market rates, and that the cost of producing cotton is given by our correspondents, almost without exception, at 8 cents a pound, it will need very little calculation to show that the laborer who makes a profit of only 2 or 3 cents a pound or $12 to $15 a bale on his cotton will have the chances too greatly against him ever to be out of debt to his merchants when he relies solely upon this crop to provide the money; and the exorbitant interest on the money advanced is not likely to be lessened so long as the merchants' risks continue to be as great as they are.

In the *Tennessee and Coosa valleys*, which are also large cotton-producing sections, a similar state of things may be observed. In Madison and Talladega counties the blacks outnumber the whites, and in both we find the product per acre falling far below the average of the region in which they are situated. Thus Madison shows a product of 0.28 bale, against the average of 0.32 for the whole Tennessee valley, and Talladega a product of only 0.36 bale, when the average for the Coosa valley region, of which it is a part, is 0.40. Wherever the black population is in excess of the white we may take it for granted that the system of large farms rented out to the negroes prevails, and the inevitable result of this system of farming thus becomes apparent in these sections also.

In the other agricultural regions of the state, and in most of the counties also of the Tennessee and Coosa valleys, the farms are, as a rule, small, and are cultivated by their owners, with the assistance of such labor as may be hired from time to time. In all these cases provisions are produced on the farm, and cotton is planted as a secondary crop. There is thus some chance for selection of the soils and for rotation of crops; and when a man cultivates his own farm fertilizers are in more general use, so that even with soils naturally much inferior to those of the main cotton-producing regions the average product per acre is much higher in these regions of small production. . . .

The concentration of the black population in the great farming regions of the state, which are also the regions of the originally most fertile soils, is amply shown by Table III; and so closely does this class of the population follow the best lands that the density of the colored population of any region might almost be taken as an index of the fertility of its soils. The white population is much more evenly distributed over good and poor lands alike, so that the proportion between the two races varies with the fertility of the soils*. . . .

The position of Alabama as a state, next to the lowest in product per acre of the fourteen cotton-producing states, has already been justly explained by Dr. Hilgard as due to the exhaustion of the soils by bad or improvident culture, and to the fact that the system of returns to the soil is not yet in general practice, as is shown by the very limited use made of fertilizers. The conditions of the different regions as above set forth furnish ample illustration of the truth of this conclusion.

INFERENCES TO BE DRAWN FROM THESE COMPARISONS.—To recapitulate, the following conclusions seem, therefore, to be plainly

---

* The negroes were originally brought together upon these great cotton-producing areas as the slaves of the wealthy planters who bought up the greater part of the best lands in the state. Since the war they have remained, practically speaking, in the same places where as laborers in the cotton-field (with which they were most familiar) they could always be sure of employment and a good living without too severe labor. The social attractions also of these great areas of negro population have not been without their influence in keeping the race together.

taught by the discussion of the data contained in the tables presented on page 60:

1. That where the blacks are in excess of the whites there are the originally most fertile lands of the state. The natural advantages of the soils are, however, more than counterbalanced by the bad system prevailing in such sections, viz, large farms rented out in patches to laborers who are too poor and too much in debt to merchants to have any interest in keeping up the fertility of the soil, or rather the ability to keep it up, with the natural consequence of its rapid exhaustion and a product per acre on these, the best lands of the state, lower than that which is realized from the very poorest.

2. Where the two races are in nearly equal proportions, or where the whites are in only slight excess over the blacks, as is the case in all the sections where the soils are of average fertility, there is found the system of small farms, worked generally by the owners, a consequently better cultivation, a more general use of commercial fertilizers, a correspondingly high product per acre, and a partial maintenance of the fertility of the soils.

3. Where the whites are greatly in excess of the blacks (three to one and above), the soils are almost certain to be far below the average in fertility, and the product per acre is low from this cause, notwithstanding the redeeming influences of a comparatively rational system of cultivation.

4. The exceptions to these general rules are nearly always due to local causes, which are not far to seek, and which afford generally a satisfactory explanation of the discrepancies.

b. Wages vs. Shares

GEORGIA

WHO ARE YOUR LABORERS CHIEFLY? HOW AND WHEN ARE THEIR WAGES PAYABLE?

NORTHWEST GEORGIA: Native whites and negroes. Wages are 50 cents per day, $8 to $10 per month with board, or $12 to $14 without board, or $100 to $150 per year, payable, according to contract, as they require it, or at the end of the season.

SOURCE: *Report on Cotton Production in the United States*, Tenth Census (1880), V: 356; VI: 438–439.

METAMORPHIC REGION: In Fannin, Europeans, chiefly English and Irish; towns, 90 per cent. white. Jackson, 1 per cent. Chinese. Mostly whites in Union, Habersham, Hart, Banks, Hall, Forsyth, Gwinnett, Cobb, Paulding, Haralson, and Heard; whites and negroes in Madison, Carroll, Rockdale, Taliaferro, Spalding, and Meriwether; mostly negroes in the other thirty-three counties. In eighteen counties wages paid are from $75 to $90 per year, or $6 to $8 per month. In other counties the average is about $100 per year, or $8 to $10 per month, in all cases with board. In Fulton $100 is paid with board, or $130 to $140 without board. Day laborers receive from 40 to 75 cents per day, and are paid weekly or daily, the latter during the busy season of the year. Payments are made according to contract, or when the laborer needs the money, final settlements being made at the end of the year when crops are sold.

CENTRAL COTTON BELT—LONG-LEAF PINE AND COAST REGIONS— Except in Glascock, Colquitt, and Berrien counties the laborers are chiefly negroes. The men receive from $5 to $10 per month or $60 to $100 per year; the women from $4 to $6 per month or $40 to $60 per year. Day laborers are paid usually 50 cents per day. Board is also furnished with the above wages, which are paid, according to contract, usually at the end of the year. "They have the free use of land, team, and implements on Saturday (a day they claim and will have) for raising crops of their own" (Twiggs).

ARE COTTON FARMS WORKED ON SHARES, AND ON WHAT TERMS? ARE SUPPLIES FURNISHED BY THE OWNERS?

The share system is practiced in all of the counties of the state to a greater or less extent, except in Dade and Union on the north, and Colquitt, Berrien, Chatham, Bryan, Wayne, and Pierce on the south.

The owner receives one-fourth the cotton and one-third of the corn for use of land alone, or one-half the crop for the use of land, implements, and teams, the laborer boarding himself. If board is also furnished, the owner receives two-thirds of the crop. In northwest Georgia, if the laborer leases new land, he takes off all timber of less than one foot diameter, incloses the land with a good ten-rail fence, and has the use of it for three years, or, if bottom land, for four years. In some counties of middle Georgia the cost of fertilizers, ginning, and baling is shared equally. In some cases tenants pay two 500-pound bales, delivered in Augusta, for the use of as much land as they can cultivate with one horse or mule; such tenants have their own plow teams, cattle, and hogs, sell their own produce, do their own trading, and disburse their own funds (*Columbia*). Labor is considered equivalent to one-third of the crop, land to one-third, and the stock, feed, and implements to one-third (*Appling*).

WHICH SYSTEM (WAGE OR SHARE) IS THE BETTER FOR THE LABORER? WHY?

In answer to this question sixty-one counties report in favor of the wage and thirty-two of the share system. The reasons are very numerous and varied.

FOR WAGES: "He is sure of his earnings, and takes no risk of crop failures when he receives wages" (twenty-two counties). Laborers usually are too poor to provide implements (ten counties). He is better and more surely paid, knows what he is to receive, and avoids trouble and division of crops (other counties). He is altogether too improvident and deficient in business and managing capabilities to succeed under the share system. Morally, the share system has greatly injured the negro race in the southern states (*Richmond, Washington*, and other counties).

FOR SHARE SYSTEM: Because shares exceed wages if the laborer is industrious; the laborer can employ his family profitably, feels more free and independent, and takes a greater interest in his crops (many counties).

MISSISSIPPI

WHO ARE THE LABORERS CHIEFLY?

Negroes, chiefly, in 25 counties, embracing the cane-hills and the Mississippi bottom regions, and some of the upland counties. Whites chiefly in 7 counties, while in the other counties of the state the two races are about equally divided. The nationalities represented are some Germans and Irish in Winston, and various in Holmes, Tippah, and Rankin counties; otherwise, all Americans.

HOW AND AT WHAT RATES ARE THEIR WAGES PAID, AND WHEN PAYABLE?

Daily wages are very generally 50 cents with board and 75 cents without board, usually at the end of the week. In Clarke, 30 cents to women and 40 cents to men, with board in each case, are paid. Monthly wages are usually from $8 to $12 throughout the state with a few exceptions, while to yearly laborers from $100 to $150, at the end of the year, or when needed, are paid to men, and a less amount to women and boys. A house and sometimes rations are also given to the yearly laborer. In many of the counties, however, the laborers work on shares in preference to regular wages. Monthly wages are paid when the time of service ends, or at the end of the season, when crops are sold, in most of the counties. Monthly payments are made in a few counties, while in many cases a portion is paid as it is needed by the laborer.

ARE COTTON FARMS WORKED ON SHARES? IF SO, ON WHAT TERMS?

The share system prevails very generally throughout the state, though in a few counties the farms are rented, the renter paying 400 pounds of lint per 10 or 15 acres for the use of land, houses, and utensils. The terms vary but little in all of the counties. If the land-owner furnishes the land, implements, and teams, he receives one-half of the crop; otherwise for the land alone he receives one-fourth to one-third of the cotton, and one-third of the corn, if any is produced. In some counties the owner furnishes the ginning and ginning material instead of the farming implements. When the laborer is boarded, and has everything else furnished to him, the owner receives three-fourths of the crop.

DOES THE SHARE SYSTEM GIVE SATISFACTION? HOW DOES IT AFFECT THE QUALITY OF THE STAPLE? DOES THE SOIL DETERIORATE OR IMPROVE UNDER IT?

In ten of the counties the system does not give satisfaction, but in the rest of the state there is but little complaint. In Marshall one or the other party complains every year. When the crop is not promising, or too liberal advances have been made to the laborer, he is likely to become dissatisfied, quit working his own crop, and hire out by the day to other farms. The staple is thought to be injured by the share system in 11 of the counties; in a few of the others it is said to improve, while in the rest of the state no change is apparent. In Holmes the negroes are very careless and indifferent as to gathering and housing their cotton; they allow a great deal of it to rot. In Sharkey the staple is two grades below that of 1860 from the same soil. In Tishomingo and Covington the staple is shorter. In Amite the laborer is usually more careful in picking when he owns a share. In almost all of the counties the soils are thought to deteriorate, in some very rapidly, unless manures are used or rotation practiced. *Issaquena:* The best cotton is grown by the "one-half-crop" system, for then the owner or his agent sees that the crop is properly tilled.

WHICH SYSTEM (WAGE OR SHARE) IS THE BETTER FOR THE LA-
BORER? WHY?

The share system is thought to be the best in 19 counties of the state. *Lowndes:* "The negro, being thriftless and improvident, will by no other system have so much for his family at the end of the year." The following summary of reasons are given: He can make more money; have garden land free of rent; can double his wages and have all the extra time to himself; he becomes interested in the results of his labor; he is more industrious and improves his habits; the entire family can be employed. In the other counties of the state the wages system is thought better. *Hinds:* "He is sure of a living, while under the share system the shiftless laborer often obtains credits to the extent of his interest in the crop and has nothing in the end. When under control, he makes more, spends less, and has a surplus of cash at the end of the year. There are exceptions, of course." The following summary of reasons are also given: He is certain of his earnings, and takes no risks of failures of crops; supplies consume his profits under the share system; he works better, and always has money. He receives his money more certainly and at shorter intervals. They cannot receive credit beyond their wages; he must work for wages, while under the share system he is indolent and careless. *Issaquena:* He is assured a livelihood as long as willing to work, his labor being in demand at good prices from January to January, at 75 cents to $1 per day. Under any other system shiftlessness prevails to a more or less extent with serious neglect of crops. Renters average three bales of cotton per hand, while with wages eight or ten will be produced, the latter thus bringing into circulation more money and creating a greater demand for the laborer's services.

33. T. Thomas Fortune, Negro Editor: Condition of the Colored Population, 1883

YOUNG AND MILITANT, *Fortune was the most widely read Negro editor of the 1880s. The New York Globe succeeded by the New York Freedman and that in turn by the New York Age, each served as his personal*

SOURCE: *Report of the Committee of the Senate upon the Relations between Labor and Capital* (Washington, D.C., 1885), II: 522–529. Hereafter cited as *Report on Labor and Capital.*

organ (the latter until 1907). The national all-Negro Afro-American League, organized in 1890, a forerunner of the Niagara Movement and the NAACP, was his brain-child; he served it as secretary and president as well as founding father.

NEW YORK, September 17, 1883.

T. THOMAS FORTUNE SWORN AND EXAMINED.

By the CHAIRMAN:

Question. Where do you reside?—Answer. In the city of New York.

Q. What is your occupation?—A. I am a journalist.

Q. What is your connection with the press?—A. Editor and proprietor.

Q. Of what paper?—A. The New York Globe.

Q. To what special interests is that paper devoted?—A. It is devoted especially to the interests of the colored population.

Q. It is the organ of the colored interests of the North, or of this city?—A. Well, it was intended to be a newspaper devoted to the interests of the citizens of New York, but it has so extended that it may be said to cover the whole ground of the United States; so that it may be said to have no local habitation, but to be rather national in its character.

Q. You have seen the resolution under which the committee is acting?—A. Yes, sir.

Q. Will you now, in your own way, make such statements of fact and such suggestions as seem to you pertinent, bearing upon the condition and the improvement of the condition of the colored population of the country, and also in regard to its relations to the white population with which it is thrown in contact?

THE COLORED POPULATION

The WITNESS. According to the census of 1880 there were in the country 6,580,793 people of African ancestry. In 1790, according to the first census, there were only 757,208. The increase of population from 1850 to 1860, under the slave régime, was 22.1 per cent.; from 1870 to 1880, 34.8 per cent. The increase is and will continue to be healthy in the state of freedom, since human effort and propagation have their greatest expansion in a state of freedom from all tyranny and narrowness. If we were freer our growth and propagation would be vastly greater. As it is, we are fettered by the

State and repressed by individuals and corporations. We are not free as other men to come and go, to make and spend, to enjoy the protection of the laws equally, or to share as other men the rights and immunities of Government. Like the Irish subjects of Great Britain, we have received everything from our Government except justice in equal degree with others of our fellow-citizens. This she has always denied and still denies to us.

This large body of our population has, since the foundation of our Republic, been a subject of the gravest moment, of the most earnest contention in the home, in the halls of legislation, and on the field of battle. But in all the conflict the negro has never received full justice at the hands of the Government, State or Federal, and he does not receive it to-day in any portion of our vast territory.

At the close of the great rebellion the negro population of the country was thrown upon its own resources, so to speak; made men and citizens at one stroke of the pen. These men were poor, ignorant beyond conjecture, cowed and debauched by the foul iniquity of human slavery, and surrounded by a hostile public sentiment which vented itself in all sorts of intolerance, in assassination, intimidation, and open robbery. Assassination for political causes has ceased because no longer necessary; but intimidation and robbery remain; so that the negro population of the South is to-day, as it was thirty years ago, a disturbing element, requiring a wise statesmanship to properly adjust it. But instead of attempting to honestly adjust, the people and the press of the country constantly talk of eliminating it from political consideration and discussion, as if it were possible to heal a cancer by leaving it severely alone.

The greatest misfortune which the Government inflicted upon us up to the close of the war was the almost universal illiteracy of the masses—illiteracy which was designed and made irrevocable by the most stringent of statutory enactments. Our intellectual and material poverty, absolute bankruptcy, was caused by the Government, which closed the book of knowledge to us and denied us the common right to accumulate. We are not responsible even to-day for the widespread poverty which obtains among us. We have not the facilities and aptitude to amass large fortunes by speculation and peculation, but we are learning to emulate the virtuous example of our white fellow-citizens in this regard.

Considering honestly our lowly beginning, the following facts are of interest. From the Bureau of Statistics we find—

SCHOOL ATTENDENCE OF COLORED CHILDREN

Enrollment of colored youths, as far as reported by the State school officers for the year 1880, 784,709; per cent. of colored youth of school age enrolled, about 48.

Colored school teachers in the United States: males, 10,520; females, 5,314; total, 15,834.

Normal schools for colored youth, 44; teachers, 227; pupils, 7,408.
High schools, or academic, 36; teachers, 120, pupils, 5,327.
Universities and colleges, 15; teachers, 119; students, 1,717.
Schools of theology, 22; teachers, 65; pupils reported, 880.
Schools of law, 3; teachers, 10; pupils, 33.
Schools of medicine, 2, with 17 teachers and 87 pupils.

STATE APPROPRIATIONS FOR COLORED SCHOOLS

According to the census of 1880, there is in the South a total school population of 5,426,890—3,758,480 being white, and 1,668,410 being colored; enrolled, white, 2,013,684; colored, 685,942. The total appropriation for school purposes by these States is set down at $12,181,602, being the beggarly pittance of $2.26 per capita. Only 31 per cent. of the white, and 26 per cent. of the colored children of Louisiana availed themselves of the advantages of the public schools, while the State appropriates the munificent sum of $529,065 for educational purposes, being $1.94 per capita; while the city of New York alone expends more than $3,000,000 per annum for the education of her youth. Four and two-tenths per cent. of the school population of New York State can't read, and 5.5 cannot write, while in Louisiana 45.8 cannot read, and 49.1 cannot write. Florida, with a school population of 82,606, appropriates only $134,880 for school purposes, being $1.63 per capita. The District of Columbia, with a school population of 38,800, appropriates $368,343, and 61 per cent. of the white and 73 per cent. of the colored school population are enrolled, the per capita being $9.49. In the District of Columbia, 5.7 per cent. of the school population cannot read, and 18.8 per cent. cannot write, while in Florida 38 per cent. cannot read, and 43.4 per cent. cannot write. These facts are suggestive.

Inadequacy of Such Appropriations

Aside from the vastly inadequate work being done in the South by the States, it should not be omitted here that Northern churches and organizations and individuals contribute annually to the education of the freedmen quite as much as the States; but the contributions from these sources are uncertain and fluctuating. Yet, after all that is done is considered, it must be conceded that ignorance is growing in the South as rank as the weeds that choke her corn and cotton. Whether it be the poverty of the people of the States, or disinclination of the people to tax themselves for the rooting out of illiteracy and the vices it breeds, I am not prepared to say; but that the evil is vast and menacing, all must concede. The rural journals of the South, which are usually ignorant of the first principles of political economy, object to popular education, on the ground that the blacks pay no taxes, supremely oblivious that the laboring classes of every country always create capital, and pay in rental the taxes of the land-owner, who has no more inherent right in ownership of the soil than the laborer. What the State refuses to pay for education it gladly pays for penitentiaries, preferring a pound of remedy to an ounce of cure.

It must not be forgotten that the teachers employed in the South labor under many disadvantages, which react with fearful effect upon the pupils. Because of the miserable compensation and the shortness of the school term, together with social isolation and political intolerance of the South, competent teachers cannot and are not always secured. The school term in the South does not average more than four months of the year, and I doubt much if the salaries paid will average $30 per month, subject to further reduction on school warrants by regular scalpers, merchants, and others. At least, such was my unfortunate experience in Florida as a teacher. And, then, these school teachers are subjected to every species of persecution from school superintendents, trustees, and the white braggarts of the town. The position of a colored school teacher in the South is not a desirable one from any standpoint. Before I would teach again in the South I would drive a dray on the streets.

I do not believe in centralization of government. I know the evils which come upon the people by merging into the hands of the few men, who must of necessity administer government, more power than they should control, and yet I am thoroughly convinced that the education of the people is a legitimate function of government—not in any sense a measure of centralization, but eminently one of self-preservation. We make lavish appropriations for harbors, forts, the Navy, and the Army, for the common defense, but illiteracy is a far more insidious foe from within than any that can or will assail us from without.

A National Board of Education Wanted

I would advocate the creation of a board of education, with four commissioners (one for each section), and I would advocate an annual appropriation of $25,000,000 to $30,000,000, to be applied according to the ratio of illiteracy. It could be applied through the superintendents of education of the several States, subject to the approval of the commissioner or commissioners, or by some other more effective and satisfactory method.

The desire of the black race of the South to take advantage of educational opportunities is too well known and too conclusively demonstrated by statistics to require more than a passing notice.

It may be pertinent to remark here that there are in this country 7,646 colored ministers of all denominations, and a church membership of nearly 2,000,000 souls.

Slave Labor and Free Labor Contrasted

It is often charged that the race is lazy, but I think the charge is absurd. If it is lazy now, what must it have been under the system of slavery? It is undeniable that the negroes of Georgia own 680,000 acres of land, cut up into small farms, and in the cotton States they own and cultivate 2,680,000 acres. Dr. Alexander Crummell, in his thoughtful reply to the misrepresentations of Dr. Tucker, of Mississippi, says, basing his statement upon accepted data, "Let us put the figures as low as 400,000 acres for each (meaning Southern) State—for the purchase of farm lands has been everywhere a passion with the freedmen—this 400,000 acres, multiplied into 14, *i. e.*, the number of the chief Southern States, shows an aggregate of 5,600,000 acres of land, the acquisition of the black race in less than twenty years." Again, I find that the Freedman's Bank, which opened in 1865 and closed in 1874, had no less than 61,000 black depositors, the aggregate of whose deposits was $56,000,000. Again, from 1857 to 1861, under slave labor, there were produced 18,230,738 bales of cotton; from 1878 to 1882, under free labor, 27,667,367 bales, being a balance in favor of free labor of 9,436,639 bales. There does not appear to be much ground for the charge of laziness to stand upon in this handsome showing.

A still more gratifying illustration is furnished in the products of South Carolina. In 1849 and 1859 she raised 654,313 bales of cotton with slave labor; in 1879 and 1882, she raised with free labor 1,153,306 bales, a difference in favor of free labor of 498,993 bales. In 1859 her wheat crop was 1,285,631 bushels, in 1882, 2,973,600 —a difference of 1,687,969 bushels in favor of free labor. In 1859 her oat crop was 936,974 bushels; in 1882, 8,094,600—a difference in favor of free labor of 7,057,626 bushels. Speaking of these marvellous and satisfactory figures the Boston Herald of a recent date says: "Free labor, protected in its rights, improved transportation, better fertilization and culture, and the subdivision of the lands are at the bottom of this wonderful growth."

I have no doubt that if comparisons were made as to the production of other States like favorable results would be shown. And yet there are men who seriously allege that the negroes are lazy. I am free to admit that a large percentum of the negroes squander much time and money in fishing, hunting and loafing; still the great mass of the people are honest, steady laborers. They must of necessity be, else how account for the steady increase of production in the South?

COMPENSATION OF FARM LABORERS IN SOUTHERN STATES

Now, in view of these facts, it will naturally be asked why the negro population continues poor and ignorant. The answer, in part, is a direct refutation of the statement made to your honorable committee on Thursday last by Mr. John C. Calhoun as to the rate of wages and how it is paid in the South. The average rate of wages of a farm laborer in the South is nearer fifty than seventy-five cents, out of which the laborer must feed and clothe his family. He seldom ever pays rent and he seldom ever sees a cent of currency. He is paid in "orders" on some storekeeper friendly to the planter. He cannot negotiate these precious "orders" at any other than the store indicated. Hence a system of fraud is connived at and practiced, to the utter demoralization and impoverishment of the ignorant, helpless laborer.

I remember an instance which strikingly illustrates the pernicious features of the "orders" system. At a place on the Suwannee River in Florida there is a large saw-mill, owned by a gentleman who also operates a large farm. This man owns the entire village and all the land for miles around, and he will not allow any one to sell on his land. He owns the only store within forty miles of his place. He pays his employés in "orders" on his store, white and black alike, and it is a rare occasion indeed when any one of them gets his hand on a real dollar bill. So expensive is it to live at this place because of the miserly monopoly of everything by the proprietor, that I have known men who had fallen out with the proprietor to walk away, having been unable, from the earnings of many months, to save sufficient to indulge the luxury of a railroad ticket. I once attended a panoramic exhibition in the little church at this place, when the bookkeeper of the firm, a very fine gentleman, stood at the door and "passed in" all his employés who desired to see the sights, noting the name of each in his little book. When they had all passed in he gave the showman an "order" for his money and told him to call at the office the following day and collect, which was done. This sort of thing breeds improvidence, but not thriftlessness, because to be improvident the "orders" must be obtainable, and they are only obtainable when the work has been performed.

SHARE-LABOR SYSTEM ON FARMS

The system of share labor is equally unsatisfactory to the laborer. He is compelled to give a lien on his unplanted or unharvested crop to be able to run his farm, and his account at the store at the end of the year usually brings him in debt. My father once kept an account in the liberal sense; that is to say, he kept an account of the things he "took up" at the store as well as the storekeeper. When the accounts were footed up at the end of the year the thing became serious. The storekeeper had one hundred and fifty dollars more against my father than appeared on the latter's book. Of course there was a wide difference of opinion, but my father settled the account according to his book and told the merchant he was at liberty to sue for the remainder. But the merchant failed to do it, and his books will show a shortage of $150 to-day if he has not balanced the account to profit and loss. But of course the mass of colored men who farm on shares or labor by the year and keep an account do not, because they cannot, keep a record of every purchase; and it is by this means that they are swindled and kept forever in debt.

I have known honest but ignorant colored men who have lost large farms, magnificently accoutered, by such thievery. The black farmers, and those in other occupations at the South, are robbed year after year by the simplest sort of devices; and the very men who rob them are the loudest in complaint that the negroes are lazy and improvident. For my part, I am surprised that a larger number of them do not go to fishing, hunting, and loafing.

Artisan Labor—Its Compensation

The artisans and laborers in the cities of the South fare better, but the wages they receive would be spurned by the white artisans and day laborers of any Northern or Western city. Masons and carpenters average not $2.50 to $5, as stated by Mr. Calhoun, but $1.50 to $3.25; other laborers receive from 75 cents to $1.25 per diem.

The statement has been made to your honorable committee that a better feeling between the whites and blacks is becoming more and more apparent, but I doubt it. There is an undercurrent of restlessness in the South which the newspapers and reform politicians attempt to smother, but nothing can smother it. The longer the blacks enjoy the state of freedom, the more education and property they acquire, the more restless they become; so that I am free to admit that the starting conclusions arrived at by Professor Gilliam in a recent article in the Popular Science Monthly will, in the main, be largely verified within the time specified by him. The man who thinks the blacks of the South will always patiently endure the wrongs heaped upon them, misapprehends that human nature which is the same in the Spartan helot, the Russian serf, and the Irish peasant.

Penitentiary Labor

The penitentiary system of the South, with its infamous chain-gang and convict features, is not equaled in inhumanity, cruelty, and deliberate fraud in any other institution outside of Russian Siberia. Even the Charleston News and Courier and the Savannah morning newspapers, which no man will claim are oversensitive as to how much a negro suffers, have declared the convict system of Alabama, Georgia, and South Carolina a disgrace to civilization. When such papers as these cry out "horror!", it is time for less hidebound papers to look into the matter. The penitentiaries of the South are full of honest men as well as thieves, for the law of the South has been purposely framed to convict the negro, guilty or not guilty. These men are sentenced to long terms of imprisonment upon charges and evidence which would not be entertained for a moment in any court of law north of Mason and Dixon's line, the object being to terrorize the blacks and furnish victims for contractors, who purchase the labor of these wretches from the State for a song. Of course this one-sided administration of justice demoralizes the ignorant blacks, as it is intended to do. The white man who shoots a negro always goes free, while the negro who steals a hog is sent to the chain-gang for ten years. During the past month I noticed three instances of the acquittal of white murderers of colored men.

Rights of Colored Men

Colored men are, generally speaking, denied the right to serve on jury in the South. Hence they never expect justice, and they always receive the full extent of punishment cunningly devised to reach their case. They hold no offices by appointment under the State governments, and, because of open intimidation and violence and fraud, they hold very few through the suffrage of their fellow citizens. Their educational interests suffer in consequence. Respectable colored men refuse to travel in the South, because corporations sell them $25 worth of accommodation and force them to accept $10 worth when they can. They refuse to be thus outrageously robbed. They cannot receive shelter in hotels and inns, and places of amusement are barred against them. All these wrongs retard the progress of the race, and make the suggestion of amicable relations ridiculous. The condition of affairs in the South is volcanic in the extreme, and is becoming more so year after year, not less because of the apparent calm.

Postal Savings Banks

I think that the establishment of postal banks would benefit the poor class of people all over the country, and especially in the South. These banks would be scattered far and wide, and the positively known reliability of the Government would secure at once confidence and conduce to economy and comparative independence among the laboring poor.

I think that national aid to education would be a national blessing.

I think that the Government should refund to the freedmen the $4,000,000, with interest, out of which they were robbed by the Freedman's Bank harpies.

I think that it would be advantageous to my race if Congress would pass the bill introduced by Congressman Phelps, of Connecticut, creating a commission to thoroughly investigate the condition of affairs in the South with special reference to the condition of the colored people. I think the report of such commission would open the eyes of the country. The people who do not want any interference into the affairs of the South are the ones who have usurped authority and who tyranically use it. Hence the urgency of the necessity for honest investigation. . . .

CONDITION OF FREEDMEN

Q. You may state anything that you would like the committee to know.—A. I think this commission should investigate the condition of the freedmen in the South, for many reasons. Of course I know this committee does not take into consideration the political condition of the people, and are dealing simply with the matter of labor and education. And yet as to the convicts in the South, who are mainly colored, I think the United States should appoint a commission to investigate their condition.

Q. Do you know anything about their numbers?—A. Not with any great exactness.

34. The Nonfarm Worker: Testimony of White and Black Southerners, 1883

THE WITNESSES who appeared before the Senate committee investigating the relations between labor and capital are identified in their testimony. Henry W. Blair, Republican of New Hampshire, was chairman

SOURCE: Report on Labor and Capital, IV: 124, 133–134, 239, 272, 450–454, 458–460, 635–637.

of the committee. James L. Pugh, who joined him in the questioning, was a Democratic senator from Alabama and formerly a prominent Confederate. In testimony not included below, except in the case of C. H. Johnson, black witnesses seized the opportunity to protest discrimination in public facilities and express concern over the 1883 civil rights decision of the Supreme Court.

BIRMINGHAM, ALA., November 13, 1883.

(Evening session.)

H. S. CHAMBERLAIN sworn and examined.

By Mr. PUGH:

Question. You reside at Chattanooga, I believe?—Answer. Yes, sir.

Q. What is your business?—A. I am a manufacturer of iron, a miner of coal, and a dealer in coal.

Q. How long have you been engaged in those pursuits?—A. Ever since the war.

Q. All the time at Chattanooga?—A. I lived in Knoxville from 1863 to 1871. I have lived in Chattanooga since 1871.

Q. What was your business in Knoxville?—A. I was in the iron business there. I am still interested in that business at Knoxville.

Q. You are a member of a company there, I believe?—A. Yes, sir; I am a member of the Roane Iron Company, and also a member of the Chattanooga and the Knoxville Iron Company, of Knoxville.

Q. What is the amount of the capital stock of those companies?—A. The capital stock of the company at Knoxville is $300,000; the capital stock of the company at Chattanooga is $1,000,000.

Q. And you are still carrying on business at both places?—A. Yes.

Q. That is, the iron business?—A. Iron and coal. We mine in both concerns; but at Knoxville we mine to sell—that is, the Knoxville company does; it is a separate organization. The Roane company sells no coal, but mines for its own use. . . .

CONDITION OF LABOR—WHITE AND COLORED

By THE CHAIRMAN:

Q. Unless something more occurs to you on these subjects of which you have been speaking, I wish that you would give us your views of the labor question, as you have had experience in dealing with it. You have employed laborers of both races, as miners and as iron workers, and I wish you would give us such facts and such suggestions as you may have in your mind in regard to the habits and characteristics of those laborers; their varying degrees of skill and of compensation; their general condition as citizens socially, and their actual intellectual and moral status as you estimate it. In short, tell us what you know about the labor question. I know you have thought about it, and therefore we shall be glad to have your views in regard to it, stated in your own way.—A. Well, directly after the war all skilled labor in our line was, of course, brought from the North. I mean in the rolling mills. We brought it all from the North, principally from Pennsylvania, but from other places also, where there were manufactures of iron. As time went on, however, more or less of the natives of this country learned the business and began to work, so that we came to employ a great many people who were born and raised in the South. I am speaking now of the skilled labor particularly. At the same time, it is true in this country, as it is all over the North, that the iron-workers, as a class, are foreigners—are not Americans. They are Englishmen, Welshmen, Irishmen, and other foreigners. That, I think, is true in Pennsylvania as it is here. At the same time, as I have said, there were a good many whites in this country who were employed in the business and we got on well with them. So far as unskilled labor is concerned, we always employed colored men. All the heavy work about the rolling-mill was done by colored labor, and the same is true of the heavy work about the mines. That is the case, I think, in regard to all these establishments throughout the State of Tennessee, and indeed through this part of the country generally. Around the furnaces, the great bulk of the labor is colored labor, and it is almost entirely so about the blast furnaces. As far as our experience goes, we have found it a good, reliable character of labor. I think it is by far the best labor that is in the South—I mean native to the South.

EFFICIENT COLORED IRONWORKERS

I have men now in my employ that have been in the employ of the company eighteen years. Of course they are older than they were, but still they seem to stay right along and to give great satisfaction. I am speaking of colored men. It has been difficult to get the colored men into the skilled work, because there was such a prejudice against teaching them the trades. That prejudice existed not only here, but all over the country, and I think it was especially strong in the iron industries. There are only a few departments of the iron business, puddling, heating, and rolling, and into these you could not put colored men, because if you did the white men would strike. You could not put in a colored puddler, because the puddlers would strike, nor a colored heater, because the heaters would strike; and so in the other departments. That is true, not only in this Southern country, but it is true also in Pittsburgh. You could not work in the colored men without having a strike on your hands. At the same time we did work them into half skilled positions, so that instead of getting the lowest wages paid they would get from $1.75 to $2 a day. That was the case at Chattanooga and at Knoxville. We had a strike two years and a half ago, and after going over the ground very thoroughly we made up our minds to put in the negro. We shut our teeth, went to work, and put him into the mill. We discharged every man we had about the mill and put the colored men into the puddling, and into the heating, and into the rolling departments—into every place about the mill. We got a few white men who were skilled to work along with them, and now we are working them right along regularly and very successfully. We find that the colored men, as puddlers (a very large class of iron workers) are fully as good as white men; their yield is as good; they are as steady workmen; they are as reliable in every way, and their product is fully as good as anything that we have got from white labor. In other departments, too, we have worked them generally with white men. We would have, for instance, a white man on one side of the rolls and a colored man on the other; we would work them in pairs in that way, and we have no difficulty about it. The colored men have worked in there, and I believe that the future labor of this country in all the industrial departments must be colored.

Q. Skilled labor as well as common labor?—A. Yes, sir.

Q. You mean in the manufacture of iron?—A. Yes, sir; I think it is coming to that, and I am very well satisfied. . . .

BIRMINGHAM, ALA., November 15, 1883.

WILLARD WARNER sworn and examined.

By the CHAIRMAN:

Question. Please state where you reside, and what public positions you have occupied.—A. I reside at Tecumseh, Ala. I am a native of Ohio. I was born and raised there, and I engaged in manufacturing, and was at the head of a large machine shop, manufacturing engines, and doing a general foundry and machine business, employing one hundred and fifty men. The only public office that I ever held there was that I was for two years a member of the Ohio senate. In the fall of 1865 I came to Alabama, but I did not become a resident of this State until the spring of 1867. I was a member of the Ohio senate at the time I came here. In 1868, I was elected a member of the Alabama legislature—the reconstruction legislature. I served some two or three weeks in that capacity, and then was elected to the United States Senate and served there until March, 1871, when I returned to Alabama and was afterwards appointed collector at the port of Mobile. In the mean time I had been appointed and confirmed as governor of New Mexico, which office I declined. . . . I am president and general manager of the Tecumseh Iron Company, in Cherokee County, in this State, which is engaged in manufacturing charcoal pig-iron.

Q. What is the extent of that manufacturing establishment? What is the cost of the plant, in round numbers?—A. Two hundred thousand dollars. Our average product is about 40 tons a day. . . . .

During the ten years that I have been at Tecumseh making pig-iron I have employed both white and black labor. Of course the preponderance of labor in this country is black, and the great majority of our laborers are black. I have found no difficulty in working white and black labor together. I have a black blacksmith, and a white man helping him, and the white man solicited the job. There is no trouble about white and black men working together; we do not think anything more about it than we would about any other two men working together. This blacksmith is a superior mechanic; one of the best blacksmiths I ever saw. In my business before the war, as a manufacturer of machinery, I employed seven or eight blacksmiths, and that experience gave me some knowledge of the business, and I say this man is one of the best blacksmiths I have ever seen. I have found the labor here permanent and steady. I have with me a great many colored men that I started with nearly eleven years ago. The colored man who put the first charge into the top of our furnace is there yet. He has been in that one position now for ten years. He helped to make the brick that built our furnace, and helped to dig the coal when it was done, and I put him on top as filler, and he has been there ever since, and I have never known him to be unfaithful in any way, and I have increased his wages once or twice, and I call him into the store at Christmas (rather than increase his wages, because it would be held to apply to others), and give him a suit of clothes or something of that kind. I have a good many men that have staid with us all the time that we have been at Tecumseh, and, as I said before, I have found them faithful, steady laborers. With some knowledge and experience of the employment of labor, both in the Northern States and in this State for now eighteen years, I think I can say with confidence that I know of no better labor in this country than the labor of this State, which is mainly black labor. I know of no better laborer than the colored laborer. We used to hear impatient people say, "Now that they have liberated the negroes, if they would only take them away." That sentiment, I think, is passing away. Our people are beginning to value the negro. He is an indispensable laborer here and people are beginning to appreciate his worth. . . .

BIRMINGHAM, ALA., *November 17, 1883.*

JAMES K. GREEN (colored) sworn and examined.

By Mr. PUGH:

Question. Where do you live?—Answer. In the city of Montgomery, Ala.

Q. What is your occupation?—A. I am a carpenter and contractor.

Q. How long have you been living there?—A. I went there the 10th day of March, 1876. I think that is the time that me and Mr. Hewitt came out of the House of Representatives together.

Q. Well you have done better as a carpenter than as a Representative, I suppose.—A. I don't say that, because I have done my best at both.

Q. How are you getting along there in your trade?—A. Well, sir, I am doing pretty well, I think. I haven't made no fortune, but I have made a comfortable living and a great many friends, I think.

"POLITICAL DOUBTS"

Q. You are doing very well all round, and are you well fixed up in life?—A. Yes, sir; in my way of fixing up. I don't own no property. I haven't been reconciled to that extent to buy any property in the South. I have always had my political doubts as to whether I should do such a thing or not, and I haven't done it, but it wasn't because I haven't been able to.

Q. You have had your political doubts as to that, you say?—A. Yes, sir. I was afraid that you folks were going to keep outcounting us, and I want to have my rights at the ballot-box.

Q. You thought the white people were going to take away your ballot and put you back into slavery, I suppose?—A. Oh, no, sir; I was never afraid of that.

Q. You have got as much right to vote as anybody here, have you not?—A. Yes, sir.

Q. Do you know of any way of taking that right away from you?—A. Only in the count.

Q. It would take a great many votes to count you out of the right to vote, would it not?—A. But it is just as well not to have the vote, unless it is counted fair. But that is not what we are to talk about now. We don't want to talk about any politics now; we just want to find out how we are getting along.

Q. Yes. Our principal inquiry is in regard to the condition of the people here, and the relations between capital and labor, and the chances a man has here to make a comfortable living and to provide for his family and improve his condition in life.—A. Well, I will go on to speak as to the chances that a colored man has, as a mechanic, in Montgomery, and I will say that it depends entirely on the character of the individual. Whenever there is plans out for buildings Mr. Hale and Mr. Philips, and any other contractors and myself have the privilege to go and look at the plans and to estimate upon them just as much as any white man has, and we do it. Sometimes we don't feel willing to run the risk of going into the business further than we are capacitated to get through with, and we give the thing up, but as to any discrimination between men in those matters it depends entirely upon the character of the individual as a man and as a mechanic. I am talking about Montgomery now. In Montgomery mechanics are like other people—just like farmers, some go up and some go down, but they all keep trying. . . .

WAGES

Around the city of Montgomery there is no big wages, but people pay all they say they will. I have been working ten or twelve hands since the 28th or 29th of last May, and I have been paying them from $10.50 to $12 a week. The lowest wages I pay is $1.25 a day.

Q. Do you think that is as much as you can afford to pay them?—A. That is all that my work would justify me to give them. We come into competition with a great many strangers coming to Montgomery, because it has the name of being very healthy, and a great many goes there in summer.

Q. Montgomery is a growing city, is it not?—A. Yes, sir.

Q. There is a great deal of building going on?—A. A good deal.

Q. And a good demand for mechanics?—A. Yes, sir.

Q. Have you stated all that you care to say?—A. Yes, sir; that is all.

BIRMINGHAM, ALA., *November* 17, 1883.
JAMES E. BUSH (colored) sworn and examined.

A USEFUL INSTITUTION

By Mr. PUGH:

Question. What is your profession?—Answer. At present I am in the intelligence bureau business in this city.

Q. What is that?—A. It has for its mission selecting labor for the city and accommodating strangers in that respect. You know this is a transitory population passing here, coming in and going out all the time, and strangers come here, and don't know where to go or to apply for situations, so I thought I could accommodate my people and others by opening an office of that kind, and I have found it to work very successfully so far.

Q. You furnish information to people who come in here seeking employment?—A. Yes, sir. . . .

Q. Have you been able to find employment for a great many persons in that way?—A. Yes, sir; for a great many.

Q. Where you have got them employment how have they generally succeeded? Have they kept their contracts?—A. Yes; the majority of them, because I tell them, "Now, here, my reputation depends on your conduct, I am responsible for you."

Q. And you think that has a good influence upon them?—A. Yes, because I say to them, "In case you do not suit these parties, if you ever want me to look you out another place, I cannot do it, but if you stay there and give satisfaction and then for any reason you want to leave later, why I can help you; but if you fail to do your duty I cannot assist you again." The object of my business is to regulate the labor and its employment throughout the city and to get these people whenever they make a contract to stand to it.

SCHOOLS—FEDERAL AID NEEDED

The chief thing that I wanted to be a witness about was the matter of schools. I have been a teacher myself for some time; I have taught in several counties in this State, and I find that one thing that has driven a great many teachers from the profession is the shortness of funds. I find that the scholastic year in this State will not average more than about seventy-five or eighty days during the year, and that of itself would prevent almost any competent man from teaching. Say I get a school to teach for three months, about sixty days, then I have got to change counties, or perhaps go to another city, if I am going to continue in the profession, and, of course, very few can do that. Another thing in connection with that is this: I find that if I teach school for three months I do not get any money from the time I begin until the term closes. That puts me at a very great disadvantage, because I have no way of getting my board or of taking care of my family in the mean time, and of course my family must have some way of living and being provided for during those three months. Now, these are great evils, and if they could be remedied, if a teacher could be paid his salary at the end of each month, so as to enable him to meet the demands of his family, it would be a great advantage to the schools. But as it is now a man who undertakes to teach for three months has necessarily to go and ask some one else to allow him to open an account, and that eats up his salary. I think that if the Government would appropriate money to carry on schools in the South it would really be a great advantage, and I think it would be their duty to make the schools industrial schools, so as to teach the people trades in connection with the schooling, so that in case they could not get anything to do in the educational line they could go to other work. I find the difficulty with most contractors now is that they are unable to figure and calculate successfully, and that is a great hindrance to taking large contracts, such as Mr. Green has mentioned. If our young men that have been educated since emancipation, had been educated in a practical way, they would be able to make such calculations as would be necessary in order to carry on business and show them how they were coming out. . . .

COLUMBUS, GA., *November 20, 1883.*
C. H. JOHNSON (colored) sworn and examined.
   By the CHAIRMAN:
Question. Where do you live?—Answer. In Columbus.
   Q. How long have you resided here?—A. About twenty-six years.
   Q. What is your business?—A. I am porter in an auction and commission house.
   Q. What pay do you get?—A. About $25 a month. . . .
   Q. Go on, now, and make any statement that you desire to make?—A. Well, I think that the condition of our people, as a general thing, has been stated very fully to you, and I do not see where it is necessary for me to go over the same ground that has been gone over to you.
   Q. Do you feel as though your people had had a fair chance to be heard by this committee?—A. I do.
   Q. You think there is nothing they want to say to us that they have not had a chance to say?—A. I do not think there is anything. I think they have talked very plain about the condition of the colored race in this city.

TIMID COLORED MEN

   Q. And you think they have said all they want to say?—A. Well, I won't say that they did that. There are some things, probably, that they wanted to say that they did not say.
   Q. Why didn't they say them?—A. Well, it is just like as it was in time of slavery. There was a great many things that they would have liked to have done, but for fear, and they have got the same feeling now, a great many of them have, and they want to say things, but they are afraid of the white people; afraid that the white people will say to them afterwards, "Look here, John, you remember the sort of remarks you made before that committee. I am done with you now." That is the case with some of the colored folks; they are afraid to say what they want to say; but I aint of that sort. Whatever I want to say I am going to say it. Unfortunately I am not an educated man, but I think, in my own judgment, I

would have been a help to my people if I had been educated, because I see a great many things going on among them that I think they ought to be advised about that they need advice about, and I do not think anybody else but a colored man could take hold of it and work it like it ought to be worked to their interests, because every man, and every nation, and every race, is bound to look out for their own people. A white man is a white man, I don't care where he is. . . .

"We Need More Power"

The great trouble with us poor colored people is that we need more power. Where are we going to get it? That is the question, as I look at it. We need more power, and if we have not got the power, there is no use to talk about negroes sitting on juries, and all that sort of thing. . . .

Q. What form of power do you mean?—A. I don't want anybody to understand me to say that I am advocating the cause that has been existing for some time around over the country about the civil rights bill. I don't see that we are just exactly prepared to stand the pressure that that civil rights bill would put upon the colored people if they had it in existence. That is the way I am thinking about it. I think this, that we want the power of having social equality amongst us, as a general thing, in the city and in the country around, and there is a great many things that ought to be looked after that cannot be—that there can't be nothing got done about except we have the power to do it.

"Social Equality" Explained

By Mr. Pugh:

Q. What do you mean by social equality?—A. I mean that when we go into places that a man has a right to go into, we want to be treated right. Suppose I get on the cars, for instance; I want to be treated fairly. As I said about the civil rights bill, if I get on the cars to ride from here to Montgomery, or to Atlanta, although I pay the same fare that you pay—they make me do that—I do not have the same accommodations. Now, I think that if I have to pay the same fare that you pay I ought to have a right to ride in the same car that you ride in.

Q. Suppose you have one just like it, won't that do?—A. Well, if it is just like it; still, it may not be the car that I want to ride in, because I ought to have a chance to ride in any one I wanted to. I think if they are going to make a law not to allow a colored man to ride in a first class car they have no right to make him pay first-class fare. That is the trouble between the colored man and the whites about this civil rights bill. I myself do not care anything about the civil rights bill; but then, as I said about social equality, I think we ought to demand our rights in that respect.

By the CHAIRMAN:

Q. Suppose you have a car just as good as the one the white folks have, but are not allowed to go into their car, will that be satisfactory?—A. But that is not going to be done. They are not going to make a law of that kind.

35. George W. Cable:
The Convict Lease System, 1884

THE CONVICT lease system existed in twelve Southern states and its victims were predominantly black men. The Redeemers had not originated the system, but their emphasis upon cutting the cost of government led to its expansion both in numbers of men and in the length of leases, which sometimes extended to ten, fifteen, or twenty years. Lessees were said to have shared their profits with state officials and party machines. Despite the force of George Cable's moral condemnation, his statistics understate the barbarity of the system. Cable followed his attack upon convict leasing with a more general one on white supremacy and segregation. He failed to realize his hopes of arousing white Southerners to put a speedy end to the lease system and take action in defense of the Negro's civil rights. His renown as the South's leading novelist did not spare him from a floodtide of abuse (see references to Cable in doc. 21).

THE CONVICT LEASE SYSTEM IN THE SOUTHERN STATES

. . . Its features [i.e., the lease system] vary in different regions. In some, the State retains the penitentiary in charge of its officers, and leases out the convicts in gangs of scores or hundreds to persons who use them anywhere within the State boundaries in the

SOURCE: George W. Cable, "The Convict Lease System in the Southern States," *Century*, V (February 1884): 582–599.

execution of private enterprises or public or semi-public works. In a few cases the penitentiary itself, its appliances and its inmates, all and entire, are leased, sometimes annually or biennially, sometimes for five and sometimes for ten or even twenty years, and the convicts worked within or without the prison walls, and near to or distant from them, as various circumstances may regulate, being transferred from place to place in companies under military or semi-military guard, and quartered in camps or herded in stockades convenient to their fields of labor. In two or three States the Government's abandonment of its trust is still more nearly complete, the terms of the lease going so far as to assign to the lessees the entire custody and discipline of the convicts, and even their medical and surgical care. But a clause common to all these prison leases is that which allows a portion, at least, and sometimes all of the prisoners to be worked in parts of the State remote from the prison. The fitness of some lessees to hold such a trust may be estimated from the spirit of the following letters:

OFFICE OF LESSEE ARKANSAS STATE PENITENTIARY,
LITTLE ROCK, ARKANSAS, January 12, 1882.
DEAR SIR: Your postal of request to hand; sorry to say cannot send you report, as there are none given. The business of the Arkansas State Penitentiary is of a private nature, and no report is made to the public. Any private information relative to the men will be furnished upon application for same.
Very respectfully,
ZEB. WARD, Lessee.
Z. J.

OFFICE OF LESSEE ARKANSAS STATE PENITENTIARY,
LITTLE ROCK, ARKANSAS, July 2, 1882.
DEAR SIR: Yours of —— date to hand and fully noted. Your inquiries, if answered, would require much time and labor. I am sole lessee, and work all the convicts, and of course the business of the prison is my private business. My book-keeper is kept quite busy with my business, and no time to make out all the queries you ask for. Similar information is given to the Legislature once in two years.
Respectfully,
ZEB. WARD.

The wonder is that such a scheme should not, upon its face, be instantly rejected by any but the most sordid and short-sighted minds. It is difficult to call its propositions less than an insult to the intelligence and humanity of any enlightened community. It was a Governor of Kentucky who, in 1873, justly said to his State Legislature: "I cannot but regard the present system under which the State penitentiary is leased and managed as a reproach to the commonwealth. . . . It is the system, not the officer acting under it, with which I find fault."

This system springs primarily from the idea that the possession of a convict's person is an opportunity for the State to make money; that the amount to be made is whatever can be wrung from him; that for the officers of the State to waive this opportunity is to impose upon the clemency of a tax-paying public; and that, without regard to moral or mortal consequences, the penitentiary whose annual report shows the largest cash balance paid into the State's treasury is the best penitentiary. The mitigations that arise in its practice through the humane or semi-humane sentiments of keepers and guards, and through the meagerest of legislation, are few, scanty, and rare; and in the main the notion is clearly set forth and followed that a convict, whether pilferer or murderer, man, woman, or child, has almost no human right that the State is bound to be at any expense to protect. . . .

If, now, we are to begin a scrutiny of this evil, we shall do well to regard it first as it presents itself in its least offensive aspect. To do this, we turn to the State prison, or prisons, of Tennessee. . . .

Here is the Lease System at its best. Let us now glance in upon it for a moment through its own testimony, as found in the official report of its operations during the two years ending December 1, 1882. At the close of that term the State held in custody 1,336 convicts. Of these, 685 were at work in the penitentiary, 28 were employed in a railway tunnel, 34 were at work on a farm, 89 on another farm, 30 in a coal-mine, 145 in another coal-mine, and 325 in still another. In short, nearly half the convicts are scattered about in "branch prisons," and the facts that can be gathered concerning them are only such as are given or implied in the most meager allusions. It appears that they are worked in gangs surrounded by armed guards, and the largest company, at least,—the three hundred and twenty-five,—quartered in a mere stockade. As the eye runs down the table of deaths, it finds opposite the names, among other mortal causes, the following: Found dead. Killed. Drowned. Not given. Blank. Blank. Blank. Killed. Blank. Shot. Killed. Blank. Blank. Killed. Killed. Blank. Blank. Blank. Killed. Blank. Blank. The warden of the penitentiary states that, "in sending convicts to the branch prisons, especial care is taken to prevent the sending of any but able-bodied men"; and that "it has also been the custom to return the invalid and afflicted convicts from the branch prisons to this prison"—the penitentiary. Yet the report shows heavy rates of mortality at these branch prisons, resulting largely from such lingering complaints as dropsy, scrofula, etc., and more numerously by consumption than by any one thing else except violence: rates of mortality startlingly large compared with the usual rates of well-ordered prisons, and low only in comparison with those of other prisons worked under the hands of lessees . . .

[The Lease System] has nothing in it to produce a knowledge of and desire for a correct and honorable and truly profitable prison management. Its interests make directly against both individual and institutional reform. The plea of self-support on which it rests, the price it pays for its privileges, whether corruptly intended or not, are a bribe to officials and to public alike to close the ear against all suggestion of better things. For example, see the report of the two inspectors of the Tennessee prisons. Excepting a letter from another hand, quoted by them, their whole biennial report is less than one hundred lines. A little over half tells of the fire and the new workshops. A little less than half is given to the praise of the Lease System, upon the lonely merit of cash returns, and to a recommendation for its continuance. For the rest, they content themselves with pointing the Legislature to the reports of the superintendent, warden, physician, and chaplain of the penitentiary, whom, they saw, "we indorse most heartily as attentive to their respective duties, and alive to every requirement of the law [which the warden reports as painfully barren of requirements] and the dictates of humanity in the discharge of their duty." However true this may be of the executive officers, it is certainly not true of the inspectors themselves. They do not certify to the correctness of a single roll or tabulated statement, or imply that they have examined any one of them. They do not present a statistical figure of their own, or recommend the taking of a single record among all the valuable registries that should be made, but are not, because the facts they would indicate are either absent or despised. Indeed, their silence is in a certain sense obligatory; for the omitted records, if taken, would condemn the system they praise, and the meager records that are given swarm with errors. It would have been hard for the inspectors to say anything worse for themselves than that they had examined the reports. The physician's is an almost unqualified denunciation of the whole establishment; the superintendent's is three-quarters of a page of generalities and official compliments; and the warden's tabulated statements confusedly contradict each other. Even the numerical counts are incorrect. . . . Such a condition of accounts might be excused in the rosters of a retreating army; but it is not to be believed, while there is room for doubt, that the people of an American State will knowingly accept such stupid and wicked trifling with their State's good name and the safety of society, or even such a ghastly burlesque of net revenue.

Yet when we pass across the boundaries of Tennessee and enter any adjoining State, excepting only Missouri, we find the same system in operation, operating viciously, and often more viciously than in Tennessee. North Carolina, during the two years ending October 31, 1880, held in custody an average of 1090 convicts. The penitentiary proper and its interior industries were being controlled under public account. Shoemaking, brickmaking, tailoring, blacksmithing, etc., the officers report, were either already profitable or could be made so, and their detailed accounts of receipts and expenditures seem to verify their assertions. The statistics of the prison are given, not minutely or very comprehensively, but intelligently as far as they go, and are valuable. . . .

The population *within* this penitentiary was generally about three hundred. About eight hundred, therefore, were scattered about in companies under lessees, and in the two years 1879–80 were at different times at work on six different railways and one wagon road. What their experiences were at these places can be gathered, by one at a distance, only from one or two incidental remarks dropped by the prison officers in their reports and from the tabulated records of the convict movement. There is no hospital record given concerning them, nor any physician's account of their sickness. When they drop off they are simply scored as dead. The warden says of them that many had "taken their regular shifts for several years in the Swannanoa and other tunnels on the Western North Carolina Railroad, and were finally returned to the prison with shattered constitutions and their physical strength entirely gone, so that, with the most skillful medical treatment and the best nursing, it was impossible for them to recuperate."

But such remarks convey but a faint idea of the dreadful lot of these unfortunate creatures. The prison physician, apologizing for the high death-rate within the walls, instances twenty-one deaths of men "who had been returned from the railroads completely broken down and hopelessly diseased." And when *these deaths are left out* of the count, the number of deaths *inside* the walls, not attributable to *outside* hardships, amounted, in 1880, to just the number of those in the prisons of Auburn and Sing-Sing in a population *eight times as large.* Ten-elevenths of the deaths for 1879 and 1880 were from lingering diseases, principally consumption. Yet, year in and year out, the good citizens of Raleigh were visiting the place weekly, teaching Sunday-school, preaching the gospel, and staring these facts in the face.

Now, what was the death-rate among the convicts working at railroad construction? The average number of prisoners so engaged in 1879 and 1880 was 776. The deaths, including the 21 sent back to die in prison, were 178, an annual death-rate of nearly eleven and a half per cent., and therefore greater than the year's death-rate in New Orleans in 1853, the year of the Great Epidemic. But the dark fact that eclipses everything else is that not a word is given to account for the deaths of 158 of these men, except that 11 were shot down in trying to escape from this heartless butchery. . . .

It only remains to be asked, For what enormous money consideration did the State set its seal upon this hideous mistake? The statement would be incredible were it attempted to give other than a literal quotation. "Therefore it will be seen," says the warden at the bottom of his résumé of accounts, "that the convicts have earned $678.78 more than the prison department has cost for the two years ending October 31, 1880." . . .

One of the peculiar temptations which the Lease System holds out to the communities employing it, as such communities are represented in the jury-box, needs a moment's careful notice. The States where this system is in vogue are now, and have been for some years, enjoying a new and great development of their natural resources and of other industries than that colossal agricultural system that once monopolized their attention. There is, therefore, a vigorous demand for the opening and completion of extensive public works,—mines, railways, turnpikes, levees, and the like,—and for ways and means for getting them done as quickly and cheaply as possible. Now, it is with these potent conditions in force that the Lease System presents itself as the lowest bidder, and holds forth the seductive spectacle of these great works, which everybody wants and no one wants to pay for, growing apace by convict labor that seems to cost nothing. What is the consequence? We might almost assert beforehand that the popular sentiment and verdict would hustle the misbehaving, with shocking alacrity, into the State's prison under extravagant sentences or for trivial offenses, and sell their labor to the highest bidder who will use them in the construction of public works. The temptation gathers additional force through the popular ignorance of the condition and results of these penitentiaries, and the natural assumption that they are not so grossly mismanaged but that the convict will survive his sentence, and the fierce discipline of the convict camp "teach him to behave himself."

But there is no need to reason from cause to effect only. The testimony of the prisons themselves is before us, either to upset or else to establish these conjectures. A single glance at almost any of their reports startles the eye with the undue length of sentences and the infliction of penalties for mere misdemeanors that are proper only to crimes and felonies. In the Georgia penitentiary, in 1880, in a total of nearly 1200 convicts, only 22 prisoners were serving as low a term as one year, only 52 others as low a term as two years, only 76 others as low a term as three years; while those who were under sentences of ten years and over numbered 538, although ten years, as the rolls show, is the utmost length of time that a convict can be expected to remain alive in a Georgia penitentiary. Six men were under sentence for simple assault and battery,—mere fistcuffing,—one of two years, two of five years, one of six years, one of seven, and one of eight. For larceny, three men were serving under sentence of twenty years; five were sentenced each fifteen years; one, fourteen years; six, twelve years; thirty-five, ten years; and one hundred and seventy-two, from one year up to nine years. In other words, a large majority of all these had, for simple stealing, without breaking in or violence, been virtually condemned to be worked and misused to death. One man was under a twenty years' sentence for "hogstealing." Twelve men were sentenced to the South Carolina penitentiary, in 1881, on no other finding but a misdemeanor commonly atoned for by a fine of a few dollars, and which thousands of the State's inhabitants are constantly committing with impunity—the carrying of concealed weapons. Fifteen others were sentenced for mere assault, and assault and battery. It is to be inferred—for we are left to our inferences—that such sentences were very short; but it is inferable, too, that they worked the customary loss of citizenship for life. In Louisiana, a few days before the writing of this paper, a man was sentenced to the penitentiary for twelve months for stealing five dollars' worth of gunny-sacks. . . .

For some years past Texas has had in custody about two thousand convicts at once. They are under the Lease System, some of whose features, at least, give dissatisfaction to the State's prison directors and to its Legislature. The working of convicts remote from the prison, though practiced, is condemned, and the effort is being made to bring the management into conformity with a statute that requires as many of the convicts as can be to be employed within the penitentiary walls. . . .

The following is from the superintendent's biennial report of October 31, 1880: "The most usual mode of punishment practiced at outside camps is by stocks. . . . Most of the sergeants, in order to make it effective, have lifted the convicts on the ball of the foot, or tiptoe, . . . jeopardizing not only health, but life. The [present] lessees . . . abolished the use of stocks at their wood camps, and I rejoiced that you [the directors] have determined to abolish them altogether. On many of the farms sergeants have been in the habit of . . . whipping, as well as permitting their guards to do so, without first obtaining an order from the board of directors, as required by law." Of illegal punishments he says: "We have been compelled to discharge sergeants and a great number of guards on account of it. . . . I am satisfied that many escapes have been caused by illegal punishments and by cursing and threats." The spirit of this officer's report does him honor throughout.

One can turn again only to leased prisons elsewhere, to find numbers with which to compare the ghastly mortality of some of these Texas convict camps. Men in large numbers, "who have contracted in the miserable jails of the State incurable diseases, or whose systems have been impregnated with diseases from having led lives of debauchery and dissipation, are put to the hardest manual labor and . . . soon break down in health." "Sick convicts are crowded into the same building containing well convicts, and cannot have proper nursing and quiet, even if they have good medical attention." "Frequently sergeants, believing that convicts are trying to play off, have kept them at work when, in fact, they

were seriously ill, . . . or have tried to physic them themselves."
On railroad construction the average *annual* rate of mortality, for
1879 and 1880, was 47 to the thousand, three times the usual death-
rate of properly managed American prisons; at plantation labor it
was 49; at the iron-works it was 54; and at the wood-cutting camps
more than half the entire average population died within the two
years. So much as to the rate. The total *number* of deaths in the
period was 256, of which only 60 occurred in the prison hospital,
the rest in the camps. Nor was any considerable fraction of them
by contagious diseases. They were from congestions of the brain,
the stomach, and the bowels; from scurvy, dropsy, nervous fever,
malaria, chronic diarrhœa, general debility, pneumonia. Thirty-five
died of gun-shot wounds, five of "wounds miscellaneous." Of
three, the cause of death was "not stated." Three were drowned,
four were sunstruck, two committed suicide, and two were killed
by the explosion of a boiler. And all was reported without a word of
apology or explanation. The whole thirty-five who were shot to
death were shot in attempting to escape "from forces at work outside the prison walls." "In nearly all these cases the verdict of a
coroner's jury has stated that the guard acted in discharge of his
duty." As to the remainder, we know not what the verdicts were, or
whether there were any; nor do we know how many vain attempts
were made to escape; but we know that, over and above the deaths,
there were treated in the prison hospital—where so few of the
outside sick ever arrived—fifteen others with gunshot wounds and
fifty-two with "wounds miscellaneous."

We know, too, by the record, that four men did escape from
within the prison walls, and three hundred and sixty-two from the
gangs outside. In the interest of the Texas taxpayer, from whom
the Lease System is supposed to lift an intolerable burden, as well
as for society at large, it would be well to know what were the
favorite crimes of these three hundred and sixty-six escaped felons
(since unreformed criminals generally repeat the same crimes again
and again), what moral and material mischief one hundred and
twenty three of them did before they were recaptured, and what
the record will be of the two hundred and forty-three remaining at
large when the terms they should have served have expired. These
facts are not given; we get only, as it were, a faint whiff of the
mischief in the item of $6,900 expended in apprehending one
hundred of them.

And yet this is the operation of the Lease System under a Governor who was giving the State prison and its inmates a far more rational, humane, and diligent attention than is generally accorded them by State executives. . . .

Even where the system enjoys the greatest favor from the State governments whose responsibilities in the matter it pretends to assume, it is rare that there is not some one who revolts and utters against it his all too little heeded denunciation. Such voices are not altogether unheard even in Arkansas, Mississippi, and Louisiana, where undoubtedly the lessees are more slackly held to account, as they more completely usurp the State's relation to its convicts than elsewhere. It is here may be found a wheel within this wheel; to wit, the practice of sub-leasing. So complete in these regions is the abandonment, by the State, of all the duties it owes to its criminal system, that in two instances, Arkansas and Louisiana, it does not so much as print a report, and the present writer is indebted entirely to the courtesy of the governors of these two States for letters and manuscript tables imparting the information which enables him to write. "The State," says the clerk of the Louisiana penitentiary, "has no expense except keeping the building in repair." "The State," writes the Governor's secretary in Arkansas, "is at no expense whatever." In Mississippi, the terms of the present lease make no mention whatever of any moral, religious, or educational privilege, or duty. "All convicts sentenced for a period of ten years or less, said lessees may work outside the penitentiary, but within the limits of the State of Mississippi, in building railroads, levees, or in any private labor or employment." One of the effects of such a rule is that a convict condemned to thirty or forty years' service, being kept within the walls, has fully three chances to one of outliving the convict who is sentenced to eight or ten years' service, and who must, therefore, work outside. Yet it is not intended to imply that the long-term convict inside the prison is likely to serve out his sentence. While among a majority of commitments on shorter periods, men, women, and children are frequently sentenced for terms of 15, 20, 30, 40, and sometimes even of 50 years, a prisoner can rarely be found to have survived ten years of this brutal slavery either in the prison or in the convict camp. In Alabama, in 1880, there were but three who had been in confinement eight years, and one nine; while not one had lived out ten years' imprisonment. In Mississippi, December 1, 1881, among 77 convicts then on the roll under 10 years' sentence, 17 under sentence of between 10 and 20, and 23 under sentences of between 20 and 50 years, none had served 11 years, only 2 had served 10, and only 3 others had served 9 years. There were 25 distinct outside gangs, and their average annual rate of mortality for that and the previous year was over 8 per cent.

During the same term, 142 convicts escaped; which is to say that, for every four law-breakers put into the penitentiary, one got away; and against the whole number so escaping there were but 25 recaptures. The same proportion of commitments and escapes is true of the Arkansas prison for the year ending the 30th of last April. In Louisiana the proportion is smaller, but far from small. A surer escape in Louisiana was to die; and in 1881 14 per cent. perished. The means are wanting to show what part of this mortality belongs to the penitentiary at Baton Rouge and what to the camps outside; but if anything may be inferred from the mortal results of the Lease System in other States, the year's death-rate of the convict camps of Louisiana must exceed that of any pestilence that ever fell upon Europe in the Middle Ages. And as far as popular rumor goes, it confirms this assumption on every hand. Every mention of these camps is followed by the execrations of a scandalized community, whose ear is every now and then shocked afresh with some new whisper of their frightful barbarities. It is not for the present writer to assert, that every other community where the leasing of convicts prevails is moved to indignation by the same sense of outrage and disgrace; yet it certainly would be but a charitable assumption to believe that the day is not remote when, in every such region, the sentiment of the people will write, over the gates of the convict stockades and over the doors of the lessees' sumptuous homes, one word: Aceldama—the field of blood.

CONCLUSIONS

There never was a worse falsification of accounts than that which persuades a community that the system of leasing out its convicts is profitable. Out of its own mouth—by the testimony of its own official reports—what have we not proved against it? We have shown:

1. That, by the very ends for which it exists, it makes a proper management of prisons impossible, and lays the hand of arrest upon reformatory discipline.

2. That it contents itself, the State, and the public mind, with prisons that are in every way a disgrace to civilization.

3. That in practice it is brutally cruel.

4. That it hardens, debases, and corrupts the criminal, committed to it by the law in order that, if possible, he may be reformed and reclaimed to virtue and society.

5. That it fixes and enforces the suicidal and inhuman error, that the community must not be put to any expense for the reduction of crime or the reformation of criminals.

6. That it inflicts a different sentence upon every culprit that come into its clutches from that which the law and the court has pronounced. So that there is not to-day a single penitentiary convict, from the Potomac around to the Rio Grande, who is receiving the sentence really contemplated by the law under which he stands condemned.

7. That it kills like a pestilence, teaches the people to be cruel, sets up a false system of clemency, and seduces the State into the committal of murder for money.

8. That in two years it permitted eleven hundred prisoners to escape.

Which of these is its profitable feature? Will some one raise the plea of necessity? The necessity is exactly the reverse. It is absolutely necessary to society's interests and honor that what the lease in its very nature forbids should be sought; and that what it by nature seeks should be forbidden. . . .

GEORGE W. CABLE

36. D. Augustus Straker:
A Black Man's View of the "New South," 1888

A NATIVE OF BARBADOS, Straker had come to the United States in 1868 and to South Carolina seven years later, just before the end of Republican Reconstruction. Trained at Howard University Law School, he soon established himself as a highly respected practicing attorney and teacher of law at Allen University. In 1887 he moved to Detroit where he continued to command respect both as a lawyer and as a Negro

SOURCE: D. Augustus Straker, *The New South Investigated* (Detroit, Mich.: 1888), iii–iv, 25–30, 33–41, 45–53, 93–97.

leader. In later years he maintained friendly relations with Booker T. Washington without forfeiting the good opinion of Washington's critics among the national Negro leadership. Proud of the Negro's intellectual achievements, he at the same time endorsed industrial education; a sharp critic of white racism, he yet believed that color prejudice would give way to the recognition of race equality. In the selection below Straker's analysis of what he viewed as the basic weakness of the "New South" of the 1880s is trenchant. The reader will note that his tribute to its achievement and promise, as well as his criticism, is written with informed conviction.

PREFACE

The publication of these views in book form is the result of many requests, verbal and written, by friends. Extracts of some of these requests I append, hoping that my readers will accept them as a sufficient and excusable reason for this attempt.

My experience in the South ranges through a period of more than a decade of years, and includes a residence in South Carolina, and various visits to other States, where I have delivered addresses and lectures on many occasions. During these years, extending from 1875 to 1887, various and vast changes have taken place in this portion of our country, sufficient to entitle said change to the title "New South." By this it is not intended to prove, as is sometimes erroneously alleged, that there is an entire transformation of the South from Old into New, so that there is no vestige of old customs, no trace of ancient laws or habits, no *indicia* of slavery or civil law, no old homesteads, nor even family cast of countenance preserved. This is not the meaning of the "New South" as treated in the following pages, but it is intended only to portray the evident changes which have occurred since the emancipation of the slaves and the reconstruction of the States engaged in civil war. These events have always produced change where they have occurred, and strange it would be, indeed, if similar results did not occur in our land. Truly has someone said that the "Old South" means all those facts and forces that characterized the geographical South, particularly as moulded by the institution of slavery. It is a political designation. But even the most inveterate conservatives and strongest partizans North and South are compelled to recognize a change and to acknowledge that the South of 1886 is not the South of 1850, 1863, or even 1870. The "New South" marks the beginning and progress of great changes, sociological and industrial, and the following pages will thus treat the topic. . . .

GENERAL VIEW

The South received an education from the North other than that taught in the school house. It received new constitutions and new methods of industry and development; but while it received these benefits, mal-administration prevailed in public affairs by the party in power to an indescribable extent, which led in 1876 to a political revolution—nay, worse, a usurpation of government. The remedy, it will be seen, was worse than the disease. . . .

But let us deal with the South more from an industrial than a political standpoint at present, as we shall return to this topic later on. The South today has, amid all its troubles, political and otherwise, made great advancement in industry, education and commerce. Our land owners are now ready and willing to utilize their lands and not let them lie uncultivated. Our farmers no longer confine themselves to the growing of cotton only, but are engaged in the more varied industry of planting corn and rice. This latter article is cultivated in South Carolina to a degree of almost perfection, as all those who visited the late Cotton Exposition, held at New Orleans, can testify, if they saw it. Manufactories begin to dot the South in all of its principal cities and towns. Who that has visited the cities of Augusta, Atlanta, Savannah and Macon, in Georgia; Charleston, Greenville and Columbia, in South Carolina; Selena, Montgomery, Birmingham and Anniston, in Alabama; the City of New Orleans; Jacksonville, in Florida; and other cities of the South, can fail to discover the great advancement in the industry of the South in the past twenty years. The hum of the spinning wheel, and the noise of the manufactories' whistles are now heard in every principal city in the South today, and the ring of the anvil follows the church bell. The spirit of industry has taken hold of our water-power and our mineral resources, and has utilized them as far as the capital of the South will admit. Along our canals are being built numerous factories, and the cotton which we now grow is no longer entirely sent to foreign parts for manufacture, but is manufactured on the spot at Graniteville, Greenville, Columbia, Charleston, Atlanta, Savannah and Augusta. This shows the need for a protective tariff for the South. From the bowels of the earth we now dig iron, coal, gold and other minerals. Our industries are more varied than is generally known. We not only manufacture cotton, but we turn the cotton seed into oil. We have successfully cultivated the tea plant. The tea farm is now reckoned among the industrial pursuits of South Carolina. Our mills are numerous. We have the paper-mill, the saw-mill, the grist-mill, moulding our future alongside of other industries. Our railroads also show the advancement of the South. The old iron rail is now supplanted by the modern steel rail, and the dog-kennel depot is supplanted in many places by the beautiful artistic building of modern days. We have the improved air-brake; we run with greater speed. I remember when, not more than ten years ago, it took twelve hours from Charleston to Columbia, a distance of 130 miles. To-day it is reached by rail in five hours. We even *kill* more people on the railroad than we did before, and then, following in the march of progressive ideas, we have our railroad attorneys to plead as a defense, "contributory negligence or common hazard." To illustrate this great advancement in industry, which characterizes the "New South," I will show in detail the advancement of the several industries I have generally mentioned as reported in South Carolina.

First, the resources which are capable of development in the State, and to which capital and skilled labor are invited, are 17,000,000 acres of land, of which only 4,000,000 are now in cultivation. These lands, such as are good, can be bought from $2 to $10 per acre. The special agent of the census on forestry estimates that there is now standing in the State 6,000,000 feet of pine lumber. Gold and silver are to be found in nearly all of the upper counties, and at present only twelve mines are being worked, and none of them have been developed to their full capacity. The water-power of the State is estimated at 3,000,000 horse-power, and only 15,000 horse-power is being used by all of the manufacturing establishments.

Now, as to advancement. In agriculture, corn has increased in twelve years 9,431,528 bushels, or 124 per cent. Oats, 7,316,377 bushels, or twelve fold the yield in 1870. Wheat, 1,150,360 bushels, or 170 per cent. Rice, 32,379,754 pounds, or 100 per cent. Cane syrup, 193,580 gallons, or 31 per cent. Sweet potatoes, 2,502,714 bushels, or 136 per cent. Irish potatoes, 303,938 bushels, or 365 per cent., and cotton has been increased 396,470 bales, or 176 per cent. The increase in manufactures has also been marvelous. The value of the total product of cotton mills in 1860 was $713,050; in 1880, $2,895,769; in 1883, $7,963,198, an increase in three years as you perceive of 175 per cent., and proof conclusive that free labor is more conducive to the prosperity of a people than slave labor. The South Carolina phosphates, which were discovered in 1867 at a place called Lambs, about twelve miles from Charleston, on the Ashley river, and which were declared valuable by the eminent scientist, Dr. St. Julien Ravenel, have increased from 20,000 tons in 1870, to 409,000 tons in 1886. There are at present fourteen land and eleven river mining companies, and they have an aggregate capital of $2,505,000, and employ 1,935 hands, and pay out $622,860 in wages. The value of their products amount to $2,190,000. Upon a royalty of $1.00 per ton, $1,279,170 has been paid into the State Treasury.

Now, as to our railroads. From the small railroad commenced in 1827 in South Carolina, which was the first effort in America to build a railroad for locomotive power, has sprung and increased to the magnificent railroad system of the present day, which embraces the South Carolina Railway Company, the Columbia, Greenville, Charlotte and Augusta, the Charleston and Savannah, the Port Royal, the Augusta and Knoxville, the Greenwood, Laurens and Spartanburg, the Wilmington and Columbia, the Greenville and Laurens, the Cheraw and Chester, and the Chester and Lenoir. The total assessed value of all railroad property in this State on the 1st January, 1884, was $15,263,366. The aggregate mileage 1,495. This is but the proof of the advancement of one of the Southern States. It is reasonable to suppose that the others are proportionate, and that the South today may, with justice, in a large degree, be called the "New South" industrially. . . .

In relation to this industrial advancement in the South, we may with profit turn our attention to the progress of the colored race therein. It is undeniable that in spite of oppression by laws and in social treatment, the colored citizen of the South has made incomparable progress. They have acquired property, real and personal, in sums of value astonishing to those who claim that they are incapable of thrift or industry. In Georgia the colored citizens pay taxes on upwards of seven million dollars worth of property. In Louisiana more than this; and in all of the Southern States they show by taxes an increase in the property they now possess. They are not so markedly advanced in industrial pursuits, such as manufactures, because the doors of technical industry are closed against them to a large extent on account of color. But this is not so strongly exercised against the colored man of the South at the present time, as heretofore. In the South, there are the colored mechanic, such as the carpenter, bricklayer, painter, tailor, shoemaker, blacksmith, wheelwright, cabinet maker and other artizans, who are employed as workmen of their trade. Indeed, in many places colored men are to be found as architects and contractors for work. The former spirit of prejudice exercised against the colored mechanic working alongside of the white, is more rapidly dying out in the South than it appears in the North. So great is the present spirit of industry in the South, that some States overstep themselves and enter upon cruelty in availing themselves of labor. This is done in South Carolina and Georgia. In the former State the shoe, cotton and hosiery factories are within the confines of the penitentiary, but South Carolina, like Georgia, is also engaged in hiring out by lease the convicts to persons for profit. This practice is not in the line of progress in the South, I must confess, and is to be condemned. By this system that convicts are leased out to contractors whose chief aim is to render his investment as profitable as he can, without regard to the life or health of the laborer, as a convict. His contract involves no interest whatever in the convict. . . . But cruel and despicable as all this is, it does not go without reproof. In South Carolina the press and the official authorities have been diligent in rebuking and arresting this uncivilized conduct; and yearly the legislature seeks to throw around the hired convict more and more protection. But the only true remedy is to abolish the cruel system altogether, and to provide for the labor of the convict within the prison walls. It is murder to hire a convict and permit him to be beaten or starved to death. The best safeguard against this cruel treatment, while the system exists, is to hang the cowardly wretch who would beat a man in chains to death. This system is the worst phase of capital against labor.

In regard to the opportunity denied the colored citizen to fully engage in the industrial pursuits, I will endeavor to show the inconsistency of the reason given for the practice exercised both in the North and the South; for this injustice is as much directed against the colored man of the North as of the South. In the South, while the colored citizen is denied admission into the manufactories, the reason given is, first, he is incapable of learning skilled labor; next, it brings him into social contact with his white brethren, yet the South utilizes this labor of the Negro convict in the penitentiary in a skilled form in making shoes, in carpentry, hosiery, tailoring and the like. In the North, the *idea* is against the equality of the Negro as a race; for he who will aid and assist the Negro to become educated as an individual in school, college or university, will close the doors of the workshop, the store of merchandise, the counting house and the printing press against him; and union leagues of trades deny him admission. Why is this? Is it because the mind of the American white citizen North and South is not yet fully educated to the principle of the "universal brotherhood of man and fatherhood of God?" In both North and South such practices belie the boasted civilization of our Anglo Saxon brethren. In the South especially it retards its advancement. What is the cruel purpose in educating the Negro in your schools of the North and then compelling him to work as a menial, or in the admitted groove of school teacher, preacher, hotel waiter or barber only? Or what benefit is it in the South to deny the privilege to the Negro of voluntarily becoming skilled in labor, where skilled labor is so much needed in developing its industries, while it is accepted in the form of convict labor? And all this distinction on account of his color. Is not this "cutting off the nose to spite the face?" I verily believe time will heal all of this, since the Negro is advancing in industry in the South in spite of all such obstacles. Let me illustrate. During the recent Cotton Exposition held at New Orleans, I forwarded a pair of pantaloons made by a colored person in Greenwood, S.C., who raised the sheep, sheared the wool, carded it, spun it, wove it into cloth, and made the pantaloons. This, to my mind, not only shows a spirit of industry, but capacity for it. The history of these pantaloons so interested the Superintendent of the Smithsonian exhibits at the Exposition, as to cause him to apply for them to be exhibited in the Institute in the City of Washington, D.C. This was granted, and they are doubtless there today. Another instance of the Negro's capacity for skilled and inventive labor, was seen in the marvelous exhibit of a complete locomotive made by a colored man of Kansas, and exhibited at the exposition in New Orleans, and he, too, not an educated Negro. In South Carolina, the bronze palmetto tree, now situate on the grounds of the State House yard, was executed by a Negro as far back as the dark days of slavery; so, likewise, was Fort Sumter erected by a Negro under the superintendency of a white architect, who instituted the plan. How far the Negro was capable to learn the skilled arts of industry was fairly tested, even when the relationship of master and slave existed; hence today our colored mechanics in the South are skilled in the several trades, and the exclusion of the race to a fuller enjoyment of those privileges which they once received as slaves, and now ask to continue as freemen, shows plainly that the denial of the privilege is based on social condition and color, and not capacity. A fuller account of Negro progress in the South will be hereafter given.

The South has assumed a new role even in its fond pursuit of agriculture, not only as shown by statistics, showing an increased produce of articles, but also in its habits. Today in the South may be seen well nigh all of the most modern machinery used in farming. The science of agriculture is taught in our colleges and universities, so that the old idea that he who labored in the field was an inferior citizen to him who labored with the pen is now an exploded idea, and not infrequently do we take a modern "Cincinnatus," and make him one of the rulers of the people. From all this is to be seen, that the South, in its new aspect of industry, needs only *capital* as the chief means of its development. It offers the fullest opportunity for this investment. Well nigh every industry of the North may be successfully carried on in the South. It is the future spot to which our overcrowded population of the North *must* bend its way. It has more unoccupied lands than any other section of the United States. Its forests of wood, its mineral resources, and its water power, only await capital and that industry which has given to America such cities as New York, Boston, Philadelphia, Chicago, Detroit and Baltimore, in which not only commerce holds sway, but in which beauty in architecture, and the growth of science, art, literature, and the spread of education are to be found. The immigration which the South needs is *not* European surplus labor, as I have shown that labor is full and efficient in this section for such purposes. What it needs is the skilled artizan, mechanic and other laborer of the North, and above all it needs Northern *push*, such as enables that section to build a railroad before a court can sign an injunction restraining it. Nothing will more effectively mould North and South into a homogeneous state than the introduction of like industries, and a common interest which money always produces, cemented by that feeling prevailing between the sections, and that good will, which General Grant in his last days so earnestly desired should take place, added to which there must be an obedience to law and order. There are many who desire that this harmonious condition should exist and wonder at its delay. I venture the reason why it is so. It is because reform and progress are inseparable in their effects. It knows no classes, no condition, no color. To be effective those who seek advancement and full harmony and progress in the South, must in the spirit of the Good Master, go out into the highway and bring in the Negro as well as the white man of the South to the feast of reconciliation and good feeling. In other words, we must not be left in the bloody chasm while others shake hands over the chasm, since there will always be discord and discontent below. . . .

I am told Northern capitalists will not come South to be socially bull-dozed. It is to be regretted that this charge is largely true whenever politics enter the question, but not otherwise. In the past every Northern capitalist coming South soon got into politics, which produced hostility and sectional strife; but gradually Northern capitalists have so benefited the South, as to call forth more liberality in exercise of their political rights while upbuilding this section, and calls into play self-preservation, expediency, policy and good sense, all of which teach the South to welcome capital without questioning its politics, and to give to every Northerner the right to be Republican or Democrat, as he chooses.

But the "New South" is not seen from an industrial standpoint only, but also from an educational view, and from a social and political aspect, each of which I shall now only briefly refer to but more fully treat hereafter. . . .

The South is unable to provide adequately for the education of its great masses. In South Carolina the taxes produce a revenue of $400,000 annually. This in some counties is supplemented by special tax and contributions as well as the many private contributions of Northern friends and societies which support and maintain private institutions of learning. Yet it is seen that other than the schools in cities, the government is unable to maintain the schools longer than three or four months in each year. The national government is in duty bound to supply this need, because we are citizens of the United States as well as the several States in which we live, and it is the duty of the federal government to secure the blessings of liberty to all of its citizens, to promote the general welfare, and insure domestic tranquility by educating its citizens as the best method of doing so. But the States themselves are not relieved from their separate responsibility as States. The South owes the Negro education as a just debt, with interest accruing for two hundred and fifty years, and there are many who acknowledge this debt, and show their willingness to pay their part; others are not, and there are those who oppose the Blair bill in Congress.

Before leaving the condition of the South as to the education of its citizens, let us briefly inquire what the colored citizen himself has done in securing an education. He has done something, and yet much remains to be done. In this respect it may be claimed, without fear of successful contradiction, that the African Methodist Episcopal Church has done more in the self-education of the colored race than any other religious denomination. In South Carolina there is Allen University, officered and instructed by colored men, engaged in the instruction of colored youth exclusively, and the institution is supported and maintained by the colored citizens themselves. So likewise is Paul Quinn, of Texas, Morris Brown, of Georgia, and several others throughout the South. The Baptists are next in this advancement. In Selma, Ala., there is the Selma University, supported mainly by the colored people themselves, and officered and instructed chiefly by colored teachers. So likewise is the Baptist Seminary of Louisville, Ky. Added to all these are the following institutions carried on by State aid and Northern bounty, but exclusively for the colored race, viz: Claflin University, at Orangeburg, the Benedict Institute, at Columbia, Clark University, Atlanta, and others, too numerous to mention, throughout the South. What benefit has been derived from this education? I answer, from these institutions of learning have come teachers capable of instructing their own race, a condition essentially necessary until the rights and privileges are equally enjoyed by all, and the Negro's inherent inferiority be disbelieved by a large number of those of the Caucasian race now engaged in teaching him. The Negro has proven himself in the South as in the North capable of the intellectual advancement of his white fellow citizen, in proportion to the advantages given him; and this brings me to the next proposition, which is the *social* condition of the South to-day, another topic to which I will briefly refer now, but more largely treat further on in these pages. . . .

As regards capital and labor 75 cents per day for the laboring class of men, and 50 cents for women must grow a class of paupers in any community, and produce petty crime. This price of labor which prevails in the South, and which will not enable the poorer classes to provide for their families, in connection with the oppressive *lien* system are the chief causes of the recent exodus of colored laborers from the South. It is not politics, except as this method of poor wages is adopted to keep dependent the employee and thus control his vote. As regards the lien system which enables the small farmer to secure agricultural advances during the maturity of his crop, although ample protection is provided by law, yet the contrivances of the merciless merchant result in causing the lienor to find, at the end of the year, after paying his landlord's rent, or his fertilizing bill, then his lien for advances at 12 per cent. per month, that he is left not money enough to buy a hat, a pair of shoes, or a single garment of clothing for his family. . . .

Another social feature of the South which blurs its progress and is a relic of the past, is the unjust discrimination of passengers on railroads. This arises from a prejudice of a Don Quixotic character, because the prejudice against color is about as sensible as Sancho's attack on the windmill. All nations at some time or other have had a species of caste prejudice, but none on the face of the globe has ever based it on color, save the American. . . .

And now let us look briefly at the political condition of the South. This, perhaps, is the worst feature of the "New South." The present political condition of the South is one which demands serious attention. The Democratic government of the South is a usurpation, as I have already said. It was wrested from the hands of a legitimate party by fraud and violence, and no Democrat of the South will deny this, but will excuse it on the grounds which have more than once presented themselves in countries for the necessity, as it is called, viz: reformation. . . . In the South to-day the vote of a majority of its citizens is suppressed; it is true, not as heretofore, by violence, but in South Carolina there *is* the Procrustean Eight Box system, and in other States other devices to suppress the ballot of the Negro. It is claimed by the Democrats of South Carolina that this system of eight boxes only demands the intelligence of the voter. Even so, it is still but a device to nullify the ballot of the uneducated voter. It may not be legally wrong, but it is morally wrong, but I believe it is both. But this too must soon pass away. In the next ten years four-fifths of the voting population of the South will have received sufficient education to enable them to read their ballots. . . .

I may have presented the bright side of the picture of the South in these general views at the expense of the dark. There are both sides in the South today, yet no one taking a retrospect of the past can fail to see progress under the influence of a new spirit in the South. But a short time ago a Southern editor, decrying the false idea that the Caucasian race would always hold sway over the Negro, exclaimed to his people, "*Hodie mihi cras tibi.*" Yes, there *is* a tomorrow for the Negro in the South, and all who see his progress in the short space of twenty years must recognize this. . . .

The Social Problem

None will deny that the labor in quality required for making cotton in the South is fully adequate to the need of producing the same, and this is seen in the fact that the cotton produced in the South since the war has greatly exceeded the amount produced before the war; and yet the producing power makes no material progress as compared with the non-producing power. I can see no other reason for this, than because capital has been, and still is, unjust to labor in the South as in a degree it is in the North, added to which there has been a greater degree of caste prejudice on account of color and former condition in the South, blocking the avenues to industry and progress. As I have said before, it is not only the political change in the administration which is daily causing thousands of colored farm hands, and even mechanics, to migrate from the South to the West, but it is also caused by unjust wages, wages which do not admit of a bare living, such as 15 cents a day, and $6 or $8 per month. These low wages is carrying out the plan, said to have been suggested by Calhoun, for the purpose of "keeping the Negro down." And how is this done in the South? Not only by paying him poor wages and giving him poorer rations, but still further denying him the opportunity for material advancement. A colored man in the South cannot purchase land with the facility of his white brother, not only because of his poor wages as compensation for his services, but because of the general indisposition to sell him land. Since the war, thousands of colored people who have commenced to purchase lands have been unable to do so and have lost what they have already paid, not only because some were defaulters in payment, but because more were the victims of the white man's original design to defraud him by some clause in the mortgage or fee simple deed, which defeated his tenure just at the time when he thought most sure he was the absolute owner. . . .

This system of discrimination between labor and capital, as seen in unjust wages and no protection, is also to be found among the few mechanics who perform operative labor in the South. It is not an unusual thing to see a white and a black mechanic, who although doing the same work, yet received different wages. Discrimination is introduced even into the precincts of the schoolhouse. A first-class colored teacher never receives the equal salary of a first-class white teacher, a practice which, upon its face, carries with it the purpose of seeking inferior teachers for one class and superior for another. The professional, on account of caste prejudice, is shut out from equal opportunity of securing an equal patronage with his white fellow, because of his color. But added to all this is the further obstruction to social progress, as seen in the closing of the doors of industry, few as they are in the South, to the colored brother because of his color, and shutting them against him in every vocation in life which is not strictly menial. How then can the social condition of the South be other than a dividing and a divergent one between the races? And the question here arises, is the present social condition of the South one of true progress— materially or socially? I unhesitatingly answer, no! The South's progress, socially, is only apparent and shadowy; it is not substantial; it cannot be with a divided and unequal people in condition and opportunity.

The present social condition of the South, as found in its white and black population, arises not so much from the habit of keeping separate these two classes on account of race or color, as by reason of the disparity in conditions and the hindrance to industrial pursuits set up by the same powerful whites against their weaker brethren—the blacks. You may say this is equally so with these two classes in the North, East and West, and yet the social condition is not the same. The principle is not different, but the facts are, and only serve to prove the truth of the principle. In the North, East and West, the largest number is the white class, and the result is in the order of the inverse ratio.

It cannot be denied that the social condition of the South in which it finds itself so far behind the other portions of our country in industry, is owing to the folly of keeping out from engaging in industrial pursuits the class of people largest in numbers in its midst. The folly of trades unions, or the spirit which denies colored persons admission to the workshops in the South, is the chief cause of Southern depression in trade, and despite the progress it has made, is the reason it has not made greater progress. It is evident that if the South could receive into its midst a large amount of capital, and would then open its avenues of industry for the large quantum of labor it possesses, in the large number of colored people in its midst, it would spring into a powerful, rich and more prosperous portion of our country, with magic and alacrity, and would be the garden spot of these United States.

37. Samuel J. Barrows: "What the Southern Negro Is Doing For Himself," 1891

THE WRITER of this report on the Negro's progress in the South was a prominent Unitarian clergyman and editor. One of the earliest friends of the Tuskegee Institute, his concern for humane causes was both vigorous and broad, encompassing Negro education, prison reform, women's suffrage, Indian rights, abstinence, and international arbitration. His enthusiasm for what the Negro had achieved in little more than a generation of freedom is infectious; his report is a tribute to the spirit of a people and a reflection of the optimism with which the South entered the nineties. It also affords a glimpse of the developing urban black middle class in the south.

For twenty-six years the Negro has had his freedom, and now the question is, What use has he made of it? I have just returned from an extended trip through the South, arranged and made solely for the purpose of getting an answer to the question, What is the colored man doing for himself? . . .

To know, therefore, what the colored man is doing for himself we must know the conditions from which he has to rise. These are hard enough, but not beyond the capacity of the Negro to break through them, as is shown in thousands of instances. Thus in Virginia and Kentucky and Tennessee the condition of things is much better than further south, and the colored man, in spite of

SOURCE: Samuel J. Barrows, "What the Southern Negro Is Doing for Himself," *Atlantic Monthly*, LXVII (June 1891): 805–815.

these obstacles, is rapidly becoming a farmowner and householder. ... A great difference is sometimes apparent in different counties in the same State. Thus in Lee County, Georgia, the people are largely laborers, working for wages. But in Marion County fifty per cent of the people own homes, and some of them have large plantations. In Sumter and Terrell counties, they likewise live mostly on farms. In the latter county, I was told that in a small city of 10,000 nearly all the colored people own their homes, and live in cabins or houses varying in size from one room to eight. The same difference is seen in Alabama. In Russell County the blacks are much behind those of Pike County, where there are better schools and more freedom from the mortgage system. In Bullock County, much government land has been preempted by the Negroes. In one section of that county the colored people are prosperous, one man of exceptional thrift owning 300 acres, twelve good mules, and four horses, and raising his own meat and potatoes. In Coffee County, the people are just beginning to rent their homes. In Elmore County, many have farms of fifty acres. In Macon County, not much land is owned. In Barbour County, land is mainly rented, but there are many who have stock. In the southern part of Randolph County, about half of the blacks own their land. In one township of Lee County, nearly all the colored people own their homes. At Notasulga, about half the people have farms ranging from twenty-five to one hundred and fifty acres. Here I learned of one prosperous woman farmer, who raises three or four bales of cotton, as well as potatoes, chickens, and cows. In the vicinity of Birmingham, farms are owned ranging from fifty to two hundred acres.

The home-buying that is going on in the agricultural districts is going on also in the cities. In Montgomery, street after street is owned by colored people. In Chattanooga, one third of the colored people own their homes. Suburban lots range in cost from $350 to $400. A cottage costs in the neighborhood of $600 to $650. In Birmingham, colored people pay $10 or $12 a month rent. A number of householders have gardens with two or three acres of land. Some were fortunate enough to purchase land before the prices went up, and have profited by the rise.

The Negro is also venturing as a tradesman. In all the large cities, and even in the smaller towns, in the South, he is hanging out his sign. Two young men have engaged in the grocery business at Tuskegee, Alabama. Their credit is good at the bank, and I was told that they were doing more for their race by their industry and thrift than could be done by any amount of talk. The colored grocers in Birmingham are sharing the prosperity of this thriving city. Near a little place which I visited in the Black Belt, a colored school-teacher, who got his education with hand and brain at Tuskegee, had bought for $225 a lot of land, and established a grocery store. At Tuscaloosa, the livery stable man who drove me owns several horses and carriages, and is doing well. Thus, in whatever direction one goes, he can find Negroes who are rising by force of education and of character. The influence of such schools as Hampton, Atlanta, and Tuskegee is felt all through the South in the stimulus given to industrial occupations. Tuskegee has turned out a number of printers, who have made themselves independent, and get patronage from both white and colored customers. One has a printing office in Montgomery. Another has opened an office in Texas. The growth of journalism and the gradual reduction of illiteracy among the colored people will make a way for many printers. In all the mechanical trades, colored men are finding places as blacksmiths, wheelwrights, masons, bricklayers, carpenters, tinsmiths, harnessmakers, shoemakers, and machinists. In Washington, colored brickmakers are earning from four to five dollars a day. Hod-carriers receive $1.50. A boy trained in the industrial department of Atlanta University has buit a schoolhouse in Alabama on contract. This boy can earn $2.50 a day with his hands and tools, and is besides a college graduate. . . .

The social progress of the Negro is well illustrated by two historic cities,—the federal capital at Washington and the former capital of the Confederacy at Montgomery. The casual traveler, who sees the alley districts and the settlements around the railroads, forms no better idea of the social development of the Negro than he does of Northern whites, if he confines his inspection to similar localities. In Montgomery, under the guidance of Dr. Dorsette, a colored physician and a respected citizen, I had an opportunity to see the homes of the colored people at their best. In some of the streets, the whites occupy one side, and the blacks the other. Occasionally the colors alternate, like the squares on a checkerboard. It is not easy externally to tell one from the other. The interiors of these homes, especially of the younger and more progressive people, are comfortably and tastefully furnished. The rooms are as high as those of their white neighbors, well carpeted and papered, while the piano or the cabinet organ suggests loftier musical tastes than that of the plantation banjo. While in most respects the movement or development of the white and colored races runs on parallel lines, in music they seem to be going in opposite directions. Though I traveled all through the South, in urban, suburban, and agricultural districts, from Baltimore to New Orleans, the only banjo I heard was played in Atlanta by a white man. . . .

The pride of the colored people in buying these homes and furnishing them is a healthful form of domestic ambition, requiring sacrifice and resolute concentration of purpose. A fine house on a corner lot was shown me which had been bought with the savings of a hackman. Even in the poorer districts it is interesting to note the ambition to improve. "I have seen these houses grow," said the doctor. "There is one in which lives an old woman. She began with one room, then built on another; then finished off one, and now has just finished off the other. It has taken her some time, but she has done it."

Immediately after the war I lived at the national capital. Thousands of destitute blacks from Virginia and further south had settled in the barracks around the city. They owned little more than the clothes on their backs, and most of these had been given to them. The change in these districts is remarkable. Large numbers of people live in their own homes. There is not much squalor outside of the alley population. Even the poorest houses have some comforts and show some endeavor to improve. A similar story may be told of Baltimore.

Standards of social position and refinement among the negroes are becoming as varied as among the whites. In some districts I was informed that a colored man had very little standing with his own people unless he had a trade or profession. It is inevitable, too, that cliques and affiliations should be formed, with the advantage and disadvantage which come from such social differentiation. Two aristocracies are appearing in the colored race,—the aristocracy of culture and the aristocracy of wealth. Fortunately, at present, in the younger generation culture and prosperity are moving together. The colored man's standard of wealth is relatively much smaller than that of the white man. There are no Negro millionaires that I know of; but there is growing up a class of men with fortunes ranging from $15,000 to $100,000. This accumulation has been going on in recent years with increasing rapidity. . . .

There are conspicuous cases of individual prosperity in nearly all the large centres and in the agricultural districts. Thus, in Montgomery, Alabama, a colored barber, originally a slave, has accumulated property amounting to $75,000 or $100,000. An ex-slave in Mississippi has bought one of the plantations that formerly belonged to Jefferson Davis. The colored people of Maryland are said to possess property to the amount of $9,000,000. In Baltimore, there are several colored men worth $15,000 each, three or four worth from $40,000 to $60,000, and the estate of a Negro recently deceased was appraised at $100,000. In Washington, also, colored men have profited by the rise of real estate, and a few are possessed of ample fortunes. These instances might be greatly multiplied from my notes.

The subject of Negro education is vast and absorbing. Among its varied aspects two are of special and correlative interest: first, What is education doing for the Negro; secondly, What is the Negro doing for education? In this paper I can refer only to the latter topic. But these questions cannot be absolutely separated. No man "receives an education" who does not get a good deal of it himself. The student is not so much inert material; he reacts on the forces which impress him. The Negroes are showing their awakened and eager interest in education by the zeal with which they are embracing their opportunities. Everywhere I found in colleges, normal institutes, and district schools fresh, live interest. In some sections, the eagerness of the colored people for knowledge amounts to an absolute thirst. In Alabama, the state superintendent of education, a former Confederate major, assured me that the colored people in that State are more interested in education than the whites are. Nothing shows better this zeal for education than the sacrifices made to secure it. President Bumstead, of Atlanta University, asks, "Where in the history of the world have so large a mass of equally poor and unlettered people done so much to help themselves in educational work?" This challenge will long remain unanswered. The students of Atlanta University pay thirty-four per cent of the expenses of that institution. A letter from the treasurer of Harvard College informs me that about the same proportion of its expenses is paid from tuition fees. If we compare the wealth represented by the students of Harvard with that represented by the colored students of Atlanta, we shall find how large a sacrifice the latter are making in order to do so much. It must be remembered, also, that at Harvard tuition fees and other expenses are mostly paid by parents and guardians; at Atlanta they are paid by the students themselves, and to a large degree by personal labor. President Bumstead calculates that for every million dollars contributed by the North at least a half million is contributed by the colored people for educational purposes. Though it is difficult to get the material for such large and general totals, it is easy to furnish a vast number of facts illustrating the truth that in the very process of getting his education the Negro is learning the lesson of self-help. Among the denominational colleges, the Livingston Institute at Salisbury, North Carolina, is a good illustration of this capacity for self-help. It receives no state aid. The colored people of the Zion Methodist Episcopal church give $8000 towards the support of this school. The students give towards their own support not less than $6000 more. The president, Dr. Price, one of the ablest colored orators of the South, is a conspicuous example of what the colored man can do for himself.

Another remarkable illustration is furnished by the Tuskegee Normal School. This institution was started in 1881 by a Hampton graduate, Mr. Booker T. Washington, on a state appropriation of $2000. It has grown from 30 pupils to 450, with 31 teachers. During the last year 200 applicants had to be turned away for want of room. Fourteen hundred acres of land and fourteen school buildings form a part of the equipment. While friends of education, North and South, have generously helped its growth, the success of the school is due largely to the executive ability of Mr. Washington and his officers. General Armstrong says, "I think it is the noblest and grandest work of any colored man in the land." All the teachers are colored. Of the fourteen school buildings, eight have been erected, in whole or in part, by the students. The school is broadly unsectarian. It is teaching the colored people the dignity of labor and how to get out of debt. It is an agricultural and industrial school combined. Its stimulating and renovating influence is felt all through the Black Belt.

One of the most important results of the excellent work done by Hampton, Atlanta, and Tuskegee is seen in the radiating influence they exert through the country in stimulating primary education. In most of the communities of the lower Southern States, the money derived from local taxation is not sufficient to keep the school more than three months in the year, and the pay of teachers is poor. The interest of these communities is so quickened by a good teacher that the people raise money to extend the school time and supplement the pay of the teacher. A few examples taken from many will illustrate. In one district in Alabama, the school time was thus extended by private subscription from three months to seven. In Coffee County, the teacher's salary was increased from ten to twenty-five dollars a month. In many cases the raising of this extra sum means a good deal of self-denial. As the State makes no appropriation for school-houses, most of the schools in the Black Belt are held in churches, which gives rise to sectarian jealousy and disturbance. To overcome these difficulties and build school-houses, additional sacrifice is required. In a district of Butler County, Alabama, the children formed a "one cent society." They brought to the teacher a penny a day. About thirty dollars was raised to buy land, and the school-teacher, a colored girl, helped to clear it and burn the brush. In one township, where the school fund is sufficient for seven or nine months, the teachers are paid thirty-five dollars a month. In Lee County, the people "supplement" for an assistant teacher. One district school which I visited, eighteen miles from Tuskegee, taught by a graduate of its institute, well illustrated the advantage of industrial education. Having learned the carpenter's trade at the normal school, he was able, with the help of his pupils, to build a fine new school-house. The girls often do better than the men. One, who teaches about twenty-five miles from Tuskegee, has now a good two-story school building with four rooms. She has two assistant teachers, who live with her in the building. She has revolutionized that section of the country. A Hampton student whom I met once applied for a school in his district, as he wished to learn to read and write. He was told that there was not a sufficient number of children. Then he offered to give a school building, if the town would furnish a teacher. With the aid of his father he carried out the plan, and established a good school. Samuel Smiles might easily make a library of books on Self-Help out of thousands of individual examples furnished by the colored people.

The interest in education is seen also in the self-denial and sacrifice which parents make to keep their children at school. This sacrifice falls chiefly on the mothers. A student told me that two thirds of the younger scholars at Tuskegee were sent by their mothers. Very often the mother is a widow. She may get twenty dollars a month, or eight, or only four, for her labor. Out of this small sum she sends to college and clothes her boy or girl. "I know mothers," said a student, "who get three dollars a month, and out of that pay one dollar for the rent, and yet send their children to school." To do this they will wash all day and half the night. Said a colored clergyman in Chattanooga: "Sometimes, when I go about and see how hard many of these mothers work, I feel almost inclined to say, 'You ought to keep your child at home;' but they hold on with wonderful persistence. Two girls graduated from Atlanta University. Their mother had been washing several years to keep them in school. She came up to see them graduate. She was one of the happiest mothers I ever saw." At Selma University, some of the students walk from ten to fifteen miles a day in going to and from the university.

There is one education which the children get; there is another which they give to their parents. The influence of the normal school reacts on the home life. The boys and girls at Hampton and Tuskegee are taught to keep house. They are not satisfied to live in the old way, when they go home. "I have seen," says Professor Washington, "the influence of the daughter so potent, when she got home, that the father has torn down the old house, and built another and better one."

The result of higher education is seen in the rise of a professional class. I remember the time when a colored doctor was a curiosity even in Washington; but colored physicians, lawyers, journalists, college professors, dentists, educated clergymen, and teachers are now to be found in all the large cities of the South. In Montgomery, Dr. Dorsette has built up a thriving practice. He has erected a three-story brick building, on the lower floor of which are two stores, one of them a large and well-equipped drug store. A hall above is used for the accommodation of colored societies. In Birmingham, there are two practicing physicians, one dentist, and one lawyer. At Selma, the practicing physician is a graduate of the university. There is also a pharmacist, owning his drug store, who studied at Howard University. There are six colored lawyers and seven colored physicians in Baltimore. The professional men command the confidence and support of their own people.

Journalism is growing slowly. There are now about fifty-five well established Negro newspapers and journals. Thirty-seven are in the Southern States; seven are monthlies and two are semi-monthlies. The aggregate weekly circulation of all is about 805,000 copies. There are other ephemeral journals, not included in this list. The largest circulation, 15,000, is claimed for the Indianapolis Freeman.

The colored people are determined to have their churches, and they subscribe, in proportion to their means, large sums to sustain them. Last year the Zion Methodist Episcopal church in North Carolina raised $84,000 to support its religious institutions. This amount represents but one State and but one denomination. . . .

The colored people do more towards taking care of their unfortunate classes than is generally realized. With all the destitution that exists, there is almost no mendicancy. When one considers how much is done in the North for hospitals, homes, and institutions of every sort, and how little in the South, it is apparent that aid must come from some other quarter. The colored orphan asylum established by Mrs. Steele in Chattanooga is, I am told, the only Protestant colored orphan asylum south of Washington. What, then, becomes of orphan children? They are adopted. I have met such children in many homes, and their love and respect for their foster parents refute the charge that the Negro is incapable of gratitude. Thus the colored people have instinctively and of necessity adopted the placing-out system for orphans, which, other things being equal, is the best disposition that can be made of them.

In other respects the colored people have developed a laudable disposition to take care of their own poor. In addition to the Odd Fellows, Masons, and Knights of Pythias, benevolent and fraternal organizations are multiplying. The city churches are feeling a new impulse to such work. Brotherhoods, Good Samaritan societies, and mutual benefit organizations are established. Members of these organizations are allowed a regular stipend when sick. In New Orleans, the colored people have started a widows' home, and have collected enough money to buy a piece of ground and to put up a respectable building. In Montgomery, I visited the Hale Infirmary, founded by the late Joseph Hale and his wife, leading colored citizens. . . .

To sum up, then, the facts which show what the Negro is doing for himself, it is clear that the new generation of Afric-Americans is animated by a progressive spirit. They are raising and following their own leaders. They are rapidly copying the organic, industrial, and administrative features of white society. They have discovered that industrial redemption is not to be found in legislative and political measures. In spite of oppressive usury and extortion, the colored man is buying farms, building homes, accumulating property, establishing himself in trade, learning the mechanic arts, devising inventions, and entering the professions. Education he sees to be the pathway to prosperity, and is making immense sacrifices to secure it. He is passing into the higher stages of social evolution. In religion the "old-timer" is giving way to the educated preacher. Religion is becoming more ethical. The colored people are doing much to take care of their own unfortunate classes. The coöperative spirit is slowly spreading through trades unions, building associations, and benevolent guilds. In no way is the colored man doing more for himself than by silently and steadily developing a sense of self-respect, new capacity for self-support, and a pride in his race, which more than anything else secure for him the respect and fraternal feeling of his white neighbors.

SAMUEL J. BARROWS

38. Farm Labor and Five-Cent Cotton: Testimony on Agriculture and Agricultural Labor, 1899–1901

IN RESPECT TO Southern agriculture the testimony heard by the Industrial Commission at the turn of the century gives striking evidence of the impact upon worker, planter, and merchant of the low cotton prices of the preceding years. All too often after 1892 the three had been dividing up, not the profits of cotton production, but its losses, even in the rich Yazoo-Mississippi delta. All suffered adversity, but the agricultural laborer was most vulnerable for he had the least bargaining power particularly in a period of general depression. In the black belt between 1890 and 1900 there was a decrease in large plantations worked by wage labor, a loss in sharecropping-share tenancy and a striking gain in money tenancy. In good times the resulting change in status for the Negro worker—from wage earner, sharecropper or share tenant to money tenant

SOURCE: Report of the Industrial Commission on Agriculture and Agricultural Labor, including Testimony, Industrial Commission, Reports, X (Washington, D.C., 1901): 75–77, 117–118, 120–121, 457–460, 816, 827.

—would have represented an advance up the agricultural ladder. In the nineties it meant only a more hopeless burden of poverty. By the shift from wage or share arrangements to fixed rentals, those who owned the cotton lands transferred to the landless laborer a larger portion of risk and loss. It did not follow that those who still worked for wages were in an enviable position; the testimony reveals the shockingly low level of their pay.

Testimony of Mr. P. H. Lovejoy, Merchant and Planter, Hawkinsville, Ga.

Washington, D.C., *June 20, 1899.*

Q. (By Representative Livingston.) What is the condition of the farmer and farm laborers of Georgia and the South?—A. I think the farmers are in worse condition than they have been. They are not prosperous in our section. They have been going back for the last 5 or 6 years. My experience in doing business with them, and then my experience with my own farm, shows that the conditions are not so good as they were years ago.

Q. Is the condition of the farm laborer improving?—A. The farm laborer can not prosper when the farmer can not prosper; it all comes under the same head. What the laborer gets he uses daily, and it leaves him without much to go on, and then the farmer is not able to help him much.

Q. What is the custom down there, hired help or crop sharing?—A. We rent, pay wages, and have crop work. We do all. We rent to some of them and share crops with some, and pay them wages; and I believe the man who gets $6 or $8 a month gets more than anybody else.

Q. The wage laborers fare better than the tenants and croppers?—A. I think so. In the last few years the products have been so cheap that it would hardly pay out. For instance, you go halves with the tenant; he furnishes the labor and you furnish the land, stock, and provisions to go with it; and his half would not pay his part of the expense.

Q. That being the case, how do the merchants South protect themselves in their advances?—A. Take mortgages on their land.

Q. And you hold the farm responsible for the crop development?—A. Yes.

Q. Then when you let the cropper run it on his own hook; how do you protect yourself?—A. We take a mortgage on the cotton crop.

Q. At what profit on these goods do you sell to these people?— A. Size him up, and if he is pretty good, we sell him pretty cheap; and if he is a hard case, we just take what he makes and quit. . . .

Q. (By Mr. A. L. Harris). Do you advance the goods to the cotton raisers on credit?—A. Yes.

Q. What margin do you charge for goods advanced?—A. We generally put a pretty good margin on cheap men because we have to take chances on them.

Q. About how much?—A. About 25 per cent.

Q. How do you charge what you call good men?—A. We sell good men at 10 per cent. We settle up what we call "papers" the 1st of September. We aim for 10 per cent clear, because you know there is a certain amount of leakage to business that no one ever found yet. You can not figure like you can when loaning money. When you loan money you know what you are doing. When you sell goods there is a leakage that has to be covered, and which you can not figure, and if you do not take care of it you will not last very long.

Q. Is that the reason why you demand such large margins from the cotton raiser?—A. Yes. You see; we take all the risk. You take the good per cent of them, we have nothing for collateral except the crop, and if they should fail and anything turns up that they do not make a crop, it is a clear loss, and so you see we have to figure for the whole crowd to pay it. . . .

Q. You have various prices, then, in the same store for the same goods?—A. Yes. If a man comes in and we make a sale, we always let him know where he stands. We tell him we will risk his agreement. We can afford to take some risk. If he wants to do it, he has the privilege to take it or let it alone.

Q. Are the merchants prosperous in the South, as a rule?—A. No, not for the last few years. It has been all we could do to tote our customers with the money made in ten years. We are toting them with it now.

Q. You are not making any money.—A. If we keep things balanced up even we are doing pretty well. . . .

TESTIMONY OF MR. L. W. YOUMANS,
FARMER AND MERCHANT, FAIRFAX, SOUTH CAROLINA.

WASHINGTON, D.C., June 22, 1899.

Q. (By Representative LIVINGSTON.) Will you give us the conditions of the landholder and the laborer in the Carolinas and the South? Are they in debt?—A. Yes; the small landholders are being forced to give up the title deeds to their land, and with the large landholders, under present conditions, it will only be a question of time until they follow suit. . . .

The charge is made against the agricultural element that they are extravagant. I do not think that will apply, especially to my experience, and right here the element of cost of the production comes in. I have heard a great deal about the protection of American labor, but I do not see any of it in my section. Take my plowmen, for instance: I employ them by the month, and they make 5½ days' honest good work each week . . . and these hands on my plantation I allow to have 2 acres of land, and the plowmen, if I do not need the animals, have the use of them on Saturday evenings. But when I settle with them at 12 o'clock on Saturday or Friday night, I pay these hands for their 5½ days' work, in addition to their rations of 1 peck of meal and 3 pounds of bacon and salt, 90 cents in trade, to be traded out in the stores at 50 per cent profit, and 20 cents in cash; that is all they get for 5½ days' labor. If I employ the labor by the day—and there is a great deal more of it than I have any need for—I pay them 30 cents, one-fourth in cash and three-fourths to be traded out at 50 per cent profit; and yet raising the crops as cheaply as that the proceeds will not meet the expense of raising.

Q. What monthly wages do you pay?—A. $5.20 for 26 days' work. . . .

Q. (By Mr. FARQUHAR.) What is the difference between the competition of the white labor and black labor in South Carolina?—A. The cotton is raised by colored people. The white people raise cotton in competition with the colored man and for the same work we do not pay any more. My whole place is arranged in so much for a day's work, and no matter who I have to plow I pay the same for the work. I have overseers and a colored foreman that I pay more. . . .

Q. Are your country merchants prosperous?—A. Not in my section. They lose money.

Q. How do your smaller banks do?—A. They are going out of the business: they have their money all tied up in real estate, and can not realize the amount of the mortgages. . . .

Q. Have any of these colored people down there acquired land

and little homes of their own?—A. It strikes me some years ago they did. I think they have been pretty well all "skinned" out. They have just about followed the small landholder. There may be some. . . .

TESTIMONY OF MR. W. L. PEEK,
FARMER, CONYERS, GA.

ATLANTA, GA., March 19, 1900.

Q. (By Senator KYLE.) How much cotton does your land produce?—A. You mean mine individually or the average?

Q. Average.—A. About a bale to 3 acres is the average.

Q. What is the cost of raising cotton?—A. When we make a bale to 3 acres it costs about 8½ cents.

Q. That includes every little item of expense?—A. That includes the cost of raising cotton and putting it on the market.

Q. That includes the wages paid to one's own children and the help around the farm that is ordinarily counted in?—A. Everything, not counting wages to children nor wife.

Q. (By Mr. RATCHFORD.) Does it include transportation?—A. Delivering at our depot.

Q. (By Representative LIVINGSTON.) Interest on land?—A. Interest on land, taxes added in, everything of that sort. Where we raise a bale to every 2 acres we can do it at about 7½ cents, and when we get a bale to the acre we can make it for about 6½ cents. . . .

Q. (By SENATOR KYLE). You have been raising cotton how long?—A. Ever since I was big enough to toddle.

Q. The average price has been what?—A. For the last few years very low. You know cotton immediately after the war was away up, but since 1872 it has been falling gradually, until last year it was 4 cents. . . .

Q. If it costs you 8½ cents, you have been raising it at a woeful loss for the last few years.—A. Yes sir; so much so that nearly everybody has lost a home in this country. I have partly escaped, but the majority of people who farm are now homeless.

Q. (Interrupting.) A man with no mortgage on his farm is able to worry along?—A. A great many have had to mortgage their land and lose it. . . .

Q. What percentage of the colored population are employed on

the farms?—I should think about 75 per cent of the colored people
in Georgia are employed on the farms.

Q. (By Mr. SMYTH.) Women, children, and men?—A. Everything; yes, sir.

Q. Quite a proportion employed in town as laborers generally?—A. Yes. Under our farming system the negroes catch at
every little thing. Prices have not been remunerative, and there is a
disposition to get away from the farm to other employment. There
is quite a disposition of both the white and colored to move
off. . . .

Q. Gone to the towns?—A. Yes.

Q. The negroes flock to the towns too?—A. Yes; very rapidly,
too.

Q. What do they do in the towns?—A. Not being a man who
lives in town, I can not tell; all sorts of work, street work, porters
on trains, brakemen, hotel waiters, and bootblacks.

Q. (By Senator KYLE.) Do they get an advance in wages?—A.
Wages are generally better than in the country.

Q. About what hours of labor?—A. The man who works on a
farm in Georgia regulates his own hours of labor—I mean the
tenant. He is not forced to a certain time—strict hours.

Q. Farming, then, is not considered a very desirable employment?—A. Not in Georgia. If we could get out the capital we have
invested in farms, as a rule, the majority of the men would go into
other business. . . .

TESTIMONY OF MR. HARRY HAMMOND,
[SOUTH CAROLINA PLANTER AND AUTHORITY ON COTTON
PRODUCTION]

WASHINGTON, D.C., *February 13, 1901.*

Q. You may state, if you please, what is the condition of labor
and capital employed in agriculture in your State and in the South
generally, if your information goes that far. As you have "a plan of
inquiry" before you, you may take up the subject as there outlined
and treat each subject as fully as you desire.—A. I have some notes
here which I will refer to. I have followed the questions in the
topical plan of inquiry. . . .

In 1886 I collected from 12 of the best cotton growers of this
region itemized statements of the cost of cotton production. They

ranged from 6.1 to 15.22; the average was 8.28. Cotton may grow everywhere between the parallels of 40° north and south latitude. Great efforts were made during the years of our war to develop it in all countries. They were not very successful. Down to 1895 the East Indian crop declined after the price reached 11½ cents, the Brazilian and West Indian after the price fell to 14 cents. Only in Russia, owing to unusual development of agriculture, and in Egypt, owing to the peculiarity of the staple, has production kept up an increase since cotton fell below 11 cents. There can be little doubt that 9 to 11 cents a pound is somewhere close to the margin of safe cost in cotton growing. If it is asked how such large crops have been grown at so much lower prices, the answer is that they have been grown on credit. The credit has been maintained by the sacrifice of other property to maintain the cotton growers. They have reduced their style of living and have abandoned many of their schools, many rural pursuits, and home comforts, to do so. I am told by visitors from other sections that our neighborhood seems exceptionally prosperous in comparison with others; and yet from my piazza I have counted in a radius of 3 or 4 miles 11 houses, once inhabited by substantial and prosperous families, which are now empty or are occupied by negro tenants, the land divided up into small cotton patches cultivated by negroes on the edge of want. Our orchards, our vegetable and flower gardens, our sheep, cattle, and horses, our servants, the repairers of our dwellings, and whatever surplus there was of other securities have all been swept up and consumed in maintaining our credit as cotton growers. . . .

Retrospect: The Nineties

IN THE 1890s Congress and the Supreme Court not only had failed to redeem the Reconstruction commitment but had carried repudiation several steps further. For the court the landmarks of reversion were the Plessy decision, legitimising segregation, and the Williams v. Mississippi decision, legitimising Negro disfranchisement through an "understanding" or "interpretation" test. Congress shared culpability. With Democrats in control of both houses and the presidency as well, in 1894 they expunged from the revised statutes the provisions for federal protection of elections originally embodied in the Enforcement Acts of 1870 and 1871. The year-end news summary of Appletons' Annual Cyclopaedia for 1894 reported that "repeal was one of the few settled points in the [Democratic] party policy" and that "next to the tariff act, this was regarded as the most important subject on which Congress took action." A political analyst two years later characterized repeal, and Republican acceptance of defeat, as having finally put to rest the "old slavery issue."[1] As the century ended, racist assumptions were both pervasive and respectable; public support for justice irrespective of race, though not dead, was minimal and ineffectual.

To the fragile political freedom of black Southerners, the decade of the nineties had added an unprecedented economic burden. Hard-won gains of earlier years had been jeopardized or lost. A belated upturn in the price of agricultural staples was as yet too tenuous to give assurance of better times ahead. And something more than a prospering agriculture would be prerequisite to future economic security for the black southerner.

The nation entered the twentieth century with the Negro in the South generally poor, disfranchised, segregated, and subjected to a rising tide of lynchings. Although a latent heritage, little remained to sustain the intent of the Reconstruction laws and amendments other than the continuing protest of blacks and the eloquent dissents of Justice Harlan. Prophetically in the fall of 1896, the American Law Review commented on the Plessy decision: "Mr. Justice Harlan delivered a strong dissenting opinion, which, whatever may be thought of it now, will do him honor in the estimation of future generations, who will study with curiosity these [Jim Crow] statutes, which will have become dead letters."

In the nation's capital on January 9, 1894, a year before his death and within weeks of his seventy-seventh birthday, Frederick Douglass had delivered an impassioned address entitled "Lessons of the Hour." Forthrightly avowing his purpose of countering the white man's view with "a colored man's view" of the relations between his people and whites in the Southern states, he pointed out that "an epidemic of mob law and persecution" was increasing in the South both in its savagery and in the number of its victims and

1. Edward P. Clark, "The Solid South Dissolving," Forum, XXII (October 1896): 263–274.

that it threatened the peace and security of the whole country. He then proceeded to demolish the Southern rationale for lynch law based upon accusations of rape. He attacked as well the fraud and hyprocrisy of those who deprived black men of their constitutional right to vote. In concluding, Douglass invoked the nation's tradition and conscience, calling upon white Americans to put aside race prejudice and to restore "the self-evident truths of liberty and equality," with which at its birth the nation had "saluted a listening world."[2]

At the Atlanta Exposition little more than six months after Douglass' death, a rising spokesman for Southern Negroes won the applause of Southern whites with a speech of contrasting mood and substance. Where Frederick Douglass openly challenged white racism, Booker T. Washington publicly championed compromise and covertly supported old goals. The veteran's passion was evocative of the old Republican commitment; the "cunning Brer Rabbit"[3] refracted the temper of the nineties.

2. Address by Honorable Frederick Douglass, Delivered in the Metropolitan A. M. E. Church, Washington, D.C. Tuesday, January 9th, 1894, on the Lessons of the Hour in which he Discusses the Various Aspects of the So-Called, But Mis-Called, Negro Problem (pamphlet, Baltimore, Md., 1894). With minor variants, the speech can also be found in Philip S. Foner, The Life and Writings of Frederick Douglass (New York: International Publishers, 1950–1955), IV:491–523.
3. Louis R. Harlan's characterization, in "The Secret Life of Booker T. Washington," The Journal of Southern History, XXXVII (August 1971): 395.

Reconstruction, the Negro, and the New South

Printed by offset lithography by Halliday Lithograph Corporation on 55# Warren's University Text. This acid-free paper, noted for its longevity, has been watermarked with the emblem of the University of South Carolina Press. Binding by Halliday Lithograph Corporation